BRECHT IN PERSPECTIVE

Edited by Graham Bartram and Anthony Waine

LONGMAN
London and New York

Longman Group UK Limited
Longman House, Burnt Mill, Harlow,
Essex CM20 2JE, England
and Associated Companies throughout the world

*Published in the United States of America
by Longman Inc., New York*

First published 1982
Third impression 1991

British Library Cataloguing in Publication Data

Brecht in perspective.
  1. Brecht, Bertolt — Criticism and interpretation
I. Bartram, Graham II. Waine, Anthony
823′.912 PT2603.R39Z

ISBN 0-582-49205-X

Library of Congress Cataloging in Publication Data

Main entry under title:

Brecht in perspective.

  Includes bibliographical references and index.
  1. Brecht, Bertolt 1898–1956-Criticism and
interpretation. I. Bartram, Graham, 1946–
II. Waine, Anthony Edward, 1946–
PT2603.R397Z57724 832′.912 81-13755
ISBN 0-582-49205-X (pbk.) AACR2

Set in 10/11pt VIP Times Roman
Produced by Longman Singapore Publishers Pte Ltd
Printed in Singapore

CONTENTS

Acknowledgements vii

Introduction viii

Bibliographical note xiii

List of Contributors xiv

Part One
THE SOCIAL, HISTORICAL AND LITERARY PERSPECTIVE

1. Brecht's Germany R. GEARY 2

2. German drama before Brecht: from Neo-Classicism to Expressionism L. LÖB 11

3. Epic theatre: a theatre for the scientific age A. SUBIOTTO 30

4. The individual and society E. SPEIDEL 45

5. Comedy and the *Volksstück* M. McGOWAN 63

6. Literature and commitment G. BARTRAM 83

Part Two
THE ARTISTIC AND THEATRICAL PERSPECTIVE

7. The German theatre as an artistic and social institution: from the March Revolution to the Weimar Republic C. DAVIES 108

8. Acting methods: Brecht and Stanislavsky M. EDDERSHAW 128

9. Brecht and Piscator H. RORRISON 145

10. Brecht and cabaret J. M. RITCHIE 160

11. Brecht in the German Democratic Republic R. SPEIRS 175

Contents

Part Three
A RETROSPECTIVE

12. The legacy for German-speaking playwrights   A. WAINE   192

13. Brecht and the English theatre   M. GERMANOU   208

Index

255

ACKNOWLEDGEMENTS

We are grateful to the following for permission to reproduce copyright material:

Associated Book Publishers Ltd (Methuen) and Avon Books for extracts from *The Political Theatre* by Erwin Piscator, translated by Hugh Rorrison. Copyright © by Rowohlt Verlag Publishing Co, 1963; Associated Book Publishers Ltd (Methuen) and Farrar Straus and Giroux Inc for extracts from *Brecht on Theatre* by John Willett Copyright © 1957, 1963 and 1964 by Suhrkamp Verlag; Modern Drama for an extract from an article by Professor J. M. Ritchie; Suhrkamp Verlag for extracts from *Gesammelte Werke* by Bertolt Brecht.

INTRODUCTION

Bertolt Brecht was a survivor many times over. He managed to establish himself as the foremost young dramatist of the Weimar Republic before the Nazi seizure of power put an end to the production of his plays; he managed in 1933 to escape into exile from almost certain persecution; a committed but independent-minded Communist, he spent the years of exile in Scandinavia and the USA rather than the USSR, and evaded the death in Stalin's labour camps that was the fate of his close friends and collaborators Carola Neher, Ernst Ottwalt and Sergei Tretyakov. After the war, equipped with Austrian passport, West German publisher and Swiss bank account, he was able to settle in East Germany, the only country that offered him the possibility of working with a theatre and a company of his own. The Berliner Ensemble, set up by Brecht and Helene Weigel in 1949, helped to assure the continuity of his legacy: not only of his writings, but also of his dramatic practice and his concept of a political theatre. Today, over a quarter of a century after his death, Brecht remains not only one of the most influential but also one of the most controversial figures of twentieth century theatre and literature.

The very vitality of Brecht's influence today, however, tends to obscure the fact that the successive upheavals that transformed Europe in the course of his lifetime have rapidly placed a great historical distance between our present, and the age into which Brecht was born and in which he grew up; and these same upheavals have continued to structure and to fragment the Brechtian legacy after his death. In a Europe split militarily, politically, socially and ideologically in two, partial and distorted images of Brecht abound. In the German Democratic Republic, his concept of a political, critical theatre has been uncomfortably accommodated on the margins of a 'positive', state-legitimated and state-legitimizing culture. In the West, his acceptance, long-delayed by the political and ideological tensions of the cold war era, has been facilitated by a separation of Brecht-the-politician from Brecht-the-writer-of-great-plays, and the upgrading of the latter at the expense of the former. As the times in which he lived and worked become ever further removed from us, so increasingly are works such as *The Caucasian Chalk Circle, Galileo* and *Mother Courage* elevated to the realm of 'timeless' art, while others such as *The Mother* and *The Measures Taken*, in so far as they are known at all, are dismissed as tediously didactic idealizations of Communist Party ideology and discipline.

Distance from a subject may create the opportunity for critical reflection and the correction of such distorted images; but it may also make room for sheer ignorance. In English-speaking countries, the distance from Brecht is not only a chronological one, but also cultural and linguistic. It has been bridged (with varying degrees of success) by translation, and by performances of his plays in translation; it has also been bridged by the availability in English of a growing number of books about Brecht's life and work. What has so far been lacking, however, is a book which seeks to build the cultural–historical 'bridge'; which attempts, in other words, to situate Brecht, for the purposes of a lay as well as an academic readership, in his historical, ideological, literary and above all theatrical context. That is the task to which *Brecht in Perspective* addresses itself.

All the chapters in this book have been written specifically for it. Though varied in scope, all have the same purpose, namely to furnish material for the understanding of Brecht as a *historical* individual, reacting to the major political and social events and ideological currents of his time, and working within particular theatrical and aesthetic traditions. To do this, we felt the need to get away completely from the customary, unitary life-and-works approach, and reconstruct instead a number of perspectives within which Brecht could be viewed. Some of these perspectives are close-up, focusing on a particular aspect of Brecht's work itself; others are far more long-range, retracing a development or a tradition back to a century before Brecht's birth. A major aim of these latter is to show how aspects of German theatrical practice that in the British or American mind are often associated uniquely with Brecht (the social relevance of theatre, the break with 'traditional' dramatic forms) do in fact have a substantial history that is largely quite independent of him.

Brecht in Perspective is addressed to students and teachers of drama and non-academic readers, as well as to the German specialist. This has to some extent dictated our choice of 'perspectives'. The focus is primarily on Brecht's place in the German theatrical tradition, and the whole of the second part of the book is devoted to various aspects of this subject. Brecht's poetry, from the literary point of view as impressive an achievement as his plays, has not been treated here; nor has the complex question of the sources of his richly varied dramatic and lyrical diction.

The opening chapter identifies those structures in Wilhelmine and Weimar society, as well as the decisive social and political developments between 1871 (the establishment of the Second German Empire) and 1933 (the Nazi seizure of power), which have undoubtedly influenced the behaviour and ideas of a man whose year of birth (1898) is almost equidistant from these two fateful turning-points in contemporary German history. The following chapter also presents a historical survey, concentrating, however, on the literary and philosophical traditions of German bourgeois culture whose identity began to take shape in the eighteenth century. Ladislaus Löb locates wherever possible the socially progressive and stylistically avant-gardist tendencies within German drama which anticipate the final and most radical break with traditional dramatic style wrought by Brecht in the 1920s.

By this time a large number of German intellectuals and artists believed that bourgeois culture was moribund. Brecht, like a good many of these men and women, devoted himself from now on in word and deed to shaping the identity of a nascent socialist culture. The changed function and substance of the new drama of the socialist age are examined in Chapters 3 and 4. Arrigo Subiotto's chapter proffers definitions of a number of key concepts relating to this drama, beginning with the central notion of 'epic theatre'. This chapter and the following one on the individual in Brecht's plays both consider his ideas on drama and on the concept of the individual as a response to a changing, complex and contradictory world, in which mass society, its scientific and technological achievements have necessitated a fundamental rethinking of man's relationship to the world. Both chapters also emphasize the extent to which Brecht's own views too were subject to constant reappraisal and consequently underwent significant changes in the course of his development as a writer and thinker.

The recognized necessity for change and the will to change, innovate and regenerate form the underlying theme of both Chapters 5 and 6, different though their subject matter is. Moray McGowan demonstrates how Brecht takes two deep-rooted traditions of German theatrical history, comedy and the *Volksstück*, which had until the 1920s been generally consigned to the domain of 'low' culture, and how he adapts and integrates them into his own philosophy and praxis, thereby broadening the base of the political theatre in Germany. The concluding chapter of the first part of the book focuses attention on arguably the single most important idea underlying Brecht's dramatic theory and practice, namely the political function of committed art and literature. Situating Brecht in the tradition of the literary and artistic avant-garde, Graham Bartram shows how, under the pressure of the social and political changes taking place in Imperial and Weimar Germany, this avant-garde increasingly moved from a stance of aesthetic revolt towards new concepts of the writer and intellectual as agents of social change.

The whole of the second part of the book adds a further and substantial dimension to the contextualized portrait of Brecht. Brecht not only wrote for the theatre, but also lived for it and by it. What styles of acting, directing and performance were prevalent in the pre-Weimar theatre and what influences did he find in the theatre culture *and* subculture of the new republic? Who were Brecht's great contemporaries as directors, and how much is he indebted to them? What was his own contribution to the German theatre as an artistic and social institution? These are the basic questions to which the authors of the five chapters in this section address themselves.

Cecil Davies's chapter on the German theatre since the mid-nineteenth century may be seen as a sequel to Chapter 2. There Ladislaus Löb introduced the work and ideas of Germany's foremost playwrights and the movements to which they belonged. In Chapter 7 we learn about the outstanding directors such as Brahm, Reinhardt and Jessner, who from approximately 1870 dominate German theatrical history. The unique institution of the 'People's Theatre' and its endeavours to broaden the social base of the German theatre are also discussed here, and Brecht's own position *vis-à-vis* this institution is critically examined. The following two chapters (8 and 9) deal with Brecht's relationship to two directors of international standing, references to whom recur regularly throughout Brecht's writings on the theatre. In comparing Brecht and Stanislavsky, Margaret Eddershaw highlights the principal differences between these two men who for so long have been considered the antipodes of contemporary European methods of stage production – the work of the Russian symbolizing the naturalistic approach, that of his German 'adversary' the anti-illusionistic style. However, she does trace in the latter part of her chapter how the two men's positions moved closer together as they overhauled their earlier theories. As regards the German director Piscator Brecht's standpoint was always much closer to his, not least of all because both of them shared the view of the theatre as a political institution, a weapon in the class struggle – an attitude far removed from Stanislavsky's more aesthetically and psychologically oriented viewpoint for example. What Piscator perhaps taught Brecht most vividly was the technical flexibility of the modern stage and its new potential for the treatment of the great complex issues such as war, revolution, inflation and the class struggle.

Despite the revolutionary nature of Piscator's politics he operated mainly within the established (bourgeois) German theatre. The urban subculture of early twentieth-century Germany, on the other hand, had imported from France a popular medium for combining entertainment and provocative social ideas in informal surroundings: the cabaret. Hamish Ritchie, in Chapter 10, evokes the atmosphere of this big-city, anti-establishment, art form to which the young, rebellious Brecht was instinctively drawn, and concludes his chapter by indicating to what extent the ambience of this medium may have permeated Brecht's dramatic technique. Chapter 11 examines the final eight years of Brecht's life, spent in the German Democratic Republic. His attitude to the new republic, its early political developments and its cultural policies, forms the first half of this chapter. The second half is concerned with the history of the Berliner Ensemble, the company he and Helene Weigel built up.

The final section of Ronald Speirs's chapter, examining the legacy of Brecht in the GDR, can be seen as part of the third and concluding section of the book, 'A Retrospective'. Chapter 12 explains how, because of the changed historical situation of Europe in the second half of the twentieth century, post-war German dramatists, while acutely aware of their indebtedness to him, have nevertheless challenged many of the assumptions, ideological and dramaturgical, on which Brecht's position is based. While embracing his political theatre as a still vital model they have done so critically – surely something of which the ever-questioning father figure of this generation would have approved. Finally Maro Germanou in Chapter 13, traces the reception of Brecht in Britain, critically highlighting the misconceptions which have accompanied his importation into this country. The need to accept and present Brecht as a political writer and not merely to see him as a technical innovator is today as pressing as the need to adapt Brecht's message to the new social and political realities of late twentieth-century Britain. Some playwrights and 'alternative groups' of the 1970s have embarked on this revision.

We would like to express our gratitude to all members of the *Brecht in Perspective* 'ensemble' for the enthusiasm they have shown for the project, their tolerance of the vagaries of their editors and their cooperation in meeting deadlines. Our thanks go also to Mrs Pat Bullock for her patient and meticulous typing of the final manuscript.

THE EDITORS
Lancaster
January 1981

BIBLIOGRAPHICAL NOTE

In referring to works by Brecht, the following abbreviations have been used throughout this volume:

GW   Gesammelte Werke, 20 vols, Frankfurt am Main, 1967. The most complete edition to date of Brecht's works.

Versuche   Versuche; Vols 1–7, Berlin 1930–32, republished in 2 vols, Frankfurt am Main, 1959.
   Vol. 8, which failed to reach publication in 1933, is also included in the 1959 two-volume edition.
   Vols 9–15, Frankfurt am Main, 1949–56.

SzT   Schriften zum Theater, 7 vols, Frankfurt am Main, 1963–64.

Aj   Arbeitsjournal 1938–1955, ed. with notes by Werner Hecht, 3 vols, Frankfurt am Main, 1973. Vol. 1 (pp. 1–506) covers the years 1938–42, Vol. 2 (pp. 507–1022) the years 1942–55. Vol. 3 contains the notes.

Tb   Tagebücher 1920–1922/Autobiographische Aufzeichnungen 1920–54, Frankfurt am Main, 1975.

Brecht on Theatre   Brecht on Theatre: The Development of an Aesthetic, trans. with notes by John Willett, London, 1964. Contains most of Brecht's major writings on the theatre apart from the *Messingkauf* dialogues, which appeared separately in 1965.

TRANSLATION NOTE

English translations followed by 'JW' or 'JW adapted' have been respectively taken or adapted from those by John Willett. Unless otherwise annotated, all other translations are original.

LIST OF CONTRIBUTORS

GRAHAM BARTRAM, b. 1946, D.Phil. (Oxon.), was Research Fellow in German at Clare College, Cambridge from 1972 to 1976. He is currently Lecturer in German Studies at the University of Lancaster.

CECIL DAVIES, b. 1918, B.A. (London), spent six years in the professional theatre after graduating. He is at present Senior Staff Tutor in Literature in the Department of Extra-Mural Studies at the University of Manchester. His publications include *Theatre for the People: The Story of the Volksbühne* (1977), and a major article on working-class theatre in the Weimar Republic in *Theatre Quarterly*.

MARGARET EDDERSHAW, b. 1943, M. Litt. (Lancaster), spent several years in professional theatre before taking up teaching. She is now Lecturer in Theatre Studies at the University of Lancaster.

DICK GEARY, b. 1945, Ph.D. (Cantab.), was Research Fellow at Emmanuel College, Cambridge, from 1970 to 1973, and has also researched at the Institute for Social History, Amsterdam. He is currently Senior Lecturer and Head of the Department of German Studies at the University of Lancaster. His publications include a book on *European Labour Protest 1848–1939* (1981), and numerous articles on European social history and social theory.

MARO GERMANOU, b. 1954, is currently researching at Essex University into Brecht's influence on English alternative theatre.

LADISLAUS LÖB, b. 1933, Dr. phil. (Zurich), has worked as a schoolteacher, journalist and university extension lecturer in Zurich, and visiting Professor of German at Middlebury College, Vermont, USA. He is at present Reader in German at the University of Sussex. His publications include *Mensch und Gesellschaft bei J. B. Priestley* (1962), *From Lessing to Hauptmann: Studies in German Drama* (1974), and numerous articles on German literature.

MORAY McGOWAN, b. 1950, M.A. (Newcastle upon Tyne), has taught at the Universities of Siegen, Kassel, Lancaster and Hull. He is currently Lecturer in German at the University of Strathclyde. His publications include articles on modern German drama and Irish literature, and he is at present working on a study of Franz Xaver Kroetz.

JAMES McPHERSON RITCHIE, b. 1927, Dr. phil. (Tübingen), has taught German at the Universities of Glasgow, Newcastle (New South Wales) and Hull. He is currently Professor and Head of the Department of Germanic Studies at the University of Sheffield. His publications include books on Benn, Brecht, and German Expressionist drama, and numerous articles on German literature from the seventeenth to the twentieth century.

HUGH RORRISON, b. 1933, M.A. (Glasgow), has studied in Vienna and Berlin and is currently Lecturer in German at the University of Leeds. He has published a translation, with notes and commentary, of Erwin Piscator's *The Political Theatre* (1980), as well as articles on German theatre in *Theatre Quarterly*, and has contributed numerous entries to the forthcoming *Oxford Companion to the Theatre* (4th edn).

ERICH SPEIDEL, b. 1932, Dr.phil. (Tübingen), is currently Lecturer in German at the University of Newcastle upon Tyne. He is the author of a number of articles on modern German drama.

RONALD C. SPEIRS, b. 1943, Ph.D. (Stirling), is at present Lecturer in German at the University of Birmingham. He is the author of articles on Brecht and Thomas Mann, and of a forthcoming monograph *The Early Plays of Bertolt Brecht*.

ARRIGO SUBIOTTO, b. 1928, Ph.D. (Aberdeen), has taught German language and literature at the Universities of Aberdeen, Keele and Stirling, and is currently Professor and Head of the Department of German at the University of Birmingham. He has written a book on *Brecht's Adaptations for the Berliner Ensemble* (1975), and articles on Brecht, contemporary drama, and twentieth-century German literature.

ANTHONY WAINE, b. 1946, Ph.D. (Lancaster), is Lecturer in German Studies at Lancaster University. He has published two books on Martin Walser and is currently working on a study of writers and politics in post-war Germany.

MORAY McGOWAN b. 1952, M.A. (Newcastle upon Tyne), has taught in the University of Strathclyde, Lancaster and Hull. He is currently critic in German at the University of Strathclyde. His publications include articles on modern German drama and Irish literature and in the field of scriptwriting on a study of Franz Xaver Kroetz.

JOHN LEONARD RITCHIE b. 1937, D. phil. (Erlangen) has taught German at the Universities of Glasgow, Newcastle (New South Wales) and Hull; he is currently Professor and Head of the Department of German Studies at the University of Sheffield. His publications include books on Brecht and German Expressionist drama, and essays, articles on German literature from the seventeenth to the twentieth century.

HUGH ROBINSON b. 1945, M.A. (Glasgow), has studied in Vienna, and until recently was a lecturer in German at the University of Leeds. He has published A translation, with notes and commentary, of Ernst in Toller's *The Roman Theatre* (1980), as well as articles on German theatre in *Theatre Quarterly* and his contribution to this anthology on Georg Kaiser is in the Zürich collection.

PETER SKRINE b. 1937, D. phil (Tübingen), is currently a lecturer in German at the University of Newcastle upon Tyne. He is the author of a number of studies on modern German drama.

RONALD C. SPEIRS b. 1943, Ph.D. (Edinburgh), was previously lecturer in German at the University of Birmingham; he is the author of studies on Brecht and Thomas Mann, and is a contributing member of the newly Ph.D. or oberton Brecht.

KLAUD SURIOTTO b. 1935, Ph.D., has carried out research in German language and literature in the Universities of Bamberg, Kiel and Stuttgart, and is currently Professor and Head of the Department of German at the University of Birmingham; his publications have appeared notably in the volume of verse (1975), and articles on German comedy, poetry drama and twentieth-century German literature.

ANTHONY WAINE b. 1946, Ph.D., is currently a lecturer in German Studies at Lancaster University. He has published two books on Martin Walser, and is currently working on a variety of subjects and politics in post-war German arts.

Part One

THE SOCIAL, HISTORICAL AND LITERARY PERSPECTIVE

Chapter 1

BRECHT'S GERMANY

DICK GEARY

Born in 1898, Bertolt Brecht lived through a period of European history which witnessed the most massive economic, political and social upheavals: he saw the carnage of two World Wars, the destruction of empires in the revolutions of 1917–18 in Austria, Germany, Hungary and most famously Russia, the emergence of mass Communist and Fascist movements throughout continental Europe, the triumph of the latter in Mussolini's Italy and the fear and the misery of the Third Reich, the division of Germany, and the cold war. It is hardly surprising, therefore, that the traditional reserve of German intellectuals towards the dirty business of politics, a reserve reflected in Max Weber's *Politik als Beruf* (*Politics as a Vocation*) and even more so in Thomas Mann's *Betrachtungen eines Unpolitischen* (*Reflections of a Non-political Man*), broke down in the inter-war period on a scale unprecedented since the 'Vormärz' (the years preceding the March Revolution of 1848) which had produced politically committed artists like Heine and Buchner. Many intellectuals now saw the need to forge a union between the hitherto discrete realms of *Geist* (mind) and *Tat* (action).

Brecht was born into Germany's Second Reich as it rose to political and economic greatness and as it experienced a rapid and spectacular process of industrial growth. That process of industrialization and concomitant urbanization formed the backcloth to much of his writing, on occasion, even, the very substance of his dramatic themes, as in *Im Dickicht der Städte* (*In the Jungle of the Cities*) and *Die Heilige Johanna der Schlachthöfe* (*St Joan of the Stockyards*). Some towns expanded at a quite extraordinary rate: Nuremberg, for example, which had a population of 83,200 in 1871, had become a significant city of 261,100 inhabitants only twenty-nine years later. Gelsenkirchen, home of Thyssen's mining interests, tripled in size between 1858 and 1871. Such rapid urban development was the result both of natural population growth and of a mass migration from the rural east to Germany's industrial heartland in the Ruhr; and it brought in its wake all kinds of economic and social problems. The sad story of low factory wages, long working hours and slum housing – the last being especially marked in Germany and symbolized by the *Mietskasernen* (tenement blocks) of large industrial towns – is well known; but equally important was the alienation experienced by the urban immigrant when he came into contact with the large, impersonal and unfriendly city. Brecht himself seems to have experienced such unease when he first moved from provincial Augsburg to metropolitan Berlin; and *Im Dickicht der Städte* certainly provided a dramatic realization of this alienation. However, it should not be imagined that rapid technological change was restricted to the earlier period of the industrial revolution. The First World War and the Weimar Republic witnessed mass mobilization on an unprecedented scale, in the military, economic and political spheres, the rationalization of business structures and the introduction of serial techniques of production such as those pioneered by Henry Ford in the United States. Such developments had a profound effect upon contemporary German intellectuals: Kaiser's *Gas* (*Gas*), Toller's *Masse Mensch* (*Masses and Men*), Brecht's belief that individualism had been swept aside by collective forces and his early fascination with America, the archetypal new technocratic society.

The process of economic modernization described above was hardly peculiar to Germany in the twentieth century; but in Germany the response to this process was in many ways more exaggerated than elsewhere. The labour movement adopted an ostensibly revolutionary programme when the SPD (German Social Democratic Party) accepted theoretical Marxism at its Erfurt congress in 1891, while the *Mittelstand* of small shopkeepers, artisans and peasant farmers who felt themselves threatened by both organized capitalism and organized labour turned to various radical reactionary organizations even before the First World War – the Army and Navy Leagues, various anti-socialist and even anti-liberal bodies – and in the period after 1918 formed the rank and file of the Nazi movement. One possible explanation for this was the very speed of industrialization. Whereas Great Britain, for example, had gone through this painful process over more than a century, Germany was transformed into a modern industrial nation almost overnight. Thus adaptation to the new order was to prove extremely difficult, especially for those who retained strongly developed ideas of the status and respect due to them, and yet found that they were being rendered increasingly marginal by the competition of both labour organizations and big business. It was precisely these status anxieties which were exploited by Hitler and his cronies and which led to the successful Nazi mobilization of the Protestant lower middle class in the early 1930s.

There were a number of other factors which rendered class conflict in Imperial and Weimar Germany more bitter than in some other industrial societies. In particular, the process of economic modernization which characterized Germany's Second Reich was not matched by political modernization: that is to say, liberalization and democratization did not

3

follow automatically from industrialization. This is not necessarily surprising: for far too long British commentators have regarded their own nation as a model of 'natural development', whereas it is arguably the British experience which is unusual, if not 'deviant'. It is none the less significant that an old, landowning, Junker aristocracy could retain power in industrial Germany until 1918 and its revolution. It meant, first of all, that the German middle class, the expected bearers of liberal values, had somehow 'sold out'. Terrified by the threat of lower-class revolt since 1848, Germany's abortive 'bourgeois revolution', won over by economic concessions and unification through a combination of Bismarckian diplomacy and Prussian military power, courted by the award of titles, a large section of the Wilhelmine middle class sold its liberal soul for a mess of feudal pottage. This was the 'feudalization' of the bourgeoisie celebrated in Heinrich Mann's novel *Der Untertan* (*Man of Straw*) and which led to cooperation between the old ruling elite and big business in a combined political struggle against the enemies of the old order and against the socialist threat in particular. Furthermore, this struggle was supported by a large section of Germany's threatened *Mittelstand* and led to the creation in 1913 of the Kartell der schaffenden Stände (Cartel of Productive Estates), sarcastically known to progressive elements as the 'Kartell der raffenden Hände' ('Cartel of Grasping Hands') to defend the status quo against both liberal and socialist opponents.

This reactionary alliance encountered only one significant and persistent enemy before the First World War: the organized labour movement and in particular the SPD, which by 1914 had a mass membership of over 1 million and was the largest socialist party in the world. In many ways the SPD was the inheritor of the traditions of the 1848 revolutions and as such it remained committed to a democratization of the Reich. However, state persecution – the party was outlawed between 1878 and 1890 and subjected to various forms of harassment thereafter – and the fact that the Imperial constitution was only pseudo-democratic – to all intents and purposes parliamentary sovereignty did not exist and the Kaiser and his entourage ruled – pushed the party in a revolutionary and socialist direction. In fact at its conference at Erfurt in 1891 the party adopted an explicitly Marxist programme and it retained a revolutionary Marxist wing at least until the split of 1917. It should not be assumed, however, that this revolutionary threat was serious before 1914. In the first place, the socialist labour movement had still not succeeded in mobilizing a numerical majority of the industrial working class by 1914: female, Catholic, Polish and unskilled workers remained outside the ranks of organized labour at this point in time. Some workers belonged to the so-called 'yellow' unions of the bosses; while Germany's largest white-collar union, the Deutschnationale Handlungsgehilfenverband, subscribed to an ideology that was anti-socialist, imperialist and racist. Secondly, many workers within the SPD were far from radical. It has ven been argued that the party's provision of social facilities, choral ocieties, cycling clubs and the like actually served to integrate its nembers into the fabric of Wilhelmine society. Certainly crime figures n SPD-dominated areas were remarkably low. What cannot be doubted s that the SPD and its affiliated trade unions underwent a process of)ureaucratization before the First World War and that this strengthened he hand of that section in the party which was more interested in :autious and piecemeal reform than social revolution. Even before the var the SPD leadership in at least some places had a decidedly *piessburgerlich* (petty bourgeois philistine) mentality; and this goes ome way towards explaining why the party had so little success in nobilizing the support of even dissentient intellectuals like Heinrich /Iann.

On the eve of war, therefore, the overwhelming majority of the)opulation had little say in the processes of decision-making in the ?eich and yet the oppositional forces were weak and confronted by a)owerful reactionary bloc. The First World War was to change all that. n the first place the war entailed a human sacrifice which led many vho had initially declared their patriotism – people like Brecht himself – o question its purpose. Towards its end Brecht was to compose his irst politically critical work, the *Legende vom toten Soldaten* (*Legend of he Dead Soldier*), in which the dead are called from their graves to :trengthen the war effort. Secondly, the war exacerbated class conflict hrough inflation, long working hours, food and fuel shortages, censor-hip and martial law, at the same time as war profiteers made vast ortunes. The increasing demand for peace, democratic reform and ocial justice led in 1917 to the split of the labour movement into two :amps (the moderate SPD and the more radical Independent Social)emocratic Party (USPD) which demanded peace without annexations), ind finally to the November Revolution of 1918, when power was eized at a local level by workers' and soldiers' councils and transferred o a coalition SPD/USPD government at the centre until democratic :lections in early 1919. Thus the old Reich was overthrown, a republic)roclaimed and parliamentary sovereignty instituted.

In many ways the November Revolution is important for what it did 1ot achieve. For a variety of reasons, principally the collusion between he SPD leadership, afraid of being displaced by more genuinely :evolutionary forces, and the army high command, the old Imperial)ureaucracy, judiciary and military were not removed; and they were to ;o on to play a major role in the destruction of the new Weimar ?epublic. Hence the new democratic order was under threat from the /ery start. Nor did Weimar see the introduction of a new social order. \llied blockade until the middle of 1919 and hyperinflation thereafter intil 1923 robbed the industrial proletariat of any economic advantage it night have gained from the Revolution and form the background to a vhole series of revolutionary insurrections of workers disillusioned with a cowardly and counter-revolutionary SPD leadership. There was the Spartacist rising of January 1919 in Berlin, the creation of Soviet republics in Bremen and Munich, insurrectionary strikes in the Ruhr, the creation of a mass Communist Party and its abortive attempts to seize power in the so-called 'March Action' of 1921 and again in 1923. Of these events Brecht had much first-hand experience and they figure in several works, especially *Trommeln in der Nacht* (*Drums in the Night*), which is based upon the Spartacist rising. Brecht himself had been elected as a member of one of the many workers' and soldiers' councils that had come into existence in the course of the 1918 Revolution. He spent time in Augsburg and Munich in 1919 when they were the centres of radical activity in Bavaria and increasingly identified with the cause of revolution, although he did not share the Utopian fantasies of many of the Expressionists like Ernst Toller.

It was not only left-wing radicalism, however, which came to the fore in Germany between 1918 and 1923. Indeed, during this period of economic and political chaos a real civil war was raging and a radical right also emerged. And again Brecht had immediate experience of this. He was in Berlin in 1920 when a group of right-wing military elements under Kapp staged a short-lived *coup d'état* and he witnessed the first Fascist demonstrations in 1923 in Munich, where, of course, Hitler's ill-fated 'Beer-Hall Putsch' was also launched in the same year. The excesses of the right reinforced Brecht's commitment to the political left and in fact the extreme left. To identify with the new Republic was never easy for a real radical; for it not only failed to deliver the goods of social revolution but also tolerated the survival of reactionary forces and a highly partial system of justice which often excused right-wing political assassins their crimes. Nor could a radical intellectual find solace in the ranks of the SPD, a party increasingly dominated by narrow-minded bureaucrats and which had played an active role in the suppression of leftist insurrections between 1919 and 1923. In fact Brecht had personal experience of social democracy's attempts to defend a rotten order when the Berlin SPD police chief Zörgiebel banned the performance of Peter Lampel's anti-Reichswehr play *Giftgas über Berlin* (*Poison Gas over Berlin*) in 1929.

From its inception the Weimar Republic had lacked support. A large section of aristocratic and upper-middle-class society looked back wistfully to the days of the old Reich. The massive inflation of the early 1920s radicalized many workers, as is testified by the growth of Communist and ultra-leftist organizations, by armed insurrections in Berlin, Saxony and the Ruhr, and by demands for socialization, and also alienated many members of the lower middle class. The apparent stability of the mid-1920s was illusory; for economic recovery was largely based on foreign finance, high structural unemployment persisted – even before the Wall Street Crash in October 1929 over 2 million workers were without jobs – and a large section of the electorate simply stayed away from the polling booths. The onset of the great depression destroyed all illusions, threw into sharp relief the absence of a democratic consensus and polarized society anew. Massive unemployment – in January 1933 the real figure stood at over 7 million and therefore included no less than one in every three of the potential labour force – drove large numbers of workers into the arms of a Communist movement which believed that the final collapse of capitalism was at hand and therefore did not hesitate to exploit the weaknesses of the Republic or to attack what it regarded as the betrayer of the working class, the SPD. At the same time Brecht was a first-hand witness to the slaughter of KPD (German Communist Party) demonstrators by the SPD authorities on May Day 1929 in Berlin, an event which further impressed upon him the bankruptcy of social democracy.

It was not only the left which was radicalized by the experiences of the depression, however. The collapse of agricultural prices led to peasant bankruptcy and in its wake the peasant embraced the cause of Nazism, especially in Protestant Germany. The ruination of small businesses, insecure at the best of times and now quite unable to survive the competition of big business, led other sections of the *Mittelstand* into Hitler's camp and by 1932 the NSDAP (National Socialist German Workers Party) was easily the largest single party in Germany. Some sections of big business (albeit a minority) also turned to the Nazis, seeing therein a bulwark against the rising threat of Bolshevism. In a sense what finally brought Hitler to power as Chancellor in January 1933 was collusion between an anti-democratic, old élite of conservative politicians, generals and businessmen on the one hand and a new mass movement called Nazism on the other.

Thus it was the depression of the early 1930s which finally undermined Germany's first experiment in democracy, a depression celebrated in Brecht's *Die Heilige Johanna der Schlachthöfe*, whose scenes recall the various stages of the business cycle through prosperity, overproduction, crisis, stagnation and finally the regeneration of the cycle. In fact, by this time it was clear that the dramatist had gained a much more scientific insight into Marxism through the collaboration of Fritz Sternberg and above all Karl Korsch. It was a Marxism more flexible, less dogmatic and far more complex than the Stalinism currently espoused by the KPD, but it and the fact that Brecht's wife was a Jewess were more than sufficient cause for flight from the rigours and evils of the new Nazi regime, a regime which regarded his work as anathema. It was on the morning after the Reichstag fire, used by Hitler as a pretext to suspend civil liberties and institute a semi-legal and in some cases unconstitutional terrorism against the left, that Brecht's flight into exile began. During that exile developments in his native and tortured land remained central to his activity as an artist. His *Furcht und Elend des Dritten Reiches* (*Fear and Misery of the Third Reich*) captures the omnipresent surveillance and the resultant human insecurity as do few other historical or literary works: it is especially strong on the invasion of even domestic privacy through the institutions of the state and the member of the family who might just spill the beans to the local Hitler Youth. In such circumstances effective resistance was to prove wellnigh impossible, although Brecht for a long time placed his hopes in some kind of proletarian rejection of the National Socialist state and even wrote his *Galileo* in part as an attempt to encourage working-class resistance. He also parodied what might well have seemed ludicrous in Nazi racial theory and policy, had it not been that these gave rise to genocide on an unprecedented scale, in his rather crude satire *Die Rundkopfe und die Spitzkopfe* (*Round Heads and Pointed Heads*), which decried the way in which such racialism distracted humanity from the realities of class struggle into vicious ethnic conflict.

Brecht's view of the Third Reich was telling in many respects. It was a state based on institutionalized violence, the violence of the Gestapo, the SS, the concentration and the extermination camps, a state which robbed its citizens of their privacy as well as their civil liberties. It was a state in which racial theory dictated programmes of euthanasia and genocide. At the same time the promised *Volksgemeinschaft*[1] was not realized, despite Nazi propaganda claims to the contrary. The Nazi state did not create a classless and harmonious society: capital became ever more concentrated into the hands of gigantic industrial empires, such as those of Krupp and Thyssen, income differentials increased, working hours extended, positions of authority, power and influence within the civil service, army and judiciary remained in much the same hands as before. The rhetoric of a 'people's community' remained rhetoric, except for a few privileged members of the only real means to social mobility, the Nazi Party itself.

The final result of twelve years of National Socialist rule, of course, was not simply a human holocaust but also the destruction of Germany itself. By 1949 the cold war had dictated the division of Germany into antagonistic military and economic camps; and this new Germany – or rather these new Germanies – bore little resemblance to what Brecht had envisaged earlier: he had placed his hopes in a proletarian insurrection in the wake of the war, a proletarian insurrection in which the workers themselves would create a different social, economic and political order. Despite his disappointment, however, Brecht ultimately decided to throw his lot in with the creation of a socialist state of some kind or other in the Soviet-dominated Eastern Zone. At times he was critical of the failings of the GDR: for example, he believed that the workers who rose in Berlin in June 1953 had something of a point, albeit not the point which Western propaganda tried to make out of that rising. For when it came to the crunch, Brecht could not give his support to a West German regime which remained committed to the capitalist order and which seemed to be tied to the apron-strings of the most aggressive and imperialist of capitalist powers, the USA, a superpower which had gone to war in Korea and which, at a much more immediate and personal level, had summoned him before the House Un-American Activities Committee while he was living there at the start of the McCarthyite era. When Brecht died, on 14 August 1956, he still identified the GDR with the socialist society of the future.

NOTE

1. Literally 'people's community'. The German term implies a form of social organization which is based upon ethnicity, which is 'natural' and 'organic' as opposed to 'artificial' and racially mixed, in which there is social harmony and no class conflict, and in which all think of themselves exclusively as Germans.

SELECT BIBLIOGRAPHY

WILHELMINE GERMANY

General
EVANS, R. J., *Society and Politics in Wilhelmine Germany*, London, 1978
ROSENBERG, A., *Imperial Germany*, New York, 1970
STURMER, M., *Das kaiserliche Deutschland*, Dusseldorf, 1970
WEHLER, H. -U, *Das deutsche Kaiserreich*, Gottingen, 1973

The right
PUHLE, H. -J., *Agrarische Interssenpolitik und Preussischer Konservatismus*, Hannover, 1966
STEGMANN, D., *Die Erben Bismarcks*, Cologne, 1970

The left
ANDERSON, E., *Hammar or Anvil*, London, 1945
GEARY, D., 'The German labour movement', *European Studies Review*, July, 1976
RITTER, G. A., *Die Arbeiterbewegung im Wilhelminischen Reich*, Berlin, 1959
ROTH, G., *Social Democrats in Imperial Germany*, Totowa, New York, 1963
SCHORSKE, C. E., *German Social Democracy*, Cambridge, Mass., 1955

THE WAR (1914–18)

FELDMAN, G., *Army, Industry and Labour in Germany, 1914–1918*, Princeton, 1966
KOCKA. J.. *Klassengesellschaft im Krieg*. Göttingen. 1973

R. Geary

THE WEIMAR REPUBLIC

BRACHER, K. D., *Die Auflösung der Weimarer Republik*, Villingen, 1964
MACKENZIE, J. R. P., *The Weimar Republic*, London, 1971
NICHOLLS, A. J., *Weimar and the Rise of Hitler*, London, 1968

On the Communist Party
FLECHTHEIM, O., *Geschichte der KPD*, Offenbach am Main, 1948

On Nazism
ALLEN, W. S., *The Nazi Seizure of Power*, London, 1966
BULLOCK, A., *Hitler*, London, 1962
WOOLF, S. J., *The Nature of Fascism*, London, 1968

THE THIRD REICH

BRACHER, K. D., *The German Dictatorship*, London, 1971
MASON, T., *Arbeiterklasse und Volksgemeinschaft*, Oplan, 1975
NEUMANN, F., *Behemoth*, New York, 1966
SCHOENBAUM, D., *Hitler's Social Revolution*, London, 1967
SCHWEITZER, A., *Big Business in the Third Reich*, London, 1964

POST 1945

CHILDS, D., *East Germany*, London, 1969
GROSSER, A., *Germany in Our Time*, London, 1971
KREJCI, J., *Social Structure in a Divided Germany*, London, 1976
STEELE, J., *Socialism with a German Face*, London, 1977

Chapter 2

GERMAN DRAMA BEFORE BRECHT: FROM NEO-CLASSICISM TO EXPRESSIONISM

LADISLAUS LOB

In his 1930 notes to the opera *Aufstieg und Fall der Stadt Mahagonny* (*Rise and Fall of the City of Mahagonny*)[1] Brecht formulates for the first time the theory of drama to which, despite subsequent modifications, he adhered throughout his life. His chief concern is to distinguish two types of theatre, which he calls 'dramatic' and 'epic'.

At the level of form, as Brecht outlines in a famous table of key phrases, 'dramatic' theatre relies on 'linear development' and 'evolutionary determinism', ensuring that 'one scene makes another' ('Geschehen linear', 'evolutionare Zwangslaufigkeit', 'eine Szene für die andere'), while 'epic' theatre moves in 'curves' and 'jumps', leaving 'each scene for itself' ('Kurven', 'Sprünge', 'jede Szene für sich'). In terms of effect 'dramatic' theatre, by keeping the 'eyes on the finish', insisting on 'suggestion' and appealing to 'feeling', 'implicates the spectator in a stage situation' and 'wears down his capacity for action' ('Spannung auf den Ausgang', 'Suggestion', 'Gefühl', 'verwickelt den Zuschauer in eine Bühnenaktion', 'verbraucht seine Aktivität'), while 'epic' theatre, by keeping the 'eyes on the course', insisting on 'argument' and appealing to 'reason', 'turns the spectator into an observer' and 'arouses his capacity for action' ('Spannung auf den Gang', 'Argument', 'Ratio', 'macht den Zuschauer zum Betrachter', 'weckt seine Aktivitat'). In the ideology of 'dramatic' theatre, where 'thought determines being', man is considered 'unchangeable' ('das Denken bestimmt das Sein', 'der unveranderliche Mensch'), while in that of 'epic' theatre, where 'social being determines thought', man is considered 'changeable and able to bring about change' ('das gesellschaftliche Sein bestimmt das Denken', 'der veranderliche und verändernde Mensch'). In short Brecht postulates that 'dramatic' theatre, through its causally coherent structure, involves the audience's emotions in the experience of the characters and thereby fosters a passive acceptance of the existing order, while 'epic' theatre, through its structural inconsistencies, distances the audience from the play and thereby promotes critical thinking and the will to change society.

11

Despite its apodictic tone Brecht's essay is not an objective analysis but a special plea for his own 'epic' theatre: consequently he mixes traditional, formal observations with unsubstantiated claims about their effects, and he arranges his sets of characteristics specifically to lead to a Marxist conclusion; he is perhaps at his most questionable when he allocates moral or spiritual idealism to the 'dramatic' mode and social realism or philosophical materialism to the 'epic' mode. Nevertheless his criteria, taken individually, afford acute insights into the way the theatre functions. Without adopting his bias, we may therefore employ them as helpful conceptual tools for a survey of the theory and practice of German drama from Neo-Classicism, when modern literature began, to Expressionism, which was the last movement to dominate the theatrical scene before Brecht arrived on it.

The foremost authority of Neo-Classicism in German literature was the Leipzig professor, Johann Christoph Gottsched (1700–66), who restored artistic merit to a stage left destitute after the decline of Baroque drama. Although he made a considerable practical impact by editing a compendium of derivative plays entitled *Deutsche Schaubühne, nach den Regeln der alten Griechen und Römer eingerichtet* (*The German Stage, according to the Rules of the Ancient Greeks and Romans*) (1740–45) he is remembered chiefly as a theorist. Influenced by the rationalist Leibniz–Wolffian philosophy of the Enlightenment and the works of French playwrights and critics such as Boileau, Corneille, Racine, Molière, Destouches and La Chaussée, he discusses the different poetic genres in *Versuch einer critischen Dichtkunst vor die Deutschen* (*An Essay concerning Poetics for the Germans*) (1730). The tragic dramatist, he legislates, must illustrate a moral axiom with an appropriate tale chosen from history, divided into five acts, and progressing through causally linked incidents; to achieve verisimilitude, he must observe the three Unities, as derived by French tragedians from Aristotle, restricting the time, place and action of each play to one day, one locality, and one main plot; to convey the message forcefully, he must maintain a serious mood, evoking the Aristotelian emotions of pity and terror by concentrating on the misfortunes of characters who belong to the highest ranks of society and who speak in dignified alexandrine verse. The comic dramatist must also observe the Unities, but since he is to edify through amusement, as in the French *comédie larmoyante*, he may include everyday expressions in his verse and depict the ludicrous quandaries of characters from the middle and lower classes.

The supremacy of Gottsched's 'regular' drama was broken by Gotthold Ephraim Lessing (1729–81), the greatest literary representative of the German Enlightenment and a herald of the approaching movements of *Sturm und Drang* (Storm and Stress) and Weimar Classicism.

Lessing's most celebrated theoretical statements occur in the essays he contributed in Berlin to the series *Briefe, die neueste Literatur betreffend* (*Letters on the Subject of Recent Literature*) (1759–65). In the seventeenth essay of the sequence he rebukes Gottsched for recommending French models, and he praises Shakespeare as a writer who comes closer to the essence of Greek tragedy while disregarding its form, whose English temperament is more congenial to Germans, and who by being a natural genius is more apt to inspire similar geniuses in Germany: this discovery marks the beginning of Shakespeare's lasting importance for a long line of German authors, which is underlined, for example, by the fact that Brecht, albeit with various reservations, refers to him more often than to any other individual. In the collection of reviews he published in Hamburg under the title *Hamburgische Dramaturgie* (*The Hamburg Dramaturgy*) (1767–69), Lessing continues to encourage German cultural nationalism by replacing French influences with those of the Greeks and Shakespeare and by expanding his novel concept of creativity. A theatrical genius, he explains, may ignore mechanical rules or historical accuracy, if his actions represent unbroken chains of causes and effects evolving from consistent characters and producing an illusion of unavoidable necessity. While all drama aims at moral improvement, comedy does so not by deriding specific vices but by sharpening the spectator's general sense of humour, and tragedy not by exalting specific virtues but by making the callous spectator sensitive and the sentimental spectator stoic: this balancing of mental faculties in the latter genre is the Aristotelian 'catharsis' which is brought about through tragic pity and fear, meaning respectively the spectator's sympathetic participation in the characters' emotions and his apprehension that he could himself become the victim of their misfortunes. The need for the emotional involvement of increasingly middle-class audiences accounts for one of Lessing's most far-reaching innovations: prompted by the *comédie larmoyante* in France and the works of Lillo and Richardson in England, he champions domestic tragedy, or *bürgerliches Trauerspiel*, which endows middle-class characters, speaking contemporary prose and beset by contemporary problems, with tragic dignity.

Among Lessing's major plays, the 'serious comedy' *Minna von Barnhelm* (1767) has been hailed as the first recognizable theatrical presentation of contemporary German individuals and society, while the blank-verse drama *Nathan der Weise* (1779) is admired as an outstanding plea for religious tolerance and human brotherhood. The evolution of social drama owes most to his two domestic tragedies: *Miss Sara Sampson* (1755), featuring elopement, murder and suicide amid uppercrust but bourgeois-tempered English people, represents the breakthrough of the genre, and *Emilia Galotti* (1772), in which the officer Odoardo kills his daughter Emilia to save her from seduction by the unscrupulous prince, introduces to it, in an Italian disguise, the conflict of upright bourgeoisie and corrupt aristocracy that was to be copied, with deliberate political implications that Lessing denies for his part, by many subsequent practitioners.

In terms of Brecht's dichotomy both Gottsched's and Lessing's rational didacticism are 'epic' features, reinforced in Lessing by the beginnings of social criticism in domestic tragedy; their insistence on moral idealism, realistic plausibility, structural cohesion and sympathetic audience–involvement, however, place them among the founders of 'dramatic' theatre. The *Stürmer und Dränger*, on the other hand, owing to their disruption of 'regular' form and their rebellion against the conventions of society, are direct forerunners of Brecht's 'epic' theatre, although their wildly emotional titanism contradicts his cool rationality.

The *Sturm und Drang*, while strongly influenced by Rousseau, idolized Shakespeare. This is best seen in the paean *Zum Shakespeares Tag* (*In Honour of Shakespeare*), written in Strasbourg in 1771 by the young Johann Wolfgang Goethe (1749–1832). Here, inspired by Johann Gottfried Herder, whose equally significant essay *Shakespeare* was also written in 1771, Goethe denounces the Unities as intolerable curbs on the imagination, and eulogizes Shakespeare for achieving inner unity by confronting individual freedom with universal necessity through widely ranging actions and magnificently natural characters that exhibit the abundance of the world and the unparalleled genius of the artist. Jakob Michael Reinhold Lenz (1751–92), who followed Goethe to Strasbourg and for whom, incidentally, Brecht had a particular admiration, advances similar views, carrying them further in some respects. Thus in *Anmerkungen über das Theater* (*Notes on the Theatre*) (1774) he argues that comedy depicts concrete social conditions, while in tragedy the Greeks demonstrated the power of divine fate through coherent plots whereas Shakespeare and other moderns demonstrate the autonomy of the individual through multifarious actions; in *Rezension des neuen Menoza* (*A Review in Defence of the New Menoza*) (1775) he repudiates neo-classical distinctions to the degree of enjoining dramatists to write tragicomedies.

Although the 1770s saw many plays by other *Stürmer und Dränger*, including Heinrich Wilhelm von Gerstenberg, Heinrich Leopold Wagner and Friedrich Maximilian Klinger, only those of Goethe and Lenz have proved durable. Goethe's *Götz von Berlichingen* (1773) is the first and greatest: based on early German history, written in colloquial though hyperbolically intense prose, moving numerous characters over wide expanses of time and place in loosely linked episodes marked by sharp changes of mood, the tragedy of the rough but honest robber-baron, destroyed by treacherous court and church officials, conveys with unique energy the author's and the movement's passionate yearning for the individual's liberation from social, moral and aesthetic constraints. *Sturm und Drang* features are also prominent in *Urfaust*, written in 1772–75 and incorporated in *Faust I* (1808), notably in the hero's boundless striving for self-fulfilment at the expense of Gretchen, the village maiden seduced by him and executed for killing her illegitimate child; *Faust* as a whole, however, is a vast poem rather than a play.

Egmont (begun in 1775, completed in 1787), on the other hand, modifies its hero's *Sturm und Drang* struggle for personal and political freedom with more objective characterization and more coherent plot development in the manner of Weimar Classicism.

Lenz is chiefly remembered for *Der Hofmeister* (*The Tutor*) (1774), in which the middle-class tutor Läuffer seduces his aristocratic pupil Gustchen, castrates himself and marries a peasant maid, while Gustchen finds an aristocratic husband and father for her illegitimate child, and *Die Soldaten* (*The Soldiers*) (1776), in which the middle-class shopkeeper's daughter Marie, seduced by the aristocratic officer Desportes, is ruined by a succession of further lovers, while her middle-class fiancé Stolzius poisons Desportes and himself. Both plays show Lenz's detestation of class prejudices and his awareness of physical, psychological and social reality, together with his habit of adding propagandist *nonsequiturs*, such as the demand for public education or military brothels. His mingling of the tragic and the comic, his diffuse actions and his abrupt ungrammatical prose anticipate the grotesque and absurd traits of twentieth-century drama.

The subsequent movement of Weimar Classicism centred on the friendship of the mature Goethe and Schiller. Inspired by both Greek and Shakespearean values, Goethe developed his classical attitude through his responsibilities in the Weimar administration, his platonic relationship with Charlotte von Stein, his scientific researches and his Italian journey, while Schiller developed his through the study of history and Kantian philosophy.

The major plays of Goethe's classical phase, apart from the *Helena* interlude (1827) which became the nucleus of *Faust II* (1832) and which briefly unites the medieval German hero with the Hellenic heroine, are *Iphigenie auf Tauris* (*Iphigenia in Tauris*) (1787) and *Torquato Tasso* (1790). Iphigenie's agonizing choice of absolute sincerity averts tragedy and wins divine blessing for human integrity; Tasso's neurotic maladjustment is balanced by his poetic talent, and his conflict with the politician Antonio is resolved in a humane society, which synthesizes passion and decorum, material security and aesthetic culture: both plays dramatize the German *Humanitätsideal* (ideal of humanity), observing the Unities, employing refined blank verse, and exploring subtle moral and psychological problems of idealized characters in rarefied Greek-mythological or Italian-Renaissance settings. While Goethe's contribution to the classical theory of drama is slight, his great classical plays thus prove eminently 'dramatic', as do many lesser plays written throughout his career, notably *Die natürliche Tochter* (*The Natural Daughter*) (1803), an expression of his conservative reaction to the French Revolution and of his Classicism at its most remote.

Unlike Goethe, Friedrich Schiller (1759–1805) expounds his philosophy in numerous substantial essays. He sees man torn between senses and reason, realism and idealism, spontaneous unity, as enjoyed by the

Greeks or Shakespeare, and self-conscious fragmentation, as experienced by most moderns. He constantly seeks freedom, conceived predominantly in aesthetic or moral terms: aesthetic freedom, or beauty, derives from the balance of opposites found in the fusion of concrete subject-matter and abstract form in art or in the rare coincidence of inclination and duty in life; moral freedom, or sublimity, implies the victory of duty over inclination. Schiller's specific theory of drama, particularly tragedy, carries on from Lessing, emphasizing passion in *Sturm und Drang* fashion, and postulating that the stage affects man's entire constitution in accordance with the harmonious *Humanitätsideal* of Weimar Classicism. This notion first appears in the seminal *Die Schaubühne als eine moralische Anstalt betrachtet* (*The Theatre Considered as a Moral Institution*) (1785) where it is accompanied by a political interpretation of drama as an instrument of judgement over the German dukes and princes who, up to the mid-nineteenth century, ruled their states with feudal authority, granting their subjects few rights and swiftly stamping on dissent: this oppositional role, assigned to the theatre by a self-liberating bourgeoisie, has remained one of its basic functions to the present day (see Ch. 7).

In general, however, Schiller concentrates on less political issues. In *Über den Grund des Vergnügens an tragischen Gegenständen* (*On the Reasons for the Pleasure derived from Tragic Subjects*) and *Über die tragische Kunst* (*On Tragic Art*) (both 1792) he stresses that the mixed sensation of pain and pleasure in tragedy results from the audience's involvement in coherent actions and consistent characters, attained if necessary by sacrificing historical authenticity. In *Über das Pathetische* (*On Pathos*) (1793), *Vom Erhabenen* (*Of the Sublime*) (1793) and *Über das Erhabene* (*On the Sublime*) (1801) he explains that the sublime in tragedy distresses the spectator by making him share the heroes' sufferings, and at the same time instils in the spectator a joyful sense of escape, either by infecting him with the heroes' own elation as they stoically accept physical or emotional ordeals for a moral purpose, or by reminding him that the anguish he and the heroes undergo is merely fictitious. In *Über den Gebrauch des Chors in der Tragödie* (*On the Use of the Chorus in Tragedy*), the preface to his most severely classical play *Die Braut von Messina* (*The Bride of Messina*) (1803), he argues that the intellectual comments and lyrical reflections of the chorus intervene between the action and the audience to defeat oppressive verism by poetic freedom. Thus the call for relentless precipitation and unfaltering participation makes Schiller a prime representative of 'dramatic' theatre, while his occasional attempts to distance the spectator from the stage come closer to the methods of 'epic' theatre than Brecht, who vehemently dislikes his idealism, would admit.

Schiller's plays, like Brecht's, dramatize their author's philosophy but have a superb theatrical vitality of their own. Unlike Brecht's, they subordinate the 'epic' assessment of society to the 'dramatic' assault on the spectator's sensibilities. While the search for classical balance appears from the beginning of the canon, the enthusiasm of *Sturm und Drang*, increasingly modified by romantic elements, persists to the end; and while the concept of freedom frequently takes stoic shapes, it also reflects political aspirations of the kind that culminated in the French Revolution of 1789. Closest to *Sturm und Drang* are *Die Räuber* (*The Robbers*) (1781) and *Kabale und Liebe* (*Intrigue and Love*) (1784), two realistically based prose plays: in *Die Räuber* the machinations of the villain Franz and the guilt and atonement of the noble outlaw Karl provide two tenuously connected episodic plots in which violent characters challenge the established order in a tragic but vigorous pursuit of individual liberation; in *Kabale und Liebe*, one of the greatest domestic tragedies in the language, the cabal of the court president and his secretary Wurm against the love of the musician's daughter Luise and the president's son Ferdinand has metaphysical overtones, but is above all a thinly disguised indictment of the political tyranny of the corrupt aristocracy over the honest if inhibited bourgeoisie, which Schiller himself experienced to his own cost in Baden-Württemberg before he moved to Jena and Weimar.

The transition to Classicism, which starts with the intricately woven tragic action, sonorous blank verse, elevated historical setting and discerning psychology of *Don Carlos* (1787), is completed in Schiller's masterpieces, the *Wallenstein* trilogy (1798–99) and *Maria Stuart* (1800). In *Wallensteins Lager* (*Wallenstein's Camp*) the colourful spectacle of the soldiers' life in the Thirty Years War is held together by frequent references to the absent general; in *Die Piccolomini* the officers' attitudes crystallize around Octavio, who conducts a clandestine campaign on behalf of the emperor, and his son Max, who admires Wallenstein and loves his daughter Thekla; in *Wallensteins Tod* (*Wallenstein's Death*) the eponymous hero assumes full stature as he stops prevaricating, converts his ambitious fancies into bold rebellion and, after the desertion of his troops, is murdered by hired assassins, while Max rushes into a fatal battle to end his divided loyalties: the trilogy expresses Schiller's philosophical dualism, but its artistic triumph rests in his unerring control of a vast historical panorama, observed with penetrating realism and suffused with an atmosphere of inexorable tragedy. *Maria Stuart*, on the other hand, distorts history to glorify sublimity, as the idealized Scottish queen is wrongfully accused of conspiring against her English rival Elizabeth, but willingly accepts her execution to expiate her earlier transgressions: an impression of tragic inevitability results from the concentrated treatment of monumental symmetries and antitheses, political intrigue and spiritual exaltation in a structure which revives the Unities and which in 'analytic' fashion carries the irrevocable events of the past unremittingly to their foregone conclusion.

The box-office success of Lessing, Goethe and Schiller was surpassed by such authors as Friedrich Ludwig Schröder, August Wilhelm Iffland

and August Kotzebue, whose sentimental prose dramas portray contemporary bourgeois society in 'dramatic' patterns and contribute to the subsequent development of nineteenth-century Realism. In the first three decades of the nineteenth century, however, serious German literature was dominated by Romanticism. Although the Romantic movement made little impact on stage, its innovations are not negligible. Romantic theory, represented chiefly by the brothers Friedrich Schlegel and August Wilhelm Schlegel, may be associated with 'dramatic' idealism in so far as it proclaims the sovereignty of mind over matter, but it shows 'epic' potential in demanding that writers mix the different genres in one poetic whole, and in promoting Shakespeare and Calderón, who were also introduced to Germans in influential Romantic translations. Romantic practice, represented in the theatre chiefly by Ludwig Tieck, appears at its most typical in two species: the Romantic chronicle play features episodic narratives borrowed from popular chap-books, a variety of lyrical styles, and pageants of legendary figures in medieval settings, extolling Catholic mysticism or chivalresque nationalism, revealing subconscious impulses, and steeping men and nature in supernatural magic; Romantic comedy withdraws from reality into fairy-tales or satirical literary feuds, and asserts poetic freedom through deliberate inconsistencies in the sequence of events, overt role-playing by the actors, addresses to the audience and other methods of underlining the fictitiousness of plays, known as 'Romantic irony'. While Brecht might dismiss the metaphysics as 'dramatic', the disjointed structure of the Romantic chronicle play is 'epic', as is the peculiar irony of Romantic comedy which directly anticipates his own technique of *Verfremdung* (distancing or alienation).

The greatest dramatist of the period was Heinrich von Kleist (1777–1811), a Prussian nobleman who after restless wanderings committed suicide near Berlin. Kleist's awareness of irrational and subconscious forces links him with Romanticism, but his stringent actions and tense, mimetic, blank verse contrast in 'dramatic' fashion with the 'epic' diffuseness of Romantic drama. As is gleaned from his letters and occasional essays, he sometimes believes that spontaneous certainty destroyed by reflection may be regained at a higher level of spiritual insight, but generally he feels, under the influence of Kant, that all human perception is inadequate: error, misunderstanding and confusion are therefore his recurrent themes. In his tragicomic adaptation of the familiar Greek myth in *Amphitryon* (1807), the failure of Alkmene to distinguish her seducer Jupiter from her husband Amphitryon proves reason, senses and emotions equally fallible. In *Penthesilea* (1808), the tragedy of the legendary Amazon queen who kills her lover Achilles and herself in extreme bewilderment demonstrates the ambiguity of passion, foreshadowing Freud's psycho-analytic concept of sado-masochism and Nietzsche's discovery of the Dionysian aspects of Greek civilization. In the medievalizing romance *Das Käthchen von Heilbronn* (*Cathleen of*

Heilbronn) (1810), prophetic dreams and telepathic intimations triumph over intellectual misconceptions, as the supposed armourer's daughter turns out to be the emperor's child and is blissfully united with the knight Strahl. In the rural comedy *Der zerbrochne Krug* (*The Broken Jug*) (1811), true knowledge overcomes deliberate obfuscation, as the judge Adam convicts himself of attempted sexual blackmail. In *Die Hermannsschlacht* (*Hermann's Battle*) (written in 1808, published in 1821), one of many German plays celebrating the Teutonic chieftain Arminius's victorious fight against the Roman occupation, anti-Napoleonic chauvinism is clothed in the unrestrained advocacy of violence and deception. Kleist's masterpiece *Prinz Friedrich von Homburg* (written in 1810–11, published in 1821), in which the eponymous hero wins a battle by disobeying the elector's orders and is pardoned after accepting his death sentence, seems to plead for the political submission of the individual to the state or for the classical cultural reconciliation of subjective and objective values; but since the chain of potentially tragic events and their happy conclusion rest on the elector's arbitrary decisions, and since the prince's initial dream of love and glory is fulfilled in a similarly dreamlike closing scene, the Kleistian mood of mysterious irrationality continues to prevail.

Leaving aside Austrian variants of Classicism, Romanticism and indigenous folk theatre in the works of Ferdinand Raimund, Johann Nestroy and Franz Grillparzer, German drama between the 1820s and 1880s became increasingly realistic. The evolution of science, the materialist neo-Hegelian philosophy of Ludwig Feuerbach and David Friedrich Strauss, the French-inspired political resistance of bourgeois liberalism against the conservative Restoration, and the subsequent attacks, led by Marx and Engels, of socialism against bourgeois capitalism, transformed earlier attempts at depicting outward reality into a new realistic style based on the empirical observation of people determined by physical, psychological and socio-economic factors in specific times and places. The first dramatists of German Realism were Grabbe and Büchner.

Christian Dietrich Grabbe (1801–1836), who died young of syphilis and alcoholism in his native Detmold, advances 'dramatic' theories in *Über die Shakespearo-Manie* (*On Shakespeare-mania*) (1827) and other essays, but his own practice is very different. His plays include a Gothic melodrama *Herzog Theodor von Gothland* (*Duke Theodore of Gothland*) and a romantically ironic comedy *Scherz, Satire, Ironie und tiefere Bedeutung* (*Jest, Satire, Irony and Deeper Meaning*) (both completed in 1822 and published in 1827), a tragic phantasmagoria *Don Juan und Faust* (1829) and historical dramas such as *Kaiser Friedrich Barbarossa* (1829), *Kaiser Heinrich der Sechste* (1830), *Napoleon oder die hundert Tage* (*Napoleon or the Hundred Days*) (1831), *Hannibal* (1835) and *Die Hermannsschlacht* (completed in 1836, published in 1838): in all these he exhibits his troubled psyche through violent incidents and overdrawn heroes, but frequently brings to bear a realistic understanding of the interaction of individuals and mass movements in history, mixing prose with verse and colloquialism with turgid hyperbole, sketching broad vistas of society in disconnected snatches, and revelling in grotesque contrasts of moods. The anti-idealistic outlook and discontinuous form of his plays make him a notable precursor of Brecht's 'epic' theatre.

Georg Büchner (1813–1837), whose death from typhus cut short a promising scientific and artistic career, combines uncompromisingly realistic qualities with anticipations of Naturalism and Expressionism. His notorious fatalism apart, his contribution to Brecht's 'epic' methods exceeds even Grabbe's. His views are theoretically discussed in his letters and his story *Lenz* (written in 1835, published in 1838). In literature he rejects the idealism of Schiller in favour of a realism, adumbrated by Shakespeare, Goethe and Lenz, which reproduces everyday life or history faithfully, regardless of morality or beauty. In politics he considers all-out class struggle as the only solution, but his left-wing radicalism, which necessitated his flight to Strasbourg and Zurich after revolutionary activities in Darmstadt and Giessen, is accompanied by the realization that the German poor are not ready to rise against the rich and mighty. Disillusioned with contemporary conditions, horrified by his study of the French Revolution, prone to the Byronic melancholy rife among post-Romantic young Europeans, he sees a ghastly fatality at work in individuals and masses alike. Determinism is the keynote of his comedy *Leonce und Lena* (written in 1836, published in 1838), which both reaffirms and parodies Romantic decadence, and his tragedies *Dantons Tod* (*Danton's Death*) (1835), and *Woyzeck* (left unfinished in 1837, published in 1879).

Dantons Tod, relying largely on authentic historical accounts, dramatizes the last days of the eponymous hero and his followers before they are guillotined by the faction of Robespierre and St Just: although Büchner appreciates the socio-economic causation of communal violence, he pictures the Revolution as a superhuman force that blindly destroys its human agents; opposing to the ideological postures of the Jacobins the cynicism, hedonism and nihilism of the Dantonists, he advocates an unflinching confrontation of the painful truth, but at the same time unveils the fatal boredom and anxiety of a society that has jettisoned idealistic comforts without finding new positive values to replace them. *Woyzeck*, based on an actual court case, indicts social injustice through the cruel jokes and degrading experiments inflicted by the captain and the doctor on the penniless, inarticulate soldier of the title, the first proletarian anti-hero of German drama, but the sexual jealousy culminating in the voices that urge him to stab his unfaithful mistress Marie link psychopathology with metaphysical mystery. Both tragedies then exhibit humanity as a passive object of irresistible compulsions in an incomprehensibly hostile universe; and both convey this pessimistic message in a multitude of self-contained episodes united not by causal continuity but by subtle correspondences and contrasts in the themes, characters, incidents and above all in the colloquial prose dialogue which thus acquires the richness of poetry.

Revolutionary aspirations are also found in the works of Heinrich Laube and Karl Gutzkow, the leaders of the *Junges Deutschland* movement, with which Büchner sympathized, but which he regarded as too intellectually moderate to be politically effective. Distrusting spiritual idealism, both men seek human fulfilment in reality, pleading for freedom of expression, sexual permissiveness, class equality and other reforms associated with bourgeois liberalism, which increased in strength from the mid-1830s but was checked by the victory of conservative establishments over the 1848 uprisings. Their demands for reform, however, do not extend to the form of drama. In both theory and practice they follow the 'regular' approaches of French Classicism as revived in the 'well-made' plays of Scribe, Sardou and Augier: although in content they are Germany's first 'committed' writers, in structure they remain traditionally 'dramatic'. Traditional 'dramatic' methods continued to dominate the theatre for several decades around the middle of the nineteenth century, as in the treatises and plays of Otto Ludwig and Gustav Freytag in Germany and the plays of Ludwig Anzengruber in Austria. These writers provide the outstanding examples of 'Poetic Realism', a compromise between objective psychological and social observation and the requirements of subjective ideas and homogeneous plots, but while they offer valuable insights into the lives of the contemporary bourgeoisie or peasantry, often with a liberal bias, they arouse little more than academic interest today.

Realistic tendencies appear in the work of Friedrich Hebbel (1813–63) but are often subordinated to a brooding Hegelesque metaphysic. In the dissertation *Mein Wort über das Drama* (*A Word on the Drama*) (1843) Hebbel, who suffered abject poverty in Wesselburen, Hamburg and Munich before he settled comfortably in Vienna, argues that tragedy must pit human nature against historical events, which may be altered if necessary, to prove that all life is a struggle between the individual and the universal: the individual cannot help asserting himself against the equilibrium of the universal, which punishes this existential rather than moral guilt by destroying him. In his prefatory note to '*Maria Magdalene*' (1844) Hebbel suggests that the universal itself changes, perhaps through its clash with the individual: great drama occurs in eras of universal change, as it did with the Greeks and Shakespeare and as it may do again in the nineteenth century, a time, he claims conservatively, of growing calls for a better foundation of the prevailing order; the great dramatist is one who succeeds best in conveying abstract ideas through concrete characters and actions, creating mounting suspense and unflagging interest. Hebbel's habit of bracketing his metaphysical speculations with the realistic, semi-autobiographical, psychological conflicts of overbearing male and resentful female protagonists underlies the 'dramatic' actions of the legend-based tragedies *Judith* (1840), *Herodes und Mariamne* (1849) and *Gyges und sein Ring* (1856). In the historical tragedy *Agnes Bernauer* (1852), in which the duke Ernst eliminates the virtuous barber's daughter Agnes to avert the war of succession that might result from her marriage to his son Albrecht, the two themes are fused more convincingly in a 'dramatic' plot that lends artistic substance to the conservative political message of the citizen's prostration before the state. In *Maria Magdalene* (1844) man victimizes woman in the person of the joiner's daughter Klara who, impregnated by the calculating clerk Leonhard, drowns herself to save her self-righteous father Anton from disgrace. As Hebbel explains in his preface, he hopes to rejuvenate domestic tragedy by deriving the conflict not from the stereotyped opposition of middle class and aristocracy but from the narrow-mindedness of the middle class itself; abandoning metaphysical dialectics, he thus achieves a bleak realistic masterpiece, which may be 'epic' in its criticism of the ossification of formerly progressive middle-class attitudes, but which is rendered powerfully 'dramatic' by the inexorable interaction of clearly outlined characters at the mercy of their own weakness and their claustrophobic, petty-bourgeois surroundings.

Realism assumed extreme proportions in Naturalism during the 1880s and 1890s, when the wealth of business and professional circles contrasted harshly with the destitution of the proletariat under the impact of spreading industrialization and urbanization, socialism was suppressed with bourgeois approval by the military-bureaucratic establishment of the newly founded Second Reich, and a materialistic outlook, based on the philosophical positivism of Auguste Comte, reinforced by the biological principles of Charles Darwin and expressed with singular refinement by Nietzsche, finally ousted metaphysical idealism. The writers of German Naturalism accordingly regarded man as entirely determined by his inherited characteristics and his physical and social environment. Influenced by Hippolyte Taine, Zola, Ibsen, Tolstoy and Dostoevsky, they held that art must devote itself to the allegedly scientific study of external reality; although they oscillated between demanding total objectivity and admitting a degree of subjective imagination, and although they were divided between pessimistic fatalism and optimistic belief in progress, they all shared a preoccupation with the sordid and miserable aspects of everyday living. The general aims of Naturalism, which evolved chiefly in Berlin and Munich, were proclaimed in many programmatic statements by such men as Wilhelm Bölsche, Karl Bleibtreu and the brothers Julius and Heinrich Hart. The most important theorist of drama in particular was Arno Holz (1863–1929). In *Die Kunst: Ihr Wesen und ihre Gesetze* (*Art: Its Essence and its Laws*) (1891) he pleads, somewhat ambiguously, for the 'second-by-second' style of 'konsequenter Naturalismus', or the utterly impersonal and complete literary reproduction of nature, while also allowing the author a personal bias; in *Evolution des Dramas* (written between 1896 and 1925, published in 1926) he hails the introduction of the language of real life and the delineation of characters instead of actions as the revolutionary innovations of Naturalist theatre. Among the practitioners of Naturalist drama Holz is best known for *Die Familie Selicke* (1890) which he wrote with Johannes Schlaf; Max Halbe and Hermann Sudermann were also much admired playwrights in their day. The foremost Naturalist dramatist, however, was Gerhart Hauptmann (1862–1946), whose work may epitomize the movement as a whole.

Hauptmann's aesthetic notions emerge from slight occasional articles, aphorisms and autobiographical sketches, rather than from sustained theoretical essays, and their ambivalence illustrates the contradictions inherent in Naturalism in general. He advocates unpolished, everyday dialogues and objectively observed, autonomous characters, rejecting plots as artificial constructions and the writer's subjective comments as untruthful intrusions, but he also argues that art must not merely copy the individual external features of natural objects but disclose their inner essence by capturing their typical characteristics, and he interprets human irrationality in increasingly metaphysical and mystical terms. Similar discrepancies occur in his politics: while he detested German nationalism and militarism, his patriotism prevented him from effectively resisting the Nazis, who displayed him as a figure-head of their 'blood-and-soil' ideology; and although his compassion for suffering humanity led him to sympathize with socialism in his youth, he preferred to remain an uncommitted individualist.

Hauptmann's best plays are those written in the Naturalist mode and set in Silesia or Berlin, where he spent the longest periods of his life. They concentrate on lower- or middle-class figures labouring solitarily under biological, psychological and social compulsions, hemmed in by meticulously described physical milieux, and involuntarily betraying rather than consciously discussing inchoate thoughts and feelings in colloquial prose ranging from standard German to broad dialect according to the speaker's status; to emphasize passive responses rather than purposeful activity, the plays dwell on static 'slices of life', with decisive events often assumed to occur off-stage or initiated by outsiders: thus they mix the 'dramatic' illusion of ineluctably determined reality with the 'epic' disjunction of characters, scenes and linguistic devices. *Vor Sonnenaufgang* (*Before Sunrise*) (1889), in which the discovery of coal in the Silesian mountains brings money-grubbing corruption to the circle of the landowning peasant Krause and the entrepreneurial engineer Hofmann, derived a scandalous success from the introduction of alcoholism, adultery and incest, but its most moving aspect is the tragedy of Krause's daughter Helene, whose pathetic hopes of escaping from her degenerate environment end in suicide when the fanatical social reformer Loth jilts her for fear of raising genetically impure children. *Das Friedensfest* (*The Family Reunion*) (1890) and *Einsame Menschen* (*Lonely Lives*) (1891) explore the emotional problems of

Berlin intellectuals stifled by the bourgeois family, while *Fuhrmann Henschel* (*Drayman Henschel*) (1898) and *Rose Bernd* (1903) unmask the disastrous effects of sexual weakness in apparently vigorous Silesian country people.

The apogee of Hauptmann's art is *Die Weber* (*The Weavers*) (1892), which turns the historical uprising of the Silesian weavers into the first and greatest mass drama in German literature. Encompassing merchant's mansion, village inn and workman's hovel, and opposing to the establishment represented by manufacturer, clergyman and police chief a crowd of individually recognizable but collectively motivated proletarians, the separate episodes unite in a relentless surge from lethargic starvation, through growing protests, to a climax of smashing and looting; a counterpoint is provided in the old pietist Hilse, who shuns violence but is killed by a stray bullet as the rioters attack the soldiers deployed against them. With his customary even-handedness Hauptmann does not indicate whether he favours revolutionary self-help or religious quietism; nevertheless the ironic ending underlines the tragic fact that destructive mass hysteria, however inevitable, is no viable alternative to capitalist exploitation and middle-class hypocrisy. Hauptmann's gift for comedy as well as tragedy is documented in *Die Ratten* (*The Rats*) (1911): in a Berlin tenement the mason's wife Frau John kills herself after losing a child she has bought from an unmarried chambermaid to replace her own dead baby, while the down-at-heel actor-manager Hassenreuter and the lapsed student Spitta argue about theatre; her plights bears out Spitta's contention that the truthfully portrayed existence of ordinary people is as worthy of drama as the heroics of elevated characters in the classical-idealistic mode championed by Hassenreuter, and the theory and practice of Naturalism merge in a brilliant tragicomedy that was Hauptmann's last unqualified success.

The early twentieth century saw the revival of classical and romantic approaches and the evolution of 'symbolistic' and 'impressionistic' methods, particularly in the plays of the older Hauptmann and Paul Ernst in Germany, and Hugo von Hofmannsthal and Arthur Schnitzler in Austria. The mainstream of German drama, however, moved towards Expressionism through Wedekind and Sternheim.

Frank Wedekind (1864–1918) shares the Naturalist's predilection for the seamy side of life, but his work as a whole is not naturalistic, as an examination of his three best-known plays may indicate. In *Frühlings Erwachen* (*Spring Awakening*) (1891), a group of small-town adolescents in the throes of sexual awakening face the incomprehension of parents and teachers; the boy Moritz commits suicide under these pressures and the girl Wendla dies of a botched abortion, but Wendla's juvenile lover Melchior, expelled from school for immorality, refuses death and walks out into life guided by a masked stranger. In *Erdgeist* (*Earth Spirit*) (1895) and *Die Büchse der Pandora* (*Pandora's Box*) (1904), the vamp Lulu crowns her escapades in the *demi-monde* of

Munich, Paris and London by seducing a succession of men, enslaving a lesbian woman, and causing the death of four husbands, before she is murdered as a cheap prostitute by the sex-killer Jack the Ripper. Admiring Nietzsche's vitalism, Wedekind extols instinct. Himself a much-travelled Bohemian until he settled down in Munich, he glorifies adventurers, perverts and criminals as superbly ruthless albeit at times tragic vindicators of nature against effete middle-class respectability. Combining techniques of the *Sturm und Drang*, Grabbe and Büchner with those of fairground entertainment, puppet-play and cabaret, he shocks his audiences by lurid distortions: his characters are caricatures; his actions disintegrate into incoherent episodes; his language mingles colloquialism and rhetoric, sultry sensuality and cynical wit; his atmospheres carry harsh dissonances of the burlesque and the melodramatic. Although his irrational individualism is unlike Brecht's Marxist rationality, his anti-bourgeois iconoclasm is close to Brecht's sentiments, and his formal innovations pave the way not only for Expressionism but also for Brecht's 'epic' theatre.

While Wedekind is distinguished by his grotesque tragicomedy, Carl Sternheim (1878–1942), who after frequent changes of residence emigrated to Brussels, is one of Germany's rare all-out satirists. In his essay *Gedanken über das Wesen des Dramas* (*Thoughts on the Nature of Drama*) (1914), he explains that the dramatist depicts the battle of divine values and human obduracy, in tragedy by setting the heroes against corruption, in comedy by placing corruption in the heroes themselves. In his plays, indebted to Molière, he concentrates on comedy, notably in the 'Maske trilogy': in *Die Hose* (*Bloomers*) (1911) the subaltern civil servant Theobald achieves solvency by exploiting two lecherous lodgers who move into his house after watching his wife accidentally lose her bloomers in a park; in *Der Snob* (1914) Theobald's son Christian marries into the nobility by means of a calculated campaign of capitalist profiteering and conservative politics; in *1913* (1915) Christian dies at the pinnacle of wealth and status, leaving the world to his even more opportunistic children. Thus Sternheim castigates the greed, lust and snobbery that he attributes to Wilhelmine Germany, chiefly at its bourgeois level. While his plots are traditionally 'dramatic', his characters appear as dehumanised automata, and his dialogues, parodying the jargon of specific classes or professions, reduce language to clipped 'telegraphic' utterances: this use of sarcastic abstraction and stylization for merciless social criticism makes Sternheim another important forerunner of both Expressionist drama and the 'epic' theatre of Brecht.

Expressionism, which lasted roughly from 1910 to 1925 and which centred on Berlin, Munich, Dresden and Leipzig, mirrors the unsettling effects of modern technology, Freudian psychology, Nietzschean philosophy, the political confrontations of right and left, and the catastrophe of the First World War (see also Chs 7 and 10). Despite individual differences, the Expressionists condemned as perniciously materialistic, the existing social order in general and the artistic determinism of Naturalism in particular; instead, they called for the regeneration of mankind, to be brought about by a new kind of art which penetrates to the spiritual essence of life by replacing external reality with the artist's private imaginative vision. The drama of Expressionism was shaped by the German influences already noted in Wedekind and by the more experimental plays of Ibsen and Strindberg. The dialogues abound in lexical, grammatical and metaphorical neologisms, often ending in the notorious, passionately inarticulate *Schrei* (cry). The protagonists are personifications of ideas, emotions or typical modes of human existence, frequently described by generic abstractions rather than individual names. The actions, which may be Utopian or apocalyptic, mystical or satirical, propelled by subconscious associations or inspired by propagandist intentions, usually highlight isolated 'stations' in the heroes' inner development in symbolic fashion: one recurrent incident is the clash of sons and fathers, signalling the rebellion of the new idealism against the old corruption. Parallel innovations in stagecraft use technological aids to provide appropriately surrealistic surroundings for the actors' frantic histrionics. Among the countless manifestos of the movement, Kurt Pinthus' review *Versuch eines zukünftigen Dramas (Towards a Drama of the Future)* (1914) explains rhapsodically how these methods jettison firmly outlined plots and rounded characters to convey a subjective world picture with explosive intensity, while Paul Kornfeld's tract *Der beseelte und der psychologische Mensch (Inspired Man and Psychological Man)* (1917) glorifies ecstasy with all the prophetic zeal and effusive rhetoric of which Expressionism was capable. The best-known Expressionist playwrights include Oskar Kokoschka, Ernst Barlach, Reinhard Johannes Sorge, Fritz von Unruh, Walter Hasenclever and Franz Werfel, all of whom, however, are overshadowed by Kaiser and Toller.

Georg Kaiser (1878–1945), who travelled widely, with longer spells in Magdeburg, Berlin and Switzerland where he died in exile, was the most prolific dramatist of the movement. While his themes and stage technique bear all the Expressionist hallmarks, his highly intellectual dialogue displays a terse sobriety and wit rarely found in his fellow Expressionists. In *Von morgens bis mitternachts (From Morn till Midnight)* (1916) the quest for individual liberation and universal solidarity fails, as the nameless bank cashier abandons his petty-bourgeois job and family for adventures in the metropolis and, discovering greed at all levels of society, shoots himself; in *Die Bürger von Calais (The Burghers of Calais)* (1914) it triumphs, as the self-sacrifice of Eustache de Saint-Pierre induces the English king to emulate his exemplary humanity by sparing the beleaguered city. The 'Gas trilogy' dramatizes similar issues, moving from the individual to the universal: in *Die Koralle (The Coral)* (1917) the billionaire hero attains personal redemption in death; in *Gas I* (1918) the failure of the billionaire's son to lead the workers back to agriculture and the success of the engineer in spurring them to increased industrial productivity illustrate the defeat of the human spirit by materialistic regimentation; in *Gas II* (1920), where the near-socialist humanitarianism of the billionaire's grandson succumbs to the rapacity of the engineer while two armies of anonymous yellow and blue figures wage a brutal war, the advance of capitalism, scientific–technological mechanization and chauvinistic militarism culminate in a gigantic explosion, annihilating mankind as a whole.

While Kaiser belonged to the politically uncommitted section of Expressionism, Ernst Toller (1893–1939), who served voluntarily in the First World War, suffered imprisonment for his influential role in the Bavarian Soviet of 1919 and committed suicide in New York, was one of its prominent left-wing activists. His major plays include *Die Maschinenstürmer* (*The Machine Wreckers*) (1922), about the Luddite riots in England, and *Hinkemann* (1923), about the plight of the returning German soldier, but his fame rests on two other plays, in which he employs Expressionist approaches to action and characterization as skilfully as Kaiser, while his dialogue has considerable depth of feeling: in *Die Wandlung* (*Transfiguration*) (1919) the autobiographical hero Friedrich leaves his middle-class home to seek community in the army, but, faced with the horrors of war, becomes a pacifist agitator and unites the people in a bloodless revolution in which love overcomes the inhumanity of the military, clerical and scientific authorities as well as of the violent radical intelligentsia; in *Masse Mensch* (*Masses and Man*) (1920) the heroine, a middle-class woman with a social conscience, agrees to lead a peaceful strike to end a war but finds herself unable to resist the spokesman of mass violence, who foments a bloody insurrection during which the workers are suppressed by the army and the heroine is executed.

Kaiser and Toller, then, exemplify most powerfully the rise and fall of the Expressionist dream. Their work, and Expressionism in general, is 'dramatic' in its emotional urgency, its spiritual idealism and its decline into tragic fatalism; it is 'epic' in its fundamental social criticism, its rejection of empirical observation and causal logic, its preference for detached scenes, distorted characters and stylized dialogues, and its modernistic innovations in stagecraft.

Returning to Brecht's *Mahagonny* notes, one remembers that in his schematic table he claims to show 'shifts of accent' ('Akzentverschiebungen') rather than 'absolute antitheses' ('absolute Gegensätze'). Accordingly, each point in the tradition of German drama is marked by a different combination rather than mutual exclusion of 'dramatic' and 'epic' elements, and Brecht has more in common with many earlier dramatists than his black-and-white dichotomy might suggest. To assist the reader in relating Brecht to the tradition, this survey will conclude with a brief summary of the most important aspects he shares with his predecessors.

In Neo-Classicism the development of aesthetic and social values still present in Brecht begins with Lessing's assault on Gottsched's rules, his discovery of Shakespeare and his introduction of domestic tragedy. The *Stürmer und Dränger*, including the young Goethe and Schiller and particularly Lenz, contribute directly to Brecht's approaches through their disruption of the Unities, their continuing emulation of Shakespeare and their violent rebellion against society as a whole. In the period of Realism, when social actuality became a dominant theme, we find Brecht foreshadowed in the discontinuous actions, unidealized characters and concrete historical motivation seen in Grabbe and in the politically radical Büchner; Laube and Gutzkow anticipate Brecht as the first committed writers of Germany. The Naturalist movement, at its best in Hauptmann, meets Brecht in its materialistic concern with socio-economic circumstances and its near-socialist criticism of the middle class, whose eighteenth-century reputation as a force of liberation had given way to accusations of conservative restrictiveness by the latter half of the nineteenth century. Situated between Naturalism and Expressionism, Wedekind is one of Brecht's most immediate forerunners, owing to his tragicomic showmanship and his anti-bourgeois anarchism. Expressionism, represented chiefly by Kaiser and Toller, comes close to Brecht with its disjointed structures, its global protest against established society, and its new stage devices.

While it is dangerous to assume an organic evolution in the history of any artistic genre, it is possible to recognize a line running straight from Lenz through Büchner to Wedekind, and thence to Brecht, whose works also bear certain similarities to those of other major writers and movements. This chapter may have indicated the extent to which he is rooted in both the comprehensive tradition of German drama and its most revolutionary strand. The chapters which follow will throw light on his remarkable individual talent.

NOTE

1. See *GW* 17,1004–16; also *Brecht on Theatre*, pp. 33–42, from which most of the English quotations of Brecht's *Mahagonny* notes have been taken. Unless otherwise stated, dates of theoretical works refer to first publication, and those of plays to first public appearance either in print or in performance. The present survey is particularly indebted to *Geschlossene und offene Form im Drama* by Volker Klotz (Munich, 1960).

SELECT BIBLIOGRAPHY

GARTEN, H. F., *Modern German Drama*, London, 1959

HAYMAN, R., ed., *The German Theatre: A Symposium*, London, 1975

KLOTZ, V., *Geschlossene und offene Form im Drama*, Munich, 1960

LÖB, L., *From Lessing to Hauptmann: Studies in German Drama*, London, 1974

MANN, O., *Geschichte des deutschen Dramas*, Stuttgart, 1963

OSBORNE, J., *The Naturalist Drama in Germany*, Manchester, 1971

ROTHE, W., ed., *Expressionismus als Literatur: Gesammelte Studien*, Berne and Munich, 1969

VON WIESE, B., *Die deutsche Tragödie von Lessing bis Hebbel*, Hamburg, 1948

VON WIESE, B., ed., *Deutsche Dramaturgie*, 3 vol, Tübingen, 1962–70

Chapter 3

EPIC THEATRE: A THEATRE FOR THE SCIENTIFIC AGE

ARRIGO SUBIOTTO

The most common term used to characterize Brecht's dramatic theory and practice is 'epic theatre', one that Brecht himself defined and promoted from the late 1920s. In subsequent years he attempted to vary and refine this description, partly because of the broad generalizations it engendered, partly because of shifts in his own attitudes to theatre. 'Dialectical' and 'scientific' were adjectives he introduced from about 1938 to adumbrate his modified and more sophisticated theatrical practice from then on. Yet 'epic' does adequately embrace the major premises of Brecht's theatre. This seeks, through careful choice of theme and formal structural means, to inculcate in the audience the detached, distancing attitude of the historian towards the events portrayed. The intention of epic theatre is thus not only to present a situation but to surprise the audience into a fresh and critical appreciation of the causes and processes underlying what is enacted.

'Epic' is, of course, a generic label for a mode of literature that has always been contrasted, for convenience, to the lyric and dramatic forms. Though it is manifestly impossible to say that a piece of writing must be purely lyrical or narrative or dramatic – there are many celebrated works that mingle the genres – it is helpful to bear in mind the dominant characteristics of a genre that particularly reflect the perspective of the author and influence the formal structure of what he writes. Thus the lyrical mode is subjective, focusing on the poet's personal feelings and reactions to external reality. The dramatic aims at the enactment of incidents and events between individuals, generally structured to involve a conflict and its solution. The author is excluded in so far as the action is cast totally in dialogue between the characters. The epic mode is regarded as the most objective; the author excludes himself from the work but is present in the form of a narrator who conveys events through description and comment. The tense of the epic tends to be past, its span often of considerable length, both in narrated and narrative time. From the *Gesta Romanorum* and the medieval lays to the modern novel the epic has appeared to be the most objective literary representation of external reality positing, as it does, an author and audience in a detached, observing relationship to the events and characters portrayed. Dictionary definitions tend to emphasize the narrative aspect with its concomitant distance from the action. In common parlance, too, the use of the epithet 'epic' implies a large-scale, panoramic span of events often covering a person's life or even several generations; essential to this is the vantage-point of the spectator standing outside the action and able to see it in its totality.

The formal aspects of epic detachment and narration are, however, only starting-points for the fundamental changes Brecht and others wished to achieve in the drama. He recognized and appreciated the tradition of epic narration in a dramatic context, from Shakespeare to crude fairground presentations of historical personages and their deeds. But these were still only a matter of technique, not of deliberate and systematic intention; that is to say, representation – not illumination – was still the aim. In 1938 Brecht wrote as the opening sentence to his important essay, *Die Strassenszene: Grundmodell einer Szene des epischen Theaters* (*The Street-Scene: Basic Model for an Epic Theatre*):

> Während der ersten anderthalb Jahrzehnte nach dem Weltkrieg wurde auf einigen deutschen Theatern eine verhältnismässig neue Spielweise ausprobiert, die sich, wegen ihres deutlich referierenden, beschreibenden Charakters und weil sie sich kommentierender Chöre und Projektionen bediente, *episch* nannte.

> (In the decade and a half that followed the World War a comparatively new way of acting was tried out in a number of German theatres. Its qualities of clear description and reporting and its use of choruses and projections as a means of commentary earned it the name 'epic'.) (JW adapted)[1]

It is true that Brecht consistently acknowledged the immense debt of the epic theatre to the pioneering work of the Naturalist movement a generation earlier, particularly in making social and political questions the explicit theme of literature. The impetus derived from the new topics of the great French bourgeois novelists began to penetrate the stage. Nevertheless, Naturalism never went beyond a surface realism and simply replaced 'fate' by 'heredity and environment':

> Ein grober und flacher Realismus, der die tieferen Zusammenhänge niemals aufdeckte .... Das Milieu wurde aber als Natur betrachtet, als unveränderlich und unentrinnbar. (*GW* 15, 214)

> (A crude and superficial realism which never revealed the deeper connections.... The environment was regarded as a part of nature, unchangeable and inescapable.)

The systematic experimentation in the 1920s aimed at a coherent use of theatre as a social art and to that end the epic drama was most actively promoted in Erwin Piscator's political theatre. Brecht almost certainly had Piscator's productions in mind when he wrote the opening sentence of *Die Strassenszene*, but although he often praised them he never perhaps sufficiently indicated how they pioneered many elements of his own drama. The reason for this may indeed lie in the fact that Piscator was solely a producer, while Brecht, as a dramatist, viewed theatrical presentation more as the creator of imaginary persons and situations. Piscator's concept of political drama was clear and forcefully formulated and practised: the task of the theatre was 'aktiv in den Gang des Zeitgeschehens einzugreifen' ('to intervene actively in contemporary events') by instructing and altering the audience. He saw three stages in this process of opening the spectator's eyes – *Kenntnis, Erkenntnis, Bekenntnis* (knowledge, understanding, conviction) – and, like Brecht, he sought fresh formal means of dramatic presentation to achieve this goal. The aim of exposing 'objectively' the workings of society, the desire to alter the spectator's consciousness, and shared political convictions made for close parallels between Piscator's political and Brecht's epic theatre.

Brecht's first and best-known contribution to a systematic theory of epic theatre appeared in 1930 in his notes to the opera *Aufstieg und Fall der Stadt Mahagonny* (*Rise and Fall of the City of Mahagonny*).[2] This was the culmination of his prolonged polemic against the established theatre that, in his opinion, was solely interested in selling superficial, mindless entertainment and side-stepped the serious concerns of the day. He called this theatre 'culinary', as it was no more mentally stimulating than was the eating of food. At this stage, and unlike Piscator who identified the function of epic theatre in a more aggressively political manner, Brecht concentrated on differentiating between the modern epic theatre and the 'dramatic' theatre he wanted it to oust. Thus, in his famous tabulation in the *Mahagonny* notes he compiled a list of contrasts between Aristotelian and non-Aristotelian forms of drama that, despite his cautionary footnote that these were not mutually exclusive characteristics but rather 'Gewichtsverschiebungen' ('shifts of accent'), was taken to be the assertion of a new dramatic dogma. In 1938 Brecht had to revise his tabulation 'because of possible misunderstandings', toning down the starkness of his initial formulation but with no radical alteration. If one remembers Brecht's caution that he was not promulgating total rejection of the 'dramatic' theatre, these notes do offer a lucid outline of the tendency in epic theatre towards an 'open' form that differed in a marked degree from the 'closed' structure of traditional classical theatre. The contrasts relate to three main areas: the 'hero' or human being as the subject of drama, the structure of the play, and the spectator. With unerring theatrical instinct Brecht unconsciously identified the crucial aspects of a drama (theme, presentation, reception) and centred his proposed changes on these. The principle that linked all three aspects into a coherent whole was the idea of *process*, that nothing is determined, absolute and fixed, but subject to influence and change. Thus Brecht attacked the prevailing conception that the hero (and all human beings) possess innate characteristics that cannot be altered by circumstances, a nature that determines his behaviour ineluctably. The consequent irresolvable conflict between the 'fixed' hero and the world, which is the stuff of classical drama, was rejected by Brecht as inappropriate and unrealistic; in its place he posited a hero subject to alteration and development, adapting to society, but also by his actions changing society. The notion that 'social being determines thought' with all its consequences derives of course from Marx's premise that being determines consciousness and not the reverse, as in classical Kantian philosophy.

Brecht created a dramatic form to match this view of the hero by breaking down the 'evolutionary inevitability' of the classical play. Instead of the inextricable interrelation of scenes where none could be omitted – a sort of organic absolute entirely enclosed in itself – Brecht allowed each scene or episode to stand independently as evidence of a process taking place rather than a psychic revelation of character. The autonomy of the separate parts of a play enabled Brecht to select such material as offered an 'assembled' explanatory presentation of people's behaviour. Instead of embodying or simulating a situation, the stage was to narrate it, with all the detachment that this implies. Indeed, it was this detachment that perhaps most concerned Brecht and has been commonly taken as the hallmark of his theatre. Certainly, Brecht castigated the established bourgeois theatre in the 1920s for encouraging the spectator to leave his reasoning powers with his hat and coat in the cloakroom and enter the darkened auditorium simply to engage in a trance-like orgy of feeling, as if he were drugged. Brecht blamed the over-emphasis on empathy for this, since it led to the pretence that the events and feelings being purveyed on the stage were real and encouraged the spectator to identify totally with them; he would wallow in emotions and would leave the theatre no more enlightened than before. Brecht had far more active designs on the spectator: he wanted him to use his critical faculties in assessing what was being enacted, and gain insights from this process that would influence his own further thinking, that is, alter his consciousness. Thus Brecht sought in the first instance to inculcate in the spectator the attitude of the observing historian who, however excited he may be by them, can stand back from the passions of personalities, register events and evidence, and come to a reasoned conclusion about a situation. But he also viewed the spectator as a person to be influenced and changed, so that the educative, instructive thrust of epic theatre, which was deliberately designed to convey an understanding of the causes underlying what was depicted, opened into a wider perspective than the play itself and aimed at 'arousing the spectator's capacity for action' or, in other words, altering his consciousness.

By the time Brecht came to revise his table of contrasts he no longer needed to define his type of drama by setting it against the Aristotelian model. After five years of exile he had lost contact with the live German theatre and was embarking on a period of intensive theoretical writing. In that same year he set out in *Die Strassenszene* his view of the essentials of epic theatre. Whereas earlier it could be inferred that the epic theatre was clearly best suited to dealing with social and political problems, public matters, Brecht now went further, unequivocally defining its function and purpose entirely in a political context:

> Die Verfechter dieses epischen Theaters führten ins Feld, dass die neuen Stoffe, die sehr komplizierten Vorgänge der Klassenkämpfe im Augenblick ihrer entsetzlichsten Zuspitzung, auf solche Art leichter zu bewältigen seien, weil die gesellschaftlichen Prozesse in ihren kausalen Zusammenhängen damit dargestellt werden könnten.

> (Supporters of this epic theatre argued that the new subject-matter, the highly involved incidents of the class war in its acutest and most terrible stage, would be mastered more easily by such a method, since it would thereby become possible to portray social processes in their causal relationships.)
> (JW adapted)

But he adds that these experiments raised a number of substantial difficulties for aesthetics. *Die Strassenszene* seems therefore to have been written to establish a close link between the practical goals of epic theatre and the expectations of traditional aesthetics. As an example of completely 'natural' epic theatre Brecht takes

> ...einen Vorgang, der sich an irgendeiner Strassenecke abspielen kann: der Augenzeuge eines Verkehrsunfalls demonstriert einer Menschenansammlung, wie das Unglück passierte. Die Umstehenden können den Vorgang nicht gesehen haben oder nur nicht seiner Meinung sein, ihn 'anders sehen' – die Hauptsache ist, dass der Demonstrierende das Verhalten des Fahrers oder des Überfahrenen oder beider in einer solchen Weise vormacht, dass die Umstehenden sich über den Unfall ein Urteil bilden können.

> (...an incident such as can be seen at any street corner: an eyewitness demonstrating to a collection of people how a traffic accident took place. The bystanders may not have observed what happened, or they may simply not agree with him, may 'see things a different way'; the point is that the demonstrator acts the behaviour of driver or victim or both in such a way that the bystanders are able to form an opinion about the accident.) (JW)

It is evident that this mundane scene that can happen spontaneously far from the aura of 'theatre' nevertheless has, as Brecht claimed, a fundamental theatrical structure: the demonstrator (actor) re-enacting to bystanders (audience) an accident (dramatic event) so that they may make an assessment and judgement of it, displays all the ingredients of Brecht's epic theatre. If the theatre wished to widen its field and show the driver in other situations besides that of the accident it would in no way exceed its model, but merely create a further situation on the same pattern. The addition rather than integration of scenes is characteristic of epic theatre, as is 'der unvermittelte Übergang von der Darstellung zum Kommentar' ('the direct changeover from representation to commentary'), and a predominant role in this is assigned to the actor. His counterpart in the street-scene, the eyewitness, must eschew perfect imitation and not seduce the bystanders by his 'Verwandlungsfähigkeit' ('powers of transformation'); he must also avoid creating pure emotions and engendering illusion, so that his audience is fully aware that here is a repetition, not a pretence of the real thing. Coupled with this is the natural attitude adopted by the demonstrator in two senses: he *is* himself *showing* the behaviour of the driver. It is also typical of the epic theatre that the demonstrator must derive his characters entirely from their actions. What aspects of the character's behaviour he gives, how thoroughly he has to imitate, is determined by his purpose; and it is his point of view (a 'committed' one, because he sees the accident in a certain light) that gives the perspective on what features of the driver's behaviour are to be picked out. In this respect the demonstrator assumes the functions of both playwright and actor in a theatrical context.

The final element that concludes this basic model of epic theatre is its practical aim. It is by no means thought of as an autonomous event giving gratuitous pleasure, rather it is intended to convey information and produce a result. The street-scene might, for instance, be transferred to a court room (and how often is the pattern of a court case the core of a Brecht play!) where a judge and jury hear evidence, weigh it up and reach a decision as to the apportionment of blame and punishment. The concluding sentences of *Die Strassenszene* stress the practical social application of both the compact street-corner vignette and the complex inventions of epic theatre on the stage:

Unser Theater an der Strassenecke ist primitiv; mit Anlass, Zweck und Mitteln der Vorführung ist es 'nicht weit her'. Aber es ist unbestreitbar ein sinnvoller Vorgang, dessen gesellschaftliche Funktion deutlich ist und alle seine Elemente beherrscht. Die Vorführung hat einen Vorfall zum Anlass, der verschieden beurteilt werden kann, der sich in der einen oder andern Form wiederholen kann und der noch nicht abgeschlossen ist, sondern Folgen haben wird, so dass die Beurteilung von Bedeutung ist . . . . Das epische Theater ist hoch artistisches Theater mit komplizierten Inhalten und weiter sozialer Zielsetzung. Die Strassenszene als Grundmodell epischen Theaters aufstellend, teilen wir ihm die deutliche gesellschaftliche Funktion zu und stellen für episches Theater Kriterien auf, nach denen bemessen werden kann, ob es sich bei ihm um einen sinnvollen Vorgang handelt oder nicht.

(Our street-corner theatre is primitive; origins, aims and methods of its performance are close to home. But there is no doubt that it is a meaningful phenomenon with a clear social function that dominates all its elements. The performance's origins lie in an incident that can be judged in different ways, that may repeat itself in different forms and is not finished but is bound to have consequences, so that this judgement has some significance . . . . The epic theatre is a highly skilled theatre with complex contents and far-reaching social objectives. In setting up the street-scene as a basic model for it, we pass on the clear social function and give the epic theatre criteria by which to decide whether an incident is meaningful or not.) (JW adapted)

One of the key elements of epic theatre that was to become indissolubly associated with Brecht's theatre and a commonplace of twentieth-century drama in general, the alienation effect, was first described in 1935 in Brecht's essay, *Verfremdungseffekte in der chinesischen Schauspielkunst* (*Alienation effects in Chinese acting*), although it had been part and parcel of his practice from much earlier (e.g. in the prologue and epilogue spoken by the actors in *Die Ausnahme und die Regel* (*The Exception and the Rule*), (1929). In *Die Strassenszene* it is given one of many later formulations, as

> eine Technik, mit der darzustellenden Vorgängen zwischen Menschen der Stempel des Auffallenden, des der Erklärung Bedürftigen, nicht einfach Natürlichen verliehen werden kann. Der Zweck des Effekts ist, dem Zuschauer eine fruchtbare Kritik vom gesellschaftlichen Standpunkt zu ermöglichen.
>
> (a technique of taking the human social incidents to be portrayed and labelling them as something striking, something that calls for explanation, and is not to be taken for granted, not just natural. The object of this 'effect' is to allow the spectator to criticize constructively from a social point of view.) (JW adapted)

As a technique the alienation effect can be easily identified, especially in Brecht's later plays, for it emerges in the major areas of the theatrical experience: in the play's structure, the disposition and contrasting of scenes and episodes; in the language, the conflict of dialogue and the contradictions highlighted between the speech and actions of the characters; in the actor's effort to play at being and to stand outside a character; and in the handling of 'sister' arts such as music, lighting and scenic design in a stage production. But the alienation effect in Brecht's theatre is not confined to formal techniques, a vehicle for the author's message (it was exploited in this mechanical way, as Brecht noted, by assorted playwrights like Thornton Wilder and Paul Claudel); it is simultaneously the content itself, namely the matter the author is structuring and his perspective on it. The social content that operates in the same way as the technique of alienation is the *Gestus*, a term Brecht devised to denote the essential theme of an incident, a scene, a whole play, and which he also defined in the mid-1930s:

> Nicht jeder Gestus ist ein gesellschaftlicher Gestus. Die Abwehrhaltung gegen eine Fliege ist zunächst noch kein gesellschaftlicher Gestus, die Abwehrhaltung gegen einen Hund kann einer sein, wenn zum Beispiel durch ihn der Kampf, den ein schlechtgekleideter Mensch gegen Wachthunde zu führen hat, zum Ausdruck kommt . . . der gesellschaftliche Gestus ist . . . der Gestus, der auf die gesellschaftlichen Zustände Schlüsse zulässt. (*GW* 15, 483f.)
>
> (Not all gests are social gests. The attitude of chasing away a fly is not yet a social gest, though the attitude of chasing away a dog may be one, for instance if it expresses a badly dressed man's continual battle against watchdogs . . . the social gest is . . . the gest that allows conclusions to be drawn about the social circumstances.) (JW adapted)

Later, in the *Kleines Organon* (*Short Organum*), Brecht indicated how the *Gestus* arises from the interaction of people, their attitudes and behaviour towards each other. The 'hands up!' *Gestus* in *Arturo Ui* as a sign of fear, surrender and total agreement or acquiescence, the figure of Shen Te 'split' into pregnant woman and bloated capitalist in *Der gute Mensch von Sezuan* (*The Good Person of Szechwan*), the predictably unpredictable behaviour of the drunk–sober Herr Puntila are examples of alienations that denote the social *Gestus* exposing the contradictions in society. Thus the integration of content with the formal means of presenting it is the distinguishing feature of the alienation technique in Brecht's works.

As Brecht in exile became more and more conscious of the complexities of human behaviour and the grey rather than black-and-white tones of social contradictions, the term epic theatre satisfied him less and less and he began to talk of the 'dialectical' theatre or theatre of 'contradictions'. As early as 1930 he had tentatively broached such a title – *Die dialektische Dramatik* – but had found that the appellation 'non-Aristotelian' better described at that time his general quarrel with traditional drama. Brecht's intensive study of Marx's dialectical materialism in 1926 bore fruit for his drama in the classic Marxist categories deployed in *Die heilige Johanna der Schlachthöfe* (*St Joan of the Stockyards*) (1929–30), and – more interestingly – the *Lehrstücke* of the same period. These didactic 'learning' plays were an experiment in articulating social and political issues in a simple, lucid but schematic form for the benefit of the performers, not for an audience. The participation of the actors in enacting and discussing a situation was a form of political self-instruction fully in accord with the intentions of epic theatre. But this unique type of drama (unique despite its echoes of the Jesuit instructional play of the seventeenth century) was ahead of its time and not easily transferable to the traditional theatre, and Brecht was clearly not yet ready to launch his drama into a new phase after dropping the ballast of the past. He needed the confidence and authority of experience to cut loose into fresh ground and propose a new general theory. This came at the time of writing his cluster of major plays between 1938 and 1943 with the bulk of the *Messingkauf* dialogues, (1939–40), subsequently more succinctly ordered in the *Kleines Organon für das Theater* of 1948. In an addendum to the *Kleines Organon* in 1954 and in *Die Dialektik auf dem Theater* (1956), Brecht referred repeatedly to the imprecision and rigidity that the term 'epic' theatre now suffered from and the need for a more adequate label:

> Hier wird versucht, die Anwendung materialistischer Dialektik auf dem Theater zu beschreiben. Der Begriff 'episches Theater' scheint immer mehr einer solchen inhaltlichen Ausarbeitung bedürftig . . . . Es wird jetzt der Versuch gemacht, vom *epischen* Theater zum *dialektischen* Theater zu kommen. Unseres Erachtens und unserer Absicht nach waren die Praxis des epischen Theaters und sein ganzer Begriff keineswegs undialektisch, noch

wird ein dialektisches Theater ohne das epische Element auskommen.
(*Versuche* 15, 78 and *GW* 16, 923)

(The attempt will be made here to describe the application of materialist dialectic in the theatre. It appears increasingly important to elaborate on the content implicit in the term 'epic theatre' . . . . An effort is now being made to move on from the epic theatre to the dialectical theatre. In our view and according to our intention the epic theatre's practice – and the whole idea – were by no means undialectical. Nor would a dialectical theatre succeed without the epic element.)

Brecht was clearly aware that epic theatre had come to be associated almost exclusively with formal aspects, focusing particularly on structural differences from traditional plays. His concern was to re-establish the significance of contradiction and dialectics in the content as well as the external mechanics of drama. Dialectics shifts the centre of gravity back to the ideas of society (political, economic, sociological) that see society as an organic process of men's living together in continual flux and change. Hence the less dogmatic, more flexible and ambiguous structures of the plays Brecht wrote after he left Germany compared with the relatively rigid illustrations of Marxist theory he favoured in the late Weimar Republic.

A further designation that Brecht used increasingly was 'theatre of a scientific age', though he felt that this, too, was not broad enough and perhaps already 'verschmutzt' ('contaminated') by the problem of the social and moral responsibility of science. In the prologue to the *Organon* Brecht calls for scientifically exact representations of human society in the theatre and several times later refers to contemporary men as 'the children of a scientific age', for our life has come to be determined by the sciences to a new and formidable extent. Sections 15 and 16 describe tersely the broad sweep of technological invention that has enabled man to make great strides towards the mastery of his environment. But Brecht accuses the bourgeoisie, brought to power by science, not only of appropriating the wealth generated by technological progress but of actively preventing the application of the sciences to the study of society, 'ein anderes Gebiet . . ., das noch im Dunkel liegt, nämlich das der Beziehungen der Menschen untereinander bei der Ausbeutung und Unterwerfung der Natur . . . . Der neue Blick auf die Natur richtete sich nicht auch auf die Gesellschaft.' ('. . . another area where darkness still reigns, namely that of the relations between people involved in the exploitation and conquest of nature . . . . The new approach to nature was not applied to society.') Thus the technological ability to make this planet fit to live on has outstripped its social structures, and the bourgeois class knows very well 'dass es das Ende ihrer Herrschaft bedeuten würde, richtete sich der wissenschaftliche Blick auf ihre Unternehmungen. So ist die neue Wissenschaft, die sich mit dem Wesen der menschlichen Gesellschaft befasst und die vor etwa hundert Jahren begründet wurde, im Kampf der Beherrschten mit den Herrschenden

begründet worden.' ('. . . that its rule would come to an end if the scientific eye were turned on its own undertakings. And so that new science which was founded about 100 years ago and deals with the character of human society was born in the struggle between rulers and
ruled.') (JW) Science, for Brecht, is now *social* science; here he refers
unambiguously to dialectical materialism, first formulated by Marx in
the mid-nineteenth century and claimed by its adherents to be the most
comprehensive 'scientific socialism'. Brecht looks to the working classes, the 'true children of the scientific age', to apply the tool of political
and sociological investigation and achieve an advance in the organization of society.

Although Brecht argued that it was no longer possible to devise accurate 'Abbildungen des menschlichen Zusammenlebens' ('representations
of men's life together') without an understanding of the social sciences,
he was careful not to shackle the dramatist. The roles of science and art
are complementary in contributing to the well-being of mankind, 'die
eine beschäftigt mit ihrem Unterhalt, die andere mit ihrer Unterhaltung'
('the one setting out to maintain, the other to entertain us') (JW). With
this Brecht introduces a dominant theme which pervades the *Organon*
and his later pronouncements: the need for *Genuss* (enjoyment) in the
theatre, that echoes and reinforces the enjoyment of thinking, of teaching and enquiring, of solving problems, of mastering reality. The
moment of 'enjoyment' was always latent in his work, but emerges
unequivocally in the *Organon*, associated closely with the idea of *Pro-
duktivität*:

> Welches ist die produktive Haltung gegenüber der Natur und gegenüber der
> Gesellschaft, welche wir Kinder eines wissenschaftlichen Zeitalters in unserm
> Theater vernüglich einnehmen wollen? Die Haltung ist eine kritische.
> Gegenüber einem Fluss besteht sie in der Regulierung des
> Flusses, . . . gegenüber der Gesellschaft in der Umwälzung der Gesellschaft.

> (What is that productive attitude in face of nature and of society which we
> children of a scientific age would like to adopt for our own pleasure in our
> theatre? The attitude is a critical one. Faced with a river, it consists in
> regulating the river, . . . faced with society, in turning society upside down.)
> (JW adapted)

The productive critical approach that the theatre's models of reality
must arouse in the audience is like 'jenen fremden Blick, . . . so
schwierig wie produktiv' ('that detached view, . . . both difficult and
productive') with which Galileo observed a swinging chandelier. Needless to say, this is achieved 'vermittels einer Technik der Verfremdungen des Vertrauten' ('by a technique of alienating the familiar')
which, as Brecht had earlier described in *Neue Technik der Schauspielkunst* (*New Technique of Acting*) (1940), science had developed for the
purpose of analysing the familiar and achieving results, and which could
be as productive in art. In contrast to his earlier more passive
definitions of the alienation effect as a formal means of facilitating

understanding of a situation, Brecht now stresses the impulse to intervention that it carries: 'Die neuen Verfremdungen sollten nur den gesellschaftlich beeinflussbaren Vorgängen den Stempel des Vertrauten wegnehmen, der sie heute vor dem Eingriff bewahrt.' ('The new alienations are only designed to free socially conditioned phenomena from that stamp of familiarity which protects them against our grasp today.') (JW) Brecht's aim is not simply to release the 'eingeschüchterte, gläubige, "gebannte" Menge' ('intimidated, credulous, hypnotized mass') from its thraldom in the auditorium of the traditional theatre, but actively to affect its presuppositions, assumptions, thinking processes.

There is thus an important distinction to be drawn between the detached, observing, 'clinical' attitude of the natural scientist and Brecht's ideal critical stance of the spectator in the theatre. To illustrate this distinction, Brecht on more than one occasion referred to the phenomenon known to physicists as the Heisenberg Uncertainty Principle, which he understood as acknowledging the impossibility of obtaining totally 'natural' conditions in which to conduct experiments: the very presence of instruments and observer affects the object under scrutiny and any measurement of a system must disturb the system under observation, with a resulting distortion and lack of precision in measurement. Brecht sees this instead as a positive virtue in his dramatic representations of reality. In the *Messingkauf* dialogues the Philosopher describes the phenomenon and relates it to the observation of society: 'Das geschieht, wenn Instrumente beobachten, was geschieht erst, wenn Menschen beobachten?' ('This is what happens when instruments observe, what could happen when human beings are the observers?') (*GW* 16, 576–7) And in the *Flüchtlingsgespräche* (*The Refugee Dialogues*) too Brecht has his physicist Ziffel describe the Heisenberg Uncertainty Principle and ironically make the connection between the physical and social worlds:

> In der sozialen Welt scheinen nun ähnliche Phänomene zu existieren. Die Untersuchung der sozialen Vorgänge lässt diese Vorgänge nicht unberührt, sondern wirkt ziemlich stark auf sie ein. Sie wirkt ohne weiteres revolutionierend. Dies ist wahrscheinlich der Grund, warum die massgebenden Kreise tiefer schürfende Untersuchungen auf dem sozialen Gebiet so wenig ermuntern. (*GW* 14, 1420)

> (There appear to be similar phenomena in social life. The investigation of social processes does not leave these processes untouched but influences them quite strongly. It operates without doubt in a revolutionary manner. This is probably why influential groups are so slow to encourage deeper investigations in the social field.)

Undoubtedly Brecht strove to induce in the spectator a detached, observant approach to the depiction on stage, but it was only objective in that it depended as much on the spectator's reasoning faculties as his emotions. A major intention of the *Organon* is to indicate ways in which Brecht's 'scientific' theatre can be harnessed to change the consciousness of the audience and hence facilitate the altering of the reality that is reflected on the stage.

The keynote of this scientific theatre is then change. Whereas the theatre as we know it shows the structure of society depicted on stage as incapable of being influenced by society (in the auditorium), Brecht calls for a type of theatre that generates new thoughts and feelings in the spectator and leaves him productively disposed, even after the spectacle is over. The uncertainty principle that would have a deleterious, distorting effect in scientific observation is positively striven for as an active corrective in Brecht's theatre – the desired aim is that the audience *should* intervene in the processes of society and should itself change its own thinking. The renowned detachment of the spectator in epic theatre has in the first instance the quality of the historian's critical view of events: he re-enacts them through description and indicates their relevance and significance through comment. This bifocal perspective is retained by Brecht through the manipulation of his material by means of alienation techniques; but while the insight into society is being mediated, the emancipatory dimension simultaneously comes into play and the audience is encouraged to adopt an actively critical stance towards the representation on stage. The audience is put into a position to see more than the protagonists, to grasp the wider context, to assess the evidence presented and adopt an attitude as to its significance. The spectator is thus not regarded as just the passive recipient of a description of circumstances, however naturalistic, but as an active and integral component of the total process of a play.

The dismemberment of social processes which lies at the core of Brecht's idea of scientific theatre rests, of course, on his confident belief in the causal nexus in society and in the possibility of analysing all social phenomena and explaining them rationally. From about 1926 Brecht had clearly agreed with and incorporated into his own arsenal Marx's postulate (formulated in the sixth Feuerbach thesis) that the human being is the sum of social circumstances ('das Ensemble der gesellschaftlichen Verhältnisse') and that there is a dialectical relationship between the individual and his social context leading to continual reciprocal change in both:

> Die Auffassung des Menschen als einer Variablen des Milieus, des Milieus als einer Variablen des Menschen, das heisst die Auflösung des Milieus in Beziehungen zwischen Menschen, entspringt einem neuen Denken, dem historischen Denken.

> (The concept of man as a function of his milieu and of the milieu as a function of man, in other words the resolution of the milieu into relationships between people, is the product of a new kind of thinking – historical thinking.)

The historical or dialectical materialism of Marxism Brecht here refers to envisages the human being only in a specific historical context, and it can quickly fall into the trap of a rigid mechanistic view of the interaction of individual and society and lead to a behaviouristic, socio-economic determinism, leaving no room at all for the essence of life, individual difference and unpredictable human actions. While retaining his faith in the rational analysis of social relationships, Brecht did nevertheless modify a tendency around 1930 to attribute socio-economic explanations to all human actions, and acknowledged in his later work idiosyncratic contradictions in the behaviour of individuals. The complex reactions of Azdak, Grusche, Shen Te, Mutter Courage, Puntila, Galileo to their situations and fellow human beings are rich in contrasts that defy resolution by causal explanations of society.

Brecht's later plays have little to do with historical authenticity and nothing whatever with naturalism. Indeed, his dominant preoccupations became the parable form and realism which, paradoxically, are intimately connected. In a revealing work-diary entry of 30 March 1947 Brecht went to the lengths of setting out in tabular form – as he had done for epic and dramatic – some contrasts between naturalism and realism, the former being merely a 'surrogate' realism (*Aj* 780). Some of these distinctions illuminate Brecht's dramatic thinking and methods. His predilection for the parable, for instance, facilitated the 'stylization' of reality and gave him the freedom to devise models of society that, unhampered by historical facts, could be structured at will to incorporate the didactic message with maximum impact. While the parable lacked the force of actual historical concreteness, Brecht was well aware that it had a vicarious authenticity that accommodates the author's intent, namely a clarification of the 'system'. In the last year of his life Brecht vigorously defended this quality of the parable in conversation with Ernst Schumacher: '. . . weil sie in der Abstraktion konkret ist, indem sie das Wesentliche augenfällig macht.'[3] ('. . . while abstracting it is nevertheless concrete since it opens our eyes to what is essential.') For all that he denied that there was an aesthetic dimension to theatre independent of its social content, Brecht recognized and exploited the fact that a fictional representation exercises the imagination and breadth of perspective more readily than the circumscribed real event. The aesthetic moment does indeed figure prominently in Brecht's dramaturgy and the *Organon* is permeated by the twin purposes of *Unterhaltung* and *Unterricht* (the classical 'dulce et utile', 'plaire et instruire'); the attaining of these goals by engaging both the intellect and the emotions of the audience is the enjoyment of realism generated by the theatre.

Time after time Brecht defined realism as a productive, 'scientifically' analytical attitude towards reality rather than a recognizable imitation of the world, and he formulated specific guidelines for realistic art:

den gesellschaftlichen Kausalkomplex aufdeckend / die herrschenden Gesichtspunkte als die Gesichtspunkte der Herrschenden entlarvend / vom Standpunkt der Klasse aus schreibend, welche für die dringendsten Schwierigkeiten, in denen die menschliche Gesellschaft steckt, die breitesten

Lösungen bereit hält / das Moment der Entwicklung betonend / konkret und
das Abstrahieren ermöglichend. (*GW* 19, 326)

(laying bare society's causal network / showing up the dominant viewpoint
as the viewpoint of the dominators / writing from the standpoint of the class
which has prepared the broadest solutions for the most pressing problems
afflicting human society / emphasizing the dynamics of development /
concrete and so as to encourage abstraction.) (JW)

The clarity of the definition does put into relief one of the limitations of
Brecht's epic theatre, in practice if not in theory, namely that it depends
entirely on the acceptance of a particular political philosophy, Marxist
dialectical materialism; any other springboard would result in a purely
formalistic employment of epic techniques. Brecht himself admitted in
1955 that actors and audience needed to share the Marxist politics of the
dramatist for the epic theatre to make sense. The question then has to be
asked: is the epic theatre limited to refining and reinforcing the already
existent historical approach, the realistically critical attitude of a Marxist
audience? A further constraint of the epic theatre is its necessary predilection for 'public' subject-matter that facilitates the exposure of the
social structures and processes, with a consequent denial or disregard of
private concerns and the intractable behaviour of individuals. Brecht's
avowed practical aim of changing society by influencing the audience
also restricts the constructs of reality presented on stage:

Das epische Theater ist hauptsächlich interessiert an dem Verhalten der
Menschen zueinander, *wo es sozialhistorisch bedeutend (typisch) ist*. Es
arbeitet Szenen heraus, in denen Menschen sich so verhalten, dass die
sozialen Gesetze, unter denen sie stehen, sichtbar werden. (*GW* 15, 474)

(The epic theatre is chiefly interested in the attitudes which people adopt
towards one another, wherever they are socio-historically significant
(typical). It works out scenes where people adopt attitudes of such a sort that
the social laws under which they are acting spring into sight.) (JW)

These programmatic limitations are both a weakness and a strength of
Brecht's theatre. On the one hand, he deliberately eschewed traditional
psychological drama, the delineation of the subtle interplay of personal
relationships for their own sake; this he saw as the nugatory business of
the bourgeois 'entertainment emporia'. On the other, he strove to realize
his vision of an audience gripped by the scientific, objective logic of the
truths about society elicited by him on the stage, an audience exercising
its intellectual faculties to understand and be enlightened by the manner
and matter of the telling, and revelling in the enjoyment of both thought
and feeling aroused by the images of society set forth before it. The
vision and the reality may be poles apart, for the statistics show that by
far the most popular Brecht plays in East German theatres since 1945
have been *Die Gewehre der Frau Carrar* (*Señora Carrar's Rifles*), *Die
Dreigroschenoper* (*The Threepenny Opera*) and *Herr Puntila und sein
Knecht Matti* (*Herr Puntila and his Servant Matti*), all with consider-

able 'entertainment' value and none an obvious model of scientific theatre. It is indisputable, however, that at the theoretical and exemplary level at least Brecht has powerfully influenced drama wherever it is socially and politically conscious, as the widespread currency of the epithet 'Brechtian' testifies.

NOTES

1. Volume and page references to the *Gesammelte Werke* for *Die Strassenszene* and other major theoretical writings by Brecht are given in the Bibliography below. The English translations are mainly taken or adapted from J. Willett, *Brecht on Theatre* (London, 1964).
2. These are detailed at the beginning of Chapter 2, 'The German Dramatic Tradition: from Lessing to the Expressionists'.
3. E. Schumacher, 'Er wird bleiben', in *Erinnerungen an Brecht*, ed. Hubert Witt (Leipzig, 1964), p. 336.

BIBLIOGRAPHY

The following are Brecht's principal theoretical works and essays, with volume and page references to the *Gesammelte Werke*.

Anmerkungen zur Oper 'Aufstieg und Fall der Stadt Mahagonny', 1930 (17, 1004 16)

Über die Verwendung von Musik für ein episches Theater, c. 1935 (15, 472–82)

Verfremdungseffekte in der chinesischen Schauspielkunst, 1935 (16, 619–31)

Vergnügungstheater oder Lehrtheater?, c. 1936 (15, 262–72)

Volkstümlichkeit und Realismus, c. 1938 (19, 322–31)

Die Strassenszene, 1938 (16, 546–58)

Kurze Beschreibung einer neuen Technik der Schauspielkunst, die einen Verfremdungseffekt hervorbringt, 1940 (15, 341–57)

Kleines Organon für das Theater, 1948 (16, 661–700)

Der Messingkauf, c. 1937–40, an unfinished collection of notes incorporating most of Brecht's theoretical ideas (16, 500–657)

John Willett's volume of translations *Brecht on Theatre* (London, 1964) includes all the above works with the exception of *Der Messingkauf*, which appeared, also in a translation by Willett, as *The Messingkauf Dialogues* (London, 1965). Willett also provides valuable explanatory notes and dating.

Chapter 4

THE INDIVIDUAL AND SOCIETY

ERICH SPEIDEL

In one of Brecht's Keuner stories Herr K. meets an old acquaintance whom he has not seen for a long time, and is greeted with the words: 'You have not changed at all.' Herr K., we are told, merely says 'Oh' and turns pale.

At first sight, this is no more than an unexpected and amusing reaction to a commonplace remark. But there is more to it than that. Behind it lies Brecht's conviction that people not only do change with time but that they ought to, and that not to have done so is nothing to be pleased about. To Brecht there can be no doubt that after some time people can no longer be expected to be their former selves. In an interview with Bernard Guillemin, published in *Die Literarische Welt* on 30 July 1926, he is reported to have said:

> ...der Mensch (kann) in zwei ungleichen Augenblicken niemals der gleiche sein.... Das kontinuierliche Ich ist eine Mythe. Der Mensch ist ein immerwährend zerfallendes und neu sich bildendes Atom. Es gilt zu gestalten, was ist.

> (Nobody can be identically the same at two unidentical moments.... The continuity of the ego is a myth. Man is an atom perpetually breaking up and reforming. We have to show things as they are.) (JW)

> [These are not Brecht's own words. Guillemin prefaced his interview with a note saying that he had 'deliberately translated into normal language all that Brecht had told me in his own manner, in Brecht-style slang' (JW).]

The sentence 'We have to show things as they are' in particular indicates the strength of Brecht's conviction and the extent to which he questions the traditional belief in the continuity and unity of the self. It is a subject to which he frequently returns in his writings, and is closely linked to his attempts to create a new type of theatre. It is therefore not surprising that Brecht's concept of the individual and his relationship with the factors which determine his social behaviour has become one of the major issues debated by Brecht scholars.

The extent to which Brecht challenges the traditional *bürgerlich* (bourgeois) concept of the individual can already be discerned in his first play *Baal*. No less an authority than the Austrian writer Hugo von Hofmannsthal recognized this when, in a prelude he wrote for the first performance of the play in Vienna on 21 March 1926, he makes the actors discuss the roles they are going to play later in the evening, and makes one of them state:

> die Zeit ist unerlöst, und wissen Sie auch, wovon sie erlöst sein möchte? Vom Individuum . . . . Sie schleppt zu schwer an dieser Ausgeburt des sechzehnten Jahrhunderts, die das neunzehnte grossgefüttert hat . . . und ich möchte so weit gehen zu behaupten, dass all die ominösen Vorgänge in Europa, denen wir seit zwölf Jahren beiwohnen, nichts sind als die sehr umständliche Art, den lebensmüden Begriff des Individuums in das Grab zu legen, das er sich selbst geschaufelt hat.[1]

> (our time is unredeemed; do you know from what it seeks redemption? From the individual . . . . It is weighed down too much by this monstrum born of the sixteenth century and fattened up by the nineteenth . . . and I would go as far as to claim that all the ominous events in Europe we have been witnessing during the last twelve years are nothing but the overceremonious way of consigning the world-weary concept of the individual to the grave it has dug for itself.)

It may have been necessary to prepare a rather conservative Viennese theatre audience for the alien and revolutionary play they were going to see; what might be surprising is to find Hofmannsthal in the role of the interpreter. He himself was deeply rooted in a traditional concept of order, advocated a spiritual rebirth of Europe and was far more attuned to the literature of eighteenth- and early nineteenth-century Classicism than to the anti-bourgeois avant-garde of his own day. On the other hand, there was still, as he put it, a 'medieval' tradition in his catholic homeland of Austria where the Reformation – one of the main ideological seed-beds of that individualism to which his *Baal* prelude refers – had had a less profound impact than in Protestant Germany. Paradoxically, this feudal legacy may have made him peculiarly receptive to the idea of the 'obsolescence' of the individual: an idea which, in the wake of the 'ominous events' referred to by Hofmannsthal – the mass carnage of the First World War, and the profound social, political and economic upheavals it brought in its train – gained wide currency among writers and intellectuals of a broad variety of political persuasions in the course of the 1920s.

Brecht's *Baal* had been inspired by a contemporary drama which in the manner of the German *Sturm und Drang* movement tried to continue the cult of the great individual, living outside society and revelling in Bohemian vice, but nevertheless reaching towards the stars in his moments of creativity. Brecht was irritated by this picture of man and decided to write an anti-play with a central figure equally anti-social, more monstrous, and totally oblivious of the existence of any divine inspiration. Baal likens human beings to plants, vegetables, sponges, fruit, drunken trees, water in a pond, and love is 'eine Kokosnuss, die gut ist, solange sie frisch ist, und die man ausspeien muss, wenn der Saft ausgequetscht ist und das Fleisch bleibt über, welches bitter schmeckt' ('like a coconut which is good as long as it is fresh, and which one must spit out once the juice has been squeezed out and only the flesh remains which is bitter') (*GW* 1, 12). Love has one dimension only, the pleasure of Baal; there is no partner, merely an object of his lust, and when the orgasm is over the object has no further value. Women have only one function – 'Du bist ein Weib wie jede andere. Der Kopf ist verschieden. Die Knie sind alle schwach' ('You are a woman like any other. The head is different. The knees are all weak') (*GW* 1, 25) – and have no identity – 'Wenn du sie beschlafen hast, ist sie vielleicht ein Haufen Fleisch, der kein Gesicht mehr hat' ('when you have slept with her, she is perhaps only flesh which has lost its face') (*GW* 1, 11). Baal longs to be at one with vegetative nature, sleep with plants, and become integrated into the cycle of life and decomposition – he wishes to lose himself in a life without consciousness.

Brecht's rejection of the traditional concept of the individual continues to mark the plays he wrote in the early and mid-1920s, and in particular *Im Dickicht der Städte* (*In the Jungle of the Cities*) (first performed in 1923) and *Mann ist Mann* (*A Man's a Man*) (1926). At this time he was fascinated by city life, its mass attractions such as boxing matches and bicycle races, and the ruthless struggle for survival among large sections of the population which left no room for individual development. Like many German intellectuals, and indeed broad segments of the middle class and even trade union leaders, Brecht had a strong admiration for the USA which, when compared with elderly Europe, was a vigorous, prosperous, youthful country and seemed to have a healthy and promising future. One of the conclusions Brecht drew from his extensive studies of the American way of life was that, in modern industrial society, man only functions as an insignificant particle in a great mass, or as an expendable cog in a machine. His behaviour depends far more on external than internal factors:

> Jene Leidenschaft der Figuren . . . ist überflüssig geworden, wo das Interesse an den Vorgängen nicht mehr vom Interesse an einem besonderen Individuum abhängt, sondern den Situationen und ihren Funktionen zugewandt ist. (*GW* 15, 193)

> (Characters ruled by passion have become superfluous now that interest in the events is no longer dependent on interest in a particular individual but is orientated rather towards the situations and their functions.)

Because man is controlled by outside forces,what goes on in the soul is no longer of interest. This depersonalization need not necessarily be negative and could even be something to be welcomed and encouraged. How Brecht sees and evaluates this process forms the essence of *Mann ist Mann*.

This play, first performed in Darmstadt on 25 December 1926, and set in a rather unrealistic and vague part of British India, presents man as entirely replaceable and exchangeable. It is mainly the story of Galy Gay, an Irish docker, an entirely ordinary and peace-loving person who is suddenly requisitioned by four British soldiers, subjected to a number of trials, threats and blackmail, until he finally loses his identity and emerges as a completely new person, perfectly reconditioned as a formidable human fighting machine who wins a battle single-handed against huge odds. The message of the play goes a good deal beyond that of *Baal*. The human being is no longer merely subjected to the dictates of his own vitality which makes him (like Baal) at worst the antisocial type *par excellence*. Galy Gay is depersonalized in a very different way. He is nothing more than the product of social pressures which are applied from outside, can be changed at will, and therefore make the individual totally adaptable to his social environment. He is entirely passive, and what we traditionally regard as the most important aspect of the self, its 'true' identity, has become entirely externalized and socialized. When he first wrote the play, Brecht by no means regarded this as something regrettable, but rather as 'eine lustige Sache, denn dieser Galy Gay nimmt eben keinen Schaden, sondern er gewinnt' ('funny because this Galy Gay does not suffer any damage but gains') (*GW* 17, 978). Significantly, his gain lies in the fact that he ceases to be a private person, and he acquires strength because he joins a large mass of people. Similarly, his extraordinary military victory can only be explained because he 'anscheinend den unbedingten Willen einer Menschenmasse ausführt' ('apparently carries out the absolute will of a large number of people') (ibid.). The value of the human being lies in numbers, not in individuality.

This seemingly uncomplicated fascination with the phenomenon of the 'mass' and the depersonalization of the individual is very much of a piece with the vigorous cultural iconoclasm and admiration for things American cultivated by Brecht in the mid-1920s. By the early 1930s, the growth of the Nazi Party and its mass appeal to the 'little man' were forcing Brecht to revise his view of the 'Menschenmasse' – a revision encouraged in any case by the direction his own aesthetic and political ideas were taking – and this development naturally produced a radical reassessment of *Mann ist Mann* and a much more critical view of its subject-matter. Brecht's assertion in 1936 that the play could also be set in Nazi Germany, with Galy Gay's transformation taking place at a Nazi Party rally at Nuremberg (*GW* 17, 987) marks the extent of this change.

Nevertheless, the *Mann ist Mann* of 1926 represents an important step forward in Brecht's development of a new kind of theatre, whose aims finally began to take a more definite shape by the end of the 1920s. What is significant in this context is Galy Gay's indifference to the sudden disruption of his identity, and his refusal to become a tragic hero:

Dieser Zeitgenosse Galy Gay wehrt sich überraschenderweise durchaus dagegen, dass aus seinem Fall eine Tragödie gemacht wird, er gewinnt etwas durch den mechanischen Eingriff in seine seelische Substanz und meldet sich nach der Operation strahlend gesund. (*GW* 15, 144)

(To our surprise this chap Galy Gay does not allow us to view his case as a tragedy, he actually gains by the mechanistic surgery on his psyche and turns up after the operation in radiant health.)

Had Galy Gay tried to resist these external pressures, in an attempt to preserve his identity, he would no doubt have been destroyed, and the play would have turned into a tragedy. But Brecht's heroes are not sufficiently interested in their selves to run the risk of destruction; to them survival, and therefore adaptability, is the far more important goal. It appears that Brecht's concept of the individual rules out any possibility of a tragedy. In his eyes, this was a step forward towards a more civilized world; the traditional drama, showing the individual in splendid isolation, and relishing his destruction, is a drama for cannibals only:

Ja, die grossen Einzelnen! Die grossen Einzelnen waren der Stoff, und dieser Stoff ergab die Form dieser Dramen . . . . Shakespeare treibt durch vier Akte den grossen Einzelnen, den Lear, den Othello, den Macbeth, aus allen seinen menschlichen Bindungen mit der Familie und mit dem Staat heraus in die Heide, in die vollständige Vereinsamung, wo er im Untergang sich gross zu zeigen hat. Dies ergibt die Form, sagen wir, eines Haferfeldtreibens . . . . Die Leidenschaft ist es, die dieses Getriebe im Gang hält, und der Zweck des Getriebes ist das grosse individuelle Erlebnis. Spätere Zeiten werden dieses Drama ein Drama für Menschenfresser nennen und werden sagen, dass der Mensch am Anfang als Dritter Richard mit Behagen und am Ende als Fuhrmann Henschel mit Mitleid gefressen, aber immer gefressen wurde. (January 1929, *GW* 15, 149)

(The great individuals! The great individuals were the material, and this material determined the form of these dramas . . . . Shakespeare, in four acts, breaks the ties binding the great individual, Lear, Othello, Macbeth, to family and state, driving him on to the blasted heath into total isolation where he has to prove his greatness in his destruction. This produces the form of, let's say, a *battue* . . . . The mainspring of this mechanism is passion, and the purpose of the mechanism is the great individual experience. Later generations will call this drama a drama for cannibals and will say that at the beginning man was eaten, in the shape of Richard III, with relish, and at the end, in the shape of [Hauptmann's] carrier Henschel, with pity, but eaten he was all the same.)

In Brecht's outline of an alternative drama, the word 'sociology' figures prominently at a relatively early stage. In June 1927 in an open letter to the Berlin *Börsen-Courier* under the title of 'Sollten wir nicht die Ästhetik liquidieren' ('Should we not liquidate aesthetics?'), Brecht suggests that the old dramatic form will be destroyed as soon as a new approach which is orientated towards sociology has taken over the stage and opened the theatre to a new public. Sociology, that is the scientific investigation of human behaviour, should replace the make-believe of art and the illusion that our actions are determined by character alone. Brecht had by this time become seriously interested in Marxism, and had discovered a remarkable affinity between his way of thinking and that of Marx; in fact he claims it was the reading of Marx's *Das Kapital* that made him understand his own plays:

> Als ich *Das Kapital* von Marx las, verstand ich meine Stücke... dieser Marx war der einzige Zuschauer für meine Stücke, den ich je gesehen hatte. Denn einen Mann mit solchen Interessen mussten gerade diese Stücke interessieren. Nicht wegen ihrer Intelligenz, sondern wegen der seinigen. Es war Anschauungsmaterial für ihn. (*GW* 15, 129)

> (After I had read Marx's *Capital* I understood my own plays.... This Marx was the only spectator of my plays I had ever had in my mind's eye. For these plays must surely interest a man with interests such as his. Not because of their brilliance but because of his. For him they were illustrations.)

What was of particular interest to Brecht in reading Marx was to find confirmed there his own feeling that the individual had become of only secondary importance, since all significant developments now depended on the movement of masses:

> Die entscheidenden Vorgänge zwischen den Menschen, welche eine Dramatik der grossen Stoffe heute darzustellen hätte, finden in riesigen Kollektiven statt und sind vom Blickpunkt eines einzelnen Menschen aus nicht mehr darzustellen. Der einzelne Mensch unterliegt einer äusserst verwickelten Kausalität... er registriert nur schwache, dämmrige Eindrücke von der Kausalität, die über ihn verhängt ist. Mit ihm als Mentor erkennt das Publikum, sich in ihn einlebend, erlebt das Publikum nur wenig. (*GW* 15, 274)

> (The decisive historical events which today's drama of great issues should be presenting take place in huge collectives and can no longer be portrayed from the point of view of a single human being. The individual is subject to a highly complex chain of causality... he receives only weak and vague impressions of the causality which is inflicted upon him. Accepting him as a mentor the audience understands little, identifying with him the audience experiences little.)

A drama which only allows the representation of individuals on the stage and fails to show the collectives as the really determining factors cannot possibly give an adequate picture of modern social reality; even worse, as it is forced to relate events to more immediate individualized causes – such as the unique character or circumstances of the hero – which are not the genuine ones, it actually misinforms its audience (GW 16, 576).

It is the motivation without gaps, the apparently immediate and direct connection between events and their (individualized) causes, and the highly subjective and therefore misleading nature of these causes that makes the traditional dramatic form inadequate for Brecht's aims. The experience of an individual can no longer sufficiently reflect the conflict between the decisive factors, the collectives, whether they are classes, armies or other large groups of people. Brecht therefore calls for a drama which breaks away from the subjectivity of the old stage, establishes in some way the objective reality, the 'Vorgänge hinter den Vorgängen' (events behind events) (*GW* 15, 256), represented by the large collectives which would allow him to show the real forces determining the modern world.

This new definition of the aims of his theatre remained unchanged from 1929 onwards, and although Brecht returned to the subject frequently in later years, it was only to restate the same idea in different terms. Where a change did occur, however, was in the way in which these intentions were to be realized on the stage, and one major factor in this development was the treatment and the representation of the individual. During the final years of the Weimar Republic Brecht wrote mainly didactic plays (*Lehrstücke*) which were meant to instruct the participants to see the world, and to act in it, in accordance with Marxist thinking. In a way this was an extension of the view that man can easily be controlled from without: if this is the case, then the right education carried out in its most effective form should quickly produce results. The key word in those didactic plays is *Einverständnis* (agreement), the need of the individual to submit to party discipline and carry out party orders. But in the years following Brecht's escape from Nazi Germany in 1933 his view of the individual's role within the collective becomes more complex. There are various references to this question in notes written between 1933 and 1941, in the *Messingkauf* dialogues (1939–40) and the *Kleines Organon für das Theater* (*Short Organum for the Theatre*) (1948), and again his theoretical statements often overlap. But these years 1938–48 were also the period when his new ideas found their expression in his most significant plays.

The most important among the didactic plays of the earlier period is *Die Massnahme* (*The Measures Taken*), first performed in Berlin on 10 December 1930, and set in a very abstract, post-revolutionary Moscow. Four Communist agitators return from their mission in China to the party headquarters and give an account of their activities to the Party, represented on the stage as *Kontrollchor*, the voice of the collective. In particular, they have to report the death of a young comrade who had been assigned to them as an assistant, but who had in spite of his willingness and indeed enthusiasm to help acted rashly against party orders on several occasions because he was overcome by pity for the suffering of the oppressed. Although he had every time admitted his mistake and promised to do better, he had finally allowed his compassion to outweigh his instructions and by revealing his identity had endangered the whole mission. The four agitators could save their mission only by killing the young comrade with his consent and destroying the body. They have now come to justify their action and to ask for, and receive, the approval of the *Kontrollchor*.

What makes the play interesting is the fact that the young comrade, who is the key figure, does not even exist as a character in his own right. He is dead when the play begins, and each of the four agitators in turn takes on his role to demonstrate his mistakes, his repentance and finally his failure as a revolutionary. It has been said that in this play the hero is no longer the subject but merely the object of the drama, and every care has been taken to ensure that there is no identification on the part of the spectator with the young comrade. In addition to this, there is a further step away from the significance of the individual: in order to carry out their mission successfully, all agitators have to go through a symbolic 'extinction' of their faces (reminiscent of the disregard of faces in *Baal*), because only as faceless men will they not be recognized by the enemy and will they become effective, reliable, will-less tools in the hands of the Party, a *tabula rasa* on which the collective as the ultimate authority can inscribe its instructions. With their faces, the agitators also erase their consciences: not what they think is right but what the Party decrees to be so should be done, and it is the ultimate crime of the young comrade that he follows the dictate of his conscience, not that of the Party, at the same time tearing off his mask and revealing his face, that is his true self. Individuality as a crime, total subjection of the self to the collective as virtue, elimination of the moral autonomy of the individual as a desirable goal – this certainly is a reversal of traditional values where the identity and personal responsibility of the human being are of paramount importance. Paradoxically, however, the issue does not end here. Although we can feel no empathy with a person we are never allowed to see, and although we are meant to, and up to a point certainly do, identify with the point of view of the *Kontrollchor*, we nevertheless witness the reappearance of the individual trying to assert his moral autonomy, and getting destroyed in so doing. *Die Massnahme* is in fact a tragedy, the only tragedy Brecht ever wrote (and one would assume perhaps against his intention), and it is interesting to note that in spite of the efforts of the playwright to prevent empathy, and to eliminate the personality of the hero, the claim to virtually absolute authority of the *Kontrollchor* appears to force the central figure into some form of resistance or self-assertion, even though the play ends with the firm demand that the individual should subject himself to the collective. Somehow it does not seem to be all that easy to eliminate the individual from the stage; efforts to do so may run into unexpected difficulties.

Die Massnahme was received with strong criticism, not least from Communists who felt that to show disregard for the individual was a misrepresentation of the Party's aims and certainly bad propaganda. In their view the whole problem ignores the reality of the Party's revolutionary struggle and is based entirely on intellectual abstraction:

In all dem spiegelt sich eine abstrakte Einstellung dem komplizierten und vielfältigen Kampf und Erfahrungskenntnissen der Partei gegenüber.[2]

(All this reflects an abstract attitude towards the complex and many-sided struggle that makes up the Party's experience.)

Brecht is even accused of an aestheticism which has lagged behind the development of progressive socialism:

Nur die Literaten, die hinter Kaffeehausscheiben Revolution machen, halten noch bei der Auslöschung der Individualität.[3]

(Only the literary men whose revolution takes place behind coffee-house windows still insist on the extinction of individuality.)

Brecht himself soon moved away from the extreme position he had taken up in this play, and in an oblique reference acknowledges that he accepts the criticism as justified:

Die Versuche, die Einfühlungstechnik so umzugestalten, dass die Identifikation nunmehr in Kollektiven (Klassen) vor sich geht, sind nicht aussichtsreich. Sie führen zu unrealistischen Vergröberungen und Abstraktionen der Personen und Kollektive zugleich. Die Rolle der Einzelpersönlichkeit im Kollektiv wird undarstellbar, obgleich gerade sie von grösster Bedeutung ist. (*GW* 15, 245)

(The attempts to change the technique of empathy so that identification becomes possible with the collectives (classes) have little chance of success. They result in unrealistic distortions and abstractions of persons and collectives alike. The role of the individual within the collective becomes unrepresentable, although this very aspect is of the greatest importance.)

His attempt to bring about an identification with the collective had caused an 'abstraction' which is contrary to the demands of the theatre. His comment that the play was intended to teach the actors rather than the audience, which in a *Lehrstück* implies that the audience may be completely ignored, turns the drama into an exercise where one vital dimension of the theatre is lost. When Brecht therefore, in the *Messingkauf* dialogues, returns to the subject of the representation of Marxism on the stage, the philosopher, his mouthpiece in the dialogues, introduces this aspect with a significant qualification:

Aber ich muss eine Einschränkung machen. Diese Lehre beschäftigt sich vornehmlich mit dem Verhalten grosser Menschenmassen. Die Gesetze, welche diese Wissenschaft aufstellte, gelten für die Bewegungen sehr grosser Einheiten von Menschen, und wenn auch über die Stellung des einzelnen in diesen grossen Einheiten allerhand gesagt wird, so betrifft auch dies eben für gewöhnlich nur die Stellung des einzelnen eben zu diesen Massen. Wir aber hätten bei unseren Demonstrationen es mehr mit dem Verhalten der einzelnen untereinander zu tun. (*GW* 16, 530)

(However, there is one reservation. This dogma deals above all with the behaviour of great masses of people. The laws it propounds apply to the movement of large human units, and although it has a good deal to say about the individual's position within these units, this refers normally only to the relations between those masses and the individual. But in our demonstrations we would be more concerned with the behaviour of individuals to one another.) (JW adapted)

This is an acknowledgement that, on the stage, the interest of the spectator is in the first instance directed towards the individualized figures, not abstract mass movements. It does not mean that Brecht has abandoned his conviction that the masses, the large collectives, are the really determining factors; as the passage quoted above confirms, these 'large human units' remain the decisive forces. But the theatre cannot ignore individuals, they must provide the equally important 'life' without which the theatre would become unattractive: 'Wo ist er selber, der Lebendige, Unverwechselbare, der nämlich, der mit seinesgleichen nicht ganz gleich ist?' ('Where is this person, full of life, unmistakably himself, he who is not quite the same as his peers?') (*GW* 16, 679) The theatre must continue to show figures who stand out as personalities in their own right, who are distinct and singular as human beings and are not merely representations or reflections of philosophical or sociological principles (*GW* 16, 615). The individual therefore becomes the indispensable counterpart of the collective, and the relationship between these two factors, one of which is crucial to the working of the theatre, the other to the understanding of our political and social realities, now becomes the crucial issue for both the theorist and dramatist in Brecht.

In order to illustrate what he means by the newly discovered interaction between the individual and the collective, Brecht introduces a concept which he borrowed like the term non-Aristotelian (by analogy to non-Euclidean), from the field of modern science, in this case from the quantum theory. It is the concept of *statistische Kausalität* (statistical causality), a new way of looking at the relationship between cause and effect. In earlier years, Brecht's attitude to this problem had been purely negative in that he denied the existence of an *absolute* cause-and-effect relationship between a person's behaviour and his character or psychological make-up. But his attempts to establish instead a similarly close link between behaviour and class or membership of a large collective had also proved to be unsatisfactory. Now the introduction of this new principle, particularly attractive to Brecht because it once again stresses the *Wissenschaftlichkeit* (scientific rigour) of his efforts, establishes a link that resolves his difficulties in the most convincing way. While the movements of the large collective can be described and predicted according to the laws of scientific Marxism, the same rule does not apply to the behaviour of the individual; it may take a broad sample of his movements and utterances before it can be decided whether and to what extent he belongs to a particular group or mass. He has therefore gained some independence and may even 'surprise' us:

Es würde uns an ihm etwas fehlen, nämlich etwas Individuelles, wenn es
allzu widerspruchslos der gesetzmässigen Bewegung der Masse folgen
würde . . . wir können bei unseren Zuschauern eine Haltung nicht
brauchen . . . die dem Individuum gegenüber (und mit ihm haben wir es zu
tun) ständig auf absolute Kausalität ausgeht, statt, wie die Physiker sagen,
auf statistische. Wir müssen in gewissen Lagen mehr als eine Antwort,
Reaktion, Handlungsweise erwarten, ein Ja *und* ein Nein; beides muss
einigermassen begründet, mit Motiven versehen erscheinen. (*GW* 15,
279–80)

(We would think him lacking in something, i.e. in individuality, if he were
to accord too readily to the laws governing the movements of masses. We
need to wean our audiences away from a way of thinking which expects the
individual (and it is him we are dealing with) constantly to be under the
control of an absolute causality instead of, as the physicists say, a statistical
one. In certain situations we must expect more than one answer, reaction, or
mode of behaviour, a yes *and* a no; both must appear to be reasonably
plausible and motivated.)

The spectator's attention is still to be directed towards the more important movements of the collectives, and he must be made aware of the
fact that the individual is no more than a small particle of such a mass
or mass reaction. Nevertheless, the relative unpredictability of the individual gives him increased significance and interest, and incidentally
opens up the way towards the creation of 'great' dramatic figures. An
example taken from Brecht's theoretical writings may illustrate the
point.

In an essay concerned with 'Die Vorgänge hinter den Vorgängen'
('The events behind the events') Brecht gives as an example the case of
evictions of the unemployed from their homes in a capitalist society.
This is an 'event' which happens on a large scale, and is of historical
interest precisely because of the large number of similar cases. One
might therefore be tempted to look at the eviction of one particular person merely as the case of a 'Mr X', i.e. as a case in which the qualities
of the individual himself are of no significance. This is indeed the way
in which this incident would be seen by the owner of the house and the
authorities. But in presenting his case it would be wrong to follow the
same attitude. From the point of view of the person concerned he is not
merely an X, he is someone with a name (here Franz Dietz), a personality which raises him above a mere number. One would therefore have to
show Franz Dietz fighting against the attempt to treat him as an X and
to rob him of his individuality. He could only do this by mobilizing a
large number of people who are in the same situation; only by collective
actions can he hope to succeed. The aim of the action however, is to
give to each member of the collective the dignity of being a person in
his own right. Franz Dietz's fight for recognition is part of the struggle
of the underprivileged against their oppressors and this, for the Marxist,
is what history is all about; at the end of this process the anonymity of

the mass and its antagonistic conflict with the particularity of the individual will be overcome (*GW* 15, 259–60).

Such a historical perspective as exemplified here does illustrate to what extent Brecht has overcome the fatalistic views of the individual and history posited implicitly in his early pre-Marxist works, but also shows how his rather crudely deterministic *Weltanschauung* in the years following his espousal of Marxism is in the process of giving way to a more dialectical view of history and individuals. With this, it becomes part of the task of the dramatist to project the contradictions of this dialectic into the dramatic action and into the presentation of the individual character; as Brecht observes:

> Seine Darstellung als eines Mitglieds einer Klasse oder einer Epoche ist nicht möglich ohne seine Darstellung als besonderes Lebewesen innerhalb seiner Klasse und Epoche. (*GW* 15, 405)
>
> (His portrayal as the member of a class or epoch is not possible without his portrayal as a particular being within his class and epoch.)

The historical figure therefore combines features which reflect the historical reality of his epoch with other features which are undoubtedly expressions of his personality. This is precisely the relationship we can expect to exist between an individual and the collective to which he belongs. Only when both factors are combined can we expect a strong and convincing figure to emerge which also sufficiently reflects the characteristics of the collective.

The dramatic figure in Brecht's work which lives up to these expectations in the most obvious way, and who is explicitly referred to by Brecht as 'eine nationale Figur' (*GW* 17, 1168) of a 'lokalhistorischen Charakter' is the estate owner in *Herr Puntila und sein Knecht Matti* (*Herr Puntila and his Servant Matti*). Puntila's enormous vitality makes him an almost legendary figure; his main objective in life is to enjoy himself to the full, which he does, sparing neither himself nor his servants, nor anyone else who happens to come near him. Whenever he is drunk – which is a necessary precondition for his enjoyment of life – his vitality leads him directly into opposition to the usual behaviour of the collective to which he belongs, that of the wealthy estate owners. The limitations that the code of behaviour of his class imposes upon him often interfere with his pursuit of pleasure, and he therefore transgresses them with impunity: he drinks and makes merry with his servants, becomes engaged to four country girls at one and the same time, rouses half the villagers from their sleep in the middle of the night in his search for 'legal' schnapps, and finally throws his upper-class prospective son-in-law out of his house, encouraging his daughter to flirt with the virile chauffeur instead. There is plenty of 'surprise' in terms of class behaviour, in his conduct.

Yet the conflict with his own class is one of appearance rather than reality. He cannot possibly turn against the class system in any serious way because his pleasures depend entirely on the existence of this very class system. Without his wealth, Puntila's vitality would not find an 'adequate' outlet in the real world, his larger-than-life vitality demanding a corresponding higher-than-average income to realize itself. Puntila needs money to pay for his servants whose presence is required at any time, day and night, so that every whim of the master can be carried out without delay. While his vitality, that is his individuality, clashes with the class system at certain points when he is drunk, his real interests at all times force him to fall in line on all important matters with the collective of which he is a member. This does not only show itself in his moments of sobriety when he turns out to be as unpleasant an employer as anyone else; it also emerges in his moments of drunkenness when he wisely refrains from conducting business or signing contracts. And when in the end his fellow estate owners threaten to boycott him unless he sacks a Communist worker, Puntila dismisses this undesirable element from his service although he is at that time drunk – even the pleasure-seeking Puntila in his inebriate state realizes that economic ruin would also mean the end of his enjoyment of life. Behind the legendary figure of Puntila we are always aware of the existence and the reality of the historical conditions, i.e. of the class to which he belongs, and in spite of all his individual eccentricities we never forget that the decisive factor in the end is not his attitude but that of the collective.[4]

The interaction between the individual and the collective reaches a more sophisticated level in *Mutter Courage und ihre Kinder* (*Mother Courage and her Children*). As the play is set in the Thirty Years War, the historical dimension is particularly obvious. Mutter Courage herself is, it is true, a humble person and far removed from the greatness of a Gustavus Adolphus or a Wallenstein. But she nevertheless stands out as a memorable and impressive figure because of her intelligence, alertness and immense vitality. She is indefatigable, hard-working, unflappable, and has the strength to carry on where others would have given up long ago – in short, she is the domineering figure in the play and the centre of her world. She is in many ways a likeable person, and her main concern to bring her children through the war unharmed certainly has our sympathy, so much so that some producers have found it easy to present her as a tragic figure who is noble and courageous but is destroyed by an anonymous and uncontrollable fate in the shape of war. Brecht's intentions were otherwise. In the first instance, it was Mutter Courage's decision to join the war in order to make a living, and she has therefore by her own will placed herself and her children under the laws of war. And secondly, she is bound to fail, in spite of all her personal efforts, because she cannot expect to escape in the long run from whatever misfortune will befall the collective to which she now belongs. This collective is the army. Of course, as she herself points out, what is a major setback for the army need not be the same for its individual members, and she did at one stage benefit from a defeat because she acquired a horse to pull the cart; it was taken away from her again after order had been restored. Even when she falls into the hands of the enemy, she can adapt to the new situation and continue business as usual. But the army is in the war to destroy or get destroyed, business is dangerous and leaves no room for pity, and Courage is not only the caring mother but also the 'hyena of the battlefield'.

The titles at the beginning of every scene remind us of the wider political and military dimensions which reflect and determine the conditions under which the army, including Courage and her children, have to live. If the destruction caused by warfare continues for a long time – the play shows us twelve of the thirty years of the war – there will be fewer material goods for everyone to share; the room for independent manoeuvre on the part of the individual will diminish. Sooner or later everyone whose spoon is not long enough to keep at a safe distance from the fighting will be affected. The disintegration of order and discipline, for example, may show itself in the rape of Courage's daughter; the general impoverishment of the collective must in turn adversely affect her business. The events on the stage show us what happens to Mutter Courage and her family, to some particular individuals; the titles inform us of what happens to the collective. As the messages of the titles get bleaker, so eventually do the lives of the individuals we see on the stage. In the end it is the development of the collective which determines the circumstances in which its members will find themselves.

The titles and the army are not the only references to a wider and more general framework we receive in this play. We are also continually reminded of the fact that expectations, attitudes or misfortunes which are expressed by or affect the figures in the play are not only experienced by these few individuals. They are also shared by a large number of people who in this war find themselves in a similar situation. These more general experiences are expressed in the songs. When Mutter Courage first enters the stage she answers the question as to who she is by one word 'Geschäftsleut' ('trader') and then bursts into a song which illustrates the predicament not only of her own case but of all people doing business in war. They are dealing with customers whose numbers decrease with every battle, and who must therefore be induced to spend all their money before the fighting begins. At the beginning of the new season in the year, in the war, and in the business the dead are of no use; trade must be done with the living. The last stanza of this song with which the play ends reinforces the point that, if Courage wants to remain in business, nothing has changed except that her own children now also belong to the useless waste the war has left behind. But this dehumanizing fact does not merely apply to her alone; behind her we must see all the others to whom the same 'fate' applies.

In the same way the song sung in the second scene by Eilif and completed by Courage illustrates the general contrast in the attitudes of the young, adventurous, carefree soldiers and of the women who stayed behind. The point of view of the young, which determines the first two stanzas sung by Eilif, gives way to that of the women who have the last word and whose fears are proved to be justified by the end of the song as well as the play. And just as Eilif and his mother allow their personal attitudes to be seen in a wider context, so Yvette, the camp prostitute, shows us in the 'Lied vom Fraternisieren' ('Fraternizing Song') that the misery of her own existence is suffered by innumerable girls whose love has led them into the same situation. The use of songs in this play reaches its climax in the fourth scene when Mutter Courage sings 'Das Lied von der grossen Kapitulation') ('The Song of the Great Capitulation'). This is the point where she, in Brecht's view, acts most despicably, because she not only persuades herself that inaction in the face of injustice from above is the best attitude, but in doing so also discourages the young soldier from lodging a justified complaint. Mutter Courage first describes the attitude of the young who think they are special, and then the resignation of later years when one's spirit has been broken. In the refrain of the song, the individual is seen as marching in a military band and contributing his 'kleinen Ton' to the music of the collective. Then, merely by changing the punctuation, Brecht turns the well-known saying 'Der Mensch denkt, Gott lenkt' ('Man thinks but God directs') into almost its opposite: 'Der Mensch denkt: Gott lenkt' ('Man thinks that God directs'), a view which is then dismissed as without substance. It is left to the spectator to conclude that if God is not in control it must be the officer commanding the band, i.e. a human being whose orders may be fallible and can be opposed. Of course there is no point in anyone acting on his own; but if the whole band decided to disobey, the officer in charge would be without power to enforce his command. The importance of the collective and of the collective action is brought out particularly strongly in this song, and so is the conclusion that if we are treated unjustly it is not the strength of authority but the weakness of those receiving and obeying orders that is to blame. The real enemy therefore is in the minds of the oppressed who capitulate because they assume far too readily that they are helpless, and the criticism of the song is directed against all who, like Mutter Courage, in similar situations persuade themselves and others that placid acceptance of orders from above is always the best option.

The play *Mutter Courage und ihre Kinder* therefore, while using one particularly strong and impressive individual and her family to illustrate the point, always carefully relates the events taking place on the stage to a far larger and wider context, constantly indicating that behind the demonstrations on the stage there are large numbers of people in the same or similar positions, with identical or at least similar motivations, interests, reactions or attitudes. The real concern of the play therefore is obviously to show the interaction between individual and collective, and to indicate that of these two aspects the collective is by far the more important factor. Thus Brecht has built up a complex framework of personal, social, economic and political forces which eventually determine the actions of individual figures. Those producers, however, who have presented Mutter Courage as a Niobe-like figure who loses her children because an inexplicable fate in the form of war has struck her have ignored the complexity of the determining factors, and have in fact returned to the one-dimensional point of view where the *statistische Kausalität* employed by Brecht has been abandoned in favour of the old *absolute Kausalität* which sees a person's actions as directly linked to character alone, attributing other occurrences that cannot thus be explained to fate.

This brings us back once more to the question of causality as the most significant single factor for Brecht's new definition of the role and function of the individual in a complex world dominated by large collectives. By introducing the concept of *statistische Kausalität* Brecht has once more underlined the 'scientific' nature of his drama which is, in his own view, the only way in which we can adopt the 'produktive Haltung gegenüber der Natur und gegenüber der Gesellschaft, welche wir als Kinder eines wissenschaftlichen Zeitalters in unserem Theatre vergnüglich einnehmen wollen' ('the productive attitude towards nature and society which we as children of a scientific age will enjoy having in our theatre') (*GW* 16, 671). But it might be worthwhile to go one step further in the theoretical speculation about the effects and the consequences of the new concept of causality in the world of Brecht's drama.

The abandonment of the old principle of absolute causality and the substitution of statistical causality has placed the individual in a new situation with far-reaching possibilities. It has in the first instance released him from the restrictions of the traditional close link between his action and an immediate motivation in his character or psyche. At the same time, however, the vacuum in motivation thus created is not filled by the new principle of statistical causality which quite explicitly is binding on the collective only, without determining the behaviour of any one particular member. Neither of the two types of causality is therefore applicable to the individual who is now standing between them, with an unexpected freedom to 'surprise' as Brecht demanded (*GW* 15, 279), and in a state of apparent non-determination. Brecht appears now to grant to the sphere of art a degree of relative autonomy *vis-a-vis* actual social and historical reality, a fact which has important repercussions for the characterization of his individuals. Their 'realism' decreases while their flexibility as role-players (and thereby their potential for demonstrating a wide range of behavioural possibilities) increases. Brecht himself certainly was not unaware of the possibilities opened up by the new situation. The creation of his famous 'split characters', notably Shen Te/ Shui Ta in *Der gute Mensch von Sezuan* (*The Good Person of Szechwan*) must be seen in the context of this development. Shen Te and her *alter ego* Shui Ta are totally unrealistic figures. The very idea that one person can split herself into two different halves entirely at variance with each other, and that she is, although living and dealing with the same people, only found out by one person, successfully fooling everybody else including her lover, is in itself entirely dependent on the suspension of all probability which is only possible in the world of fairy-tales and legends.

The development of this figure illustrates to what extent Brecht exploits all aspects of the 'aesthetic state' and its implications in the building up of a character. At first Shen Te is a nondescript person, a prostitute whose only characteristic seems to be that she is unable to say no. Then the gods enter her life and present her with the instruction to be good: there is now a moral obligation which ought to decide her further conduct. There should be no problem; Shen Te is only too willing to obey the new command which in any case seems to suit her natural inclination. But the gods have also, albeit reluctantly, provided Shen Te with some money to give her a start in her new life. This is where the real conflict begins: as Shen Te is determined to do good and needs her money for this purpose she invests it; but once she has done so she is forced to protect her investment, because if her business is ruined she will no longer be able to help anybody. In order to protect her capital, however, she has very much against her will to adopt certain practices of the capitalists in the disguise of her cousin Shui Ta. The economic pressures under which she finds herself now constitute an entirely different type of motivation or causality: with her first success as a capitalist, other members of this class take notice of her, and so Shui Ta slowly adopts the characteristics of the new class to which 'he' now belongs. While Shen Te still intends to return and to help those in need, Shui Ta develops more and more in the opposite direction. This even affects Shen Te's relationship with her lover, whose selfishness further complicates her already difficult position: while Shen Te would like him to realize his dream of becoming a pilot, Shui Ta discovers in him all the characteristics of a despicable bully and offers him every opportunity to further his own good fortune at the expense of others. Shen Te/ Shui Ta herself is driven further along the same path when she discovers that she is pregnant and realizes that she must protect her unborn child against the dangers of a hostile world. The conflict remains unresolved, as does the question as to what sort of person Shen Te/Shui Ta 'really' is. Her dilemma not only demonstrates the social, economic or moral pressures which dominate human life; it also reflects to what extent Brecht has exploited the possibilities offered by the new freedom in building up complex, contradictory characters on the stage. The probability of character portrayal has given way to the creation of fictitious figures who, precisely because there is no restriction on the play of the author's imagination, demonstrate the supra-individualistic attitudes of which Brecht wants his audiences to become aware.

There is, then, a clear development in Brecht's attitude towards the concept of the individual. His first plays are in this respect entirely negative: his heroes are either, like Baal, at the mercy of their instincts and vitality and have become completely anti-social, or they are, like Galy Gay, so much a product of social pressures that the identity and continuity of the self disappears and is replaced by total adaptation to the environment. With his conversion to Marxism, this latter de-individuation is no longer a fact but an ideal, and anyone who like the young comrade in *Die Massnahme* resists the abandonment of his personal convictions is cast in the role of an undesirable relic of the past who must be destroyed. At the same time Brecht does here allow the hero to offer some resistance to external manipulation, and this eventually leads to a more complex portrayal of the individual's role. As the laws of Marxism describe the movements of large collectives, they can predict the actions of the majority of their members only. In particular, the replacement of 'absolute causality' (which links the actions of a dramatic figure entirely to his character) by 'statistical causality' (which applies to the actions of a majority in a given collective only) leaves the individual in a state where there is no immediate determination of his actions at all, thus allowing the author complete freedom in the creation of his figures. They need no longer conform to psychological probability nor to class characteristics, they may even, like his 'split characters', move freely from one to the other. They are, as the German writer Martin Walser has remarked, fundamentally fictitious: 'Realistisch ist nur die Tendenz, das Bewegungsgesetz. Die Figuren aber sind aus dem Stoff, aus dem die Märchen sind und die Legenden'. ('The only realistic thing is the tendency, the law governing the development of events. The figures, however, are of such stuff as fairy-tales are made of, fairy-tales and legends.') Although Brecht set out to destroy the traditional concept of the individual, and to replace art by sociology, he did in the end create impressive dramatic figures and, in so doing, art.

NOTES

1. 'Das Theater des Neuen: Eine Ankündigung', in Hugo von Hofmannsthal, *Gesammelte Werke in Einzelausgaben*, Herbert Steiner, ed. *Lustspiele IV* (Frankfurt am Main, 1956). pp. 405–26 (p. 419).
2. Reiner Steinweg, ed. *Die Massnahme*, (Frankfurt am Main, 1972), p. 355.
3. Ibid., p. 401.
4. See Chapter 5 below for a discussion of *Puntila* as comedy and as *Volksstück*.

COMEDY AND THE *VOLKSSTÜCK*

Moray McGowan

COMEDY

'Not by wrath, but by laughter do we slay.'

FRIEDRICH NIETZSCHE

'Ein Theater in dem man nicht lachen soll, ist ein Theater, über das man lachen soll.' ('A theatre in which you're not supposed to laugh is a theatre about which you have to laugh.')

BERTOLT BRECHT (*GW* 16, 644)

Brecht's view of comedy is absolutely central to his work. It is fundamental both to his theatrical theory and to the social philosophy his plays reflect. An understanding of this point will provide an approach to virtually all his plays as well as explaining why, despite his much professed liking for popular forms of art, he rejected the *Volksstück* or German popular comedy, and wrote only one play which he called a *Volksstück*.

Brecht was attracted to comedy from the beginning of his writing career as a means of revolt both against the classical German dramatic tradition, which regarded tragedy as the highest form of theatre and comedy as being very much secondary, and against the dominant literary movement of the time, Expressionism. Brecht mocked earnestness wherever he found it; he knew that the serious could be comic, and throughout his career he insisted on the comic's right and ability to make serious statements about society.

The central role of comedy in Brecht's plays lies in its complex, two-way relationship with *Verfremdung*, theatrical alienation in the Brechtian sense defined in Chapter 3 of this book. Brecht himself repeatedly stressed this relationship:

Der V-Effekt ist ein altes Kunstmittel, bekannt aus der Komödie.... (*GW* 16, 652) gewisse verfremdungen stammen aus dem zeughaus der komödie, das 2,000 jahre alt ist. (*Aj*, 912) Allgemein angewendet wird der V-Effekt in der Komödie, besonders der niedrigen. (*GW* 15, 366)

(The alienation effect is an ancient artistic device, familiar to us from comedy . . . certain alienation techniques come from the 2,000-year-old arsenal of comedy . . . the alienation effect enjoys widespread use in comedy, especially low comedy.)

The first element in this reciprocal relationship between comedy and *Verfremdung* is the way in which comedy can be used to generate *Verfremdung*. Tragedy depends on our acceptance that the tragic hero's fall is inevitable, since the social, moral or metaphysical forces against which he struck out are immutable, and thus it works primarily on our emotions. Comedy on the other hand appeals to the intellect; indeed the philosopher Henri Bergson thought it was a wholly intellectual activity. Comedy depends, in William Hazlitt's words, on 'the incongruous', the gap between 'what things are and what they ought to be', on what Fritz Martini calls 'die spannungsgeladene Dialektik zwischen Sein und Schein' ('the tense interactivity between being and appearance').[1] Comedy is about paradoxes and absurdities in society and behaviour, about things not being what they seem; moreover it is essential that the audience should recognize this gap between *Sein* and *Schein*. Comedy would seem a good vehicle for Brecht's critical and didactic purposes, since it can be used to encourage critical distance and reflection in the audience.

It does not always do this, of course. The Whitehall farces of Brian Rix or the television sitcom, be it the *Dick van Dyke Show, On the Buses* or *Love Thy Neighbour*, or the average contemporary *Volksstück* of the Ohnsorgtheater or Komödienstadel companies, all generate laughter precisely through an illusionistic avoidance of any effect that might prompt the audience to critical reflection. In this kind of more or less apologetic, affirmative comedy, as the East German playwright Peter Hacks puts it, 'Die Welt wird vergoldet durch ein Wir-sind-ja-alle-Ferkel-Gefühl' (roughly: 'a feeling that we're all pigs at the same trough together makes us feel the world is a fine place, really').[2]

Hacks distinguishes this from critical comedy, which demonstrates the negative aspects of the society or situation under scrutiny, and implicitly or explicitly calls for their removal. Obviously it is this latter type of comedy that interested the Marxist Brecht, and of which he was thinking when he wrote that 'Humor ist Distanzgefühl' ('humour is a feeling of distance') (*GW* 18, 3), for a critical distance from the events being portrayed is essential in order to recognize that they are changeable: as Louise Bird remarks, a salient feature, a precondition, of critical comedy is 'the feasibility of change'.[3] The writer of critical comedies wants us to see that the world not only should be, but *could* be different.

A tragedy like *Romeo and Juliet*, and the typical romantic comedy in which the two lovers are thwarted until it is discovered that the boy, to whom the girl's wealthy parents had objected because of his poverty, is to inherit a substantial sum from a maiden aunt, at which point all obstacles to their marriage fall, both have the same message: that the world as it is will have its way in the end. The tragedy ends tragically because the moral fibre of the hero will not brook compromise; the romantic comedy ends happily not because the world and its values are changed but because individual fates are manipulated until they meet the scheme of things.

From this perspective it is clear that Brecht does not totally reject traditional theatre, and indeed he repeatedly stresses that many of his ideas have their roots there; rather, his attack is on the philosophy of tragedy as a philosophy of inevitability (an attitude not restricted to tragedy, as we have seen), and on the fatalistic attitude it engenders in the audience.[4] As early as 1921 Brecht condemned tragedy as part of the bourgeois ideology in whose interest it was not to countenance the possibility of change. 'Die Tragödie basiert auf bürgerlichen Tugenden, zieht daraus ihre Kraft und geht ein mit ihnen' (*Tb* 131). ('Tragedy is founded on bourgeois virtues, draws its strength from them and decays as they decay'.) Thus when Brecht asserts 'dass die Tragödie die Leiden der Menschen häufiger auf die leichte Achsel nimmt als die Komödie' ('tragedy is prone to treat the sufferings of humanity less seriously than comedy'), he means that tragedy accepts suffering, whereas comedy, or at least critical comedy, indicates where change is necessary and possible, and thus takes up a more 'responsible' attitude towards the suffering it observes (*GW* 17, 1178).

Critical comedy presupposes a Utopia, in fact. Brecht's comedy is an attempt to grasp the world intellectually, to render experience relative, not absolute as in tragedy, to compare the real with the ideal to the cost of the former, or, from the perspective of the optimistic socialism of the later Brecht, to compare the present with the future Utopia.[5]

In establishing the relationship between comedy and *Verfremdung* in Brecht's work, we find ourselves talking less and less about theatrical forms and more and more about Brecht's attitude towards society. And rightly so, for while it is true that Brecht employed comic techniques and structures to achieve *Verfremdung*, it is much more fundamental to recognize that he employed *Verfremdung* to show the comedy of society. 'Comic' and 'tragic' were for Brecht less aesthetic categories, more ways of looking at life, the tragic view being that conditions as they were were inevitable and unchangeable, the comic view that they were laughable, because unnecessary. Even this reformulation is inadequate, since in fact the comic was not a 'way of looking' for Brecht, *but what he saw*. To understand this fully we should briefly consider the place of comedy in the Marxist philosophy of history.

According to Marx, 'the last phase of a world-historical form is its comedy'.[6] As historical change occurs, those elements in society who stand to lose by change, or think they do, or fail to recognize that change is taking place, try to prevent it or act as though it is not happening; they cling to anachronistic attitudes and structures. From Marx's perspective, the antics of the ruling classes in the 1840s and 1850s, for example, were farcical and absurd because they were anachronistic, and in particular Louis Bonaparte became 'the serious buffoon who no longer takes world history as a comedy [which Marx saw as the correct view] but his comedy for world history'.[7] In the contemporary world, the retired officer type represented by *Private Eye*'s Colonel Gussett is comic because he clings to Britain's long-past colonial greatness, the House of Lords in all its splendour is comic because of its inappropriateness in its present form to a modern democracy. But Marx's analysis goes much deeper: because of the paradoxes and contradictions inherent in capitalism such as its creation of an industrial proletariat which is essential to its development but which none the less will eventually overthrow it, capitalism is itself fundamentally comic. Marx is evidently judging his own time from, as he sees it, a superior position of insight into the true nature of capitalist society and historical development.

The same facility of being able to view the present from the perspective of a Utopian future enables the Marxist Brecht to write comedies about Hitler, *Der aufhaltsame Aufstieg des Arturo Ui* (*The Resistible Rise of Arturo Ui*), or about racism, *Die Rundköpfe und die Spitzköpfe* (*Round Heads and Pointed Heads*). From Brecht's perspective these subjects are comic in the sense outlined above, which is not to say that they are funny or harmless, of course; anachronisms can be doubly dangerous because their defence requires irrational rather than rational justifications. Brecht never underestimated the vicious nature of National Socialism, but in *Arturo Ui*, by presenting Hitler as a comic opera gangster trying to corner the Chicago greens market, Brecht enables us to view his rise to power from a more critical perspective. This critical perspective enables us to see the comic nature of Fascism. The play's title speaks of Ui's 'aufhaltsame Aufstieg', his resistible rise. It need not have happened. Brecht's concern is not to *reduce* the stature of the Nazi leadership by making them look ridiculous – he stresses in his notes on the play that great crimes do not make great men (*GW* 17, 1178) – but to show that they are *inherently* ridiculous. As Peter Giese says, 'das Komische also ist im Dargestellten selbst und entsteht nicht erst durch die Darstellung'.[8] ('The comic, therefore, is inherent in the reality represented, and is not first created by the representation'.) The comedy on stage causes the historical events portrayed to be *verfremdet*, made strange in such a way as to lead the audience to the experience of *Verfremdung*, of critical distance, towards the reality being treated. Critical distance in turn enables the audience to recognize society as at present constituted as 'komisch, weil... historisch, d.h. durch eine andere Gesellschaftsordnung lösbar' ('comic, because capable of being replaced in the course of the historical process, that is by another social order') (*GW* 2, 489). By means of *Verfremdung*, by for example setting *Die heilige Johanna der Schlachthöfe* (*St Joan of the Stockyards*) in an imaginary Chicago, or *Der gute Mensch von Sezuan* (*The Good Person of Szechwan*) in a totally mythical China, Brecht could present the capitalist society of his day as a historical form, as a point in time not an eternal truth, and by writing from the viewpoint of a Utopian social-ist future he could show capitalism as anachronistic and therefore comic, its absurdity being a provocation to the audience to change it, and the point of the style (i.e. of *Verfremdung*) being to ensure that the inherently comic is clearly recognized as such. In Lessing's words, comedy is 'Übung unserer Fähigkeit, das Lächerliche zu bemerken' ('training in the ability to notice the ridiculous') (*Hamburgische Dramaturgie*, 29. Stück). This, the general development of his audi-ence's ability to recognize the comic, because incongruous, elements or structures of their society, is as important to Brecht as the specific indictments that specific plays make.

Brecht's comedy is therefore not only not comedy for its own sake. It is also not simply comedy for the purpose of achieving *Verfremdung*, critical distance. His comedy is not dependent on certain theatrical effects and techniques, but is a reflection and a function of an incongru-ous and paradoxical social structure; it is not so much a theatrical form as an interpretation of society and a statement of social purpose.

THE POPULAR

Was Brecht a 'popular' writer? His well-documented preference for popular forms of art stems partly from a sincere belief that they could provide an alternative to the sterility of German classical theatre and the bombast of Expressionism. But many of his pronouncements also reveal a delight in antithesis and iconoclasm for their own sake: 'Ich lese aus Mangel an Schundromanen die Bekenntnisse des Augustinus.' (*Tb* 212) ('Due to the shortage of smutty novels I'm reading the Confessions of St. Augustine.') In 1934 he declared: 'Ich bin Stückeschreiber. Eigentlich wäre ich gerne Tischler geworden.' (*Tb* 219) ('I'm a playwright. Really I would have liked to be a carpenter.') This seems most unlikely. Brecht's anti-bourgeois stance was not that of a proletarian, as he him-self admitted. He was an intellectual from a comfortably middle-class fam-ily, and he *used* popular forms and techniques to create his own, indi-vidual, often intellectual theatre.

The concept of the 'popular' was still more problematic for Brecht in 1940, when he wrote his *Volksstück, Herr Puntila und sein Knecht Matti* (*Herr Puntila and his Servant Matti*). The National Socialists had been practising tyranny in the name of the *Volk* since 1933. The ideol-ogy of *Volkstümlichkeit* (roughly: appropriateness to the broad mass of the people) was being used to justify both countless brutal acts and a multitude of more petty deceptions of the German people, such as the

Volkswagen scheme. For the Nazis, the words *Volk* and *völkisch* referred to the racial nation, and were part of the ideology that supported the persecution of the Jews. The National Socialists thus provided a principal reason for Brecht's deep scepticism about any term that included *Volk*, and one of the purposes of his play *Furcht und Elend des dritten Reichs* (*Fear and Misery of the Third Reich*) was to destroy this Nazi myth of a harmonious, classless *Volksgemeinschaft* (national community).

In an essay written in exile in 1938, 'Volkstümlichkeit und Realismus' ('Popular culture and realism') Brecht tries to clarify his position as a writer towards the 'popular'. He rejects the term *volkstümlich* as currently used. 'Der Begriff 'volkstümlich' ist nicht allzu volkstümlich' (*GW* 19, 323). ('The term 'appropriate to the broad mass of the people' is not very appropriate to the broad mass of the people'.) The characteristics of the *Volk* have been particularly falsified by the attribution to it of unified, unchanging values that transcend class or economic circumstances. We must, therefore, Brecht argues, reject *Volkstümlichkeit* as an ahistorical, static concept that has become a tool to oppress those strata of society it claims to represent.

However, 'gegen die zunehmende Barbarei gibt es nur einen Bundesgenossen; das Volk, das so sehr darunter leidet' ('against increasing barbarism there is only one ally: the people, who suffer so much from it') (*GW* 19, 323). So, because the *Volk* are essential allies in the fight against Fascism, Brecht also calls for a new definition of *Volkstümlichkeit* as that which serves the best interests of the people:

> Volkstümlich heisst: den breiten Massen verständlich, ihre Ausdrucksform aufnehmend und bereichernd / ihren Standpunkt einnehmend, befestigend und korrigierend/den fortschrittlichsten Teil des Volkes so vertretend, dass er die Führung übernehmen kann, also auch den andern Teilen des Volkes verständlich / anknüpfend an die Traditionen, sie weiterführend / dem zur Führung strebenden Teil des Volkes Errungenschaften des jetzt führenden Teils übermittelnd. (*GW* 19, 325)

> (Popular means: comprehensible to the broad masses, using and enriching their means of expression / taking up, supporting and correcting their viewpoint / representing the most progressive elements of the *Volk* in such a way that they can take over its leadership, and therefore also comprehensible to the other elements of the *Volk* / building on and carrying forward the traditions / communicating the achievements of the now leading elements of the *Volk* to those elements who are aspiring to leadership.)

Thus Brecht's conception of popular art in 1938 was one which employed the idiom of the people and was concerned to deal with issues that directly affected them, but which was not content to portray their world in a static way. Instead it aimed to focus attention on, and to expand the possibilities for development that were latent in the masses. For Brecht, of course, this meant the development towards socialism. This did not lead Brecht to create glowingly positive proletarian heroes of the kind that occur in the socialist realism of Soviet Russian and GDR literature. Precisely in order to be *volkstümlich* in his sense, Brecht had to base his analysis on the reality of capitalist society as the *Volk* of his day experienced it. Thus while the Nazi ideology of *Volkstümlichkeit* was for him the epitome of all that was dishonest in such a concept, yet his Marxist belief in the masses as the repository of the progressive forces in society meant that he had to generate a new version of *Volkstümlichkeit* to replace the old one.

POPULAR COMEDY: THE *VOLKSSTÜCK*

In 1940 Brecht completed his *Volksstück Herr Puntila und sein Knecht Matti*, and the accompanying 'Anmerkungen zum Volksstück' ('Notes on the *Volksstück*'). From the latter one can see that Brecht's attitude to the *Volksstück* is comparable to that he held towards the concept of *Volkstümlichkeit*: in its existing form it was profoundly unsatisfactory since it promoted a false image of the *Volk* and had become an instrument for their oppression, but because, for Brecht, the *Volk*, the people, the broad masses, were the class in which the future rested, it was necessary to mould a new *Volksstück* worthy of the name.

The *Volksstück* in its existing form is, says Brecht, generally 'krudes und anspruchloses Theater' ('crude and undemanding theatre) and scholars and critics ignore it or treat it disdainfully.

> Da gibt es derbe Spässe gemischt mit Rührseligkeiten, da ist hanebüchene Moral und billige Sexualität. Die Bösen werden bestraft, und die Guten werden geheiratet, die Fleissigen machen eine Erbschaft und die Faulen haben das Nachsehen. Die Technik der Volksstückschreiber ist ziemlich international und ändert sich beinahe nie. (*GW* 17, 1162)

> (There one finds coarse gags, mixed with sentimentality, coarsely simplistic morality and cheap sexuality. The bad get punished, the good get married, the industrious inherit and the lazy face the consequences. The technique of the *Volksstück* writer is fairly international and almost never changes.)

Brecht maintains it would be pointless to try to revive the old *Volksstück*. 'Es ist nicht nur völlig versumpft, sondern hat, was bedenklicher ist, niemals eine wirkliche Blüte erlebt.' (*GW* 17, 1163) ('It is not only completely stagnant, but, and this is more of a cause for scepticism, it has never experienced a real blossoming.') What was this *Volksstück* genre that attracted such a decisively negative verdict from Brecht? And was this verdict justified?

The *Volksstück* still awaits definitive description or even a single satisfactory history. There is no equivalent term in English. The slightly inaccurate term 'popular comedy' has been used so far, since 'folk play' misleadingly suggests simple amateur festivities, for which the German is *Volksschauspiel*, and 'popular theatre' as a genre is often ephemeral and unscripted, and may take place outside the conventional theatre, and many of its forms are non-literary. The *Volksstück*, in contrast, is today a literary genre which, although it retains some elements of popular theatre, is largely formalized, scripted and integrated into the established theatre.

It was not always so. The *Volksstück* is widely regarded as having developed principally from the *Wiener Volkstheater* (Viennese popular theatre). This theatrical tradition had developed in the eighteenth century as an alternative to the *Burgtheater* or court theatre.[9] The ordinary people, or *Volk*, which in this period included large sections of the new bourgeoisie, sought in the *Volkstheater*, besides entertainment, an expression of their interests, which the high drama of the *Burgtheater* held to be beneath consideration.

The plays of the *Volkstheater* borrowed eclectically from medieval secular and religious drama and from the Jesuit theatre, from the baroque opera, from English, German and Italian travelling players, from the *commedia dell' arte*, the comedies of Molière and Goldoni, primitive stand-up comedians and popular slapstick and from the Germanic tradition of vigorous comedy to which the sixteenth century *Schwänke* (farces) of Hans Sachs belong. They even borrowed from the court theatre itself, in so far as they often parodied the noble sentiments and grand actions of high drama. *Stegreifkomödie*, improvised comedy on the basis of a skeletal plot, was common, as were light and sound effects, visual comedy, disguise and plays within the play. There was little psychological subtlety in the characterization. Constant themes were the young's attempts to marry against the opposition of the old, master–servant relationships, father–son conflicts, and amorous motifs such as cuckoldry.

A central figure, developed particularly by the actor/manager Josef Stranitzky, was the comic Hanswurst, who appears regardless of the plot of the particular play. Part clown, part fool, part sycophant and part schemer against his master or the authorities, he participates in the action yet stands outside it and comments on it, repeatedly breaking the illusion of a closed form by means of songs, monologues, asides and local references.

The eighteenth century *Volkstheater* had a loose, empirical approach to the solution of dramaturgical problems, and an ambivalent if not completely antagonistic attitude to high culture. It was witty and iconoclastic ensemble theatre, the author being just one productive contributor among many. The text, if there was one at all, was a sketch for production, not a sacrosanct model to be slavishly reproduced. This theatre made free use of adaptations and satirical or parodic references to contemporary events and to other works of literature, and was in its use of songs, slapstick, music and the Hanswurst figure, generally anti-illusionistic. All these approaches and techniques have parallels in Brecht's theatrical theory and practice. But *Volkstheater* and *Volksstück* are not the same thing, and as the former developed into the latter it changed crucially, and, from Brecht's viewpoint, disastrously.

Almost as soon as the *Volkstheater* emerged as a significant popular medium, it became subject to the pressures of censorship and commercialization, which encouraged a process towards increasing formalization and schematization of plays and towards uncritical entertainment. To satisfy the censors, precise texts had to be produced. To satisfy commercial pressures, the theatres employed salaried writers to churn out plays, which inevitably led to schematized production and tame imitations. Between 1804 and 1835, for example, three playwrights, Adolf Bäuerle, Josef Gleich and Karl Meisl, wrote about 500 plays altogether. Entrepreneurial theatre managers became increasingly important, notably Karl Carl, who like a nineteenth century Lew Grade, temporarily near-monopolized the ownership of the Viennese suburban theatres. Both the outstanding nineteenth century authors of Viennese popular theatre, Ferdinand Raimund and Johann Nestroy, worked for Carl.

Raimund's plays represent the apex and yet also the last fling of the *Zauberstück* (magic play), in which, typically, the mortal hero is given a chance to live a different life by fairies who use magic to effect a radical change in his circumstances. In *Der Bauer als Millionär (The Peasant as Millionaire)* (1826) for example, a bad fairy maliciously arranges for the peasant Wurzel to find a treasure. He moves to the town and becomes an extravagant, drunken bully, who tries to force his daughter to marry a rich suitor. Eventually the forces of good triumph. Wurzel's daughter marries the poor fisherman she loves and Wurzel becomes a peasant again, to his delight. In the final song he repeatedly praises 'Zufriedenheit' ('contentedness'). In *Der Verschwender (The Wastrel)* (1833), the concluding message is 'Genügsamkeit' ('being satisfied with what you've got'). Raimund's plays seem to plead for moral rectitude and acquiescence in one's lot within the existing economic and social structure. This is a message that later *Volksstücke* were to echo, without Raimund's unquestioned artistry, and was one of the main things Brecht objected to in the genre.

Johann Nestroy's position is much more critical. He discarded the *Zauberstück* and the *Besserungsstück* (morally improving play), a form that shared the morality of the *Zauberstück* without the magic, or he parodied them mercilessly, as in *Der böse Geist Lumpazivagabundus (The Wicked Fairy Lumpazivagabundus)* (1833) in which overindulgence and hedonism triumph over thrift and diligence. Conflicts may now be based on class interests rather than moral character; they are at any rate conflicts with real, not magic forces, and there is no guarantee that the balance of good and evil will be restored at the end.

In *Freiheit in Krähwinkel (Freedom in Krähwinkel*: synonymous with provincial small-mindedness) (1848), his satire on the 1848 Revolution in Vienna, Nestroy mocks the bombast and vacuity of the petty-bourgeois characters with upper-middle-class aspirations, such as the small businessmen. But he clearly supports their right to more freedom, and he warns of the still present spirit of reaction.

The example of Nestroy shows that some nineteenth century *Volksstücke* had a definite emancipatory, critical role in strengthening the self-respect of the *Volk*, in so far as they showed lower-class characters who were intelligent, responsible, expressive and opposed to the forces of reaction. Nestroy's work seems to contradict Brecht's assertion that the *Volksstück* never had a blossoming; but to take note of it would have complicated the black-and-white nature of his argument. Like Nelson, Brecht could be blind when it suited him. Certainly, Nestroy's rejection of fatalism, his portrayal of an awakening social and economic consciousness in his lower- and middle-class characters, his verbal alienation techniques and his use of songs that reflect satirically rather than illustratively on the main action, suggest that Brecht was much closer in spirit to Nestroy than he admitted.[10]

However, Nestroy was exceptional. The *Volkstheater* was becoming increasingly predictable and conservative as the century progressed. It ceased to be a term that encompassed a wide range of theatrical forms. For example, operetta developed as a separate genre, taking with it most of the musical elements of the Viennese popular theatre. The *Volksstück* itself hardened into a single literary genre. It could now be defined as a play, usually a comedy, usually in dialect or a stage language making use of dialect for comic effect and the establishment of a milieu, set among the ordinary people of a specific town or rural area, and having as its subject their everyday concerns: love and marriage, inheritance, the problems of small businesses and the like. The plays tend to be anachronistic repetitions of stock situations with occasional superficial modernization. This line of development, which continues unbroken in the televised *Volksstücke* of today, was the principal source of Brecht's dissatisfaction with the genre, since these plays deal with the everyday concerns of the *Volk* in terms of those eternal rules which Brecht noted in his 'Anmerkungen': the good are rewarded, the bad punished, etc. The *Zauberstück* died under Nestroy's stiletto thrusts, but its morality emerged unscathed and lives on here.

The *Volksstück* became increasingly irrelevant to the real socio-economic status of the actual *Volk* or mass of the population. Indeed many critics of the genre argue that this kind of play is quite devoid of the positive, emancipatory qualities of *Volkstheater* or popular theatre, and that it was only after these plays had ceased to be *Volkstheater*, in any sense of theatre that stood in a relationship of intimate, mutual fertilization with the *Volk*, the common people, that they came to be called *Volksstücke*.[11] And it is true that though the term existed at least from the early nineteenth century, it was not widely applied until much later; Nestroy, for example, hardly used it. But even if we accept its applica-

tion to the products of German-language popular theatre from the beginning (and though this survey has as yet concentrated on Viennese examples, other German-speaking areas developed similar traditions), it is
none the less true that the hardening of the *Volksstück* into a particular,
largely static genre took place while the *Volk* itself was continuously
developing away from the more or less common starting-point of the
mid-eighteenth century.

The development of the *Volksstück* was not, however, uniformly one
of degeneration into trivial or reactionary cliche. There has always been
an impulse in the tradition towards serious politically, socially or morally engaged theatre. Nestroy has been mentioned. Ludwig Anzengruber's plays, set mostly among the Austrian peasantry, treat moral
conflicts from a critical, anti-clerical perspective. His tragedies, in particular, like *Der Meineidbauer (The Perjured Peasant)* (1871), or *Das
Vierte Gebot (The Fourth Commandment)* (1877) begin a South German
tradition of critical *Volksstücke* with tragic outcomes. This tradition runs
through Ludwig Thoma's *Maria Magdalena* (1912), in which villagers,
egged on by the clerical authorities, drive a father to kill his dishon-
oured daughter, to Martin Sperr's *Jagdszenen aus Niederbayern (Hunting Scenes from Lower Bavaria)* (1966), in which a mentally deficient
homosexual is hounded to his death. The tradition is paralleled in North
Germany by plays like Fritz Stavenhagen's *Jürgen Piepers* (1901).
These plays, like those of Nestroy, could be called critical *Volksstücke*
in so far as they take the topographical and sociological setting of the
Volksstück but attempt to show the reality behind the idealized façade.

But what Brecht was really objecting to when he attacked the *Volksstück* was not the theatre of Stranitzky, Nestroy or Anzengruber, but the
conventional, ossified *Volksstücke* and farces he had experienced
directly in the 1920s. Whatever literary historians may say about
'Weimar culture', this was still the golden age of the comedy, the farce
and the operetta.[12] Zuckmayer's *Der fröhliche Weinberg (The Jolly Vineyard)*, to be considered below, is regarded as having blown Expressionism off the stage in a gale of laughter in 1925.[13] Other major successes were the (still popular) comedies of Curt Goetz, such as *Hokus
Pokus* or *Die Tote Tante (The Dead Auntie)* or Bruno Frank's *Sturm im
Wasserglas (Storm in a Teacup*: a gripping saga of a lapsed dog
licence). The theatres suffered particularly from the slump after 1929
and sought safe commercial works that satisfied their audience's perhaps
understandable escapist desires. This experience inevitably coloured
Brecht's view of the *Volksstück* in the following decade, and led him to
overlook the positive elements of its tradition, remembering instead the
trivia that had flooded the theatres at the time when he, ultimately for
other reasons of course, had been forced to abandon them.

The trivial *Volksstück* as defined above plays among the peasant farmers, labourers, employees and small tradesmen of a locality unsubtly
defined by the stage décor and the dialect. The titles usually indicate the

milieu, as in *Der Bauerndiplomat* (*The Peasant Diplomat*: this is meant to be a contradiction in terms and to hint at impending jollities), or the theme and its message: *Liebe geht durch den Magen* (*The Way to a Man's Heart is Through his Stomach*). The characters often have woodenly comic names: Priggenpahl or Klootscheeter in the North German plays, Zitzelsberger or Streitbichler in the South German ones. Ho ho. The regional mileu is not now established to highlight local problems but as a signal to the audience to expect primitive, ridiculous characters and primitive, ridiculous plots. Though it is rarely stated openly, a subliminal message is communicated here: to those who do not see themselves as part of the *Volk*, it is that this is what the *Volk* is like; to those who do, it is that this is what life is like.

Maximilian Vitus' *St Pauli in St Peter* (1938), which, as the title suggests, concerns the problems caused when a North German lady of uncertain virtue visits her penfriend in his rural Bavaria, repository of unsophisticated respectability, August Hinrichs' *Wenn der Hahn kräht* (*If the Cock Crows*) (1933) and Hans Müller-Schlosser's *Schneider Wibbel* (*Tailor Wibbel*) (1913) are all set in timeless 'good old days', and were all performed throughout the Nazi period and continue to be so today, more or less unchanged. Despite Hinrichs' close association with National Socialism, his play was chosen by the Ohnsorgtheater, a company specializing in the production of North German *Volksstücke* for television, for their 100th broadcast in 1977. Vitus, who continued to write during the Nazi period, is one of the regular authors of the South German equivalent, the Komödienstadel. Müller-Schlosser's play was filmed in 1939 and he himself wrote an operetta libretto version in 1938.

Thus, even if these plays were in no sense Nazi propaganda – indeed the very ridiculousness of so many of the *Volk* in the *Volksstück* was at odds with the Nazi image of the noble peasant – they were perfectly acceptable as mass entertainment in the Nazi period, and for this reason too were anathema to Brecht.

Karl Schönherr and Richard Billinger are two writers whose *Volksstücke* do imbue the *Volk* with irrational qualities which bring them within the embrace of the Nazi *Blut und Boden* (blood and soil) mythology. Plays with revealing titles like *Volk in Not* (*A Nation in Need*) (1916), *Erde* (*Earth*) (1907), and especially *Glaube und Heimat* (*Faith and Fatherland*) (1910) made Schönherr one of the most performed playwrights of his period in German-speaking Europe. By 1925 *Glaube und Heimat* had reached its 100th printing. Billinger's *Stille Gäste* (*Silent Guests*) (1934) is characterized by feeble jokes, primitive exposition, anti-modernity and a decrying of the degenerate, overfed, city types in contrast to the healthy peasantry. The happy end brings a double marriage and the proverb 'Je kleiner das Nest, desto schöner die Fest' ('the smaller the place, the better the festivities'), to underline the point about where the true, untainted qualities of the German *Volk* are to be found.[14]

In 1925, many critics felt that Carl Zuckmayer had successfully revived the moribund *Volksstück* with *Der fröhliche Weinberg;* it was enormously successful, enjoying 500 separate productions in the eight years after its première. Gunderloch, a Rhineland vineyard owner, wants his daughter Klärchen to marry only a man virile enough to impregnate her. He is a typical *Volksstück* farmer/father figure: loud, plain-spoken and proud of it, full of homespun wisdom but young enough still to be a ladies' man. Klärchen is wooed by Knuzius, an arrogant young student, who, it seems, may have difficulty fulfilling Gunderloch's condition. Secretly her heart beats for Jochen, a Rhine bargee. After much boozing and archetypal farce business, Klärchen and Jochen are wed, and Gunderloch too, and even Knuzius, take brides.

The play satirizes excessive nationalism and militarism. It attracted violent protests and scandal until it was eventually banned by the National Socialists. None the less it never really breaks out of the *Volksstück* tradition. The implicit message is that the happy end will be yours 'wenn das Herz echt ist' (if the heart is true') (20)[15], and if you follows your nature. Zuckmayer's *Volk*, is regionally and not class-determined. It is certainly not the real *Volk*, in the sense of the broad mass of the population of Weimar Germany, but instead draws its members from the ranks of the traditional *Volksstück*. Jochen, the bargee, declares: 'Mitgift, Erbschaft and Familiengut... das brauche wir heut nit mehr! Mir komme von unne ruff, un schaffe's uns selber!' ('Dowry, inheritance, family estate... we don't need all that today! We're going to come up from below, and make it ourselves!') (58) At the end of the play, however, he marries into inherited wealth. Gunderloch too can only flout morality and convention because of his economic independence as a rich landowner. His claim that 'die herrgottgschaffe Natur' ('God-created nature') (62) determines events is thus at best a self-deception. The happy end includes the sparrows, allowed to pick grapes undisturbed for a day, and it embraces even the right-wing nationalists, who join in the festivities. Thus real conflicts in 1920s Germany are touched upon, but papered over with a false harmony.

Thus, though Brecht ignored, perhaps wilfully, some of the positive elements of the *Volksstück* tradition, his harsh verdict on the genre as he found it seems justified. But we should also consider the attempts by Brecht's contemporary, the Austrian Ödön von Horvath, towards the end of the Weimar period, to regain the lost critical potential of the *Volksstück*. If the *Volksstück* is to be a living form, Horvath recognized, it must change as the *Volk* changes. For Horvath the contemporary *Volk* of the Weimar period were the urban masses, who now consisted 'zu neunzig Prozent aus vollendeten oder verhinderten Kleinbürgern' ('90 per cent complete or frustrated petit-bourgeois') (4,662),[16] an amorphous class trying to maintain or to pretend to middle-class values and aspirations in an economic situation in which they had become increasingly proletarianized.

Horváth's three major *Volksstücke*, *Italienische Nacht* (*Italian Night*) (1930), *Geschichten aus dem Wiener Wald* (*Tales from the Vienna Woods*) (1931) and *Kasimir und Karoline* (1932), between them treat petty-bourgeois behaviour as manifested in grass-roots party politics, family life and especially male–female relationships. Though Horváth claimed to hate parody, *Geschichten aus dem Wiener Wald* is particularly clearly a counter-model to the sugary legend of 'Vienna' perpetuated by operetta and the *Volksstück*. Mean, brutal reality and kitsch are harshly juxtaposed. Thus in one scene a woman kills her grandson's unwanted child by exposing it to the draught, while she twangs waltzes on her zither. The sadism and suppressed sexuality associated with pig-killing in this play contrast markedly with the lusty celebration of similar events in *Der fröhliche Weinberg*.

Language is a crucial element in Horváth's *Volksstücke*. He believed that the language of the contemporary masses was characterized by the complete infiltration of dialect by *Bildungsjargon* (cultured jargon). The characters should therefore not speak dialect, but standard German peppered with this jargon. However, they should speak it 'so wie jemand, der sonst nur Dialekt spricht und sich nun zwingt, hochdeutsch zu reden' ('like someone who otherwise only speaks dialect and is forcing himself to speak standard German'). This tension brings out what Horváth calls the 'Komik des Unbewussten' ('the comedy of the subconscious'), the contradiction, visible to the audience despite and because of the speaker's attempt to hide it even from himself, between *Sein* and *Schein*, or *Sein* and *Bewusstsein*, between his real situation and how he perceives it (4,663).

Horváth sincerely wanted the *Volk* to be not only the subject of, but also the public for his plays. His aim was to bring the situation of the majority on stage so as to give this majority insight into themselves and their environment. But in order for the audience to see those social causes of behaviour which the characters on stage do not see, this false conciousness being part of what Horváth wants to convey, the audience requires a consciousness advanced beyond that of the people on stage. And so Horváth's *Volksstücke* are not perhaps ultimately plays for the *Volk* at all, however telling a picture they may give the sophisticated reader or theatre-goer of the state of consciousness of the masses in the 1920s and 1930s.

After a long period of neglect, Horváth's acerbic cameos were rediscovered by directors and audiences in the 1960s. In particular, his studies of false consciousness as revealed in language, related as they were to the sociology of the Frankfurt School, impressed younger writers like Peter Handke, seeking a radical critical stance but eschewing a specific political platform, and, moreover, viewing Brecht as part of a cultural establishment to be overcome. To these writers Horváth seemed much more sophisticated than what they saw as Brecht's simplistic, over-optimistic models of society. The critical *Volksstücke* of the 1970s, too, such as those of Franz Xaver Kroetz, seemed closer to Horváth than Brecht. [17]

Horváth tried to show the social–psychological influences on the *Kleinbürger* that made them receptive to Fascism. This was what the *Volk* was up to in the Weimar period, not romping in vineyards or chauffeuring bucolic landlords. However, his plays remain in the *Volksstück* tradition of showing slices of life, a certain class or area as it earns its bread, boozes and couples, but not the whole cake, nor how the cake is baked. They are ultimately somewhat circular, even fatalistic, offering criticism but no alternative. Brecht, as we know, wanted more.

In his 'Anmerkungen zum Volksstück', Brecht states his intention to develop a new *Volksstück* in keeping with its noble name, which, in accordance with his redefinition of *Volkstümlichkeit*, would take the side of the *Volk*, the ordinary people. Many of his plays, such as *Mutter Courage* (*Mother Courage*), *Der kaukasische Kreidekrys* (*The Caucasian Chalk Circle*) or *Schweik im zweiten Weltkrieg* (*Schweyk in the Second World War*) would fit this criterion. They are not *Volksstücke* in any formal sense, although Brecht frequently, as part of his espousal of popular forms in general, used *Volksstück* motifs, such as the wedding party in *Die Kleinbürgerhochzeit* (*The Petty Bourgeois Wedding*), *Die Dreigroschenoper*, *Der kaukasische Kreidekreis* and *Der gute Mensch von Sezuan*, usually by parodying them and reversing their morality. Rather, these plays might be called *Volksstücke* in so far as they take ordinary people as their central figures and take their side.

What then makes *Puntila* specifically a *Volksstück*? If the criterion is the partisan support of the interests of the common people, or the attempted demonstration of the Marxist tenet that the working class are the driving force in social change, as established in Brecht's redefinition of *Volkstümlichkeit* and the *Volksstück*, then it is no more a *Volksstück* than many other of his plays. It only becomes one when analysed in terms of its use of the motifs, language and setting of the genre, that is, in purely formal terms. This, however, does not deny the critical effectiveness of the play, which stems in part precisely from its arousal and reversal of conventional expectations.

The play is a loosely connected series of scenes about the lusty, expansive, bibulous landlord Puntila. His daughter Eva is being wooed by the insipid but well-connected attaché Eino Silakka, but she hankers after Puntila's chauffeur Matti. There are drunken carousings, sexual adventures, squabbles with neighbours over property, talk of land, landscape and inheritance, an engagement party, milkmaids, farm-hands, a hiring fair and numerous other *Volksstück* ingredients. In terms of the basic situation, the figures, setting, language and stage business, *Puntila* commits itself more than almost any of Brecht's plays to a specific genre. But in almost every case Brecht subverts the traditional *Volksstück* motif to produce a radically critical perspective.

77

This is perhaps clearest in the case of Puntila himself. Like Falstaff and Tartuffe, Puntila alternates pious proclamations with unscrupulous egotism. When drunk he proposes universal brotherhood, offering work on generous terms to labourers and marriage indiscriminately to local women; generally supporting the value system postulated at the happy end of a conventional *Volksstück*, in fact. When sober, however, he is ruthless and calculating, and cancels all his promises.

But Puntila sober, for all his ruthlessness, is at least honestly conforming to the rules of capitalist exploitation. Puntila drunk is spiriting up a falsely harmonious human brotherhood, which in actual fact *also* conforms to these rules, is part of the exploitation process. Puntila uses his drunkenness to pretend to be and enjoy the fruits of something he does *not* really want to be, since he knows it would go against his material interests. Brecht thus demonstrates in the figure and behaviour of Puntila not only the paradox of the benevolent capitalist, but also that the benevolence itself is inherently dishonest. Puntila may be a vital, even attractive character, but his role in society is a contemptible one.

The figure of Matti too has many traditional *Volksstück* elements. As a virile man of the people he is preferred by Eva to the effete attaché. As the clever servant who nurses his master through the scrapes his vitality and lack of circumspection get him into (though as we have seen Puntila drunk is far from innocent), Matti belongs, like Jeeves, or Frankie Howerd in *Up Pompeii*, to a tradition that reaches back through Hanswurst and the *commedia dell'arte* to Plautus. However, Matti has a proletarian awareness of the class basis of Puntila's behaviour. It is this awareness, and not a character defect, that makes him less 'attractive' than Puntila; unable, for example, to share the latter's eulogy of nature:

PUNTILA: O Tavastland, gesegnetes! Mit seinem Himmel, seinen Seen, seinem Volk und seinen Wäldern! (*Zu Matti:*) Sag, dass dir das Herz nicht aufgeht, wenn du das siehst!

MATTI: Das Herz geht mir auf, wenn ich Ihre Wälder seh, Herr Puntila. (*GW* 4, 1707)

(PUNTILA: O Tavastland, blessed land! With its skies, its lakes, its people and its forests! (*To Matti:*) Admit your heart leaps when you see that!

MATTI: My heart leaps when I see *your* forests, Mr Puntila. [my italics])

Matti's tiny modification reveals the true economic basis of Puntila's poetic waxings; Matti never loses his grip on the material realities, because he cannot afford to.

So too when Puntila tries to marry Eva to Matti instead of the spineless attaché, like Gunderloch giving the bargée Jochen preference over the student Knuzius, it is Matti who resists, despite his erotic interest in Eva. In Brecht's Finnish source, Eva marries the chauffeur, but the latter turns out actually to be a *Doktor* and therefore one of her class. The social conflict is thus doubly neutralized, since the happy end is a marriage of social equals now restored to their 'rightful' station. In *Puntila*, however, the *Volksstück* plot of the willing lovers thwarted by the father is completely reversed (*GW* 4, 1676 ff).

Brecht had a dual purpose in parodying the *Volksstück*: first to emphasize the negative lessons, that oil and water do not mix, that capitalists cannot be trusted, and second, to show that the expectations of a happy end awakened by the use of *Volksstück* ingredients require social and economic change for their realization. Puntila, for example, may be almost a human being, 'but, finally, there is no magic potion, not even alcohol, which can humanize men within the conditions of capitalism'.[18] Brecht thus aims in *Puntila* to contrast the make-believe world of the traditional *Volksstück* with the reality of exploitation, dehumanization and class struggle, and also to suggest that social revolution could produce the very happy end for which, the popularity of the *Volksstück* shows, its audience longs.

In sociological terms, Brecht's *Volk* in *Puntila* is no more typical of the proletarian masses of twentieth-century Germany than Zuckmayer's. However, the fact that Brecht's *Volksstück* is set in Finland, a country about which he knew little, reminds us that it does not really matter where it is set: Brecht was not writing a guidebook to a colourful locality. What he has to say about the *Volk* concerns universally applicable social and economic mechanisms. In 1979 an Indian theatre company was adapting *Puntila* for their local audience, and the actor playing Puntila remarked: 'Ich habe angefangen, einen Landlord von *Punjab* zu gestalten, und habe in den Proben erfahren, dass ich den *Landlord* von Punjab zeigen muss.' ('I began by trying to create a landlord from *Punjab*, but I realized in rehearsal that I must demonstrate a *landlord* from Punjab')[19] This recognition that what matters is not real or pretended ethnic authenticity, whether local or imported, but social representativeness, is the essence of Brecht's *Volksstück*.

Brecht's view of the world as comic, because changeable, conflicted directly with the *Volksstück* as he found it, largely because the latter employed a static, ahistorical concept of the *Volk* that ignored the economic and social dimension of class, or tried to paper it over with a false harmony. Brecht's concern in the late 1930s was to redefine the *Volk* and *Volkstümlichkeit*, and then, with *Herr Puntila und sein Knecht Matti*, to redefine the *Volksstück* in terms which would permit realistic, critical comedy, so that the *Volksstück* could take its place among the techniques in Brecht's arsenal of comic method, and be an adequate means of communicating Brecht's view of society as comedy. But he wrote only one *Volksstück*; perhaps, ultimately, the form resisted the reformer.

NOTES

1. Hazlitt quoted in J. L. Styan, *The Dark Comedy*, 2nd edn (Cambridge, 1968), p. 40; Martini, *Lustspiele – und das Lustspiel* (Stuttgart, 1974), p. 22.

2. Peter Hacks, 'Das realistiche Theaterstück', *Neue deutsche Literatur*, **5**, No. 10 (1957), 98.

3. Louise J. Bird, 'The comic world of Bertolt Brecht', *Forum for Modern Language Studies*, **4** (1968), 248–59 (p. 252).

4. cf. Bird. op. cit., p. 248. Brecht would have rejected adamantly Eugène Ionesco's fundamentally fatalistic view of the comic too, which is fairly representative of that of the dramatists of the 'Absurd': 'the comic alone is capable of giving us the strength to bear the tragedy of existence' (quoted by Martin Esslin, *The Theatre of the Absurd*, 3rd edn (London, 1974), p. 159).

5. cf. Bird, op. cit., p. 252.

6. 'Contribution to the Critique of Hegel's Philosophy of Law. Introduction', in Karl Marx and Friedrich Engels, *Collected Works* (London, 1975), Vol. III, p. 179.

7. 'The 18th Brumaire of Louis Bonaparte', in Karl Marx and Friedrich Engels, *Selected Works in 2 Volumes* (Moscow, 1962), Vol. I, p. 296.

8. Peter C. Giese, *Das 'Gesellschaftlich–Komische'. Zu Komik und Komödie am Beispiel der Stücke und Bearbeitungen Brechts* (Stuttgart, 1974), p. 56.

9. This is true only within a narrow time-scale. From a wider perspective, it is the *Burgtheater* and the bourgeois theatre in general that is the exception, since in the 2,500-year history of European theatre, *Volkstheater*, popular theatre, has been the rule. See Siegfried Melchinger, *Drama zwischen Shaw und Brecht*, 3rd edn (Bremen, 1954), p. 50.

10. See Roger A. Crockett, 'Nestroy and Brecht: aspects of modern German folk comedy', Diss. (University of Illinois, 1979), Also G. S. Slobodkin, 'Nestroy und die Tradition des Volkstheaters im Schaffen Brechts', *Weimarer Beiträge*, **24**, No. 9 (1978), 99–117.

11. See for example Ludwig Hoffmann, 'Nachwort,' in Hoffmann, ed., *Volksstücke*, (Berlin [GDR], 1967), p. 392.

12. Volker Klotz has recorded over 1,250 farces performed in the German theatre between 1880 and 1930; see 'Geschlechterfronten, Blossstellungskämpfe, Fassadenkunststücke. Diagnostische Bemerkungen zum Bühnenschwank', *Theater heute*, **17**, No. 10 (1976), 18–26.

13. See Günther Rühle, *Theater für die Republik* (Frankfurt am Main, 1967), p. 667; Jost Hermand, Frank Trommler, *Die Kultur der Weimarer Republik* (Munich, 1978), pp. 229–35.

14. Richard Billinger, *Stille Gäste* (Berlin, 1934), p. 89.

15. Page references to *Der fröhliche Weinberg* will be from Zuckmayer, *Meisterdramen* (Frankfurt am Main, 1966), and will be made in the text.

16. References to Horváth's works will be to the *Gesammelte Werke*, 4 vols. (Frankfurt am Main, 1971), identified in the text by volume and page number.

17. Kroetz, the most prominent and prolific writer of critical *Volksstücke* in

the 1970s, in fact told the present writer in a conversation in September 1980 that he felt the term was no longer useful.

18. Edward M. Berckmann, 'Comedy and parody of comedy in Brecht's *Puntila*', *Essays in Literature*, **1** (1974), 258.
19. Quoted by Fritz Bennewitz, 'Mit *Puntila* kontra ethnisches Show-Theater', *notate* (Informations- und Mitteilungsblatt des Brecht-Zentrums der DDR), February 1980, p. 2.

SELECT BIBLIOGRAPHY

ON COMEDY

BIRD, LOUISE J., 'The comic world of Bertolt Brecht', *Forum for Modern Language Studies*, **4** (1968), 248–59

GIESE, PETER C., *Das 'Gesellschaftlich-Komische'. Zu Komik und Komödie am Beispiel der Stücke und Bearbeitungen Brechts*, Stuttgart, 1974

WEISSTEIN, ULRICH, Die Komödie bei Brecht' in Wolfgang Paulsen, ed., *Die deutsche Komödie im 20. Jahrhundert*, Heidelberg, 1976.

ON THE *VOLKSSTÜCK*

DOPPLER, ALFRED, ed., *Das Österreichische Volksstück*, Vienna, 1971

FRANCOIS, JEAN-CLAUDE, 'Brecht, Horváth and the popular theatre', *New German Critique*, **18** (1979), 136–50

HEIN, JÜRGEN, ed., *Theater und Gesellschaft. Das Volksstück im 19. und 20. Jahrhundert*, Düsseldorf, 1973

HEIN, JÜRGEN, 'Formen des Volkstheaters im 19. und 20. Jahrhundert', in Walter Hinck, ed., *Handbuch des deutschen Dramas*, Düsseldorf, 1980, pp. 489–505. See also the bibliography on pp. 581–4

HINTZE, JOACHIM, 'Volkstümliche Elemente im modernen deutschen Drama. Ein Beitrag zur Theorie und Praxis des Volksstücks im 20. Jahrhundert', *Hessische Blätter für Volkskunde* (1970), 11–43

HOFFMAN, LUDWIG, ed., *Volksstücke*, Berlin (GDR), 1967

KARASEK, HELLMUTH, 'Die Erneuerung des Volksstücks', in H. L. Arnold and T. Buck, eds, *Positionen des Dramas*, Munich, 1977, pp. 137–69

KÄSSENS, WEND and MICHAEL TÖTEBERG, 'Fortschritt im Realismus? Zur Erneuerung des kritischen Volksstücks seit 1966', *Basis*, **6** (1976), 30–47

MÜLLER, GERD, *Das Volksstück von Raimund bis Kroetz. Die Gattung in Einzelanalysen*, Munich, 1979

POSER, HANS, 'Komödie als Volksstück: Zuckmayer, Horváth, Brecht', *Neophilologus*, **62** (1978), 584–97

SCHLECHTER, PIT, '. . . ab nach rechts . . . . Zur Trivialität des volkstümlichen Theaters', *Zeitschrift für Literaturwissenschaft und Linguistik*, Beiheft 2: *Literatur für viele* (1976), 169–89

URBACH, REINHARD, *Die Wiener Komödie und ihr Publikum: Stranitzky und die Folgen*, Vienna and Munich, 1973

M. McGowan

ON *PUNTILA*

BERCKMANN, E. M., 'Comedy and parody of comedy in Brecht's *Puntila*', *Essays in Literature*, **1** (1974), 248–60

HERMAND, JOST, '*Herr Puntila und sein Knecht Matti*: Brechts Volksstück', *Brecht heute. Jahrbuch der internationalen Brecht-Gesellschaft*, **10** (1971), 117–36

POSER, HANS, 'Brechts *Herr Puntila und sein Knecht Matti*: Dialektik zwischen Volksstück und Lehrstück', in Hein, *Theater und Gesellschaft* (see above), pp. 187–200

SPEIDEL, ERICH, 'Brecht's *Puntila*: a Marxist comedy', *Modern Language Review*, **65** (1970), 319–32

Chapter 6

LITERATURE AND COMMITMENT

GRAHAM BARTRAM

In the late 1920s, at the age of about thirty, Brecht became a Communist. He remained one, without ever actually joining the Communist Party, until his death in 1956. His work as a writer, producer and intellectual was both moulded and sustained by this political commitment, to the extent that it is not really possible to grasp the full meaning of his plays or his work in the theatre without being attuned to the Marxist philosophy and the Marxist aesthetic on which both are based.

In Chapter 1 of this book Dick Geary has examined the dramatic social and political changes that took place in Germany between 1870 and 1950. Brecht's conscious repudiation of his middle-class origins and his profession of solidarity with the revolutionary proletariat were on one level simply the response of a socially aware individual to the violent upheavals of war, revolution and civil war in which he was involved either directly or as a close witness. To understand Brecht's commitment more fully, however, we need also to situate it more precisely, in a cultural and ideological context. It was a remarkable attempt by a leading twentieth-century German dramatist and intellectual to define and fulfil his responsibility *as an independent writer* towards the society of which he was a member.

'Commitment', when used nowadays in a literary–political context, is generally taken to mean active adherence to left-wing or 'progressive' values. Though this assumption is in some respects misleading, it does reflect the fact that over the last sixty years or so it has mainly been left-wing artists and intellectuals who have made political *engagement* an explicit theme of their artistic theory and practice. Those equally significant writers who have espoused the values of the right and sometimes the extreme right – Ezra Pound and T. S. Eliot are two notable examples – have not on the whole seen their function as artists as one directly linked to their political beliefs. Brecht is clearly a 'typical' committed writer in this generally accepted left-wing sense. Furthermore, his continuing loyalty to the Communist Party makes him a committed writer in the narrower, party-political sense as well. But if we wish to understand his politicization in its historical context, and if in particular we are to compare his conception of the writer's role with that of his predecessors, it would be foolish to restrict the discussion of commitment to the question of party-political allegiance. The whole problem is far wider, and has roots reaching much further back into the past, than this narrow focus would tend to suggest.

Indeed, it is possible to go to the other extreme and to argue that practically all literature is 'committed' – in the sense that writers have always possessed basic values and assumptions that underlly their work and shape it in ways of which they may be largely unaware. True though it is, this latter point yields a concept of commitment that is far too broad to be of any practical use. Commitment can perhaps best be understood as arising out of a writer's or an intellectual's *conscious* questioning of his social role, and as involving his equally conscious decision to play an active part, either through his literary activities or simply as an individual human being, in the shaping of social and political events.

Seen in this light, the issue of commitment is essentially a product of the modern, i.e. post-medieval, age. In the Europe of the Middle Ages – and here certain parallels suggest themselves with the state socialist regimes of today – the writer's social role and ideology were to a large extent dictated by the feudal society in which he lived, and its all-embracing, theologically underpinned world-view. With the growth of the economic, social and political power of the middle class and the concomitant collapse of this basically theological *Weltanschauung* under the successive assaults of Protestantism and the Enlightenment, litera-ture, like philosophy and the natural sciences, gained a new measure of autonomy, a new sphere of freedom. By the end of the eighteenth cen-tury it was invested with a dual role. On the one hand it articulated the new secular values of an increasingly dominant middle class: universal humanism, critical rationalism, the belief in individual freedom and in human progress. On the other hand, it also became the vehicle of the Romantic movement's reaction *against* the Enlightenment and its politi-cal, social and philosophical values. In the wake of the violent upheaval of the French Revolution, European Romanticism lamented the split that the Enlightenment, and particularly the critical philosophy of Immanuel Kant, had brought between man's moral and sensual nature, between his rational faculties and his emotions, and contrasted the individual's frag-mentation in the present with his supposed 'wholeness' under the unified theological world-view of medieval Catholicism.

Romanticism contained a powerful element of reactionary nostalgia for a lost past, and for its aristocratic and religious values – a nostalgia that not infrequently led Romantic writers to embrace the Catholic faith. Simply to label Romanticism as an expression of political and ideologi-cal reaction is, however, to distort its nature quite drastically, and in particular to ignore its most vital contribution to the self-image and self-definition of the modern writer. For both in Romanticism proper, and also, most remarkably, in that monumental synthesis of Enlightenment and Romantic ideas achieved in the works of German Classicism – of J. W. von Goethe (1749–1832) and Friedrich Schiller (1759–1805) – there began to emerge an essentially new and exalted concept of the nature and purpose of art. Accepting that man had now entered a secular, bourgeois age, writers such as Goethe, Schiller and their visionary contemporary Friedrich Hölderlin sought *in art itself* a means of recuperating in symbolic form that understanding of man as a harmonious, sensual–rational whole that Kant's rational critique of religion had seemingly destroyed. The art of German Classicism in fact embodies not a reactionary but a powerfully Utopian moment; it does not seek to reverse the philosophical achievements of the Enlightenment or the material achievements of the dawning industrial–capitalist era, but rather offers a permanent critique of social reality, measuring man's shortcomings in modern society against a quasi-religious yet undogmatic and 'open-ended' ideal of what he *might* become. The Marxist Brecht naturally rejected the metaphysical dimension of this world-view–witness, for example, his parody of Schiller's idealist language in *Die Heilige Johanna der Schlachthöfe* (*St Joan of the Stockyards*). But the Utopian, socio-critical role that it assigns to art and the 'aesthetic state' is one with which his own theatre has a great deal in common.[1]

The 'modern' concept of the writer's mission and social role has its historical roots in this aesthetic developed by German Classicism in the immediate post-Enlightenment era. By the closing decades of the nineteenth century, however, the transformation wrought by industrial capitalism on the social and economic landscape of Europe, and the equally profound changes that had taken place in the attitudes and values of the European bourgeoisie, had made writers' consciousness of their 'modernity' – their belonging to an essentially bourgeois and secularized age – far more acute, and from both a social and an aesthetic point of view far more problematical, than it had been in the early 1800s. The rapid modernization and technologization of industry, the growth of monopoly capitalism, and the expansion of some towns and cities into vast industrial conurbations, had produced a 'mass' society in which the average individual seemed increasingly a passive victim of social forces of which he had little understanding and over which he had virtually no control. The claim of writers like Schiller to a vital and active social role for art had presupposed that the bourgeois individuals whose sensibilities were to be transformed by the writer would in turn exercise a civilizing influence upon society at large; once the relationship of the individual to his society came to be seen as a largely passive rather than an active one, art's own pretensions to a 'civilizing' social role seemed correspondingly less and less plausible.

This was the social and historical situation that gave birth to the phenomenon of the literary and artistic avant-garde, and the closely related trend in modern European culture which, lasting from about 1870 to the end of the 1930s, acquired early in its development the name 'modernism'. The writers of the avant-garde were a minority who defined themselves and their work in conscious opposition both to the prevailing social and economic trends of modern industrial capitalism and, with still greater vehemence, to the mainstream bourgeois culture of their day, which they saw as profoundly philistine and materialistic. Clinging fervently to a belief in the vital importance of the artist's activity, they rejected the superficial, 'decorative' use to which culture was put in modern bourgeois society as a betrayal and trivialization of art. They themselves developed new ways of seeing and means of expression whose radical originality was meant to shock the bourgeois out of his complacent attitudes and at the same time resist assimilation to any merely decorative social function. Avant-gardism demanded, in effect, a permanent revolution in artistic form, since the stylistic innovations of avant-garde artists were often quickly absorbed into the mainstream of bourgeois culture and lost their 'scandalizing' impact. The great representative figures of modernism – artists such as Cezanne and Picasso, composers such as Schoenberg and Stravinsky, the poets and novelists Mallarmé, Proust, Joyce, Kafka, Musil and Broch – produced works whose originality and integrity of vision have survived the dissipation of whatever initial shock effect they may have had. But the enterprise of the avant-garde was constantly attended by the twin dangers of empty formal innovation for the sake of sheer effect on the one hand, and retreat into total incomprehensibility – the logical conclusion of 'art for art's sake' – on the other.

The anti-bourgeois revolt of the nineteenth-century literary avant-garde was predominantly an aesthetic, not a political one. It had in general little sympathy for, or interest in, the challenge to the bourgeois–capitalist order presented by the organized working class. With a few early exceptions, among them the painter Gustave Courbet (one of the first representatives of the French avant-garde), modernist writers and artists in the nineteenth century shared with large sections of their educated bourgeois public a growing disillusionment with the political and philosophical legacy of the Enlightenment, whose optimistic belief in progress and the value of the natural sciences was seen to have brought not the promised liberation of the individual, but instead his enslavement to the new tyrannies of a shallow scientific positivism on the one hand, and the conformist and increasingly rationalized 'mass society' on the other. European intellectual life at the turn of the century was dominated by anti-positivist, irrationalist currents of thought, which went hand in hand with pessimistic or nihilistic views of historical change, and a tendency to reject both industrial capitalism and working-class socialism as equally malign products of the modern age.

In Germany, owing to the social and political factors described in Chapter 1 above, these intellectual and ideological tendencies were particularly pronounced. The attitudes of the late nineteenth-century avant-garde, despite its anti-bourgeois stance, in fact had much in common with the world-outlook and values of its middle-class public. The retreat of the German *Bürgertum* from progressive political activity after its failure to carry through a political revolution in 1848 had its counterpart in the educated middle class's concept of *Geist* (mind, spirit, intellect) as something to be kept separate from the sordid realities of *Realpolitik*; and this apolitical stance of the *Bildungsbürgertum* was in turn reflected in an aestheticized form within the self-appointed spiritual élites of the modernist movement.

Where, however, a distinction – albeit a fuzzy rather than a clear-cut one – should be made, is between the anti-bourgeois stance of the German avant-garde on the one hand, and on the other the anti-bourgeois, anti-capitalist and often anti-Semitic ideologies that began to gain ground among the middle and lower-middle classes in the Second Reich. These racialist–nationalist (*völkisch*) ideologies were unhappily much the more significant in social and political terms, in that they made considerable inroads into the discontented petty bourgeoisie – a process in which, as George Mosse has shown, the numerically large and socially influential intelligentsia of school and university teachers played a significant role. The subsequent political mobilization of these groups took them towards organizations of the extreme right, including the Nazi Party. The intellectuals and writers of the avant-garde were in comparison a small minority, and even in the Weimar Republic they remained on the margins of middle-class society and culture. They too, as we shall see, became politically active in the period 1910–33, but their commitment was (with one or two exceptions) to the politics of the left.[2] A major landmark in this politicization of German modernism is the politically committed yet aesthetically experimental theatre of Bertolt Brecht.

The movement of German modernism from an 'aesthetic' revolt in the *fin de siecle* period towards its later, more political concept of the artist's role was a complex and often contradictory process, and one that was far from embracing all the members of the avant-garde. That this was so is due in no small part to the pervasive and lasting influence on the German avant-garde of its main intellectual progenitor, the philosopher and cultural critic Friedrich Nietzsche.

Nietzsche's writings, from *The Birth of Tragedy* (1872) to *The Genealogy of Morals* (1887), present a broadside attack on the philistinism of *bürgerlich* culture in Bismarck's Germany and a radical critique of Christian–humanist moral values, while at the same time elevating art into a supreme mode of being and experience. 'Art', however, no longer has the civilizing relationship to *bürgerlich* culture and society optimistically ascribed to it by the Classicism of the 1790s (the unfortunate Schiller, having been distorted by nineteenth-century German culture into the poet of nationalism and conventional right-mindedness, is mocked by Nietzsche as a 'Moraltrompeter', a moral tub-thumper). Instead, true art, exemplified for the early Nietzsche in the operas of Richard Wagner, is seen as subversively *anti*-bourgeois, embracing the destructive side of man's nature, and giving form to an ultimately nihilistic view of the universe. Nietzsche denied the possibility of objective knowledge and initiated the tradition of irrational and subjectivist *Lebensphilosophie* (vitalism), which was to play a crucial role in the development of the human sciences in Germany through the first half of the twentieth century. Many of his concepts and images filtered in vulgarized form into the broad stream of middle-class ideology and helped to feed that very philistinism he had been attacking. But his irrationality, his invocation of *Leben* (life) as a chaotic and amoral force against the moribund superficiality of contemporary culture, and his anti-democratic scorn for the conformist 'herd' also exerted an enduring influence on the writers and artists of the avant-garde.

Nietzsche's career, from the publication of the academically highly unorthodox *Die Geburt der Tragödie* in 1872 to his final collapse into insanity in 1888, was that of an 'outsider'; styling themselves in his image, many of the avant-garde literati of Imperial Germany became solitary individuals on the margins of a hostile or indifferent society. The Naturalists of the 1880s, with their interest in the lot of the proletariat and of the then banned Social Democratic Party (SPD), admittedly represent an exception to this general trend; but their romantic image of socialism, often closely wedded to a Nietzschean élitism, made them highly suspicious to the SPD leadership, and their alliance with the party was tenuous and short-lived. The last decade of the nineteenth century saw among the avant-garde a marked reaction against their movement, with the rise of the cult of the dandy, the Bohemian and the aesthete, and the formation of small, exclusive literary coteries, of which the 'George-Kreis', the circle of writers gathered round the Symbolist poet Stefan George, was the most famous and influential.

George's vision of the artist's calling was from the outset an exalted, quasi-religious and unpolitical one; and so it was to remain until his death in exile in 1933. His circle, whose members included not only poets but also historians and literary critics, was still a major influence on the cultural scene in the closing years of the Weimar Republic; and both directly and indirectly his élitism left its imprint on the cultural–critical attitudes of the neo-Marxist Frankfurt School.[3] But despite the extensive influence which he enjoyed within the circles of the literary intelligentsia, the social role which he allotted to the poet was essentially one of a self-imposed isolation; and already in the pre-war era this 'ivory tower' conception of the poet's mission was coming under fire from a new generation of the avant-garde, whose violent revolt against the complacent materialism of Wilhelmine culture contained in itself the seeds of a far more active form of social involvement than the Symbolists ever contemplated.

This was the Expressionist movement, which dominated the German avant-garde from about 1910 to 1922. Stylistically, Expressionism was part of a wider European movement in the arts (influences and parallels include Fauvism and Cubism in France, Futurism in Italy and Suprematism in Russia) against the Naturalism and Impressionism of the preceding decades. Bringing together avant-garde tendencies in music (e.g. Schoenberg), painting (e.g. Kokoschka, Kandinsky, Franz Marc) and literature (e.g. the poets Heym, Stadler, Trakl; the dramatists Sorge, Hasenclever, Toller and Kaiser), it sought to free the artist from the conventional perception of surface reality; its fragmentation of verbal and visual imagery, together with its synthesis of different art forms, revolutionized twentieth-century aesthetics more profoundly than any other movement before or since. This extraordinarily fruitful *artistic* legacy of Expressionism was, as we shall see, one which Brecht was to have no hesitation in appropriating for the purposes of his politically committed 'dialectical' theatre.

In its social import, however, literary Expressionism's assault on the philistine *Bürger* was from the start shot through with violent contradictions. The poet's longing to be at one with all mankind, expressed in the 'O Mensch!' ('O Man!') pathos of Werfel's work, or the ecstatic proclamation of the spiritual renewal of society through the poet in such plays as Sorge's *Der Bettler* (*The Beggar*), were juxtaposed and sometimes mingled with strong currents of nihilism and despair. Such contradictory extremes are an index both of Nietzsche's influence on the movement and of the profound cultural and social pessimism of the Expressionists themselves. Their prophecy of the advent of the 'New Man' (cf. Nietzsche's 'superman') was an apocalyptic one, deriving its intensity from their total rejection of the society in which they lived, and their conviction that it was heading for self-destruction. Unlike the Italian Futurists with their cult of the machine, German Expressionists abhorred modern technology as an instrument for the enslavement of the individual (cf. Kaiser's *Gas* trilogy) and as the product of a totally materialistic concept of 'progress'. In terms of political ideology, their image of the ideal society (in so far as they had one) owed more to anarchism, with its stress on the liberation of the individual, than to socialism; and their view of the present as a time of crisis was diametrically opposed to the optimistically progressive outlook of the SPD. Expressionists were in fact as alienated from the by then thoroughly bureaucratized SPD as they were from the other institutions of Wilhelmine Germany, and their Utopian longings found no kind of political expression in the pre-1914 period.

The will to become socially and politically involved was, however, most certainly present in the Expressionist movement in the pre-war era, and was indeed the main impetus behind the writings of the loose grouping of Expressionist intellectuals known as the 'activists'. One of the first, most lucid, and most unambiguously democratic statements from the activist camp came in the form of a polemical broadside entitled *Geist und Tat* (*Mind and Action*), published in 1910 by the author and essayist Heinrich Mann. His short but powerful piece became a rallying-point for the movement, many of whose members came to revere Mann (born in 1871) as a mentor and father-figure.

Heinrich Mann's literary career, like that of his younger brother Thomas, had begun before the turn of the century. Both brothers had rebelled against their respectable upper-middle-class background to become writers; both had in the 1890s come heavily under the sway of Nietzschean ideas and attitudes. Heinrich's one previous foray into literary politics – a twenty-month spell in 1895–96 as editor of the right-wing journal *Das Zwanzigste Jahrhundert* – would certainly have done little to prepare his readers for the stance that he was now in the process of adopting, and which was to bring him into bitter public conflict in the war years with his more conservative brother. For *Geist und Tat* was an attack, from a clearly left-wing standpoint, on the apolitical and implicitly anti-democratic values of Germany's literati. And, more specifically, it was a critique of that Nietzschean tradition which had up to that point been such a major influence in Heinrich's intellectual and artistic development.

Inspired above all by the crucial intervention of the French writer Emile Zola in the Dreyfus affair, Mann in his essay contrasts French intellectuals, with their long tradition of involvement in radical politics, with the sorry spectacle presented by their politically quiescent counterparts in Germany. German writers have in Mann's view betrayed their essential task: the rational critique of authority and power. But their betrayal is to some extent caused by factors beyond their control; for just as the social involvement of French intellectuals has depended on the existence of a democratically active bourgeois public, so conversely the failure of German intellectuals to combat *Macht*, power, is due in part to the fact that they are generals without an army. The *Volk*, the people, has abandoned the goal of a liberal parliamentary democracy in favour of a secure but politically servile existence under the wing of the semi-autocratic Kaiserreich, and in so doing it has left its would-be progressive intellectuals in the lurch. The result: a widening gulf between *Geist* – the realm of ideal constructs, theoretically admired but practically ineffectual – and the crude, materialistic reality of *bürgerlich* life; and the channelling of writers' protest into an ultimately harmless Nietzschean aestheticism, whose sneering contempt for the ideals and institutions of 'Western' (i.e. French or British) democracy betokens a virtual capitulation to Germany's still undemocratized status quo. Mann ends his essay with a ringing call to intellectuals to abandon their ivory tower for a new alliance with the *Volk* against *Macht*. Their task is to restore to the people their self-respect, and to lead them into action against the established order.

In its left-wing critique of Nietzsche, Mann's essay displays a political self-awareness that was at this time new among the German avant-garde. Its central concern – the restoration of a progressive socio-critical role to the intelligentsia – foreshadows the work of Brecht. But Mann's abstract and highly generalized references to *Geist* and *Volk* themselves betray the extent to which his thought is still influenced by that apoliti-cal tradition that he is attacking. His intention is to salvage *Geist* from the distortions to which it had been subjected in the Second Reich, and to restore to it some of the force it had possessed in the Enlightenment era. But in so doing he invokes a unified *Volk* that is hard to relate con-cretely to the class-divided society of his own day, and credits a socially isolated minority of independent intellectuals with a power to influence events which – as his own essay suggests – they do not in fact possess.

The 'activists' meanwhile began to make a growing impact on the pre-war scene, one of their main forms of expression being the political–cultural magazine. Franz Pfemfert founded *Die Aktion* in Ber-lin in 1911; in the same year Erich Mühsam, anarchist and cabarettist, and the author of a famous poem 'Der Revoluzzer' attacking the faint-heartedness of German social democracy, launched the improbably named *Kain: Zeitschrift für Menschlichkeit* (*Cain: A Magazine for Humanity*) in Munich. He was its sole contributor. The year 1913 saw the start of two more activist magazines, *Die Revolution* and *Die weis-sen Blätter*, the latter of which was later to become, under René Schic-kele's editorship in Zurich, one of the main focal points of German pac-ifism during the war years.

When war was declared in 1914, these activists were among the small minority of German *Literaten* who with their outspokenly pacifist position sounded a discordant note in the great symphony of patriotic fervour. For young intellectuals, particularly those whose alienation from the dominant culture of Wilhelmine Germany had taken them towards right-wing, pseudo-mystical or 'back-to-nature' groupings such as the Wandervogel youth movement, the outbreak of war came as a welcome release from the unheroic conformism of *bürgerlich* society; Expressionist artists and poets (many of whom, e.g. Ernst Stadler, August Stramm, Franz Marc, were killed in action) tended to see it as a realization of their apocalyptic forebodings. Few people in 1914, how-ever, could have had any real idea of the extent of the social and politi-cal changes that were to transform the face of Europe over the coming four years.

The actual events of 1914–18 and the period of virtual civil war that followed marked what many Weimar intellectuals were later to look back on as a 'Zeitenwende', an epochal change. This perspective is as fundamental to the Communism of Brecht, and his view of the relation-ship between individual and society (see Ch. 4), as it is to the militaris-tic nationalism propagated through the 1920s and early 1930s by a wri-ter who in many ways was Brecht's antipode – the war diarist Ernst Jünger. Both these writers derive their radically different political com-

mitments from the massive military, economic and industrial collectiv-
ization of human individuals that had brought the Wilhelmine era and its
bürgerlich values to an end. However, an essential aspect of Brecht's
and, to a lesser extent, Jünger's commitment is that they mark long-
term responses, arrived at over a period of years, to the upheavals of
war and revolution. This was a phenomenon very different from the
politicization of writers and intellectuals that took place within the
Expressionist era, and particularly under the immediate impact of the
war itself.

The wartime politicization of the Expressionist generation was in part
a direct response by writers to their horrific experiences in the trenches.
Thus, Ernst Toller and Fritz von Unruh, who had both gone into the
war as convinced patriots, became pacifists, and wrote plays (Toller's
Die Wandlung, The Transfiguration, von Unruh's Ein Geschlecht, A
Family) that reflected their conversion. But this change of attitude on the
part of individuals gained its main political significance from the much
broader-based resistance to the war that from the end of 1915 was growing, particularly among the working class, within Germany itself. With
the founding of the far-left Spartakusbund under the leadership of Karl
Liebknecht and Rosa Luxemburg in 1916, the secession of the anti-war
USPD (Independent Socialists) from the SPD in 1917 and the creation
of the KPD (German Communist Party) in January 1919, left-wing intellectuals, writers and artists were confronted with political organizations
that, unlike the SPD, could genuinely claim to be radical or revolutionary, and for whose leaders (particularly Liebknecht and Luxemburg)
many of them felt considerable respect. A number of writers, Toller,
Hasenclever and Pfemfert among them, joined the USPD, others such
as Ludwig Rubiner the KPD. Toller not only wrote Die Wandlung, but
distributed scenes from it to striking Krupp workers in Munich. And in
the increasingly revolutionary political situation of the years 1916–18,
Expressionist drama – even that written before the war – frequently took
on a quite new political dimension. The left-wing diarist Harry Graf
Kessler experienced a performance of Hasenclever's Der Sohn (written
in 1913 but first performed in 1916) as a sign of

> ...den Übergang der deutschen Intellektualität von einem fast reinen
> Kultur-Revolutionarismus, wie ihn Nietzsche...vertrat, zum praktischen,
> politischen und wirtschaftlichen Radikalismus, dessen Extrem augenblicklich
> die Spartakusbewegung ist.[4]

> (...the abandonment by German intellectuals of the purely cultural
> revolution...represented by Nietzsche, in favour of a practical, political and
> economic radicalism, whose extreme form is at the moment to be found in
> the Spartacist movement.)

In the revolutionary events of 1918–19, played out against the back-
drop of the Bolshevik Revolution of October 1917, the political
involvement of the Expressionist playwrights and artists and of the
activists such as Heinrich Mann and Kurt Hiller reached its climax. This

involvement took two broad forms, which for most intellectuals were mutually exclusive. On the one hand, there was the possibility of work-ing *within* the new forms of political democracy that enjoyed a brief existence in 1918–19. As the anarcho-socialist Gustave Landauer observed in 1919:

> Dem Volk und dem Dichter tut es in der Tat not, dass sie zusammenkommen. Der Dichter aber ist nicht immer Dichter, und es wird gut und natürlich sein, dass er als einer unter vielen, als Mensch unter Menschen zu den Beratungen seiner Gemeinde und seines Volkes geht.[5]
>
> (Writer and people do indeed need to come together. But the writer does not spend all his time writing, and it is only right and natural that he should attend the meetings of his community and his people as one among many, as a human being among other human beings.)

Many intellectuals, Brecht among them, took part in the workers' and soldiers' councils or soviets that sprang up in many parts of Germany in November 1918, without necessarily being 'committed' to this revolutionary form of democracy; indeed, the Central Congress of Councils that took place in Berlin voted (much to the disgust of radicals such as Toller) to transfer power to a future constituent assembly. Quite a different order of commitment and revolutionary optimism was, how-ever, generated by the events in Bavaria in February–May 1919. Here the revolutionary government set up in November 1918 under the Inde-pendent Socialist Kurt Eisner gained the support of a large number of left-wing intellectuals. Following Eisner's assassination by the right-wing Count Arco-Valley on 21 February 1919, a *Räterepublik* (council republic or soviet) was set up in opposition to the parliamentary regime, which fled to Bamberg. The Communists, led by Eugen Leviné, hung back from involvement until the last minute; most of the intellectuals participating in the soviet were idealists with anarchist leanings and often strong pacifist convictions: Toller, Mühsam, Landauer.

They paid dearly for their commitment. When in May 1919 the soviet was crushed by the counter-revolutionary militia, the *Freikorps,* Landauer was brutally murdered, Leviné shot, and Toller, brought to trial on charges of high treason, escaped with five years' 'fortress arrest' (of which he served all but one day) only because his honourable motives, attested by a string of witnesses including Thomas Mann and Max Weber, were allowed in mitigation. Mühsam was sentenced to fifteen years, of which he served six. Not only were these anarchists physically defeated; their dreams of a Utopian future to be born out of love and non-violent struggle were also destroyed by the violent mass events (cf. Toller's play *Masse Mensch*) in which they were caught up and over which they had little control.

In stark contrast to this direct involvement in the political revolution were the activities of those radicals who, rather than working within the soldiers' and workers' councils, decided in November 1918 that the hour of *Geist* had finally arrived, and accordingly constituted themselves, in major cities throughout Germany, into self-appointed *Räte geistiger Arbeiter* (councils of intellectual workers). The first was set up in Berlin under the leadership of Kurt Hiller, whose activist publication *Das Ziel* (*The Goal*) had first appeared in 1916; its programme, invoking *Geist* as the sole means of liberating humanity and calling for a fusion of Marx and Nietzsche, in fact owed a lot more to Nietzsche than it did to Marx. It was élitist, individualistic and, in its inflated idea of the power of *Geist*, quite out of touch with reality. Heinrich Mann's address to the Munich council, of which he was chairman, was somewhat less exalted in tone, but likewise placed far more importance on 'Radikalismus des Geistes' ('spiritual radicalism') than on mere economic developments. Riding on the wave of revolution but for the most part condemning the Revolution and the masses as 'ungeistig', the councils of intellectual workers, their lofty pronouncements hearkened to by no-one but themselves, were soon faced with the fact of their own impotence, and disbanded in June 1919.

Many of the members of the *Räte geistiger Arbeiter* were radicals for whom the parliamentary constitution of the Weimar Republic represented in itself a betrayal of their ideals. Others, such as Heinrich Mann, were willing at first to believe that at least the structures of the new republic were essentially democratic, and that the task of *Geist* would henceforth be to implant the spirit of democracy in the hearts and minds of the German people. In Mann's case, however, this trust in Weimar's institutions was progressively undermined, and finally destroyed by the devastating impact on the middle and working classes of the inflation crisis of 1923.[6]

As well as becoming alienated, either instantly or gradually, from the parliamentary system of Weimar, radical intellectuals also lost their commitment to political parties. This was due largely to the changes that took place in the parties they had joined. The USPD split and was swallowed up, the bulk of the membership going to the KPD in 1921, the remainder joining the SPD in 1922. The KPD, which had begun as a party with strong anarcho-syndicalist tendencies, became rapidly bureaucratized, and from the mid-1920s came increasingly under the influence of Moscow. Many of its left-wing members, including intellectuals such as Franz Pfemfert, editor of *Die Aktion*, seceded in 1919 and founded the KAPD (Communist Workers' Party). This, however, disintegrated into warring splinter groups and was finished as an effective political force by 1923. Thus, of the two major left-wing parties remaining at the end of this process, the conservative SPD was even more unattractive to radicals than it had been before the war, while the KPD, bereft of the intellectual figureheads of Liebknecht and Luxemburg and now truly a mass working-class party, presented an image of stolid orthodoxy that most middle-class intellectuals found distinctly uninviting.

Despite all this, it would be wrong to imagine that those intellectuals who had been politicized by war and revolution simply succumbed to political apathy in the post-Expressionist era. Admittedly the new mood of *Sachlichkeit*, the 'New Objectivity' or 'New Sobriety', had no place for that Utopian *mélange* of Marx and Nietzsche proclaimed by Kurt Hiller in 1918. But the continuing precariousness of the Republic, and the economic and social stress to which it was subjected even during its relatively stable phase (1924–28), made it much less easy for writers to return to the ivory tower, Thomas Mann's 'machtgeschützte Innerlichkeit' ('inwardness protected by power'), from which the war had expelled them. With the growth of Fascist and Communist movements committed ultimately to the destruction of the Republic, neither the power of the newly established political order nor the inwardness of the private individual was really secure any longer. Thomas Mann himself, alarmed particularly by the fanaticism of the extreme right in the period 1918–23, moved from an initial conservative hostility to Weimar via lukewarm support to an active commitment, in essays and political speeches, to the Republican order. In his 'Deutsche Ansprache' ('German address') delivered after the Nazi gains in the September 1930 elections, he appealed to the *Bürgertum* to resist the Nazis' rabid nationalism, to overcome its horror of socialism by distinguishing between moderate social democracy and Moscow-oriented Communism, and to support the SPD, which he now saw as the true and only viable guardian in the political arena of traditional middle-class values.

Thomas Mann's politicization was, however, that of an instinctive conservative, seeking – much to the scorn of Bertolt Brecht – to preserve a *bürgerlich* tradition against the threat of revolution from both left and right. If, on the other hand, the political involvement of avant-garde radicals such as his brother Heinrich was sustained beyond 1923, it was in part because the enthusiasm of 1918–19 had spawned not only the short-lived councils of intellectual workers but also more long-lasting organizations and groupings of artists and intellectuals that continued through the 1920s to provide an effective focus and vehicle for their commitment. Two of these may serve as examples: the Weimar (later Dessau) Bauhaus, and the political–cultural journal *Die Weltbühne*.

The Bauhaus was a school of art, design and architecture established in Weimar in 1919 with the support of the new socialist government of Thuringia and with the architect Walter Gropius as its director. It was unique in its fusion of the previously separate Academy of Fine Arts with the School of Applied Arts and Crafts in Weimar – a breaking-down of barriers which, as its first manifesto made clear, was one of the guiding ideals of its founders:

> Architekten, Bildhauer, Maler, wir alle müssen zum Handwerk zurück! Denn es gibt keine 'Kunst von Beruf'. Es gibt keinen Wesensunterschied zwischen dem Künstler und dem Handwerker . . . .
> Bilden wir also eine *neue Zunft der Handwerker* ohne die klassentrennende Anmassung, die eine hochmütige Mauer zwischen Handwerkern und

Künstlern errichten wollte! Wollen, erdenken, erschaffen wir gemeinsam den neuen Bau der Zukunft, der alles in einer Gestalt sein wird: Architektur *und* Plastik *und* Malerei, der aus Millionen Händen der Handwerker einst gen Himmel steigen wird als kristallenes Sinnbild eines neuen kommenden Glaubens.[7]

(Architects, sculptors, painters, we must all return to the crafts! For there is no such thing as 'professional art'. There is no essential difference between the artist and the craftsman . . . .

Let us therefore form a *new guild of craftsmen* without that presumptuous class division which in the past has sought to build an arrogant wall between craftsmen and artists! Let us together will, devise and create the new building of the future, which will unite everything within a single form, architecture *and* sculpture *and* painting, and which, fashioned by millions of craftsmen's hands, will one day rise towards heaven as a crystalline symbol of a new faith as yet unborn.)

Many of the Utopian ideas contained in this founding manifesto, in particular the project of a 'new building of the future' that would unify all the arts and crafts within an architecturally conceived whole, were first formulated by Gropius and his fellow architects Bruno Taut and Adolf Behne in the revolutionary *Arbeitsrat für Kunst* (Art Soviet), formed, like the intellectual workers' councils, in November 1918.[8] The influence of the Expressionist *Sturm* group, founded in 1910, and particularly artists like Kandinsky (who was to join the Bauhaus in 1922), played a quite crucial part in the Art Soviet's wildly ambitious and impractical conception of its social impact and social role. The Bauhaus itself was to remain committed to the idea that the applied arts, and in particular that socially most unavoidable of the applied arts, architecture, could contribute in a vital fashion to the creation of a new social order. In time, however, the strongly individualistic emphasis and anti-technological bias of the school's first years were replaced by a growing interest in working in cooperation with industry to design objects of a functional beauty that could be manufactured with the techniques of mass production. This movement from a Utopian individualism to a more sober coming to terms with the realities of industrialization and the mass society is part of the general trend from Expressionism to *Sachlichkeit* in the Weimar period, and provides an illuminating parallel to Brecht's own development towards an emphatically rational yet idealistic form of social commitment in the late 1920s.

Though Gropius explicitly rejected party-political commitment the Bauhaus had clear left-wing sympathies. Gropius himself, for example, sculpted a memorial to the victims of the right-wing Kapp Putsch and later designed a (never-to-be-built) theatre for Piscator. Because of this, and because of its avant-gardism, the Bauhaus was under attack by the right throughout the Weimar Republic. Political harrassment forced it to move to Dessau in 1925, and after a further move to Berlin in 1932 it was closed down by the Nazis in 1933.

Die Weltbühne (*The World-Stage*), overshadowing the somewhat less radical journal *Das Tage-Buch*, was the major organ in the Weimar Republic of the politically disaffected intellectuals of the radical left, and as such gathered round itself a circle of writers who, without having any coherent political programme, nevertheless presented to the outside world a kind of political–cultural corporate identity. The prehistory of the journal is symptomatic of the times: under its original title *Die Schaubühne* (*The Stage*) it had begun life in the Wilhelmine era as a non-political, cultural–aesthetic publication, focusing on the theatre as the well-spring of a spiritual transformation of society. Under the impact of the events of 1917–18, however, its founder and editor, Siegfried Jacobsohn, changed both the name and the character of his journal, increasing its political content dramatically. Edited by Kurt Tucholsky from Jacobsohn's death in 1926 until October 1927, and by the prominent pacifist Carl von Ossietzky from 1927 until its suppression in 1933, *Die Weltbühne*, whose contributors also included the Expressionists or erstwhile Expressionists Heinrich Mann, Kurt Hiller, Walter Hasenclever, Ernst Toller and Erich Mühsam, stood for the kind of libertarian–leftist ideals which since the demise of the USPD had not had a political party to represent them. It became progressively disenchanted with the policies of both SPD and KPD, whom towards the end of the Weimar era it was urging to unite in a revolutionary struggle against the Nazi threat.

The call fell on deaf ears; and from 1933 *Weltbühne* intellectuals became prime targets of Nazi persecution. Mühsam was tortured for seventeen months and finally murdered in July 1934; Ossietzky, after years in prison and concentration camp, died of tuberculosis in 1938. Toller, Hasenclever and Tucholsky all committed suicide in exile. Heinrich Mann, on the other hand, faced with the unpalatable but finally inescapable fact of the German middle class's capitulation to Hitler, came to see the USSR as representing the only realistic hope for a better future. Following the Communist International's adoption in 1935 of the new 'popular fronts' policy aimed at bringing together Communist, left-radical and social-democrat opponents of Fascism, Mann was elected President of the German Popular Front, the *Volksfront*, on its foundation in 1936. Though he never became a Marxist, his support for Stalin remained unshaken by the Moscow Show Trials and even survived the Stalin–Hitler pact of 1939. After the war Mann made up his mind to return from America to live in the GDR, but died in Santa Monica in 1950 before he was able to put this plan into effect. His ashes were later taken to East Germany, where he is today celebrated as one of the spiritual founding fathers of the socialist state.

The Bauhaus and the *Weltbühne* thus represent means whereby the commitment of the Expressionist movement was perpetuated into the post-Expressionist years of the Weimar Republic. Brecht, in spite of his clear left-wing sympathies in the closing years of the war, never identified with that movement, either in an aesthetic or a political sense. His sceptical distance from it was expressed at the time, both in his parody of Expressionism in *Baal*, and in the withdrawal of Kragler, the anti-hero of *Trommeln in der Nacht* (*Drums in the Night*) from revolutionary activity into private life. When later as a Marxist Brecht began to develop his own variety of political theatre, the result bore the stamp of a vigorous and optimistic rationalism – a radical break with Expressionism's individualistic and pathos-laden rebellion against the realities of the modern industrial age.

In the light of the widespread alienation of radical intellectuals from party politics after 1923, Brecht's commitment to the KPD in the late 1920s may seem to represent a rather untypical development. He was, however, by no means alone in taking this step. A number of writers and artists joined the Party at that time, including the dramatist Friedrich Wolf, author of the anti-abortion-law play *Zyankali* (1929), the avant-garde composer Hanns Eisler, who cooperated with Brecht on a number of major works, beginning with the didactic play *Die Massnahme* (*The Measures Taken*) (1930), Ludwig Renn, whose novel *Krieg*, based on its author's experiences as an officer in the First World War, appeared in 1928, and Anna Seghers, whose *Aufstand der Fischer von St Barbara* (*Revolt of the Fishermen of St Barbara*) was published in the same year.

The years 1929–33 following the brief interlude of apparent stability were of course to see a growing politicization and polarization of artistic and literary activities in response to the economic and political crisis. The Kampfbund für deutsche Kultur (Militant League for German Culture), founded by the Nazi Alfred Rosenberg in 1929, went on to the offensive against both socialism and modernism in the arts, while on the left the Communist cultural periodical *Die Linkskurve*, whose first number also appeared in 1929, launched bitter attacks on left-wing intellectuals such as Tucholsky who refused to align themselves with the Party.

The commitment of Brecht, Eisler, Wolf, Seghers and Renn, however, falls in the period 1926–28, the period of relative calm preceding the final crisis, and so cannot be seen as a response to the crisis itself. Nor is it comparable to the politicization of the Expressionists, for whom the new left-wing parties of 1917–18 had symbolized the possibility of an immediate and radical transformation of society. The situation in 1926–28 was not a revolutionary one, and the Communist Party to which these writers committed themselves was for its part pursuing much more moderate policies than it had done in the Expressionist era.

Brecht himself came to Communism neither through a sudden access of revolutionary zeal nor through an identification with the sufferings of the proletariat (*Mitleid*, sympathy, was one of the emotions he most distrusted), but as the end result of a lengthy study of Marx. Marx's theories sustained him in the conviction, already reached in the mid-

1920s and reflected in *Mann ist Mann* (*A Man's a Man*) (1926), that in the mass society of the post-war era, collectivized by war, revolution and industrialization, *bürgerlich* culture and its liberal individualism had finally become obsolete. Marxism, however, not only seemed to confirm this bankruptcy of bourgeois culture, but pointed a way forward out of it; and this was what made it so attractive to Brecht.

The reason for this lies in Brecht's development as a dramatist and an intellectual. He was not satisfied with making a career for himself in the theatre of the Weimar Republic – an aim that would have been, indeed was, quite adequately achieved by the provocative cynicism of his earlier plays, up to and including *Die Dreigroschenoper* (*The Threepenny Opera*) (1928). More ambitiously, he claimed for writers and intellectuals a vital role in shaping and changing social reality. The bourgeois theatre had, he considered, abandoned its social function and devoted itself to purveying either trivia or short-lived emotional experiences, whose net effect was to confirm the audience in their comfortably passive attitude *vis-à-vis* society. To this he opposed his Marxist concept of a 'dialectical' theatre that would present man and society as understandable and alterable. Contemporary thought he likewise saw as 'folgenlos' ('inconsequential'), reduced either to a technical rationality maximizing the capitalist's profits ('die Vernunft im Dienste der Rationalisierung') or to an impotent critique of society, condemned simply to mirror the social contradictions that it was attempting to master (*GW* 20, 166). To this he opposed his Marxist practice of 'eingreifendes Denken' ('thought-that-intervenes') (*GW* 20, 158–78).

Brecht thus continued to see himself primarily as a dramatist, producer and intellectual even after his commitment to the Communist movement. His alliance with the revolutionary working class, and the method of Marxist dialectic, offered him a means of being 'productive' – a key word for Brecht – by endowing his theatre and his thought with the legitimacy and the social vitality that bourgeois culture had seemingly lost. What, he once asked himself, is the material interest that makes intellectuals participate in the class struggle alongside the proletariat?

> Die einzige Erklärung ist, dass die Intellektuellen nur durch die Revolution sich eine Entfaltung ihrer (intellektuellen) Tätigkeit erhoffen können. (*GW* 20, 53)
>
> (The sole explanation is that it is only through revolution that intellectuals can hope for a development and expansion of their (intellectual) activities.)

For Brecht the dramatist, however, commitment involved not simply the propagation of a new, revolutionary Marxist message, but a Marxist-inspired restructuring of the very *form* of the drama itself. The resulting theory and practice of epic theatre, and the part played in its development by Brecht's predecessor and colleague Erwin Piscator, are discussed in Chapters 3 and 9 of this book. What should be emphasized here, however, is the wider debt that this politically revolutionary theatre owes to the aesthetic revolution achieved by the literary and artistic avant-garde in the period 1910–30.

It was a debt which Brecht himself not only freely acknowledged but also used as an argument when in the late 1930s he defended his own concept of socialist art against the sterile dogma of socialist realism. In seeking historical precedents for the *social function* and the kind of audience he wished his theatre to have, Brecht admittedly ignored the modern avant-garde and instead looked back a full century and a half to the theatre of the eighteenth-century Enlightenment, of Diderot in France and Lessing in Germany. This was the theatre of a rising middle class; a theatre that had addressed itself to a progressive bourgeois public, and in so doing had self-confidently combined 'pleasure' or 'enjoyment' on the one hand, with 'instruction' – the articulation of the bourgeoisie's revolutionary moral and social values – on the other: the kind of synthesis that Brecht saw as notably lacking in the theatre of his own day. When, however, he came to consider the actual *forms* that a modern political theatre should evolve, then the social isolation of the avant-garde, and the fact that it often seemed to propagate an aesthetic revolution rather than a social and political one, were less important; what mattered was its essential modernity – the fact that it had developed its new resources and techniques of expression as a response, albeit in Brecht's view a confused one, to the contemporary crisis of capitalist society.

Thus, while criticizing Expressionism as an unproductive revolt of art against reality, whose practitioners 'sich nur von der Grammatik befreit hatten, nicht vom Kapitalismus' ('had merely freed themselves from the rules of grammar, not from capitalism') (*GW* 19, 304), Brecht also declared that he could learn far more from Expressionists such as Kaiser, Sternheim and Toller than from such classic nineteenth-century authors as Tolstoy and Balzac, whose heroes moved in a world so different from that of his own (and the Expressionists') experience. In 1928 he chose Joyce's *Ulysses* (translated that year) as one of his four 'books of the year', and a decade later listed Joyce's use of 'inner monologue' alongside the documentary montage of Don Passos, the narrative techniques developed by the modernist writer Alfred Döblin, and indeed the *Verfremdung* (alienation) of Kafka's narration, as elements that contemporary socialist writers should take over from the avant-garde novel and exploit for their own purposes (*GW* 19, 361).

Brecht clearly did not regard these techniques developed by the avant-garde as solely the product of idle fancy or of a superficial desire to appear 'radical' and shock the philistine bourgeoisie. They were in fact the only adequate means available to the contemporary writer of seizing the modern world in all its complexity. The modernist novel's fragmentation of external reality and of the individual psyche, and its abandonment of the rounded characters and coherent plots of nineteenth-century realism, were in part a reflection of the radically disruptive social forces to which men were exposed in a highly industrialized and technologized era. In these circumstances it could not, Brecht asserted, be the business of politically committed writers simply to sweep aside these artistic products of the modern age as 'decadent' and model their works on those of the nineteenth century, in a regressive attempt to return to the 'good old days' of the individual hero and a reassuringly comprehensible world. The fact of modern mass society had first to be accepted, if its dehumanizing aspects were to be overcome (*GW* 19, 297–8); correspondingly, forms of literary realism would have to be developed that could not but be strikingly different from those of 100 years earlier.

Brecht's Marxism, unlike that of his neo-Hegelian Marxist contemporaries in the Frankfurt School, was of an uncompromisingly optimistic and forward-looking kind: he saw the world-wide crisis that capitalism had been plunged into in the late 1920s as the birth-pangs of a future socialist society. His age he regarded as one of transition, an end but also a new beginning. And while the Utopian vision of the Expressionists had been based on a total rejection of the present reality of industrial capitalism, Brecht, following the Marxist view of history, took a much more positive view of the economy and society of his own day. Capitalism, though doomed, was nevertheless developing 'productive forces' ('Produktivkräfte') which would eventually burst asunder its outmoded social and economic structures and replace them with socialist ones.

For Brecht, these 'productive forces' were not to be found in the realm of economic production alone. As someone who was first and foremost a writer and dramatist, he was deeply committed to the view that art itself was a kind of 'production', not simply mirroring a given social reality (the function to which Communist literary *historians* were apt to consign it), but an active, material part of that reality, and potentially able to contribute towards changing it. This helps us to understand why Brecht's attitude to the avant-garde, though critical, was ultimately a positive one; just as he was keen to exploit the resources of advanced technology (including the radio) for his theatre, so too he regarded the technically most advanced art of his age (in so far as it was not mere spurious gimmickry) as potentially the most 'productive' for the politically committed writer (*GW* 19, 361).

Brecht's systematic attempt, beginning in the late 1920s, to appropriate the experiments of the avant-garde for the purposes of political art, had had some important precedents in the period immediately following the revolutions of 1917–18. There was in the first place the upsurge of avant-garde art in Russia after 1917 – the Proletkult movement; the graphics of El Lissitzky; the poetry of Mayakovsky; the theatre of Meyerhold; and Constructivism, whose attempts to integrate art and technology later made a major impact on the work of the Bauhaus. There was of course the political theatre developed by Piscator from

1919 onwards, and influenced, directly and indirectly, both by the Proletkult movement and by Meyerhold's work. And there was the Berlin wing of the Dada movement, which had in 1917–18 brought together in the metropolis a number of avant-garde writers and artists committed both to left-wing Communism and to the politicization of art. These included John Heartfield (who had anglicized his name), and his brother Wieland Herzfelde, directors of the Communist publishing house, the Malik Verlag; the writer Franz Jung; and the painter and caricaturist George Grosz.

Dada, which originated in an 'unpolitical' form in the wartime performances of a group of poets in the Cabaret Voltaire, Zurich, was at one and the same time an extension of Expressionism, carrying its fragmentation of language, its anti-bourgeois aggression and its mixture of despair and millenial hope to a new extreme; and an anti-art reaction *against* Expressionism, whose overblown pathos served, in the view of the Dadaists, to perpetuate the essentially bourgeois concept of the sanctity of the work of art. The Communist Dadaists of Berlin, whose politicization was unique in the Dada movement, developed techniques, such as the photomontage of John Heartfield and the combination of text and image in Grosz's paintings, which anticipated Brecht both in their self-conscious exploitation of contemporary technology and in their anti-illusionistic form, and which were used in magazines such as *Die Pleite* (*Bankrupt*) to present a bitter indictment of the politics and society of Weimar Germany from an extreme left-wing standpoint. The beginnings of Piscator's political theatre date from his close association with the Berlin Dadaists in the immediate post-war period – and later John Heartfield, George Grosz and Franz Jung all worked with him, the first two as designers (see particularly Heartfield's work for the Proletarisches Theater of 1920–21, and Grosz's animated cartoons for the 1928 *Schwejk* production), the last as playwright.

These Berlin Dadaists were all committed to the KPD in the earliest, most militant-revolutionary stage of its existence; Brecht from the late 1920s equally explicitly allied his theatre to the Party's cause. For their part, however, the Party's cultural theorists tended from the outset to treat the political art or anti-art of the avant-garde with considerable suspicion. The cultural iconoclasm of Grosz, Heartfield and Jung and the early experiments of Piscator were fiercely attacked in the party organ *Die Rote Fahne* (*The Red Flag*) by critics who saw their own function as one of preserving intact the progressive bourgeois classics of an earlier era until such time as the proletariat, having achieved its revolution, would annexe them as part of its rightful cultural legacy. The ideological revolution propagated by the left-wing Communists as an essential counterpart of political revolution, the efforts of Heartfield and others to create a proletarian art here and now rather than postponing it until the arrival of Communism, were dismissed as the wild dreams of anarchistic *Literaten*, exploiting the working-class movement for their own fanciful ends. In this, the cultural theorists of the KPD were echoing the judgement which their predecessors in the SPD had passed on the Naturalist movement some thirty years previously.

From the mid-1920s the KPD, following the Comintern line, adopted a more positive cultural policy, fostering the growth of a whole range of proletarian organizations, sporting, theatrical, choral, etc., in opposition to those established by the SPD, and approving the formation in 1928 of the Bund proletarisch-revolutionärer Schriftsteller (League of Proletarian-Revolutionary Writers) under the leadership of the ex-Expressionist Johannes R. Becher. In the USSR, however, the cultural freedom that had blossomed in the post-revolutionary era had during the 1920s been progressively eliminated; artistic activity was brought under the control of the Party bureaucracy, avant-garde experimentation systematically suppressed as a product of bourgeois decadence, and literature given the task of monumentalizing the achievements of the Soviet people in general and the Party under the leadership of Stalin in particular. The Moscow line was of course faithfully followed by the KPD, both in Germany and, after 1933, in exile; the orthodoxy Moscow preached and, in the USSR, enforced, was one which ran counter to Brecht's most vital convictions concerning the artist's social role. A visit to the USSR in 1935 was enough to convince him that a longer stay there would be fruitless; and his later writings on Expressionism and on realism, countering the Stalinist dogma of 'socialist realism' officially proclaimed in 1934, can be read on one level as an extended defence of the artist's freedom against the dictatorship of the Party bureaucracy and its cultural apologists.

Brecht never lost his faith in the possibility and indeed the necessity of combining literary creativity and political commitment. But the commitment was not one whose terms could ultimately be dictated by anyone other than Brecht himself. Admittedly, he was willing to listen to advice from people whose judgement he respected, and to alter his plays accordingly. Furthermore, he regarded art as a collective rather than a purely individualistic enterprise – a concept that took on a concrete reality in his work in the theatre, where so much depended upon the cooperation of a team, both at the stage of composition and in the actual realization of the work in performance. Clearly, his belief in artistic freedom was not based on the traditional romantic concept of the work of art as a unique and unchangeable product of a single, individual genius. But, as we have seen, Brecht the theatre-worker held tenaciously to the view that art, including his art, was a specific form of *production* in its own right. If it were to function productively as an agent of social change, it would have to be allowed to do so in its own particular fashion, without being supervised by Party officials interested primarily in reinforcing their own authority. Those who demanded 'affirmative' works of art conforming to a predetermined political formula and a conservative aesthetic, rather than the critical and problemati-

G. Bartram

cal 'thought-experiments' that Brecht was engaged in, were seen by him as 'enemies of production' whose dictates, if enforced, could only spell sterility for the artist.[9] This was a fate that Brecht succeeded in eluding in the years of Weimar and exile, but which – partly through reasons of official repression, partly because he for his part supported the newborn socialist state – he was not altogether able to escape in the GDR.

NOTES

1. For a discussion of the 'aesthetic state' as exemplified in Brecht's later plays, see Chapter 4 above.
2. The most notable exception was the poet Gottfried Benn, who for a while welcomed the Nazi seizure of power in 1933. In embracing barbarism, however, he mockingly distanced himself from his fellow avant-garde writers, 'die Intellektuellen' – and so was, in a sense, the exception that proved the rule.
3. See Martin Jay, *The Dialectical Imagination* (London, 1973), pp. 9, 23, 94, 178.
4. Harry Graf Kessler, *Tagebücher 1918–1937* (Frankfurt, 1961), cited by Franz-Joachim Verspohl, 'Autonomie und Parteilichkeit: 'Asthetische Praxis' in der Phase des Imperialismus', in Michael Müller et al., *Autonomie der Kunst: Zur Genese und Kritik einer bürgerlichen Kategorie* (Frankfurt am Main, 1972), pp. 199–230 (p. 214).
5. Cited by Eva Kolinsky, *Engagierter Expressionismus: Politik und Literatur zwischen Weltkrieg und Weimarer Republik* (Stuttgart, 1970), p. 205.
6. See David Gross, *The Writer and Society: Heinrich Mann and Literary Politics in Germany, 1980–1940* (Atlantic Highlands, New Jersey, 1980), pp. 207–18.
7. Cited in Herbert Bayer, Walter Gropius and Ise Gropius, eds, *Bauhaus 1919–1928* (Stuttgart, 1955), p. 16.
8. See Chapters 3 and 4 in Marcel Franciscono, *Walter Gropius and the Creation of the Bauhaus in Weimar: The Ideals and Artistic Theories of its Founding Years* (Urbana/Chicago/London, 1971).
9. See 'Conversations with Brecht' in Walter Benjamin, *Understanding Brecht* (London, 1977), pp. 105–21 (p. 118).

SELECT BIBLIOGRAPHY

THE *BÜRGERTUM* AND ITS WORLD-VIEW

LUKÁCS, G., *The Destruction of Reason*, trans. Peter Palmer, London, 1980
MOSSE, GEORGE L., *The Crisis of German Ideology*, London, 1966

104

SAGARRA, EDA, *A Social History of Germany 1648–1914*, London, 1977
STERN, FRITZ, *The Failure of Illiberalism*, New York, 1972; particularly 'The political consequences of the unpolitical German' (pp. 3–25)

CULTURE AND SOCIETY IN GERMANY FROM 1870

HAMANN, RICHARD and JOST HERMAND, *Epochen deutscher Kultur von 1870 bis zur Gegenwart*, 5 vols, Munich, 1971–76
PASCAL, ROY, *From Naturalism to Expressionism: German Literature and Society 1880–1918*, London, 1973
REISS, H. S., *The Writer's Task from Nietzsche to Brecht*, London, 1978

CULTURE AND SOCIETY IN THE WEIMAR REPUBLIC

HERMAND, JOST and FRANK TROMMLER, *Die Kultur der Weimarer Republik*, Munich, 1978
LAQUEUR, WALTER, *Weimar: A Cultural History 1918–33*, London, 1974
ROTHE, WOLFGANG, ed., *Die deutsche Literatur in der Weimarer Republik*, Stuttgart, 1974
SONTHEIMER, KURT, *Antidemokratisches Denken in der Weimarer Republik*, Munich, 1968
TAYLOR, RONALD, *Literature and society in Germany 1918–1945*, Brighton/New Jersey, 1980.
WILLETT, JOHN, *The New Sobriety: Art and Politics in the Weimar Period 1917–1933*, London, 1978
WILLIAMS, C. E., *Writers and Politics in Modern Germany (1918–1945)*, London, 1977

WRITERS, INTELLECTUALS AND LEFT-WING COMMITMENT

General
ADORNO, THEODOR W., 'Engagement', in T.W.A., *Noten zur Literatur III*, Frankfurt am Main, 1965, pp. 109–35.
Aesthetics and Politics: Debates between Ernst Bloch, Georg Lukács, Bertolt Brecht, Walter Benjamin, Theodor Adorno, London, 1977
CAUTE, DAVID, *The Illusion: An Essay on Politics, Theatre and the Novel*, London, 1971
CAUTE, DAVID, *The Fellow-Travellers: A Postscript to the Enlightenment*, London, 1973
MARCUSE, HERBERT, *The Aesthetic Dimension: Towards a Critique of Marxist Aesthetics*, London, 1979
WILLIAMS, RAYMOND, *Marxism and Literature*, Oxford, 1977

In the Weimar Republic
ALBRECHT, FRIEDRICH, *Deutsche Schriftsteller in der Entscheidung: Wege zur Arbeiterklasse 1918–1933*, Berlin/Weimar, 1970

BENJAMIN, WALTER, *Understanding Brecht*, trans. Anna Bostock, London, 1973

BRÜGGEMANN, HEINZ, *Literarische Technik und soziale Revolution: Versuche über das Verhältnis von Kunstproduktion, Marxismus und literarischer Tradition in den theoretischen Schriften Bertolt Brechts*, Reinbek, 1973

DEAK, ISTVAN, *Weimar Germany's Left-Wing Intellectuals: A Political History of the 'Weltbühne' and its Circle*, Berkeley/Los Angeles, 1968

FÄHNDERS, WALTER and MARTIN RECTOR, *Linksradikalismus und Literatur: Untersuchungen zur Geschichte der sozialistischen Literatur in der Weimarer Republik*, 2 vols, Reinbek, 1974

GALLAS, HELGA, *Marxistische Literaturtheorie: Kontroversen im Bund proletarisch-revolutionärer Schriftsteller*, Neuwied/Berlin, 1971

KÄNDLER, KLAUS, *Drama und Klassenkampf: Beziehungen zwischen Epochenproblematik und dramatischem Konflikt in der sozialistischen Dramatik der Weimarer Republik*, Berlin/Weimar, 1970

Part Two

THE ARTISTIC AND THEATRICAL PERSPECTIVE

THE GERMAN THEATRE AS AN ARTISTIC AND SOCIAL INSTITUTION: FROM THE MARCH REVOLUTION TO THE WEIMAR REPUBLIC

CECIL DAVIES

When Brecht declared in 1952 that art – including, of course, the art of the theatre – should be a means of education, but that its aim was entertainment, he was placing himself firmly in the mainstream of the two-centuries-old German dramatic tradition whose classic expression is found in Schiller's essay of 1785, *Die Schaubühne als moralische Anstalt betrachtet* (*The Theatre Considered as a Moral Institution*):

> Die Schaubühne ist die Stiftung, wo sich Vergnügung mit Unterricht, Ruhe mit Anstrengung, Kurzweil mit Bildung gattet.
>
> (The theatre is the establishment where entertainment is united with instruction, rest with exertion, pastime with education.)

This view has been reiterated by one of the most brilliant of living German theatre critics, Günther Rühle, who wrote in 1967 that if the German theatre has a tradition it is not one of style or playing, but of social function.

As the inner character of the German theatre has been determined by the German genius, so has its outward structure been determined by German political history. Because of the fragmentation of Germany before its unification under Bismarck in 1871, and its division into East and West after the Second World War, the country has for much of the time lacked a theatre capital comparable with London or Paris, and though Berlin assumed this position between 1871 and 1945 the strength of the theatre is remarkably evenly distributed not only throughout Germany itself but the whole German-speaking area. It is no accident that the standard High German that culturally unites speakers of diverse dialects from the borders of Scandinavia to those of the Balkans is known as *Bühnendeutsch* (stage German), for despite the failures from the time of Lessing onward to establish a German National Theatre, the theatre has been and remains a powerful agent for the cultural unity of the German-speaking peoples.

It was not always so. In the seventeenth century and the early eighteenth century German theatre presented two virtually unrelated aspects:

the crude mimes and impromptus of the strolling players, and the court theatres dominated by spectacular opera and the French language. It was the literary critic J. C. Gottsched (1700–66) and the great actress-manager Friederike Caroline Neuber (1697–1760) who in the 1730s brought about the turning-point of German drama by establishing a theatre culture dominated by German-language literature, which was taken up by the newly emancipated middle classes to create a powerful tradition of bourgeois theatre. This in turn led to the building of the great nineteenth-century municipal theatres, and thus to civic pride in the theatre. The municipal theatre came to be regarded as an essential feature of a self-respecting community, like the town hall and the fire station, and regular theatre-going, dignified with Sunday best and a sense of occasion, became an accepted and serious part of bourgeois life.

Such an established and respectable theatre was naturally prone to fall into habits of uncreative traditionalism, routine acting, conventionalized scenery and artificial rhetoric, and its significant history, particularly in the four decades from the Year of Revolutions in 1848 to the founding of Otto Brahm's Freie Bühne in 1889, is primarily that of individuals who worked for reforms and of companies dedicated to reformed prac-tices. The latter became possible after the introduction in 1869 of the new industrial code (*Gewerbeordnung*) which established freedom to pursue any trade or profession (*Gewerbefreiheit*) as a basic right, and thus permitted independent theatre managements to operate. Though it was by no means obvious at the time, all the important reforms were tending in the same direction – away from stylized convention and towards naturalism in its many manifestations. Heinrich Laube (Director of the Vienna Burgtheater, 1850–67) asserted the supremacy of the spoken word, taught his actors both an unaffected conversational style for contemporary drawing-room plays and a theatrically effective gran-der manner for the classics, and simplified his scenery to a visual sobri-ety that would not distract the audience from the text. His friend Richard Wagner's struggles, especially after 1864, to create the *Gesamtkunstwerk* (unified work of art) did something surprisingly simi-lar for opera. In spite of the vast orchestra, the mythical story-material and Joseph Hoffmann's conventionally conceived and painted scenery, the production of *The Ring* at Bayreuth was realistic in a totally new way. For his music-drama Wagner demanded singers who were also actors. Much of his own energy went into their training, and he demanded of them naturalism in movement and expression. His 'last request' to the singers before the opening of the first production of *The Ring* was,

Nie dem Publikum etwas sagen sondern immer dem andern; in
Selbstgesprächen nach unten oder nach oben blickend, nie geradeaus.

(Never say anything to the audience, but always to the other actor; in
soliloquy looking down or up, never straight out into the audience.)

The meticulous search for visual historical accuracy in the productions of Charles Kean at the Princess Theatre, London (1851–59) powerfully attracted German directors, including George II, Duke of Saxe-Meiningen, who took charge of his own court theatre in 1870. He, with his wife, the actress Ellen Franz, and his director, Ludwig Chronegk, made the Meiningen Players, with their stress on ensemble playing and the uniquely individual contribution of every supernumerary in every crowd and of every element in every individually designed setting, a decisive influence upon theatrical production from Moscow to New York. Above all, as regards the German theatre, it was from Chronegk that Otto Brahm learnt what he applied to his productions of the new naturalistic drama.

The professional and commercial freedom after 1869 had its dark side, of course, in bankruptcies and underpaid actors. Oscar Blumenthal said sadly: 'In dem Tabaksqualm der "Nikotinbühnen" ersticken allmählich die Hoffnungen der Sanguiniker, welche von der Theaterfreiheit ein goldenes Zeitalter der dramatischen Volksdichtung erträumt hatten.' ('The hopes of the optimists who had dreamed of a Golden Age of popular, national, dramatic poetry arising from theatrical freedom, are gradually being suffocated in the thick tobacco smoke of the "nicotine theatres".') However, the new freedom gave scope for artistic as well as commercial enterprise, especially in Berlin, now capital of the German Empire. In 1883 Adolph L'Arronge, a dramatist, founded the Deutsches Theater. The Company included August Förster, a pupil of Laube's and Josef Kainz, already well known from the Meiningen tours. Its reputation soon rivalled that of the Royal Theatres. Inspired by its success Oscar Blumenthal founded the Lessing Theatre in 1888, and in 1889 Ludwig Barnay, one of the original company of the Deutsches Theater, created the Berliner Theater out of an operetta house – and these were only the most outstanding of a considerable group of privately run theatres.

Meanwhile many of the greatest plays of the new naturalistic dramatists (e.g. Ibsen, Strindberg, Tolstoy), though written during the 1880s, remained, in spite of these theatrical developments, virtually unplayed in Germany, partly because of managerial timidity, but largely because of the severe political censorship. In this situation Otto Brahm, already a notable theatre critic, founded in 1889 his theatre club, Die Freie Bühne (The Independent Theatre) which, because its performances were private, was free of censorship, and because of the prestige of its founders and prominent members, attracted the services of some of the best actors of the day. The Freie Bühne was dedicated to the production of the great naturalistic contemporaries both German and European, and its foundation is in effect that of the modern German theatre, while the influence of Brahm's own style as director, both in the Freie Bühne and, from 1894 to 1904 as *Intendant* (director) of the Deutsches Theater, was immense and lasting. What we know of the first Freie Bühne production (Ibsen's *Ghosts*), really, though not nominally, directed by Brahm, provides vital keys to our understanding of this style. The author's text was restored to the supremacy established by Gottsched and Neuber instead of being subordinated to the demands of scenic spectacle or slow, rhetorical acting. It was neither cut nor altered. In unity of style the production was compared favourably with those of the Meiningen Players; reality, plainness and simplicity characterized every aspect; non-essentials and exaggeration were avoided; silent expressiveness was a noteworthy feature, and the critic Frenzel drew attention to the *Kunstpausen* (artistic pauses) – though he thought them too long! These pauses indicated that Brahm was inaugurating a new stage style, giving the actor time for the psychological effect of word and action to get through to the audience – and this nine years before Stanislavsky's *Seagull*. In a distinguished cast the most highly praised was Emmerich Robert, from the Vienna Burgtheater, as Oswald. The writer and critic Theodor Fontane praised his presentation of a character and a psychological study of neurosis, not just of a 'sick man'. Thus Brahm restored the human element to that central position in the theatrical experience where Schiller had placed it and from which it had been largely displaced during the nineteenth century by elaborate scenery and virtuoso acting. Schiller concludes the essay already quoted by declaring that the effect of theatre on the individual is to leave room for one perception only: that of being a human person. Despite the great and obvious differences between Brahm's naturalistic and Brecht's epic theatre, the person is the central object of study in both. As Brecht says in his *Mahagonny* notes:

Der Mensch ist Gegenstand der Untersuchung.

(The person is the object of investigation.)

Brahm's second production was the first production of the first play of the central figure of German Naturalism, Gerhart Hauptmann's *Vor Sonnenaufgang* (*Before Sunrise*). This, and not *Ghosts*, was for him the real 'new beginning' and the great breakthrough of Naturalism into the German theatre. Although, without losing any essential meaning, Brahm softened Hauptmann's text a little and tactfully eliminated, for example, the off-stage 'cry of a woman in childbirth', the impact of the consistent Naturalism was evidently quite shocking, even though many of the audience had already read the published play and articles about it. The detailed realism of the Act II farmyard setting provoked Frenzel's sarcastic comment that the dunghill and the crowing cock had been left out: but he also disliked the social realism and called the play an offence against morals, sentiment and taste, – a view evidently shared by a certain Dr Kastan who, during the long scene involving the off-stage childbirth, stood up in his seat waving a pair of obstetric forceps and shouting, 'Sind wir denn in einem Bordell?' ('Are we in a brothel, then?'). Brahm's production of Hauptmann's most famous naturalistic play, *Die Weber* (*The Weavers*), was also in low key, for although an explosive production would have provided good publicity for the Freie Bühne, it would have delayed police permission for public performance. In this way Brahm again showed his respect for the author and his play.

Brahm's decade at the Deutsches Theater confirmed and developed the characteristics of his leadership shown in the first two Freie Bühne productions as broadly cultural rather than specifically theatrical. That is to say, he was more concerned with the relationship of drama to contemporary life than with innovations in acting and production.

> Ich gehöre zu den kämpfenden Naturen, und freudig arbeite ich, um die neuen Formen der Dichtkunst durchzusetzen, um dem Theater, das die Fühlung mit dem modernen deutschen Leben zu verlieren droht, seine volle Bedeutung für unser geistiges Leben zurückzugewinnen. (Brahm)
>
> (I belong to the fighting natures, and I work joyfully, in order to carry through the new forms of poetic art so as to win back for the theatre, which threatens to lose touch with modern German life, its full importance for our spiritual and intellectual life.)

His theatre became really an Ibsen–Hauptmann theatre, plus such modern authors as could be played in the same style. Druing these 10 years Brahm put on 45 modern authors, with 10 plays of Ibsen and 14 of Hauptmann, but none by Strindberg, Wilde, Wedekind or Shaw. He soon allowed the number of classics produced to fall rapidly, and of the 24 classical productions during this period, 13 were taken over unaltered from L'Arronge's notebooks. Brahm even adopted L'Arronge's trick of presenting classics uncut on the first night and afterwards omitting whole scenes in the interests of length. In fact, he evaded the whole dramaturgical problem of finding a modern style for classics. Even in modern plays he tended to cut lyric–romantic passages in order to make them approximate more to Naturalism. Cuts and changes were often made during rehearsal, not in the study, and because Brahm was the personal friend of many of the authors, he could discuss changes with them, usually declining to suggest the actual alterations himself: 'Das müssen Sie machen, ich bin kein Dichter.' ('*You* must do that: I'm no poet.') This director–author relationship anticipated much modern practice.

The centrality of the 'person' implied the centrality of the actor – but not of the star personality. In Brahm's new acting style the actor was to be wholly absorbed and submerged in his role and must not play 'cat and mouse' with it or move in and out of character for the sake of theatrical effect, and the individual performer was to keep within the framework of the production as a whole. The highest art was to express on the stage the unique spirit of the actual play presented. Thus even the emphasis on the quality of individual acting was subordinated to that of the ensemble. For him there were no 'parts', only the total effect of the play – yet this supremacy of the artistic object over the artist did not lead to the suppression of the actor as a person. Brahm developed a corporate fellowship among the members of his company, and deliberately offered long contracts which included such practical matters as sick-pay and help for dependents after an actor's death. Like Chronegk, Brahm did not type-cast, and expected every actor to play the part best suited to him. He did not carry a large company: 38 in his first season at the Deutsches Theater, and subsequently under 35, compared with companies of over 50 and 60 at the Lessing and Schiller Theatres. On the whole the Naturalistic plays had smaller casts than classics, but more important to Brahm was the fact that the ensemble could be better achieved in a smaller company.

In spite of the progressive ideas and social purpose expressed in the naturalistic plays it presented, the Freie Bühne was a middle-class association, and the initial average price of its seats (3.50 marks, plus 1 mark subscription) was far too high for working-class people, members of the rapidly expanding urban proletariat, with an average wage of 20 to 25 marks per week. Even in the mid-nineteenth century, when two-thirds of its population was rural, Germany was socially and educationally the most deeply divided country in Western Europe. Between 1850 and 1910 its population nearly doubled, but its urban population quadrupled, so that by 1891 there were over 150,000 factory workers in Berlin alone, and Bismarck's politically unified Germany was socially more deeply divided than ever. The working-class social democratic movement was from its beginnings educational and cultural as well as political, and recognized the particular importance of drama. A one-act play (now lost) by Friedrich Engels was performed at a German workers' festival in 1847, and Ferdinand Lassalle, the principal founder of the German social democratic movement, published in 1859 a tragedy, *Franz von Sickingen*, which used the subject of the Peasants' Revolt to examine reasons for the failure of the March Revolution of 1848. The publication led to a fascinating exchange of letters between Lassalle, Marx and Engels. The great body of working-class drama during the 1860s and 1870s, however, did not concern itself with historical subjects or exceptional individuals, but through agitation pieces, election farces, festival items, *tableaux vivants* and strike plays, with much satire and comedy, dealt with actual contemporary social and national questions, glorified the collective ideal and had heroes with such names as Roth (Red), Fels (Rock) or Frei (Free). The plays were not performed in theatres but in trade-union and left-wing political clubs. For the amateur actors the political and histrionic motives were inextricably interwoven. The middle classes, of course, had no idea of what went on in workers' clubs.

During the period of Bismarck's anti-socialist laws (1878–90) the workers' plays had to disguise their political message, and historical subjects again became popular in the clubs – along with classics and a great deal of light rubbish. The clubs, too, had to disguise themselves as purely social or as literary and debating societies with harmless-sounding or even absurd names. Through these a genuine interest in contemporary literature often developed: Ibsen, Tolstoy and Zola were read and discussed. The members were excited by the expressions of Darwinism and determinism in what they began to see as 'real' art, whose themes, if not socialist, were nevertheless strongly social and were closely related to the theories of environmental influence and historical determinism which were the mode of thought of the Marxist left. Naturalism was adopted as the art of the socialist working class. A club called Alte Tante (Old Aunt) discussed plays produced by the Freie Bühne and decided to seek corporate membership of the association. With this in mind a delegation approached Dr Bruno Wille, a left-wing free-lance writer and lecturer, who was so inspired by the club's enthusiasm that instead of helping it to obtain corporate membership (which he considered to be impracticable) he himself founded a 'Freie Bühne' for working-class people – the Freie *Volks*bühne (Independent *People's* Theatre) – whose first performance, Ibsen's *Pillars of Society*, was given on a Sunday afternoon in October, 1890. This marriage of theatrical Naturalism and social democratic aspiration, this historic conjunction of the artistic and the social in a theatrical institution, is in practical and symbolic terms the uniquely significant event in all subsequent German theatre history. Through it Naturalism reached a new, popular audience; working-class theatre acquired an open and ultimately legal existence; ideological theatre was popularly established; and mass block-booking through audience organizations became a characteristic feature of German theatre-going. The Freie Volksbühne provided the soil out of which the work of a Piscator and a Brecht could grow. It built up over the next three decades a large body of regular theatre-goers primarily drawn from artisans and the lower-paid white-collar workers, with a leadership basically committed to social democracy and open to admit developments and experiments in dramatic style and content.

From the beginning two attitudes to the theatre had been current among social democrats. Some saw theatre as part of the cultural heritage from which the workers had been cut off and which under socialism they would inherit; others saw it as an instrument of social change. Bruno Wille's motto for the Freie Volksbühne, 'Die Kunst dem Volke' ('Art for the People') epitomizes one attitude, and a comment by Béla Balázs on left-wing amateur theatre of the 1920s, the other:

> Ein Kampftheater, das ungeheure Aufopferung forderte, das viele Helden und Märtyrer und eine heroische Geschichte hatte, welche einmal die deutschen Schulkinder lernen werden. Denn es wollte nicht Bühnenstile ändern, sondern die Welt.

> (A Theatre of Struggle, that demanded enormous sacrifices, that had many heroes and martyrs and an heroic history, which German schoolchildren will learn some day. For it didn't want to change theatre-styles, but the world.)

Representatives of both these attitudes were among the founding members of the Freie Volksbühne and it is hardly surprising that within two years ideological differences, reinforced by personal frictions, led to a split in the movement. On the one side Wille stood for literature and dissemination of culture, on the other Julius Türk saw the association as a weapon in the class struggle. Moreover, Wille belonged to the opposition which broke away from the Social Democratic Party (SPD) at the Erfurt conference in 1891 and formed itself into the short-lived Verein unabhängiger Sozialisten (League of Independent Socialists), while Türk remained within the official party (SPD). When Wille was massively defeated at a general meeting of the Freie Volksbühne in October 1892, he and his friends withdrew and formed the Neue Freie Volksbühne (New Independent People's Theatre). After bitter conflicts the two bodies gradually drew closer to each other again but were not finally reunited until 1920. Under Siegfried Nestriepke this new united Volksbühne held to the original ideals of Bruno Wille, but the old dichotomy reappeared in the conflicts between Nestriepke and Piscator.

Brahm's almost immediate successor at the Deutsches Theater was Max Reinhardt, a magnificent eclectic in whose work practically every important theatrical tendency of the age is represented and carried forward from Wilhelmine to Weimar Germany. An Austrian – in contrast with the northern Brahm – he had as a young man absorbed the spectacle and the grand manner of the Vienna Burgtheater. As a brilliant actor of old men he had learnt under Brahm the principles of unexaggerated truth, ensemble playing and unconditional respect for the author's text. He gained early experience in satirical cabaret in his own Schall und Rauch (see Ch. 10 p. 164) which he established even while acting for Brahm. Freed from Brahm's control (at a cost of 14,000 marks for breach of contract) he had quickly discovered his ability to direct actors in parts which he himself could not actually play, and to attune them to each other. After his first big success in 1903 with Gorky's *The Lower Depths* (in German *Nachtasyl, Night Shelter*) which he, playing Luka, in fact directed, though the nominal director was Vallentin, who also played Satin, he moved to his great series of classics, beginning with Lessing's *Minna von Barnhelm* and including his famous Shakespearean productions. In these he anticipated the emotive–spectacular side of Expressionism (which he also later shared in the mass-theatrical effects of his Grosses Schauspielhaus, opened in 1919) and the technical developments of the 1920s. Reinhardt's spectacles and his use of crowds and choruses were, unlike those of Expressionism, fundamentally naturalistic and were normally non-ideological in intention. They may properly be seen as deriving from the Meiningen Players. In particular he applied new technical possibilities to plays in episodic and 'open' form (e.g. Strindberg, Büchner, *Faust II*), and thus led the way towards the visually exciting narrative (*episch*) productions of Piscator, and so ultimately to Brecht's epic theatre, very different though that

C. Davies

was. Reinhardt more than any other director was responsible for bringing Wedekind's plays upon the stage, especially with his historic, albeit heavily cut production of *Frühlings Erwachen (Spring's Awakening)* at the Kammerspiele in 1906 (fifteen years after it was written), a production which finally and conclusively established Wedekind as a serious dramatist. Reinhardt revived the name Schall und Rauch for a post-war cabaret for which Grosz designed and where Walter Mehring's early songs were performed.

Although the 'prodigal genius', as Herbert Jhering called Reinhardt, had no specific ideological orientations, either artistic or political, he played a vital role in the development of the Volksbühne movement. In 1903 before Reinhardt had been widely recognized as an outstanding artist, the chairman of the Neue Freie Volksbühne, Dr Joseph Ettlinger, established a relationship with him which later, thanks to the enterprise of Heinrich Neft, the treasurer, enabled the Neue Freie Volksbühne with a virtual monopoly in cheap seats for Reinhardt productions in both the Deutsches Theater and the Neues Theater, to grow from a tiny society to a mass organization. When the Volksbühne's own theatre, the Theater am Bülowplatz (now the Luxemburgplatz), which was opened on 30 December 1914, was threatened with closure because of the war, it was Reinhardt who took it over and saved it for the movement through those years. Thus came about that fruitful partnership of the basically social democratic and working-class Volksbühne movement with the popular and non-ideological theatre of Reinhardt, which the left regarded in the words of the title of Jhering's pamphlet as *Der Volksbühnenverrat (The Betrayal of the Volksbühne)*, and which is still so regarded in the German Democratic Republic. More justly the partnership may be seen as providing a broad and reliable foundation for the exciting but often unstable experiments of the 1920s.

In the highly wrought emotional atmosphere of the war years the theatre reflected with special intensity the internal conflicts, tensions and changing attitudes of society. The final revulsion against the war was expressed in Reinhard Goering's *Die Seeschlacht (Naval Battle)* (1917) and Fritz von Unruh's *Ein Geschlecht (A Family)* (1918), both of which owed their Berlin performances in 1918 to the patronage of Reinhardt. In the following year Karl-Heinz Martin produced Ernst Toller's *Die Wandlung (Transfiguration)* at his important, though short-lived, political theatre Die Tribüne. *Die Wandlung* showed, in Expressionistic style, the conversion of a young man from being an enthusiastic supporter of the war to being a pacifist – the story, in fact, of the author himself, as well as that of many others. Reinhard Goering, for example, had volunteered in 1914, and von Unruh was a Prussian officer and son of a Prussian general. Over a year earlier, Toller had printed and distributed scenes from the play as an anti-war pamphlet and had had parts of it performed in support of the Munich munition workers' strike. Expressionism with its Whitmanesque verse, its often inflated rhetoric, its dis-

116

torted, 'exploded' settings, its grotesquerie and its passionate idealism became the dominant style of the anti-war pacifists and revolutionaries. Hasenclever's *Der Sohn* (*The Son*) (written 1913), Sorge's *Der Bettler* (*The Beggar*) (written 1911–12), Kornfeld's *Die Verführung* (*Seduction*) (written 1913), Kaiser's *Gas* trilogy (written 1917–19), were outstanding productions of this time (1917–20). As well as the overtly political material, the 'generation gap' was a theme important in this movement. Toller's second play, *Masse Mensch* (*Masses and Man*) again objectified the author's subjective struggles – this time between the moral demands of revolution and those of pacifism, for Toller embodied in himself the major ethical and political controversies of his own lifetime. Jürgen Fehling's production of this play (1921) at the Volksbühne, set on a flight of steps, with choric speech and movement and a dream-like atmosphere, was declared by the keenest left-wing theatre critic of the day, Herbert Jhering, to be the season's best production.

Even while the Expressionist movement was at its height the reaction against it and against the mass emotionalism associated with it was growing. Similarly Reinhardt's spectacular and stirring production of Romain Rolland's *Danton* at the Grosses Schauspielhaus in 1920 provoked a bitter poem from Kurt Tucholsky, who contrasted the revolutionary fervour of the audience with the lack of any resulting political action. In the theatre as in every branch of the arts at this time, there was a trend away from Expressionism to what became known as *Die Neue Sachlichkeit* (The New Sobriety), and the cool, critical tones of Brecht's first plays, *Baal* and *Trommeln in der Nacht* (*Drums in the Night*), were closely in harmony with the new movements in art and poetry. Brecht, like Toller, had been converted from a pro-war to an anti-war attitude but was five years younger than him. He therefore missed active service in the war and was too young to be caught up in the wave of Expressionism. Nevertheless, the effect upon him of his experience as a medical orderly in the Augsburg military hospital, expressed in the bitter *Legende vom toten Soldaten* (*Legend of the Dead Soldier*), was indelible, and *Baal* is written as much in reaction against the bourgeois cult of the hero's life as against Hanns Johst's Expressionist play *Der Einsame* (*The Solitary*), about the nineteenth-century Romantic poet Grabbe. The influence of Wedekind, especially as cabarettist, also contributed to Brecht's bypassing the Expressionist movement. From him Brecht derived the art of using realistic detail, verbal and visual, in a non-naturalistic framework.

For others the war experience broke down the barrier between art and life. 'Von der Kunst zur Politik' ('From art to politics') is how Piscator heads the first chapter of *Das politische Theater* (*The Political Theatre*) in which he describes how his experience of 'front theatre' turned him away from 'pure' art for ever. He banned the word 'art' in the Second Proletarian Theatre (1920) and declared that his plays were proclamations intended to lead to political action on contemporary events. His designer was Helmut Herzfelde who, with no knowledge of England or English, had changed his name by deed poll to John Heartfield in protest against wartime anti-British propaganda. Heartfield, Dadaist and Communist, worked for three years (1920–23) as chief designer for Reinhardt. He designed for Toller's *Die Maschinenstürmer* (*The Machine Wreckers*) (1922) directed by Karl-Heinz Martin, and for Piscator's revue *Trotz alledem!* (*In Spite of Everything!*) (1925) and his production of Friedrich Wolf's *Tai Yang erwacht* (*Tai Yang Awakes*) (1931). He was an important graphic artist and the first and greatest exponent of the art of montage. His propaganda montages, especially those created for the *Arbeiter-Illustrierte-Zeitung* (*Workers' Illustrated Paper*), developed this into the characteristic art-form of the left during the Weimar Republic period. The debt owed by Piscator's productions and Brecht's plays to Heartfield's montage art is incalculable. Brecht's tabulated contrasts between dramatic and epic theatre in his *Mahagonny* notes include:

Wachstum   : *Montage*

(*Development* : *Montage*)

New styles of drama imply new styles of acting. Prototype of the new generation of actors was Werner Krauss, who when young had acted with Wedekind and who made his mark as Fourth Sailor in Goering's *Seeschlacht* in 1918. 'Werner Krauss ist so besessen von seinen inneren Erfahrungen, dass er mit vertauschten Sinnen spielt. Es ist, als ob er die Töne sähe und die Gebärden hörte', wrote Jhering. ('Werner Krauss is so possessed by his inner experiences that he plays with his senses interchanged. It is as if he saw sounds and heard gestures'.) Such synaesthesia is, of course, a characteristic of Expressionist poetry. The young actors seized upon the rhythms and expression of the roles in the new texts and carried these rhythms over into the performance of classical roles. And as the décor of the Expressionist designers broke down the old perspectives and destroyed the theatre of illusion, so, suddenly, it seemed, the directors were ready to discover new unities of scene and action. The old unities were replaced by 'open' form which, though as old as Reinhold Lenz and Büchner, now in the open and questioning society of the 1920s came into its own at last. In large theatres and small, the Tribüne and the Grosses Schauspielhaus, directors in their productions broke through the barrier of the proscenium arch which in the illusionist theatre had divided the world of the play from that of the audience, and brought play and audience into a new, creative relationship.

Because of the changes in acting and production styles demanded by the work of the younger dramatists the post-war period was rich not only in new plays but in new interpretations of the classics. In seeking to underline the contemporary significance of these, imaginative directors went far beyond what had normally beeen thought of as 'interpretation'. Leopold Jessner, *Intendant* of the Staatliches Schauspielhaus in Berlin from 1919 to 1930, began to interpret Shakespeare and other classics boldly – an 'estimable vandal' ('schätzenswerter Vandale'), Brecht called him. Although, like Reinhardt, Jessner had taken as his starting-point Brahm's theatre, basing productions firmly on the interpretation of the author's text, he had moved from it in a different direction. Where Reinhardt put on the stage characters, colours and moods, Jessner, sweeping aside psychological detail, presented in simple, concentrated form the fundamental characteristics of the typical. He was more interested in the idea behind the story than in its outward nuances. Despite his cavalier treatment of the classics and the originality and vividness of his visual effects, he was, as he himself declared, 'ein Regisseur des Wortes und nicht der Decoration' ('a régisseur of the word and not of the décor'). Typical of Jessner's work is his *Richard III* production of November 1920. In his hands the play was neither a history nor the study of a psychopath, but the vision of a headlong career up the 'one-way street of power' (Kortner). Jessner used a huge staircase upon whose ups and downs Richard's fate was played out both literally and symbolically – the famous 'Jessner steps' or 'Jessner stage'.

> Hier wurde dem Publikum nicht mehr ein schleimiger hinkender Intrigant vorgeführt, sondern der neue 'Held', der von Ehrgeiz gestachelt bis zur letzten Stufe des Throns über Leichen weg emporsteigt. (Jessner)
>
> (What was presented to the audience here was no longer a slimy, limping intriguer, but the new 'hero' who, goaded by ambition climbs his way up over corpses to the final rank of the throne.)

Jessner saw his task as that of bodying forth in direct and uncluttered theatrical presentation the basic ideas underlying the author's text.

Inspired – or, rather, provoked – by Jessner's example, Brecht reworked Marlowe's *Edward II* (1924) in 'open' form, seeking to distance the audience from the action. Both his methods and his end-product were, however, very different from those of Jessner, who continued to be clearly related to the Expressionists. Brecht was prepared to rewrite and reconstruct the play radically, to use it as raw material for his own conceptions and to show little respect for the intentions of the original author. The setting by Caspar Neher was simplified and stylized, and Brecht used non-naturalistic visual effects such as coating the soldiers' faces thickly with chalk to indicate their fear before battle. At the same time he insisted on realistic detail, as in the hanging of Gaveston, and on absolute emotional truth in speech and action. Although scarcely anyone outside the company realized it, the seeds of a new way of writing plays and a new style of acting came into being in this production, despite its imperfections. At the time, too, it was to some extent eclipsed by a version of the play, now lost, associated with the name of Karl-Heinz Martin, which had been presented a few months before by the Schauspieler Theater (Actors' Theatre), an anti-commercial professional group set up in June 1923 by a number of prominent Berlin actors. Erich Engel's production of Shakespeare's *Coriolanus* (1925) was seen by Brecht as a decisive attempt at epic theatre. In September 1926 Piscator produced Schiller's *Die Räuber* (*The Robbers*) in Jessner's Staatliches Schauspielhaus. He turned the play on its head, cutting and altering ruthlessly and with utter lack of regard for the author's intention so that Spiegelberg, in Trotsky make-up, could become the Communist hero of the play. The production raises in acute form the question as to whether a director can, without immorality, try to make a new work through his production, or whether the proper course is not for a poet to write a new play, as Goethe wrote a new *Iphigenie auf Tauris*. Julius Bab wrote of Piscator's production:

> Der Versuch eines Regisseurs mit seinen Mitteln eine neue Dichtung zu schaffen, ist ästhetisch so aussichtslos, dass er ein wenig ans Unmoralische streift. Denn (wohl in Unklarheit über sein eigenes Handeln) weiter behauptet er, Schiller zu inszenieren, und das grenzt dann doch an eine Fälschung.

> (A director's attempt to create a new poem with the means at his disposal is aesthetically so hopeless that it verges a little on immorality. For (perhaps not clear over what he is doing) he further asserts that he is staging Schiller, and that borders upon falsification.)

Less extreme than this production, but nevertheless showing the same desire to squeeze contemporary rather than eternal truth from the classics, was Jessner's own *Hamlet* three months later, in which the external background of court intrigue became far more important than the internal psychological struggle and which was so directed that the audience was strongly aware of actual parallels with modern German history – Claudius, for instance, as Kaiser Wilhem II, Polonius as Bethman-Hollweg. Brecht himself throughout his career not only freely adapted existing plays but also wrote new works on old models, always with the aim of giving contemporary (and, as time went on, Marxist) significance to the older play. Though some of these reworkings are among his weakest productions they also include the masterpiece of the 1920s *Die Dreigroschenoper* (*The Threepenny Opera*), in which Weill's reinterpretation of the conventions of operatic music are as important as Brecht's text – a fact borne out by the poverty (in spite of Casparius' wonderful photography) of the film version, where the musical element is minimized and the action depicted realistically.

The changed, post-war democratic Germany with its government of the centre, assailed from the very start by the forces of the extreme left and right, was mirrored not only in the artistic but also in the social character of its theatre. The 'Royal' theatres became 'state' theatres, still officially subsidized but now lacking the aura of the court. Provincial theatre, already well established, acquired new life. The Volksbühne immediately became a national movement in keeping with the political emancipation of the German people. It did not, as the Communist left alleged, become an association of the well-to-do, but primarily of the higher grades of artisans and lower grades of white-collar workers and their families. Large theatres were the order of the day. The Volksbühne Theatre on the Bülowplatz, with almost 2,000 seats, was the largest in Berlin when completed in 1914, and Reinhardt's Grosses Schauspielhaus (1919) was another 'mass' theatre: these had to be filled, a factor which naturally affected their policies. When Piscator left the Volksbühne in 1927 to establish the Piscator-Bühne, he needed a theatre with 3,000 to 3,500 seats in order to pay for his expensive productions, but had to put up with the Theater am Nollendorfplatz with only 1,100 and so had to charge what he himself admitted were 'Kurfürstendamm prices of the Communist theatre'. Thus ironically he played to an audience wealthier in part than that of the Volksbühne, which he had criticized for what he regarded as its political timorousness, but which in fact, economic factors apart, was its deliberate policy of not becoming a propaganda theatre.

In contrast with the wealthy, who paid up to 100 marks for a seat on the opening night of the Piscator-Bühne (3 September 1927, the play being Toller's *Hoppla, wir leben!* *'Hurrah, we're alive!'*) were the members of the special sections of the Volksbühne, whose programme was arranged to include a high proportion of visits to Piscator's theatre.

> Neben den feinen Leuten, die Frack und Smoking zur Feier des Abends gewählt und ihre Damen mit den schon frühzeitig ausgemotteten Winterpelzen und vielleicht schon bezahlten Perlenkolliers geschmückt hatten, standen, kattungekleidet, mit Wandervogelhosen und Schillerkragen, die Gott sei dank sehr gesunden und sommerlich gebräunten Jünglinge und Mädchen, die von der bevorzugten und sonst überall sichtbaren Premierengesellschaft deutlich und standesgemäss abgesondert bleiben wollten.

> (Along with the fine folk who had chosen tailcoats and dinner-jackets to celebrate the evening and had decked out their ladies with winter furs prematurely taken out of moth-balls and pearl chokers that had perhaps been paid for by now, stood – wearing cotton clothes, with hiking shorts and open-necked shirts – the very healthy (thank God!) lads and girls, with summery sun-tan, who clearly and in accordance with their status wished to remain detached from the privileged first night society which was otherwise everywhere in evidence.)

This sharp division in the audience was remarked upon by several critics. Stefan Grossmann, the editor of *Das Tage-Buch*, wrote:

> Sieben Uhr: Auffahrt der Autos, Anmarsch der Windjacken. Im Gedränge war es unklar, was heute Festkleid war, Smoking oder Kniehose und Leinenjoppe. Ein Mann kam in Frack mit weisser Weste, es war der Vertreter des Polizeipräsidiums, er, der Festlichste von allen.

> (Seven o'clock: the cars drive up, the anoraks advance. In the crowd it wasn't clear what constituted evening dress today – dinner-jacket or shorts

121

and cotton top. One man came in tails and white waistcoat: he was the representative of police headquarters, the dressiest person of all!)

Neither group represented the audience of ordinary workers and their families that Piscator really wanted to reach, and Hans W. Fischer concluded his critique:

> Zu einem Theater, wie es sich Piscator wünscht, fehlt jetzt nur noch das Publikum, das genau dieses Theater braucht und trägt: ob es vorhanden ist, entscheidet nicht die Premiere, sondern die – nahe – Zukunft!

> (The only thing now still lacking for a theatre such as *Piscator* wants is the audience that needs and supports precisely *this* theatre: whether that audience can be found, is not decided by the first night, but by the future – the near future!)

In the event that audience was apparently not found.

Piscator fully documented his own view of his relationship with the Volksbühne in his book *Das Politische Theater* (1929), Ernst Toller was the 'opposition speaker' on behalf of the Piscator supporters at the stormy annual national conference of the Volksbühne held at Magdeburg in June 1927, and Brecht had already made his attitude clear in 1926. The monthly periodical *Die Scene* had asked a number of young writers, including Toller, Hans J. Rehfisch, Johannes R. Becher and Brecht for their opinions concerning the Volksbühne, and had published the replies in its June 1926 issue under the heading 'Die Volksbühnenbewegung und die junge Generation' ('The Volksbühne movement and the young generation'). Brecht's reply is unequivocal:

> Die Volksbühne... hat nur den alten, überholten Theaterbetrieb auf andere Weise weitergeschleppt und ist heute nichts weiter als ein nichtsnutziger Verschleiss von Theaterkarten an ihre Mitglieder, die auf Gnade und Ungnade einer Kommission verfallen sind. Was kann eine Kommission schon leisten? Nichts! (*GW*, 15, 102)

> (The Volksbühne... has simply perpetuated the old, outmoded theatre-business under a different guise, and is nowadays nothing but a redundant organization peddling tickets to its members, who are dependent upon the whims of a commission. What can a commission do? Nothing!)

When the storm broke in 1927 over Piscator's production of Ehm Welk's *Gewitter über Gottland* (*Storm over Gotland*), Brecht was if anything even more fiercely critical. To the accusation that the play was politically committed, Brecht retorted that other Volksbühne productions were also 'committed':

> Sie haben die klare Tendenz zur Verdummung des Publikums, zur Verflachung der Jugend, zur Unterdrückung freier Gedanken gezeigt. (*GW*, 15, 103)

> (They showed a clear commitment to stupefying the audience, feeding trivia to young people and suppressing freedom of thought.)

Brecht concluded that nobody interested in a really vital theatre would continue to support the Volksbühne.

When the following year Jhering published his pamphlet *Volksbühnenverrat* (*The Betrayal of the Volksbühne*) Brecht numbered it (in answer to a questionnaire) among the four best books of the year,

> .... Weil sie einen Versuch darstellt, das Theater als öffentliche Angelegenheit zu betrachten und darauf Einfluss auszuüben. (*GW* 18, 66)

> (... because it represents an attempt to consider the theatre as a public concern and to bring influence to bear upon it.)

The sixteen-page pamphlet, which was also cited at length by Piscator in *Das Politische Theater*, argued that the original ideals of the Volksbühne had been betrayed over the years by its officers and committee. Jhering took his stand with Piscator and with those who, even from the foundation of the movement, had seen it as an instrument for political change rather than as a means of bringing culture to the underprivileged. He saw the alliance with Reinhardt as the turning-point for the Volksbühne, the break in the movement, the betrayal and the beginning of what he believed to be its decline. Reinhardt was in Jhering's view the natural enemy of the Volksbühne movement and the alliance an emergency action, an error to be righted in the future. That the Volksbühne leaders came to accept Reinhardt's eclectic 'luxury' theatre as the true way for it to follow was, he thought, the betrayal. As we have already noticed, Jhering could not but recognize Reinhardt's genius. Similarly he could not deny the status of 'classic' and 'recognized greatness' to Friedrich Kayssler, the Volksbühne's theatre director from 1918 to 1923. He objected, however, to the almost religious reverence with which Kayssler demanded the art of the theatre to be regarded, and believed such reverence led to sleep and theatrical death. For Kayssler's successor, Fritz Holl, who had in fact first invited Piscator to direct a play at the Volksbühne theatre, Jhering even lacks respect as an artist. Under him, he says, shapelessness succeeded shapelessness and the theatre's programme became one long play of colour and form, sometimes under one title, sometimes under another.

Another change in the theatre as Brecht found it was its freedom. In Wilhelmine Germany, right to the end, theatre had been subject to censorship, the Volksbühne in particular had suffered from police harassment, and the fight against the censor would undoubtedly have become more intense had not war broken out. In the post-war political atmosphere social and political questions ranging from naval mutiny to the abortion law could be raised in the theatre, and what came to be called the *Zeitstück* (the play concerned with immediately contemporary problems) became one of the most significant genres between 1920 and 1933. Toller's *Hinkemann* (1923), the tragedy of a soldier castrated by a war wound; Bruckner's *Verbrecher* (*Criminals*) (1928), with a multiple setting that exposed a whole cross-section of society; Wolf's *Cyankali*

(*Cyanide*) (1929) and Credé's '*§218*' (1929), both attacking the anti-abortion law, are but a few examples out of many *Zeitstücke*, whose authors included Rehfisch, Weisenborn, von Horváth, Mühsam and others. Toller's *Der entfesselte Wotan* (*Wotan Unchained*) (performed in Russia in 1924, in Germany in 1925, but published in September 1923, less than two months before Hitler's Munich Putsch) is a terrifying anticipation of the Nazis. (In 1926 Fehling used Hitler make-up for the part of Wotan.) It is written as a comedy, but the God Wotan in a Prologue from Valhalla warns the audience:

> O Publikum! Lach nicht zu früh!
> Einst lachtest du zu spät
> Und zahltest deine Blindheit mit lebendgen Leibern.
> Lach nicht zu früh!
> Doch – lach zur rechten Zeit!

(O Audience, don't laugh too soon. Once you laughed too late and paid for your blindness with living bodies. Don't laugh too soon! Still – laugh at the right time!)

No account of the theatrical scene as Brecht found it would be complete without some reference to the amateur dramatic movement of the social democratic and Communist left. Until 1928 the social democratic societies were organized largely within the Deutscher-Arbeiter-Theater-Bund (German Workers' Theatre Union). In that year the Union was taken over by a carefully organized Communist majority and became, as the Arbeiter-Theater-Bund-Deutschlands (Workers' Theatre Union of Germany), the German section of the Moscow-based International Workers' Theatre Movement, and the seceding social democrats formed the Arbeiter-Laienspieler-Verband (Workers' Amateur Players' Union) (1930) with support from the SPD.

For the use of social democratic amateur groups the Leipzig publisher Alfred Jahn brought out during this period scores of one-act and full-length plays on working-class themes – socialism, capitalism, contemporary political events, the church, the abortion law, free love and so on. Apart from plays like these (which naturally varied enormously in quality), the working-class amateur movement developed several characteristic theatrical forms: the *Massenspiel* (mass play); *Sprechchor* (speaking chorus); Living Newspaper, and *Lehrstück* (teaching piece). The most important *Massenspiele* were those performed in Leipzig each August from 1920 to 1924. The first of these was *Spartakus*, in which an amateur cast of 900, under professional direction, presented a pageant of the revolt of Roman slaves to an audience of 50,000. Supported by the Independent Social Democratic Party, the pageants continued until 1924. Two were based on outlines provided by the imprisoned Ernst Toller, but the final productions were less immediate in their impact than the earlier ones. The *Massenspiele* were largely inspirational in their effect.

The *Sprechchor* (the word is applied both to the speaking choirs and the works they performed) developed from recitations given at workers' festivals. From solo recitation came group and dramatized recitation of existing poems. Then works began to be written specifically for *Sprechchor* performance. Some were written by intellectuals like Toller, others by poets from the working classes, such as Bruno Schönlank. The majority of *Sprechöre* belong to the '*O Mensch!*' ('O Man!') school of poetry associated with Expressionist drama and their impact is primarily emotional. They continued to be popular with social democratic groups right up to the end of the Weimar Republic. Sometimes they developed into elaborate performances with speech, movement, scenery, and lighting and sound effects. The Communists wanted something more didactic and concrete, and in 1923 the leader of the central *Sprechchor* of the Communist Party of Germany (KPD), Gustav von Wangenheim, wrote and produced his *Chor der Arbeit* (*Chorus of Work*). Although this is quite a remarkable piece of work the *Sprechchor* form did not lend itself to didacticism and direct propaganda, and the dramatic art of the far left found its most appropriate expressions in Living Newspaper and *Lehrstücke*.

Piscator's brilliantly successful *Revue Roter Rummel* (*Red Revue*) of November 1924, in which he used both professional actors and working-class amateurs, led in the following year to a proliferation of amateur Red Revues of varying quality. From these grew the agitprop groups which presented left-wing revues all over the country. A renewed impetus was given to this movement when the Moscow 'Blue Blouses' toured Germany in the autumn of 1927 with their so-called Living Newspaper. (The programme – no actual script survives – suggests that 'Living Magazine' would have been a more precise description.) The agitprop groups now gave themselves names like Red Blouses and Blue Blouses, and adopted many of the Russians' ideas and techniques. One of these was the inclusion in the revues of short didactic scenes. The importance of these was quickly realized. The relative merits of mass drama and short scenes were debated in the pages of *Arbeiter Bühne* (*Workers' Theatre*), the journal of the now Communist Arbeiter-Theater-Bund-Deutschlands. From these grew the short didactic play, the *Lehrstück*, as an independent form. It was given literary status by Wolf, Wangenheim and of course by Brecht himself.

In conclusion, two theatrical moments, each from a celebrated *Zeitstück*, may serve both to actualize and symbolize the state of the German theatre as an artistic and social institution in the 1920s. The first is the closing scene of Piscator's production of Alfons Paquet's *Fahnen* (*Flags*) in 1924, his first production for the Volksbühne and the first play to be called by its director *An Epic Drama* (*Ein episches Drama*). (The author called it *A Dramatic Novel* (*Ein dramatischer Roman*).) This play virtually renounced dramatic form to allow the plain facts to be narrated and presented, so the director believed, clearly and objectively with accompanying slide-projections like the subtitles of the silent cinema. Yet this production, claiming to present sober fact, actually played on mass emotion just as Reinhardt's *Danton* production had done, and was basically different from the coolness, detachment and stimulus to constructive thought aimed at by Brecht in *his* conception of epic theatre. At the end of the play when the three great black flags which give it its name were dipped over the coffins of the martyred workers, 'brach ein Beifall los, der fast etwas Revolutionäres an sich hatte' ('a round of applause broke out which almost had something revolutionary in it'). These are Piscator's own words. Once again, however, revolutionary theatre did not lead to revolution, but its techniques for rousing mass emotion were adopted by the forces of the right in the great, banner-hung Nuremberg rallies of the Nazis.

The second moment is from Toller's *Hoppla, wir leben!* the first production (1927) of the Piscator-Bühne, which opened before that strangely mixed audience of conspicuous wealth and youthful radicalism described in the press. The hero of the play, Karl Thomas, is, like Toller himself, a post-war revolutionary. After the failure of revolution he is condemned to death and then with his friend Wilhelm Kilman, pardoned. But he suffers a breakdown and spends eight years in an asylum (as Toller spent five years in a fortress), returning to the outside world in 1927 to find that Kilman is a minister in the new state, obliged to compromise with reactionaries and capitalists. In despair Thomas, now a waiter, plans to shoot Kilman. Kilman and his wife are having a working dinner with a prominent banker in a private room of the Grand Hotel, with Thomas as waiter. Thomas reveals himself to Kilman, who tries to pass off the embarrassing situation. He and the banker offer Thomas money:

> (*Karl Thomas, der mit der einen Hand den Revolver in der Tasche umkrallt, sieht fassungslos auf das Geld, zuckt, angewidert, die Schultern, so als wenn er der Tat müde wäre und will sich umdrehen.*)
>
> KARL THOMAS: Es lohnt sich nicht. Du wirst mir grenzenlos gleichgültig.
>
> (*Da öffnet sich leise die Tür. Student im Kellnerfrack kommt herein. Hebt den Revolver über Karl Thomas Schulter. Dreht das elektrische Licht aus. Schuss.*
> *Schrei.*)
>
> BANKIER: Licht! Licht! Der Kellner hat auf den Minister geschossen.
>
> (*Vorhang*)

(Akt III Sz. II)

> (*Karl Thomas, who is clawing at the revolver in his pocket with one hand, looks disconcertedly at the money, shrugs his shoulders in disgust as if he were weary of the affair and wants to turn round.*)
>
> KARL THOMAS: It's not worth while. You've become a matter of complete indifference to me.

*(Then the door opens softly. Student in waiter's jacket enters. Raises
revolver over Karl Thomas' shoulder. Switches off the electric light.
Shot.
Cry.)*

BANKER: Light! Light! The waiter has shot at the Minister.

(Curtain)

The student is a Nazi who wants to shoot Kilman, 'Weil er ein Bols-
chewik, weil er ein Revolutionär ist. Weil er unser Land an die Juden
verkauft.' ('Because he is a Bolshevik, because he is a revolutionary.
Because he is selling out our country to the Jews.')
'Ist die Welt ein Irrenhaus geworden?' ('Has the world become a mad-
house?'), cries Thomas.

The scene dramatizes not only the situation of the German government during the Weimar Republic, constantly driven into compromises
and always bitterly attacked from left and right, but also the situation of
the theatre, in which non-revolutionary progressives, like the management of the Volksbühne, were attacked from the right by bodies like the
Grossdeutsche Theatergemeinschaft (Great German Theatre Society)
and from the left by Toller himself, Piscator, the Communist Party, and
by Brecht as well – the very people to be driven into exile or to suffer
eclipse or extermination under the Nazis, along with all that was worthy
and humane in the German theatre.

SELECT BIBLIOGRAPHY

BAB, J., *Über den Tag hinaus: kritische Betrachtungen*, ed. H. Bergholz. Ver-
öffentlichungen der deutschen Akademie für Sprache und Dichtung, Darmstadt, 1960

BRAULICH, H., *Die Volksbühne: Theater und Politik in der deutschen Volksbühnenbewegung*, Berlin, 1976 (A Communist view)

DAVIES, C., *Theatre for the People: The Story of the Volksbühne*, Manchester,
1977

JHERING, H., *Von Reinhardt bis Brecht. Eine Auswahl der Theaterkritiken
1909–32*, edited with an introduction by R. Badenhausen, Reinbek, 1967

KNILLI, F., and MÜNCHOW, U., *Frühes Deutsches Arbeitertheater 1847–1918:
Eine Dokumentation*, Munich, 1970

MELCHINGER, S., *Max Reinhardt*, Hanover, 1968

OSBORNE, J., *The Naturalistic Drama in Germany*, Manchester, 1971

RÜHLE, G., *Theater für die Republik 1917–1933 im Spiegel der Kritik*, Frankfurt am Main, 1967

RÜHLE, G., *Theater in unserer Zeit*, Frankfurt am Main, 1976

SIEPMANN, E., *Montage: John Heartfield, vom Club Dada zur Arbeiter-
Illustrierten-Zeitung*, Berlin (West), 1977

TÜTEBERG, M., *Heartfield*, Reinbek, 1978

WILLETT, J., *The New Sobriety, 1917–1933: Art and Politics in the Weimar
Period*, London, 1978

ACTING METHODS: BRECHT AND STANISLAVSKY

MARGARET EDDERSHAW

> 'It is easy to dream and create theories in art,
> but it is hard to practise them.'
>
> KONSTANTIN STANISLAVSKY

There can be few theatrical figures of the twentieth century who have been surrounded by more debate or who have been followed by more avid disciples than Brecht and Stanislavsky. Both men have had enormous influence on the practice and development of Western theatre during this century: Brecht on staging methods and playwriting, Stanislavsky on the training and techniques of the actor. And their names are constantly linked because of the way they, apparently, neatly represent two directly opposed viewpoints, viewpoints that come at either end of the spectrum of possibilities of the way a play makes its communication with its audience.

Let us consider how these viewpoints manifest themselves in the playhouse. How can we tell the difference between a Stanislavskian and a Brechtian performance?

Imagine we are members of an audience awaiting the start of a conventional play to be performed by a company of Stanislavsky-trained actors. The lights in the auditorium dim and the proscenium arch curtains in front of us open to reveal what to all intents and purposes is a 'real' location, for example, a room fully decorated, furnished and lit. 'Life' is going on in this room: 'real' people come and go, moving 'naturally' in their seemingly real environment, talking to each other, carrying out their activities and behaving towards each other in a manner that convinces us of their actuality as people. These people are not aware of us, it seems; we are privileged voyeurs, peeping through an imaginary 'fourth wall', perhaps uneasy about making our presence felt. A part of us 'believes' that what we see is as real as our own lives: we suspend our disbelief. We are moved, amused or shocked by those we observe, reacting emotionally and mentally to them as we would if we met them outside the theatre.

As we follow the characters' experiences, we see them change in mood, age or outlook in a way that persuades us that time is passing and that events are taking place (including those we do not actually witness). And we perceive these changes as part of a cause and effect pattern in which people's psyches, the way they are, contribute to what happens to them; the 'meaning' of their stories lies in the interaction of character and fate. As the story progresses, the events in the characters' lives become more complicated, conflicts that occur are more pronounced, and a stage of momentous decision for the principals is reached. Then a resolution is arrived at – by accident or design – and the story comes to a natural end, be it sad or happy. At that point the characters disappear behind their curtain, and we are released from their story and their emotions to our actual world, to an auditorium suddenly lit.

Now let us take our seats for a Brechtian play. When we sit, the playing area is plainly visible – even the stage machinery and the playhouse wall beyond the scanty set. The set itself will provide a background for the actors and a token description of their location, but is clearly a set. The actors at first perhaps mingle with the audience at the bar or chat with the musicians, and the beginning of the performance is signalled by their donning part of their costume in front of us. The band starts to play harsh, emphatic music, provocative and not atmospheric, and the actors advance to the edge of the stage to sing to and at us. At the end of the song one of the actors announces the first scene which is to follow and then several others 'switch' into acting the first episode of the play, outlining the story. The acting is, as it will be throughout, in an almost cartoon style, using sparse vocal effects and clear, diagrammatic gestures; mimicry rather than behaviour. During the scene the actors at some points appear to be speaking to each other in a relatively realistic way as though we were not present, and at other moments they address us directly, implicating us in the play's action and involving us in the performance. When the episode is finished the actors indicate this by simply becoming themselves, becoming actors again. Our attention is constantly being demanded and redirected by the rapid changes from dialogue to song, from humour to a more serious tone. We never forget we are in the theatre and at the same time we are constantly made aware that what the actors are showing us has a basis in real life; it relates to the processes by which we control our own lives. And at the end of the play, when the episodic action has allowed the full demonstration of a particular point, the actors again put off their roles to invoke our ratification of the statement they have made. And we are sent out of the playhouse to act upon our new knowledge.

Naturally, these two theatre 'accounts' are necessarily simplified but should serve to remind us that it is ultimately the end-product, the audience's experience in the playhouse, that matters and not the theories which lie behind that end-product. And both Stanislavsky and Brecht were men of the theatre first and theorists second, and they codified the theoretical basis of their views on theatre only after years of practical experimentation.

Stanislavsky's forty years of theatre research were carried out with the Moscow Art Theatre, a company he founded in 1898 with the Moscow literary critic and drama teacher, Nemirovich-Danchenko. Both men disliked the contemporary theatre in several of its aspects: its lack of seriousness and artistic integrity, its 'star' system, its neglect of adequate training for actors and rehearsal for plays, and its moribund repertoire. And so they began the Moscow Art Theatre with the explicit aim of correcting these faults. Within a year their company was famous for its achievements in a style of production that was markedly naturalistic. And it became almost instantly known for its interpretations of the plays of the great contemporary writer, Anton Chekhov.

Stanislavsky's primary concern was with the actor, and in particular with the methods by which the actor could attain a 'truthful', convincing performance. He therefore evolved his so-called acting 'System' which, he insisted, was not something new but was merely a codifying of what most great actors had done and still did. It drew together into a coherent whole an approach for the 'non-genius' actor who could not and should not rely on inspiration alone to create a satisfactory performance. The principle objective of the System was thus to aid the actor in creating an illusion of actuality on stage and in convincing the audience that he was portraying a real person, that his feelings and thoughts were exactly those of the character he embodied. Embodiment becomes the key to this particular style of acting.

The System is elaborated in three books, *An Actor Prepares* (1937), *Building a Character* (1949) and *Creating a Role* (1961), the latter two published posthumously. In *An Actor Prepares* Stanislavsky attempted to systemize the psychological and emotional preparation an actor needed both for his personal development and for the creation of a particular role. In *Building a Character*, the physical and vocal training and techniques required to communicate the varied aspects of a role to an audience were summarized. And in the third book, *Creating a Role*, Stanislavsky gave detailed examples of the application of the System, as formulated in the previous books, to specific roles. This last book also contains developments and amendments in the approach to acting which were the results of the author's maturing experience. The System, as described in the three books, itself falls into three parts.

In simple terms, the first part of this threefold System, the 'internal' preparation of the actor, focuses on the development of the actor's imagination, observation, concentration and emotions. The preparation includes training exercises for the actor in imagining himself in the 'given circumstances' of an imagined character, so that by means of what Stanislavsky called the 'creative if', the actor could go on to imagine how that person would feel and behave *if* those circumstances were real rather than fictional. This is, of course, what most actors did and do when trying to portray a character; Stanislavsky was stressing the importance of training and practice to sharpen the actor's ability to do this accurately and well, and to repeat it at will. And a further important aspect is the detailing of exercises which will enable the actor to be able to recall and re-create past emotions and experiences of his own that are analagous to those required for particular moments in the 'life' of his role. This Stanislavsky termed 'emotion memory'.

Stanislavsky's fierce criticism of many contemporary actors who 'played to the gallery' or were only concerned with the audience's reaction to them personally (as performers rather than as the characters they played) led to considerable emphasis in the System on the actor's concentration (that is, concentration on his fictional role rather than on his stage presence). In *An Actor Prepares*, there is a discussion of the problem for the actor of the 'black hole', that fourth wall through which the audience watches and by so doing tends to distract the actor, causing him to lose his mental and emotional involvement in his part. Stanislavsky advised that to combat this the actor must strive to achieve what he called 'public solitude', the kind of concentration which enables the actor to behave as though no one were watching him.

By developing his inner resources, the actor reaches a state of preparation in which he can achieve 'the subconscious through the conscious'. By this phrase Stanislavsky denotes the kind of inspired acting in which conscious preparation gives way to unconscious achievement, when acting is lifted on to a higher plane than that of mere technical competence, and the truthful embodiment by the actor of his role occurs.

The 'external' preparation of the actor, that is of his body and voice, occupies in an equally detailed form the second part of the System. Here, Stanislavsky stresses the importance of physical relaxation, body awareness and self control by all of which the actor achieves clearer, more exact and truer-to-life movements when behaving in character. Stanislavsky then goes on to examine the part played in what we now call 'body language' of rhythm, tempo and selectivity of gesture. Finally he gives a detailed plan for the training of the actor's vocal resources, with an emphasis on diction, intonation and expressiveness.

The third part of the System, the means by which an actor works on a text for performance, has been perhaps the most influential (and the most contrary to Brechtian theory). At the onset of rehearsals, the actors are urged to find the 'super-objective' of the play they are to perform. The super-objective is the essence of the meaning of the play which can be expressed in one, mutually agreed sentence. This sentence then acts as the guide-line for the whole production. By encapsulating a particular interpretation of the play text, it clarifies the purpose and logical sequence of each action and of each scene of that production and confers a unity of effect on the whole.

Secondly, each actor has to find his character's 'through-line', the dominant motivating force which prompts the character's actions throughout the play. The through-line is also to be expressed in one sentence (a sentence containing an active verb in order to provoke action), so that the actor can see his character's behaviour and actions as a coherent shape or pattern. For example, an actor playing Macbeth might choose as his through-line: 'I want to obtain and keep the crown of Scotland whatever the cost'. He would then relate all Macbeth's actions, however divergent, to this central notion.

The Stanislavsky actor is then asked to divide each of his scenes into 'units of action' and give these units headings which express the character's stated or unstated intentions at those particular moments in the story. To continue the Macbeth example: in Act I, Scene III, the actor of Macbeth might divide the opening into such units as: 'Ride with Banquo to Forres; Find out who the witches are; Question the witches further.' By breaking his part into small units and analysing each of them, the actor is, Stanislavsky argues, better able to understand and handle his role in the early stages of rehearsal, and by gradually adding the units together he moves nearer and nearer to an appreciation of the logical development of the whole role. Notice how this idea presupposes a unity within the role set down by the playwright which comes from a psychologically derived notion of the character as a real human being.

Having analysed the material provided for him in the script, the Stanislavsky actor is now expected to extend his 'knowledge' and understanding of his role by exploring through improvisation the 'experiences' of his character which may be imagined or are known to have happened before the play begins and which take place 'offstage' during the play. In this way the actor is able to create an 'unbroken line of life', by means of which during the actual performance, even when off-stage, he remains 'in character' and thus creates a continuity of emotional response for his character by recalling the imagined experiences. These techniques are clearly of great importance in a method of acting that aims to persuade the audience that the actor *is* the character he portrays.

However, the actor as character is an aspect of the System which is often misunderstood. Stanislavsky was careful to point out that, while attempting to achieve inner, psychological 'truth' for, and emotional involvement in, his character, the actor must not 'lose' himself entirely in his part. This in any case would be psychologically dangerous. But it is also of artistic and practical value to maintain a kind of dual consciousness, and Stanislavsky quotes one of his favourite actors, Tommaso Salvini, on this theme:

> An actor lives, weeps and laughs on the stage, and all the while he is watching his own tears and smiles. It is this double function, this balance between life and acting that makes his art.[1]

On a more mundane level, the same 'double function' ensures that the actor can monitor what he is doing, check how the audience is reacting, and be ready to adapt when something unrehearsed occurs.

The value of the System can, of course, only really be seen through an examination of its application, for, as Stanislavsky frequently reminded his actors, the System was 'only the means for the realistic embodiment of the dramatist's ideas... not an end in itself'.[2] Both the System and Stanislavsky's whole approach to theatre were based on an aesthetic idealism, something rare in the days when he founded the Moscow Art Theatre. He tried to change not only the attitudes to theatre of the actor but also of the audience, who, in his view, must develop a new reverential attitude to the performance. His account of the difficulties the company encountered with the new, post-revolutionary audience of 1917 is revealing:

> We were forced to begin at the very beginning to teach this new spectator how to sit quietly, how not to talk, how to come into the theatre at the proper time, not to smoke, not to eat nuts in public, not to bring food into the theatre and eat it there, to dress in his best so as to fit more into the atmosphere of beauty that was worshipped in the theatre.[3]

To begin with Stanislavsky met comparable problems in persuading the actors to pursue his 'System'; they felt threatened, puzzled or were simply incredulous. And despite the early success and fame brought to the company by the Chekhov productions between 1898 and 1904, Chekhov himself frequently criticized the acting. Watching the actors in rehearsal, the playwright remarked on the naturalistic fussiness of Stanislavsky's new kind of performer: 'They act too much. It would be better if they acted a little more as in life.'[4] But the company was given an enthusiastic reception for their first tour abroad in 1906, though it is worth noting that Stanislavsky's methods of actor-training were still at an early stage. In his autobiography Nemirovich-Danchenko cites a German reviewer:

> To the impression created by the Muscovites, it is possible to juxtapose only the very best that we have known to date in the art of representing human beings and in the craft of directing all means of the stage.[5]

Despite such reviews Stanislavsky was not satisfied. Even fifteen years later, when the work of the Moscow Art Theatre was based entirely on the System, he continued to criticize the actors for too often accepting what he called 'empty theatrical self-consciousness for true inspiration'.[6]

Transmission of the methods of the company also met problems. Actors tried to put the System into practice without fully understanding it. In 1933, while working on *An Actor Prepares*, Stanislavsky wrote to the dramatist, Gorky, that he hoped the book would

> put an end to all the silly talk about my so-called 'System', which in the form it is taught now merely cripples the actor.[7]

And gradually the results and benefits of the System as exemplified by the Moscow Art Theatre became appreciated by theatre practitioners in the rest of Europe and in the USA. This led to the founding of many studios and drama schools which based their work and training on the System, the most famous of all being the Actors' Studio in New York, which numbers among its well-known 'sons', Marlon Brando. But theatre 'revolutions' take time, and even in the late 1950s the differences between actors in the British theatre and those of the Moscow Art Theatre were keenly apparent to the critic, the late Kenneth Tynan, who noted the Russian actors' effective embodiment of character:

> They (the Moscow Art Theatre actors) have become, with long rehearsal, the people they are playing: they do not need, as our actors do, to depend on the lines alone for their characterisation. We act with our voices, they with their lines . . . . This is not verbal acting, like ours, but total acting.[8]

It is evident here that Stanislavsky's ideal of the illusion of actuality had been achieved. The Moscow Art Theatre had come to represent the pinnacle of 'slice of life' acting.

It was, of course, against the naturalistic tradition, which appealed to the emotions and depended on the audience's 'suspension of disbelief', that Brecht set his own style of critical, thought-provoking theatre. He was intent on avoiding the creation of illusion and on blocking an audience's will to empathize with the characters. To Brecht, naturalism as an artistic principle expressed a bourgeois view of life, and, as he says in a poem of 1939, he saw naturalistic actors as 'dealers in narcotic drugs'.[9] He wanted to break the 'trance' he saw such performing induce and to replace the cathartic purging of the audience's emotions through empathy with a more critical, objective assessment of the events presented. In his essay 'On experimental theatre' (1939) Brecht summed up his objections thus:

> A style of acting had been evolved which could do more to stimulate illusions than to give experiences, more to intoxicate than to elevate, more to deceive than to illumine.[10]

Illusion, to Brecht, appeared as delusion. And Stanislavsky, as the arch representative of naturalistic acting, was an obvious target. On reading of Stanislavsky's death in 1938, Brecht expressed his opinion of the Russian director succinctly, if vehemently: 'The Order of Stanislavsky is a sink collecting every popery in the dramatic arts.'[11]

Brecht's most sustained attack on naturalistic theatre in general and on Stanislavsky in particular is contained in *The Messingkauf Dialogues*, in which the main 'characters', the Actor, the Dramaturg and the Philosopher, discuss the differences between 'dramatic' theatre, the theatre Brecht associated with Stanislavsky, and 'epic' theatre, Brecht's own kind. The Dramaturg remarks ironically:

What he (Stanislavsky) cared about was *naturalness*, and as a result everything in his theatre seemed far too natural for anyone to pause and go into it thoroughly. You don't normally examine your own home or your own eating habits, do you?[12]

The same spokesman goes on to pour scorn on the System's efforts to invoke the actor's imagination in the attainment of a 'truthful' performance by improvisation:

There's an account of some well-known exercises for actors, designed to encourage natural acting, which includes the following drill: the actor places a cap on the floor and behaves as if it were a rat. This is supposed to teach him the art of inspiring belief.[13]

It is easy, of course, to decry work taken out of context; but the System's 'inner' technique and its objective of helping the actor to 'be' his character was, not surprisingly, like the proverbial red rag to Brecht, who, in any case, doubted any actor's ability to achieve in performance, by a creative process, consistently authentic emotions:

Stanislavsky provides a whole list of devices, a whole *system* of devices, by means of which this 'creative mood' can be produced afresh at each performance. Usually the actor does not succeed for long in really feeling like the other person. He soon begins, in his exhaustion, to copy certain external features of his carriage, or tone of voice, and thereby the effect on the audience is appallingly weakened.[14]

Brecht's criticisms did not rest with those of Stanislavsky's theatrical style. More fundamental in a way was his awareness of a lack of political message in the work of the Moscow Art Theatre. Stanislavsky saw the function of theatre as entirely an artistic one: 'the very least utilitarian purpose or tendency, brought into the realm of pure art, kills art instantly'.[15] And while he was dedicated to art in the theatre, Brecht intended theatre importantly to function as a tool of social and political change, which formed the basis and motivating force of Brecht's 'epic' programme.

It is more difficult to summarize Brecht's theatrical theory than Stanislavsky's, partly because Brecht's ideas were reactions against the prevailing tide and were, therefore, often negative responses, and partly because those ideas are not expressed in a unified, coherent 'system'. They are mostly collected in the *Schriften zum Theater* that constitute Volumes 15 to 17 of the 20-volume *Gesammelte Werke* (1967). In addition, a number of Brecht's poems about theatre often provide simple and clear illustrations of notions expressed elsewhere.

As one of the fundamental aims of Brecht's 'epic' theatre was to make the audience critically aware of the social implications of the situations presented on the stage, instead of merely being involved with the characters, all aspects of a performance – the script, the setting, the acting and the auditorium – were controlled by what Brecht called the *Ver-*

fremdungseffekt which may be translated as 'alienation effect' or better, 'distancing effect'. The intention was to 'alienate' or 'distance' the audience emotionally from the characters and their story by breaking with the traditional 'illusions' of naturalistic theatre and by constantly reminding the audience that they were in a theatre watching actors. And this was to be achieved in a number of ways.

Firstly, Brecht wanted the atmosphere in his theatre to be similar to that of a sports arena, and the spectator could then be expected to sustain the kind of dispassionate, critical awareness that Brecht saw and admired in the crowds at sporting events. In contrast to the well-behaved Moscow Art Theatre audience, the Brechtian spectator was even to be encouraged to smoke. And this change in atmosphere was to be aided by the use of an open, platform stage with no front curtains and with minimal scenery. The mechanics of the production were not to be hidden or disguised and so the reverential or polite hush invoked by the sudden revelation of an illusion of reality could not occur.

Secondly, unlike his Stanislavskian counterpart, the Brechtian actor was to be aware, and show his awareness, of the presence of the audience. (In this, of course, the actor was assisted by Brecht's own plays that required the performer to address the audience directly.) In addition, Brecht insisted that the actors should avoid treating the audience as a single unit:

> He asked them to think of their audience as a divided group of friends and
> enemies, rich and poor, and to *divide* their audience accordingly by
> addressing themselves to one part of the audience now, to another part the
> next moment.[16]

Thirdly, and this is the key difference between Brechtian and Stanislavskian acting theory, Brecht wanted his actors to 'distance' themselves from their roles; instead of embodying the characters, they were to *demonstrate* them. A result of this is the reduction of the actor's emotional involvement in the part and consequently of the audience's empathy. To clarify this idea, Brecht offered the analogy of the witness of a street accident who, in his description, imitates the participants just enough to make his story clear.[17] The Brechtian actor, then, '*shows* the character, he *quotes* his lines, he *repeats* a real-life incident'.[18]

Brecht argued that this distance between the actor and his role also enables the actor to be critical of his character and to share that criticism with the audience. For illustration of this, Brecht referred to an actor whom he greatly admired, Charlie Chaplin. If Chaplin were to play Napoleon, Brecht mused (a part, incidentally, that Chaplin longed to create), he would not be concerned to impersonate Napoleon physically but would seek to show the Corsican tyrant objectively and critically as a political idea. And it is worth noting that in his autobiography, Chaplin himself stressed an anti-Stanislavsky approach:

> I abhor dramatic schools that indulge in reflections and introspections to

evoke the right emotion. The mere fact that a student must be mentally operated upon is sufficient proof that he should give up acting.[19]

In addition to separating the actor from his part, Brecht also insisted that the actor should make his own awareness of himself as a performer apparent to the audience. He derived this notion from watching Chinese actors, Mei Lan-Fang and his company, in Moscow in 1935. Actors of this kind, Brecht said:

openly choose those positions which will best show them off to the audience . . . . At the same time (the actor) also observes his own arms and legs, adducing them, testing them and perhaps finally approving them.[20]

The Brechtian approach to a character, it necessarily follows, is very different from the Stanislavskian approach. Whereas Stanislavsky required his actor to find a 'through-line' which apparently rationalized divergencies, Brecht stressed the need for the actor to emphasize the inconsistencies contained within any particular role, so that, in a sense, the actor made 'an inventory' of the role instead of a presentation of it as a finished and coherent whole. The resulting 'contradictory' approach was important in revealing the 'social' truth of the part as opposed to the 'psychological' truth; it allowed the audience to witness and understand the dialectic of the individual and his society:

The dramatic (Stanislavskian) actor . . . has his character established from the first, and simply exposes it to the inclemencies of the world . . . the epic actor lets his character grow before the spectator's eyes out of the way in which he behaves.[21]

All the emphasis, for Brecht, then, is on the notion of social truth, in contrast to Stanislavsky's inner truth. And so for Brecht, only the end-product of the actor's performance, what is shown to the audience, not the processes which go into that performance, was of importance. Carl Weber, a director who worked with Brecht, emphasized Brecht's single-minded concern:

Brecht never cared how his actors worked. He didn't tell them to go home and do this or that or to go behind the set and concentrate. He didn't give a damn about the mechanics they used, he just cared about results.[22]

And this reminds us that Brecht, unlike Stanislavsky, was playwright first, director second, and actor not at all; and his company, the Berliner Ensemble, was founded primarily in order to facilitate the perfect staging of Brecht's own plays. The focus in 'epic' theatre is transferred from the actor to the script, or from performer to what is performed.

In fact, the company may well have been hardly aware of Brechtian dramatic theory as they rehearsed his plays. Lotte Lenya, the great actress who worked with Brecht in the 1920s and 1930s and was the wife of Kurt Weill, composer of music for many Brecht plays, makes this clear in her account of the first time she saw Brecht after the war:

> Now at that time, there was a big to-do about epic theatre – everything was
> epic, everything was *Entfremdung* [*sic*] – alienation. I said, 'To hell with
> that, I'm singing "Surabaya Johnny" the way I always sang it' . . . . Right
> in the middle of it, I stopped for a second and said, 'Brecht, you know your
> theory of epic theatre – maybe you don't want me just to sing it the way I
> sang it – as emotional as "Surabaya Johnny" has to be done?' . . . . He said,
> Lenya, darling, whatever you do is epic enough for me.'[23]

Of course, this is not to say that in rehearsal Brecht did not try to help
his actors achieve 'epic acting'. He devised a number of rehearsal
exercises to get the actor to maintain a distance between himself and
the role he plays. Five exercises are mentioned particularly. First, the
actors were told to say their lines in the third person, using 'He/She
said' and turning direct speech into reported speech, thus inviting the
actors to see their roles as other than themselves, as objects to be contemplated. Secondly, the actors had, before delivering their character
lines, to speak aloud the stage directions that referred to them. The
effect here was to strengthen their awareness of the narrative in which
their roles were embedded. Thirdly, they were invited to paraphrase the
poetic language of the play in colloquial speech, which in effect prompted them to view the playscript in a new and critical light. Fourthly, the
actor, in rehearsing a scene, was told to precede each thought expressed
in the dialogue or each action with its dialectical opposite, thus enabling
him to define the various alternative choices available to his character
which he, the actor, may make clear to the audience. Fifthly, the actor
was instructed to swap parts with a fellow actor or actress in a shared
scene so that each was able to view his character – as played by the
other – from the outside.

The work of the Berliner Ensemble was widely acclaimed. Even Lee
Strasberg, director of the Stanislavsky-based Actors' Studio, admired
the acting as being 'stripped of all mannerisms, of anything whose purpose is to show the actor's skill'.[24] And George Devine, director of the
Royal Court Theatre, in response to the Ensemble's first performances
in London in 1956, remarked that there was none of the 'clichéd acting'
which he saw in the contemporary London theatre.[25] Many reviewers of
the time, in fact, seemed more enthusiastic about the acting than the
plays. In particular, critics appreciated the performances of the now
legendary Helene Weigel.

Weigel had worked with (and then married) Brecht before the war
and she loyally supported him during the years of exile in Europe and
America. Brecht wrote several leading roles for her and her practical
criticism in rehearsal provided him with a constant source of stimulus. It
is probably true to say that without Weigel the Berliner Ensemble would
not have happened. Besides playing many major roles, she also had
overall responsibility for the running of the company. Kenneth Tynan
summed up her performance talents succinctly:

She is a great actress; she has eyes like the glint of hatchets, a clarion voice, and a physical technique as supple as that of Martha Graham.[26]

Brecht frequently indicated that Weigel achieved much that he required of an 'epic' performer and Tynan saw the achievement of 'epic' acting in her playing of Mother Courage in 1956: 'her performance is casual and ascetic; we are to observe but not to embrace her'.[27] In other words, Weigel made no bid for the audience's sympathy and denied the possibility of empathetic involvement.

By the time of this London performance Brecht had died, but the Berliner Ensemble continued with Weigel in charge. Her approach to acting and performance remained consistent with Brecht's 'epic' concept; she acted according to the belief that 'the psychology generally used in the theatre is very inferior, old-fashioned and useless'.[28]

Although the ideologies and theories of Stanislavsky and Brecht seem widely different, in practice they consistently overlap. Both men had a close relationship with the actors in their respective companies and both were concerned to further the aesthetic development of theatre. Both required the actor to have a good intellectual and emotional understanding of his role and of the whole play, and to develop a wide-ranging technique for its communication. Both companies rehearsed for long periods, until, in fact, the production was considered 'ready' for an audience.

Similar in many respects, too, was their actual approach to a text. Actors in each case were urged to remember and utilize their first reactions to a script; to discuss together the overall meaning and purpose of the play; to divide the play into small units for analysis and rehearsal, giving each unit a descriptive title; to ascertain and make clear their character's motivations, exploring them and the relationships with other characters by means of improvisation; to speak aloud in rehearsal the play's subtext, that is, the actual and often contradictory ideas in the characters' minds underlying the words and actions; to be selective and precise in the use of physical gesture and expression, and of costume and props; and in the late stages of rehearsal to take care to find the correct rhythm and tempo for performance.

Consequently, it is not surprising to find that actors themselves spotted important points of contact between the two approaches. One of Brecht's 'epic-trained' actresses in the Berliner Ensemble, Angelika Hurwicz, told Brecht that on reading *An Actor Prepares* she discovered 'parts which appeared quite important, which I have made use of for years now'.[29] And she noted close links in the actual rehearsal methods of the two men:

Brecht is by no means hostile to drama exercises aimed at ensuring the truth to life and the warmth of the presentation of the role; in fact he regards them as a pre-requisite. Brecht simply starts with what Stanislavsky calls the 'super-task' (i.e. 'super-objective') of the actor.[30]

Her suggestion here, that Brecht goes beyond Stanislavsky rather than in a totally different direction, is supported by Brecht's essay called (note the title) 'Building a Character'. Here he outlines three phases for the actor.[31] In the first phase, the actor 'loses himself' in the character; in the second, he searches for the subjective truth of the character; and in the third, he attempts to see the character from the outside. The Stanislavsky actor works through the first two of these phases, too, but though Stanislavsky stressed that the actor must also be able to see the character from the outside, he should not usually make this evident to the audience, except in a comic or satiric play.

Something of this *rapprochement* between Stanislavsky and Brecht is also apparent in the way they both in later life revised and modified their theories and responded to criticisms. For example, it irked Stanislavsky to have his work described as 'naturalistic'; this was seen by him as a kind of failure:

> We often have been and are still accused of falling into a naturalistic expression of detail in our pursuit of the realism of life and truth in our stage actions. Whenever we have done this we were wrong. It is definitely bad and inartistic; it misrepresents our desired attempt to create a realistic performance.[32]

In later years Stanislavsky also expressed a revised view of the relationship of art and politics:

> Politics is an integral part of our lives now. This means that the director's horizon includes the government's structure, the problems of our society. It means that we, the directors of the theatre, have much more responsibility and must develop a broader way of thinking.[33]

There were modifications, too, in actual practical approaches. Stanislavsky came to be very much against the 'static representation' of a character and asked his actors to show characters 'as if in the process of formation'.[34] Perhaps even more interesting is the fact that Stanislavsky also allowed that it was possible 'for the actor to become the character and at the same time to disapprove of him or accuse him'.[35] And in the last few years came the most radical *volte face* of all, when Stanislavsky changed from advising the actor, as he pursues his character, to work from his inner feelings to outward expression to proposing that the actor should use physical actions to stimulate and re-evoke the emotions appropriate to that moment in the play. This last significant development of the System, known as 'the method of physical actions', also invited the actor to pay more attention to the plot of the play. It required him to work through the narrative in rehearsal in considerable detail in order to strengthen his awareness of its sequence and shape. In effect, this was to move the emphasis away from character towards story.[36]

Brecht recognized the modifications that Stanislavsky was making in the direction of his own ideal theatre. He remarked: 'Stanislavsky's "method of physical actions" is most likely his greatest contribution to a new theatre',[37] and even went so far as to list in *Theaterarbeit* (1952) 'Some of the things that can be learnt from Stanislavsky'. The list includes the feeling for a play's poetry, the sense of responsibility to society (seeing the actor's art as having social significance), the importance of ensemble playing and of truthfulness, the need for unity of style, and the importance of the further development of art.[38] These notes are often regarded as a superficial and conciliatory gesture by Brecht towards the much respected Soviet director, but it is evident that he, too, was in the process of moderating his theories.

Brecht's own most significant revised opinion is on the subject of the emotional charge in theatrical performance. He comes to admit that it is neither desirable, nor indeed possible, to eliminate all the actor's emotional involvement with his role or all the audience's empathy. On the contrary, he was increasingly aware that it was artistically important to leaven dry didacticism with the life-blood of human emotion. He notes that:

> Our mistakes are different from those of other theatres. Their actors are liable to display too much spurious temperament; ours often show too little of the real thing. Aiming to avoid artificial heat, we fall short in natural warmth. We make no attempt to share the emotions of the characters we portray, but those emotions must none the less be fully and movingly represented.[39]

This highlights one of the key paradoxes of Brecht's theatre. If his actors conveyed too much 'natural warmth', then the audience became involved emotionally. Some critics, for example, regarded Helene Weigel as 'a superb, Stanislavsky-trained actress',[40] and even her performance of Vlassova in *The Mother*, one of Brecht's most didactic and austere pieces, moved the audience to tears. Sometimes it was not the actor who was at fault, Brecht decided, but the play text. When the press wrote that *Mother Courage and Her Children* demonstrated 'the moving endurance of the female animal',[41] thus failing to criticize Mother Courage for her mercenary involvement in the war, Brecht rewrote the end of the play to deflect sympathy from the title character.

In fact, Brecht never felt that 'epic' acting had been fully achieved in his lifetime. It may be that, in many ways, the 'alienation' Brecht wanted is more the concern of the director (or in Brecht's case, of the playwright) than of the actor. In any case, his notion of 'acting in quotation marks' is not easily carried through. The difficulty for the actor lies in combining *realistic* portrayal with the required critical comment. Brecht provides rehearsal exercises but nowhere does he describe what 'epic' acting should feel like for the performer. His oft-quoted exhortation to his actors to act 'dispassionately, without involvement' has, therefore, frequently led actors to suppose that Brechtian acting means *less* acting rather than a kind of restrained, 'cool' acting.

Another problem the Brechtian actor encounters in seeking an objective and less empathetic reception by the audience is the fact of the essential 'immediacy' of a live performance. Brecht's hope for a style of acting that appears to narrate a story that has already happened, and is therefore in the past, is at odds with the 'here and now' of each performance. As Charles Marowitz puts it: 'Objectivity may be a journalistic virtue; but it's an artistic impossibility.'[42] Eric Bentley, critic and Brecht collaborator, puts his finger neatly on perhaps the obvious answer:

> Epic theory cannot always be taken literally. It does not even square with
> Brecht's practice. He does not eliminate stage-illusion and suspense; he only
> reduces their importance. Sympathy and identification with the characters are
> not eliminated; they are counterpoised by deliberate distancing.[43]

To sum up, the Stanislavskian actor is usually required to give a continuous presentation of his character from that character's viewpoint and in his performance shows no apparent awareness of the audience. The Brechtian actor steps in and out of demonstrating his character (or characters), he makes contact with his audience, and is required to place more emphasis on the situation and on the social significance of that situation than on his character perceived as a psychological reality. Neither approach is in itself appropriate for all styles of theatre; it would be unhelpful for an actor to attempt to find psychological motivation for a Beckett character or to apply 'epic' theory to a play by Coward. The Stanislavsky approach, however, can be applied successfully to a far wider range of material than Brecht admitted. Brecht's own theatre was essentially satirical but Stanislavsky was not the slave of one theatrical style; the plays he successfully directed included not only naturalistic pieces but melodramas, farces and operas. It is true that in the area of human psychology Stanislavsky is very much of the nineteenth century; some of his views on 'character' are over-simple for the complexities of the post-Freudian world. None the less, the Stanislavsky System is still widely taught in drama schools and practised in today's theatre, where the predominant mode of acting is 'naturalistic', a mode seen to its best advantage in the popular 'theatre' of television. Stanislavsky showed the way to fuller, deeper character acting and then Brecht added the dimensions of detachment, criticism and social significance. Thus, rather than being at opposite poles, as is often assumed, their practices, if not their theories, are on the same continuum. On this, Brecht can have the last word. After seeing and being impressed by a production at the Moscow Art Theatre in 1955, he said:

> Now I shall have to defend Stanislavsky from his supporters. Now I shall
> have to say about him what people say about me – that the practice
> contradicts the theory.[44]

NOTES

1. K. Stanislavsky, *An Actor Prepares*, trans. E. Hapgood (London, 1937), p. 267.
2. N. Gorchakov, *Stanislavsky Directs*, trans. M. Golding (New York, 1968), p. 193.
3. K. Stanislavsky, *My Life in Art* (London, 1924), p. 554.
4. V. Nemirovich-Danchenko, *My Life in the Russian Theatre*, trans. J. Cournos (London, 1937), p. 160.
5. Ibid., p. 285.
6. Stanislavsky, *My Life in Art*, p. 571.
7. E. Duerr, *The Length and Depth of Acting* (New York, 1962), p. 482.
8. K. Tynan, *Tynan on Theatre* (London, 1964), p. 276.
9. J. Willett and R. Manheim, eds. *Brecht Poems*, Part III (London, 1976), p. 340.
10. B. Brecht, 'On experimental theatre', in *Brecht on Theatre*, trans. J. Willett (London, 1964), p. 133 (see *GW* 15, 294).
11. Quoted by K. Völker, *Brecht Chronicle*, trans. F. Wieck (New York, 1975), p. 86.
12. B. Brecht, *The Messingkauf Dialogues*, trans. J. Willett (London, 1965), p. 23 (see *GW* 16, 516).
13. Ibid., p. 14 (see *GW* 16, 505).
14. B. Brecht, 'On Chinese acting', *Tulane Drama Review*, **VI** (Fall 1961), 132 (see *GW* 16, 623).
15. Stanislavsky, *My Life in Art*, p. 380.
16. C. Marowitz, T. Milne and O. Hale, eds, *The Encore Reader*, (London, 1965), p. 148.
17. See 'Die Strassenszene' (*GW* 16, 546–58), p. 549 and Chapter 3 above.
18. Brecht, *The Messingkauf Dialogues*, p. 104.
19. C. Chaplin, *My Autobiography* (London, 1964), p. 227.
20. B. Brecht, 'Alienation effects in Chinese acting', *Brecht on Theatre*, p. 92 (*GW* 16, 620).
21. *Brecht on Theatre*, p. 56.
22. C. Weber, 'Brecht as director', *Tulane Drama Review*, **XII** (Fall 1967), p. 112.
23. *The Listener*, 24 May 1979, p. 709.
24. R. H. Hethmon, ed., *Strasberg at the Actors' Studio*, (New York, 1966), p. 390.
25. Marowitz et al., *The Encore Reader*, p. 15.
26. *Observer*, 26 June 1955.
27. *Observer*, 2 September 1956.
28. 'Dialogue: Berliner Ensemble', *Tulane Drama Review*, **XII** (Fall 1967), p. 112.
29. B. Brecht, 'Notes on Stanislavsky', *Tulane Drama Review*, **IX** (Winter 1964), p. 162 (see *GW* 16, 852F).
30. H. Witt, ed. *Brecht as They Knew Him*, (London, 1975), p. 132.
31. Brecht. 'Notes on Stanislavsky', p. 159 (see *GW* 16, 843F).
32. Quoted by Gorchakov, *Stanislavsky Directs*, p. 143.
33. Ibid., p. 16.

34. L. I. Coger, 'Stanislavsky Changes His Mind', *Tulane Drama Review*, **IX** (Fall 1964), p. 65.
35. S. Moore, *The Stanislavsky System* (London, 1966), p. 98.
36. See S. Moore, 'The method of physical actions', *Tulane Drama Review*, **IX** (Summer 1965), p. 92.
37. Brecht, 'Notes on Stanislavsky', p. 160 (see *GW* 16, 844).
38. See *Brecht on Theatre*, p. 236 (Also *GW* 16, 859F).
39. Ibid., p. 248.
40. M. Billington, *The Modern Actor* (London, 1973), p. 202.
41. M. Esslin, *Brecht: A Choice of Evils* (London, 1959), p. 204.
42. C. Marowitz, *The Method as Means* (London, 1961), p. 108.
43. E. Bentley, *The Playwright as Thinker* (London, 1967), p. 219.
44. Witt, *Brecht as They Knew Him*, p. 213.

SELECTED BIBLIOGRAPHY

BRECHT

BRECHT, B., *Brecht on Theatre*, trans. J. Willett, London, 1964
BRECHT, B., *The Messingkauf Dialogues*, trans. J. Willett, London, 1965
ESSLIN, M., *Brecht: A Choice of Evils*, London, 1959
WILLETT, J., *The Theatre of Bertolt Brecht*, London, 1977

STANISLAVSKY

EDWARDS, C., *The Stanislavsky Heritage*, New York, 1965
GORCHAKOV, N., *Stanislavsky Directs*, trans. M. Goldina, London, 1968
MAGARSHACK, D., *Stanislavsky on the Art of the Stage*, London, 1950
NEMIROVICH-DANCHENKO, V., *My Life in the Russian Theatre*, trans. J. Cournos, London, 1937
STANISLAVSKY, K., *An Actor Prepares*, trans. E. Hapgood, London, 1937
STANISLAVSKY, K., *Building a Character*, trans. E. Hapgood, London, 1950
STANISLAVSKY, K., *Creating a Role*, trans. E. Hapgood, London, 1963

MODERN THEATRE

BILLINGTON, M., *The Modern Actor*, London, 1973
BROOK, P., *The Empty Space*, London, 1968
HAYMAN, R., *Techniques of Acting*, London, 1969
MOROWITZ, C., *The Method as Means*, London, 1961

Chapter 9

BRECHT AND PISCATOR

HUGH RORRISON

'There will be a day when our names, yours, Brecht, and mine, will be together under the rubrique [*sic*] of the EPIC THEATRE, and the world will know what it meant for our days and will mean for the future.'[1]

PISCATOR

'lass mich dir, der Ordnung halber, mitteilen, dass von den Leuten, die in den letzten 20 Jahren Theater gemacht haben, mir niemand so nahe gestanden hat wie du.'[2]

BRECHT

('for the record I want you to know that of all the people who have been involved with the theatre over the last twenty years nobody has stood as close to me as you have.')

Brecht was an avid follower of events in the Berlin theatre on both sides of the curtain from the moment he first set foot in the capital in 1921 and he knew Piscator's work at the Volksbühne, his version of *Die Räuber* (*The Robbers*) at the Staatliches Schauspielhaus, and probably Piscator himself by March 1927 when Piscator's single-minded attempts to develop political theatre made his position at the Volksbühne untenable. He had turned Ehm Welk's *Gewitter über Gottland* (*Storm over Gottland*) (which had been accepted by the management as an innocuous fifteenth-century pirate piece about Klaus Störtebecker) into a political play by inserting a specially made film which presented the action as a stage in the inexorable march of Communism. The management cut politically sensitive parts from the production and a wide range of literary and theatrical figures signed a declaration of solidarity with the director's right to work uncensored. Brecht's name was not among them. It was, however, listed the following winter, to Brecht's chagrin, when Piscator's Communist aide Felix Gasbarra announced to the press the composition of the 'dramaturgic collective' which he was to lead at the newly opened Piscator-Bühne. The editing and documentation of scripts were crucial for Piscator's production technique, and it was intended that Gasbarra and the other staff dramaturg Leo Lania would consult sympathizers like Johannes R. Becher, Döblin, Walter Mehring,

Erich Mühsam, Toller, Tucholsky and the film critic Béla Bálazs where appropriate. Brecht was incensed at the suggestion that he should work under Gasbarra and strutted up and down the stage of the Theater am Nollendorfplatz shouting, 'My name is my trademark and anybody who uses it must pay for it.'[3] He informed Piscator that whereas he was happy to be his comrade he was not his dramaturg. Despite this inauspicious start, a working relationship developed and Brecht attended rehearsals at the Piscator-Bühne and offered suggestions and constructive criticism, and Piscator reciprocated when Brecht's association with Ernst Josef Aufricht's Theater am Schiffbauerdamm began the following year.

Brecht's best-known contribution to the work of the Piscator-Bühne is his work on the adaptation of Jaroslav Hasek's *Die Abenteuer des braven Soldaten Schwejk* (*The Adventures of the Good Soldier Schwejk*) for the stage. Grete Reiner's German translation of the novel only appeared in 1926, but by 1927 Max Brod and Hans Reimann had secured the rights and produced a dramatization. This proved to be a flimsy, 'well-made' barrack-room comedy with none of the original's cutting edge, so Piscator decided to produce his own version, and accordingly set up a training camp at Neubabelsberg on the southern outskirts of Berlin. Here, punctuated by bouts of jogging and pistol-shooting which Brecht, whose interest in sport stopped short of actual participation, observed from a hotel window with a cynical smile, Piscator, Gasbarra, Lania and Brecht reread the novel and selected the series of episodes best suited to recreating Hasek's whole view of life on the stage, for it was Hasek's satirical vision, his view of society in Austria/Hungary during the First World War that interested Piscator. Eventually Brod and Reimann were introduced to the new version and persuaded to accept it.

The stroke of genius which gives the production its place in theatrical history, though it must be said that it was the inspired performance of Max Pallenberg that carried it on the stage, came when Piscator observed that the novel is in continual flux because Schwejk (Piscator's spelling), a wholly passive figure in himself, is constantly being shunted around by the authorities. He then hit on the idea of conveying this visually by making Schwejk march on a conveyor belt. With the addition of a second parallel belt on which props and supporting characters rolled on and off behind him, the translation of Hasek's comic style from page to stage was assured.

The set was simple, consisting simply of two pairs of white flats connected overhead by white borders and closed by a white backcloth. On this screen, to complete the effect, George Grosz's cartoon illustrations of the bureaucracy with which Schwejk tangles were projected. *Schwejk* was epic theatre in the sense that it staged a novel without doctoring the plot to fit traditional dramatic structure and demonstrated that it was possible to tell the story in a string of independent scenes, a lesson that was not lost on Brecht.

The prompt-book for *Schwejk* is lost, but four typed copies of the script survive in the Bertolt-Brecht-Archiv with an accompanying sheet indicating the collaboration of Piscator, Lania, Gasbarra and Grosz. This is a more accurate attribution of the authorship than Brecht's later claims (*Aj* 576, *SzT* 5, 139) to have written the script himself, especially when one considers that some of the chosen scenes and even parts of the dialogue were taken from the original Brod/Reimann version. Brecht's claim probably reflects the fact that on this one occasion he was a full-time member of the script collective rather than an occasional observer.

Brecht made a small but characteristic contribution to Leo Lania's *Konjunktur* (*Boom*), the fourth Piscator-Bühne production, and the only script generated wholly within the Piscator team. It started out as a comedy with an English entrepreneur exploiting a Chinese Communist general, but the subject was soon changed to the international exploitation of a fictitious oil strike in Albania. This too was to be a comedy, with a starring part for Tilla Durieux who had been instrumental in setting up the financial backing for the Piscator-Bühne. Frau Durieux was enthusiastic when she read the draft of the first two acts, and this meant that when it became clear to Piscator at the third rewrite that a big subject was being wasted on a trivial comedy he could neither abandon the project nor even cut the leading lady's part without offending his backer. This was just one of the paradoxes of running a Communist theatre with capitalist finance.

The play started on a bare stage with two tramps stumbling upon a natural oil spill, and built up to a point where the stage was filled with shacks and derricks, a couple of cars and even a live donkey, as international interests wrestled for control of the field, notably Frau Barsin (Tilla Durieux) of the Soviet Nafta concern. At the preview an invited audience from the KPD (German Communist Party) and the Soviet embassy and trade mission pointed out to Piscator that a Communist theatre should not impute to a Soviet agency economic imperialism indistinguishable from the practices of the capitalist West, a flaw which Piscator had, remarkably, failed to spot. He agreed to withdraw the production rather than jeopardize his political credibility, and it was at this point that Brecht, who had watched developments with some glee, stepped in. Given two days he could, he said, rewrite the ending. Frau Barsin would be unmasked as an imposter who had all along been working for South American interests. His offer was accepted, and the production went on but was a commercial failure.

The weakness of Lania's script had become clear when the dramaturgic team began to research the background:

> The more intensively we explored the subject and the problem the greater the
> difficulties became. Together we worked our way through volumes of
> literature, statistics and industrial reports, and it gradually became clearer
> that the subject of *Boom* had in it the germ of an economic comedy in the

grand manner, that the subject had possibilities which opened up new perspectives for the theatre.[4]

Study in depth was a normal part of any production at the Piscator-Bühne, and it is clear that as Piscator familiarized himself with the ramifications of the oil business and the management of the market, he realized that this subject would lend itself to a satire on the workings of capitalism. Had it not been for his obligation to Tilla Durieux and his desperate need to put a production on the stage of the Lessingtheater to bring in cash, Piscator would, he implies, have developed this project, undaunted, probably even encouraged by its complexity, for, as Bernard Reich points out, Piscator liked to work on a large canvas.

Dass jetzt die unmittelbaren Zusammenstösse von Gruppen und Klassen zum Gegenstand der dramatischen Darstellung werden sollten, ergab sich als die einfachste Folgerung. Das Piscator-Modell bevorzugte deshalb Schauspiele grossen Formats. Dort, wo das Spannungsfeld eng und begrenzt war, wurde es durch den Regisseur, der ohne weiteres die Funktion des Stückeschreibers einnahm, verbreitert: durch Einschübe, Anzeigen, Tabellen, Reportagen, Filmeinblendungen usw. Das Feld der Ereignisse war ihm nie breit genug, und bei historischen Stücken dehnte er den geschichtlichen Hintergrund bis an die denkbar äusserste Begrenzung aus.[5]

(That now the direct collision of groups and classes must become the subject of the dramatic presentation was the straighforward conclusion. The Piscator-Model thus preferred plays of large format. Where the field of tension was narrow and limited it was expanded, using insertions, announcements, tables, reports, film clips, by the director, who did not hesitate to assume the function of the playwright. The field covered by events could never be wide enough for him, and for historical plays he expanded the period background to the furthest conceivable limits.)

At about this time Brecht was working on a comparable subject, *Joe P. Fleischhacker*, which was listed in the Piscator-Bühne's advance publicity for production under its earlier working title *Weizen (Wheat)*. It was to have dealt with the world grain market, and Brecht too set about his homework, but in a different fashion.

Für ein bestimmtes Theaterstück brauchte ich als Hintergrund die Weizenbörse Chicagos. Ich dachte, durch einige Umfragen bei Spezialisten und Praktikern mir rasch die nötigen Kenntnisse verschaffen zu können. Die Sache kam anders. Niemand, weder einige bekannte Wirtshaftsschriftsteller noch Geschäftsleute – einem Makler, der an der Chicagoer Börse ein Leben lang gearbeitet hatte, reiste ich von Berlin bis nach Wien nach – niemand konnte mir die Vorgänge an der Weizenbörse hinreichend erklären. Ich gewann den Eindruck, dass diese Vorgänge schlechthin unerklärlich, das heisst wieder einfach unvernünftig waren. Die Art, wie das Getreide der Welt verteilt wurde, war schlechthin unbegreiflich. Von jedem Standpunkt aus, ausser demjenigen einer Handvoll Spekulanten, war dieser Getreidemarkt ein einziger Sumpf. Das geplante Drama wurde nicht geschrieben, statt dessen begann ich Marx zu lesen. Jetzt wurden meine eigenen zerstreuten praktischen Erfahrungen und Eindrücke richtig lebendig.[6]

(For a certain play I needed the Chicago Grain Exchange as background. My idea was that I would make a few enquiries of specialists and practitioners in the field, and that way I would quickly get the knowledge I needed. Things turned out differently. Nobody, neither a number of well-known writers on economics, nor some businessmen – I went from Berlin to Vienna to track down a dealer who had spent a lifetime trading on the Chicago Exchange – none of them could adequately explain to me what went on at the Grain Exchange. I got the impression that the goings-on were downright inexplicable, unreasonable. The way grain was distributed throughout the world was quite inconceivable. From any point of view, except that of a handful of speculators, the grain market was a swamp. The projected drama was never written, and instead I began to read Marx. Now my own scattered experiences and impressions really came to life.)

Brecht is looking for a pattern in the events and wants to understand their logic, so he turns to experts in the expectation that they will be able to summarize the essentials for him, whereupon he in his turn will devise the appropriate, simple dramatic structure. When it transpires that the matter only makes sense from one angle, that of the speculators, he turns to the study of Marxism in the hope of finding another, more acceptable way of looking at, among other things, world grain trading. This search for lucid principles had nothing in common with Piscator's technique of montage which was kaleidoscopic and involved the simultaneous presentation of live action, film and statistical projections. He bombarded the audience with a mass of complementary and contradictory information, allowing them then to make their own connections. Bernhard Reich recollects that Piscator's production of Walther Mehring's *Der Kaufmann von Berlin* (*The Merchant of Berlin*) which used this additive technique, added up to a fairly complete social panorama of Berlin during the inflation of 1923, which, he adds, gave the impression of having been submitted to a Marxist method of examination. Piscator, if this is true, was successful in his aim of putting the material across, at least to Reich who was a sound judge in these matters.

Piscator was concerned then with presenting large subjects, and he was happy to improvise and experiment in staging them, starting, as he repeatedly tells us, from scratch every time in his quest for the appropriate scenic form for each new production. Brecht as a playwright was primarily concerned with the form of the play though the margin by which this is so is a matter of debate, whereas what interested Piscator at heart was the form of the staging. He was after all a director.

In a clear reference to Piscator, Brecht noted in 1928 (*SzT* 1, 205–6) that it was the director rather than the writer who had begun to use the theatre as a weapon in the class struggle, employing new means like jazz and film. At this stage he felt that this trend was passive and reproductive and hence anti-revolutionary, so that he could only view it as the final stage in the bourgeois–naturalistic theatre. Piscator would hardly have agreed.

The Piscator-Bühne collapsed in May 1928, and in some reflections prompted by Leopold Jessner's production of Sophocles' *Oedipus* which opened on 4 January 1929, Brecht concluded that the season so far, with productions of P. M. Lampel's *Revolte im Erziehungshaus* (*Revolt in the House of Correction*) and F. Bruckner's *Die Verbrecher* (*The Criminals*), indicated that Piscator had been influential in introducing new subject-matter into the theatre rather than, as had previously been supposed, in the matter of form. From a formal point of view Jessner's technique in *Oedipus on Colonus*, 'where he tells the story with great theatrical effect' (*SzT* 1, 208) points the way ahead. This leads Brecht to consider the future form of the drama.

> Unsere dramatische Form beruht darauf, dass der Zuschauer mitgeht, sich einfühlt, verstehen kann, sich identifizieren kann. Platt gesagt, für Fachleute: ein Stück das etwa auf der Weizenbörse spielt, kann in der grossen Form, der dramatischen, nicht gemacht werden . . . . Wie muss also unsere grosse Form sein?
>
> Episch. Sie muss berichten. Sie muss nicht glauben, dass man sich einfühlen kann in unsere Welt, sie muss es auch nicht wollen. Die Stoffe sind ungeheuerlich, unsere Dramatik muss dies berücksichtigen. (*SzT* 1, 208)

> (Our dramatic form depends on the audience going along with it, feeling its way in, being able to understand, to identify. To be blunt, for people in the business: a play that chances to take place in a grain exchange cannot be done in the grand, the dramatic form . . . . How then must our grand form look?
>
> Epic. It must make a report. It must not believe that it is possible to feel one's way into our world, it must not even want this to happen. The subjects are monstrous, our drama must bear this in mind.)

Brecht's observation of Piscator's attempts to deal with contemporary political and economic subjects and his own failure to complete *Joe P. Fleischhacker* had prompted him to recognize in Jessner's *Oedipus* the germ of a new grand form, the epic drama, which he himself was later to develop, but that is another story.

Also published in 1929, Piscator's ideas on the drama, which he summarizes under the heading, 'Sociological and Political Theory of the Drama' are more humble in scope, amounting to no more than 'a new angle from which to approach the staging of half-formed or even totally incomplete dramatic subjects', rather than a prescriptive dramaturgy in the traditional sense. This new angle is, he says, based on a new conception of man and a number of techniques of staging. War and revolution have put an end to bourgeois individualism and eclipsed the 'interesting hero' of traditional drama. He cites Tasso and Hamlet as characters whose once sublime emotions and souls have become ridiculous on the stage, now that the First World War has shifted the focus of interest from the individual to the masses.

> The epoch whose social and economic conditions have in fact perhaps deprived the individual of his right to be a man, without affording him the higher humanity of a new society, has raised itself on a pedestal as the new

hero. It is no longer the private, personal fate of the individual, but the times and the fate of the masses that are the heroic factors in the new drama.[7]

The new heroic factor is the fate of the masses, in the sense both of the conditions historically imposed on them and of their new Communist destiny to which Piscator's political theatre was to contribute, and this can perhaps best be illustrated by taking a detailed look at Piscator's transformation of *Rasputin, or the Czarina's Conspiracy*, a bloodthirsty political thriller by Alexey Tolstoy and Peter Shchegolev which had run successfully in Leningrad in 1924, into a grand panorama of war and revolution, *Rasputin, the Romanovs, the War and the People which Rose Against Them*.

The insight which crystallized the form in which *Rasputin* was staged came from Piscator's reading of the *Memoirs* of the French ambassador to St Peterburg, Maurice Paléologue. It was here that Piscator saw,

> that not even the smallest political ploys and moves made by Rasputin could be explained without reference to English policy in the Dardanelles or military moves on the Western front. The concept of a globe on which all events are closely bound up with one another and are mutually interdependent took hold of my imagination.[8]

The theatre of action was the world and this was symbolized by a hemispherical set, a dome built of gas piping and silvered balloon cloth which the designer, Traugott Müller, built on the revolving stage. It had flaps which opened to reveal acting segments on two levels, and this would have facilitated rapid scene changes if the construction of the dome had matched the conception. As it was it just worked, and Alfred Kerr described it as a 'trundling tortoise of tent-cloth'.[9] A screen could be lowered in above the dome, there were two projectors trained on the dome itself, there was a front gauze for projections, and there was a tall 'calendar' screen on each side of the proscenium arch on which statistics and other data could be shown.

A team of researchers drew up a calendar on the basis of available books and documents, and on the basis of chronological coordinates established by this means, eight new scenes were inserted among the eight scenes of the original script which were retained. The following outline shows the new material in italics and indicates the original structure of the play in Roman numerals.

1. Vyrubova's room at Tsarskoe Selo (I)
2. *Pub on the outskirts of Moscow showing public gloom and desperation after the reports of losses in the field* (film).
3. *Three emperors scene.*
4. *Lenin at Zimmerwalden (Switzerland) in March, 1916, the deliberations of the revolutionary leaders counterpointing the mouthings of the imperialist puppets in the previous scene.*
5. Rasputin's house (II) where Rasputin asserts the need for peace. (*Film: French counter attack at Verdun, Russian losses on the Düna and Berezina*).

6. *Three tycoons scene. The opposing arms manufacturers, Krupp, Creusot and Armstrong state that they are fighting to save the German spirit, democracy and civilisation, and freedom, respectively. (film: belching chimneys of arms factories).*

7. *Haig and Foch scene. Generals blandly discuss tactics against projections of carnage in the Western front with superimposed captions, such as, 'Losses: half a million. Gains: 300 square kilometers.'*

8. *Russian deserter scene, written by Brecht, Lania and Gasbarra to illustrate demoralization in the ranks.*

9. Czar's headquarters (III, i and ii). Czar writes to his wife of the healthy and invigorating life he is leading at the front. *Projections of mutilated Russian corpses.*

10. *Duma*

11. Prince Yussoupov's study (IV, i).

12. St. Petersburg nightclub with floor show (IV, ii).

13. Yussoupov's palace (IV, iii), Gory murder of Rasputin.

14. Czarina's room (V, i, ii, iii). Czarina plans the arrest of revolutionaries. *Film of the sealed train bringing Lenin back to Russia runs overhead. Lenin acts decisively as soon as he arrives.*

15. *Soviet Congress at Smolny with Lenin speaking. Soviet Revolution. Internationale.*[10]

The original plot remained, but it was punctuated by scenes reflecting the state of the proletariat (the Moscow pub scene and the Russian deserter scene). All the lines spoken by public figures were based on documentary evidence. Piscator's defence in a legal action brought against him by the ex-Kaiser was that his Kaiser on the stage said nothing that the real Kaiser was not on record as having said in real life. The three emperors deplored having been forced into the war while at the same time appealing for patriotic support. The revolutionaries in Switzerland unmasked the emperors' hypocrisy. Then the three tycoons, the men who wielded the real economic power, depict the war as a national crusade, while their factories, working at full blast on film behind them, make their material profit from the war explicit. As the Czarina plans to restore order, a film shows her fate rolling across Europe towards her in a sealed train. The whole action climaxes in Lenin's seizure of power, and the evening ends with a rendering of the *Internationale*, a feature of several Piscator productions.

The use of film which Piscator had developed consistently in various productions since first using still projections in *Fahnen (Flags)* in 1924 reached a peak of complexity in *Rasputin*. Piscator categorizes its three functions as didactic, dramatic and commentary. The didactic film presented the kind of material one might normally expect to find in the programme notes. The prologue to the evening consisted of shots of the Czars shown in historical sequence on the main screen, with appropriate captions such as 'died suddenly', or 'died by his own hand', or 'died insane', which were flashed on the calendar screen on either side of the stage while film on the lower part of the dome showed the brutalized condition of the people under the oppression of the priesthood and the aristocracy. This potted history of Czarism in league with the Orthodox Church showed one of the root causes of the Revolution. As it ended Erwin Kalser as Nicholas II stepped out on to the stage and postured under a towering projected silhouette of Rasputin, and the production moved from film into a live scene, an effective transition from one medium to another, and the kind of effect Piscator enjoyed.

The dramatic film was used to advance the story quickly, showing in one scene mutinous forces advancing on the palace while the Czarina was still pleading with the ghost of Rasputin for advice.

The film commentary largely took the form of captions and data projected on the calendar, and was addressed directly to the audience to draw their attention to important developments in the action, to spell out the implication of pronouncements made by public figures and even as direct agitation. As generals Haig and Foch bandy strategy with one another at headquarters, atrocity footage from the battle of the Somme is shown with the comment, 'losses – half a million dead: military gain – 120 square miles'. The Czar pens a letter to his wife extolling the life at the front while shots of Russian corpses come up on the screen.

The production lasted four hours and made considerable demands on the audience's concentration. The original play was embedded in an elaborate context of international events, and as the lines were spoken they were commented upon and often contradicted by silent film and projections, while an apparatus of facts and figures flashed up on screens beside the stage. To Hans Reimann, who was backstage one night in connection with the *Schwejk* adaptation, the sheer bulk of the information presented was something of a joke. He himself was something of a wag, so he strolled across the stage in his hat and coat to see what would happen. Neither the audience, nor the actors, nor the stage manager noticed him, though the fireman seemed mildly suspicious.

In an article called 'Drama and history' Leo Lania summed up the ideas behind this propagandistic presentation of recent history.

Historical drama is not the tragedy of the fate of some hero or other, it is the political document of an epoch . . . . Historical drama is not just a matter of education: only if it has a life of its own can it bridge the gap between then and now and release the forces which are destined to shape the appearance of the present and that of the immediate future . . . . The Peasants' War, the French Revolution, the Commune, 1848, 1813, the October Revolt – only in relation to the year 1927 can we experience these things . . . . This basic attitude towards historical drama means a complete revision of traditional dramatic form; not the inner arc of dramatic events is important, but the most accurate and comprehensive epic account of the epoch from its roots to its ultimate ramifications. Drama is important for us only where it can be supported by documentary evidence. Film, the constant interruption of external events by projections and film clips, are a means of achieving this documentary breadth and depth; they are inserted between the acts and after decisive turns of events and provide areas of illumination as the searchlight of history penetrates the uttermost darkness of the times.[11]

For the purposes of political theatre historical drama must document an epoch and bring it to life on the stage, a distant echo of Büchner. The emphasis is on detail, and film is an essential ingredient for adequate coverage. But historical drama must also analyse that epoch so as to liberate in the spectator the forces that will shape the future. This is consistent with the line pursued by Piscator from his earliest political productions for the Proletarian Theatre which in 1920 announced as its intention,

> Subordination of all artistic aims to the revolutionary goal: conscious emphasis on and cultivation of the idea of the class struggle.[12]

The faith in Marxism which Piscator brought back from the Western front in 1918 remained unshaken throughout the Weimar Republic, without, it should be stated, making him a slavish conformist or even a reliable front man for the KPD of which he was a member. The depth of his conviction is revealed in touching reiterations of his belief that his Marxist analysis of the facts on the stage was not an interpretation but a revelation of the truth. After the Second World War this conviction gave way to a more conciliatory attitude.

> Once I believed commitment was truth: the others were wrong and my side was right. Today one should at least be able to demand the right to say 'truth is neutral'.[13]

The characteristic feature of Piscator's productions was an attempt to contextualize whatever action lay at the heart of the piece, so that he ended up with long sequences of loosely related scenes which he marshalled with the help of an array of theatrical techniques, to which he would sometimes refer as 'Maschinentheater'. This to his mind was 'epic theatre' even after Brecht's development of alienation effects, gestic acting and other refinements had given the term another meaning which had wide currency. In a passage inserted in the revised edition of *Das Politische Theater* in 1963 he wrote that he had begun to develop epic theatre in *Fahnen* in 1924, and offered the following as his final definition of it:

> Briefly, it was about the extension of the action and the clarification of the background of the action, that is to say it involved a continuation of the play beyond the dramatic framework. A didactic play (*Lehrstück*) was developed from the spectacle-play (*Schaustück*).[14]

Piscator was not, as John Willett rightly observes, the innovator in the field of acting that he was in staging and dramaturgy, and the development of epic, gestic, demonstrative acting was Brecht's independent achievement. Nonetheless Piscator was aware of the need for a new style and looked to political commitment to produce a new breed of actor:

> One who draws his whole strength from his involvement in the common

cause. In the course of time this attitude will produce a new form of acting.[15]

This is a hope rather than a formula, and Piscator took his ideas a little further. He was aware of the need to harmonize the acting in his theatre with the bare wood, canvas and iron of his constructivist sets which clashed both with stock characterization and with the subtly modelled, poetic style he associated with Friedrich Kayssler, two Berlin styles he seems to have found to be widespread and offensive. Seeking a name for the style he wants, he hits on the term 'neorealistic', which he qualifies as hard, unambiguous, unsentimental, unfalsified and open, all of which, he hastens to add, has nothing to do with the Naturalism of the 1880s.

> Of course we do not require professional naturalness, but a performance so scientific and so clearly analysed by the intellect that it reproduces naturalness at a higher level and with a technique just as intentional and calculated as the architecture of the stage. Every word must be as central to the work as the centre is to the periphery of a circle. That everything on the stage is calculable, everything fits together organically.[16]

The stress on reason, scientific objectivity and calculated relationships must have struck a sympathetic chord in Brecht. Piscator was frequently annoyed when critics belittled his ability to lead actors, and he protested that he was being blamed for imprecision that stemmed from the short-comings of the actors' training, and was merely thrown into relief by his productions. Brecht's trenchant view was that he was better than his notices but worse than he himself thought, being more tolerant of clashes of acting style within his productions than was consistent with sound taste.

On a practical level Piscator tells us how he prepared the actors for Toller's *Hoppla, wir leben* (*Hoppla, Such is Life!*)

> Each actor had to be quite conscious of the fact that he represented a particular social class. I remember a great deal of time was spent at rehearsals discussing the political significance of each role with the actor concerned. Only when he had mastered the spirit of the part in this way could the actor create his role.[17]

Fruitful though this must have been for the actor's understanding of the play, it helped to distribute emphasis rather than to develop a new style. In *Hoppla* the playing of the Weimar establishment was speeded up for caricatural effect, so that the normal pace of the proletarian figures stood out with dignity. Gerhard Bienert, one of the few surviving actors from the Piscator-Bühne, cannot recollect that anything other than straight, realistic acting was required of him – but then he had to confess in the same conversation that he could not make sense of Brecht's alienation either.

The Piscator-Bühne season of 1927–28 saw Piscator's career at its peak. He directed five more productions in the Weimar Republic, notably Carl Crede's *§218*, a *Zeitstück* attacking the law on abortion. It was cheaply and simply mounted by a *Kollektiv* of ex-Piscator-Bühne actors and ran for some 300 performances. This, however, was theatre on a shoestring and it did not satisfy him. He was, Brecht reports, 'like a bacteriologist whose microscope has been taken away' (*Brecht on Theatre*, p. 69). At the beginning of 1931 Piscator was directing Friedrich Wolf's *Tai Yang erwacht* (*Tai Yang Awakes*) in the obscurity of the seedy, old Wallner Theater while Brecht was staging an elaborate, wholly experimental revival of *Mann ist Mann* (*A Man's a Man*) with all the resources of the Staatliches Schauspielhaus. Brecht went on to become an international celebrity at the Berliner Ensemble, while Piscator, in spite of his achievements at the New York Dramatic Workshop and his breakthrough with documentary theatre at the Freie Volksbühne in the early 1960s, never really regained his 1920s eminence. Neither, however, did he ever wholly reconcile himself to not being at the top, which may explain why a certain sourness creeps into his attitude to Brecht, while Brecht continues to treat him with considerable generosity.

The two men's inverse career structures are naturally not the whole explanation. During the period of their European exile, Piscator (1931– 38 in the Soviet Union and France) and Brecht (1933–41 in Denmark, Sweden and Finland) were in intermittent contact, assuring each other of their willingness to collaborate on a film or a play, should it be possible to set up an appropriate project. While he was in Paris, Piscator was constantly involved in negotiations for a stage version of *Schwejk*, either in New York or in Paris, or for a Schwejk film, either in the USA or in Europe. He cabled Grosz in New York who replied that he and Hanns Eisler had had a good laugh over Piscator's suggestions, and that Piscator was too wedded to the big time ('zu sehr ans grosse Geldverdienen gewöhnt') to be able to work with the kind of people who would be interested in *Schwejk* in the USA, people as bereft of influence as they were of cash. Wieland Herzfeld pointed out from Prague that Schwejk as a figure was *passé* and would anyhow involve interminable lawsuits. Piscator replied with unconcealed displeasure

Die *Schwejk*aufführung ist berühmt, und wenn ich heute entsprechend Angebote bekomme, ihn zu verfilmen oder zu inszenieren, so ist das eine Berufsangelegenheit. Ich werde ihn selbstverständlich so machen, dass ich ihn politisch vertreten kann. Wird gar der *Schwejk* in Amerika gemacht, so ist das für mich eine Existenzfrage von grösster Bedeutung, wie Du zugeben wirst.[18]

(The production of *Schwejk* is famous, and if I accordingly get offers to film it or restage it, then that is a professional matter. I will naturally do it in such a way that I can stand by it politically. If *Schwejk* were even to be done in America then it would be quite crucial for my living, as you will agree.)

Brecht was kept abreast of developments, and these culminated in 1937 in a film scenario which was sent to Brecht who appraised it in some detail. He was, he said, prepared to join the project at the drop of a hat, but nothing came of it.

The subject of a new version of *Schwejk* cropped up again in 1943 when Piscator and Brecht discussed an updated *Schwejk* in New York. At the same time E. J. Aufricht approached Brecht about collaborating with Kurt Weill on a musical version of *Schwejk* and, though this project was abandoned, Brecht drafted *Schweyk im zweiten Weltkrieg* (*Schweyk in the Second World War*) on the train back to Santa Monica. When Piscator heard, indirectly, of Brecht's by then completed new play he was incensed and contemplated legal action. He remained convinced that although he had not secured the legal rights to the subject he had a moral right, and Brecht had in effect stolen it from him. It is doubtful whether his attitude to Brecht ever recovered from this shock.

In 1947, writing from Santa Monica, Brecht sounds out 'lieber pis' ('dear pis') about returning to Germany, saying he cannot imagine a revival of 'grosses, politisch reifes Theater' ('great, politically mature theatre') without him, but suggesting that each head a separate theatre. Piscator's reply, presumably asking why they should not work in the same theatre is lost, but Brecht's next letter explains that he needs

> ... einen ganz bestimmten Darstellungsstil, der sich von deinem unterscheidet – Das ist der ganze Vorbehalt, und es scheint mir produktiver. Gerade du kannst nicht an eine mechanische Einteilung in Stückeschreiber und Inszenator glauben. Wir arbeiten nichtsdestotrotz auf der gleichen Linie.[19]

> (... a quite definite style of acting which is different from yours – that is my entire reservation, and it seems to me more productive. You would be the last person to believe in a mechanical separation of playwright and director. We are working none the less on the same lines.)

Piscator replies to 'lieber Berthold' [*sic*] that he is closer to him than any other playwright. Two years later Brecht offers him a production of O'Casey or Lorca, or better still Nordahl Grieg's *Die Niederlage* (*The Defeat*) as the opening production of the new Ensemble under Helene Weigel's direction. It was now or never. Piscator's reply is full of uncertainty; there were too many imponderables, an allusion to the political situation in East Berlin, for him to make so decisive a break.

The correspondence lapsed, and when, two years later, Piscator returned, it was to the Federal Republic.

It is clear from this exchange that Brecht still considered that their similarities far outweighed their differences, though he reserved the right to do his plays his own way. He had reason to know what Piscator might do to them. During the lull which followed the collapse of the Piscator-Bühne in 1928 Piscator, Brecht and Fritz Sternberg discussed a revival of *Trommeln in der Nacht* (*Drums in the Night*) which Piscator proposed to tie in with the failure of the Revolution, using an elaborate set to show a cross-section of Berlin. In 1945 Piscator rehearsed an off-Broadway production of *The Private Life of the Master Race* (*Furcht und Elend im dritten Reich*) which was to set the play in context with, among other things, a discussion of dictatorship and democracy, leading to a further discussion of the principles of epic theatre before the actual play came on. When Brecht demurred, Piscator walked out, pronouncing himself 'unable to afford the luxury of an artistic failure'. Oddly enough the *Mother Courage* which Piscator directed in Kassel in 1960, after Brecht was dead, seems to have followed Brecht's model fairly closely. Finally, if Brecht had reservations about Piscator's directing, Piscator, for all his assurances that Brecht was a kindred spirit, found that his plays tended to be arid and intellectual.

What finally did Brecht get from Piscator? A working example of Marxist political theatre which aimed to instruct and induce change through rational, scientific analysis, which tackled big, new subjects and exploded the traditional form of drama. Brecht's use of songs may derive from the introduction of Mehring's chanson 'Hoppla wir leben' into Toller's play, Mother Courage's revolve from Schwejk's conveyor belts, Brecht's half-curtain from Piscator's projection screens, and so forth, as Piscator was inclined to think. But these are details, and probably it is best to say that in Piscator Brecht found an inspiration and a relevant example which he subsequently developed along quite individual lines.

In his generous assessment of Piscator's theatre in the *Messingkauf Dialogues* Brecht calls Piscator one of the greatest men of the theatre of all times, the man who electrified the stage and brought it into the technological age. His restructuring and staging of inadequate texts entitled him to be called a playwright, though he scarcely wrote so much as a scene himself. He provided, says Brecht, 'Anschauungsunterricht', object lessons for the times. He did the same for Brecht.

NOTES

1. *Erwin Piscator 1893–1966*, Exhibition Catalogue (Berlin, 1971), p. 81. Piscator's dedication on a portrait sent to Brecht on 1 August 1941, reproduced in the catalogue of the 1971 Piscator exhibition at the Akademie der Künste, West Berlin.
2. Brecht to Piscator, dated March 1947, unpublished letter in the archive of the Akademie der Künste, West Berlin.
3. Erwin Piscator, *The Political Theatre* (London, 1980), p. 196
4. Ibid., p. 274.
5. Bernhard Reich, *Im Wettlauf mit der Zeit* (Berlin, 1970), p. 223.
6. Reinhold Grimm, *Episches Theater* (Cologne/Berlin, 1966), p. 51. Quoted after Werner Hecht's paper, 'Brechts Weg zum epischen Theater'.
7. Piscator, *Political Theatre*, p. 187.
8. Ibid., p. 232.
9. Ibid., p. 235.

10. Ibid., p. 222–3.
11. Ibid., p. 229–30.
12. Ibid., p. 45.
13. Erwin Piscator, Diary 14, entry for 17 January 1955, quoted after John Willett, *The Theatre of Erwin Piscator* (London, 1978), p. 190.
14. Piscator, *Political Theatre*, p. 75.
15. Erwin Piscator, *Schriften II* (Berlin, 1968), p. 29. Translated in Willett, op. cit., p. 118.
16. Piscator, *Political Theatre*, p. 121.
17. Ibid., p. 214.
18. Herbert Knust, *Materialien zu Bertolt Brechts 'Schweyk im zweiten Weltkrieg'* (Frankfurt am Main, 1974), p. 139. Knust presents a selection of Piscator's correspondence relating to *Schwejk* on pp. 137–146.
19. Unpublished letter dated March 1947 in the archive of the Akademie der Künste, West Berlin. There are four of Brecht's letters and three of Piscator's between February 1947 and March 1949 in this file.

SELECT BIBLIOGRAPHY

GRIMM, REINHOLD, ed., *Episches Theater*, Cologne/Berlin, 1966
KNUST, HERBERT, ed., *Materialien zu Bertolt Brechts 'Schweyk im zweiten Weltkrieg'*, Frankfurt am Main, 1974
MEWS, SIEGFRIED and HERBERT KNUST, eds, *Essays on Brecht*, Chapel Hill, 1974
PISCATOR, ERWIN, *Schriften I/II*, Berlin GDR, 1968
PISCATOR, ERWIN, *The Political Theatre*, London, 1980
REICH, BERNHARD, *Im Wettlauf mit der Zeit*, Berlin GDR, 1970
WILLETT, JOHN *The Theatre of Erwin Piscator*, London, 1978

Chapter 10

BRECHT AND CABARET

J. M. RITCHIE

Why has cabaret assumed such significance that since the appearance of the United Artists' film of that name, it has come to be the key to the decline and fall of the Weimar Republic? By way of partial explanation what perhaps needs to be said for a start is that the source of that particular film was a series of books by Christopher Isherwood, who almost in the style of German post-First World War New Objectivity recorded in little prose sketches his outsider's view of this world before it was destroyed by National Socialism. In a remarkable process of literary exploitation over the next decades these narrative sketches passed through a protean sequence of permutations involving a play, a film, a musical, and finally a film of the musical with the American star Liza Minelli acting the part of the incompetent English girl Sally Bowles in Berlin. By this time the song element had become all-important for the atmosphere of decadence the film was intended to convey, decadence which came across so convincingly that doubts as to whether Berlin was ever really like that, or cabaret ever really like that, now seem utterly irrelevant. Nevertheless, there was an element of truth in the film. Germany always was and still is *the* theatre-crazy country and though perhaps after the First World War 'those who wished to enjoy the true and noble pleasures of the theatre made the journey to Paris, where the most advanced and stimulating theatre in Europe was flourishing and playing to full houses',[1] Berlin did have certain counter-attractions, as the presence there of English intellectuals like Auden and Isherwood indicated.

The reasons for their presence and for the fascination which Berlin exercised at the time were many and varied and not all connected with the cabaret theatre. Many intellectuals thought they saw in the new Germany a nation somehow purified by war, marching forward to pure democracy; others saw the very opposite; Berlin, as the film suggests, did become notorious and attractive for its immorality. Christopher Isherwood, for example, commented as follows on the enticing difference between Paris and Berlin:

Berlin was a complete contrast. Outwardly it was graver, stiffer and more formal; inwardly it was far more lurid and depraved. For a runaway Briton it was a more congenial refuge than Paris because it recognised vice, and cultivated it in all its forms with humourless Prussian thoroughness.[2]

Whatever the reasons, Berlin enjoyed a cultural Golden Age at this time, 'a period of violence, a Renaissance age of gangsters and aesthetes, Savonarolas, Cellinis and Borgias',[3] and some of the excitement of these Roaring Twenties was encapsulated in the minor form of the cabaret. The war seemed to have broken down all the traditional barriers, removed all the braking and modifying processes and thrown the whole country open to a *nouvelle vague* in every sphere of life. This was the age which saw the spectacular triumph of Expressionism in literature, music, painting and the cinema. Expressionism was no little avant-garde group of isolated artists but a tidal wave which swept all before it, evoking in the end an equally violent reaction against it, culminating in the Nazi banning and burning of all such 'decadent' art, and cabaret, which had close connections with the avant-garde, was also denounced as decadent. Significantly too the Roaring Twenties proved to be not only Germany's Golden Age of Cabaret: they also developed into a Golden Age of the Theatre in general. The names of Erwin Piscator and Max Reinhardt, the great producers, still conjure up an age of theatrical excitement and experimentation, despite the fact that the plays and authors of the period have largely failed to find their place in the enduring repertoire of contemporary Germany, and that only the memory of these hectic cabarets remains alive.

Before focusing particularly on possible connections between Brecht and the cabaret perhaps something needs to be said about the connections between cabaret and Expressionist theatre. The outstanding feature of the theatre of German Expressionism is the great wealth of material and great diversity of style and subject-matter which it produced. This diversity makes the Expressionist play difficult to characterize, but one thing was always true – it was always deliberately unsettling. This was to be a feature too of the drama of Brecht who, while rejecting Expressionism in general, was among the first to see the positive features of this new revolutionary drama for a scientific age. It had no plot, no characters, no time-scale, no action, no personal psychology, no motivation, no exposition, no realistic background. In a Brecht play, too, it is often difficult to discern a continuous plot line: characters do not develop, they are deliberately constructed and contradictory, indeed split down the middle; the time-scale is often vague as in *The Caucasian Chalk Circle*; place is equally confusing; while what would have been exposition in a traditional play is often presented by a commentator addressing the audience directly. The Expressionist play proceeded by a process of reduction – everything was reduced to the bare minimum, language was pared down to the language of the telegram. The play became abstract, geometrical, dialectic, where it did not explode entirely into formlessness. It was intended to have the explosive power of a clenched fist, intended to be a fever expressed in cold clear language – a vision. All the 'unrealistic' effects banished by the realist–naturalistic school were reintroduced, such as long monologues addressed straight at the audience and exaggerated gestures.

Obviously the impact of the whole was disturbing for the poor bourgeois in the audience. All the things he normally looked for in a play seemed to have been deliberately removed. Yet even for the most naive theatre-goer there were great compensations, apart from the simple excitement of being part of an artistic revolution. There was the great development in the exploitation of the resources of the theatre – the use of pageantry, choreography, light and colour effects, mime, music and song, all of which could be readily transferred to the small cabaret stage. The theatre became much more theatrical and much less academic than it had ever been before in Germany. Perhaps it produced few great plays and playwrights, but it did clear the ground for what was to come. Brecht's career in the theatre is inconceivable without consideration of the Expressionist and post-Expressionist New Objectivity generation from which he sprang.

One of the features of the theatre in Germany after the First World War was that it seemed to move in at least two directions at the same time: it soared upwards to the loftiest heights to proclaim the current ideals of the time, while at the same time sinking to the lowest depths and becoming anti-art. The theatre of the age was highbrow, obscure, difficult, engaged in technical experiments; but at the same time there was an appreciable move in the opposite direction into the most popular of art forms. People were fascinated by circuses, beercellars, and the theatre in all its forms. As far as music was concerned there was an equally appreciable move towards jazz. This reflected a general European movement. Willet gives the French background and notes:

> Other German musicians associated with this group carried the French experiments a good deal further, both inside and outside the actual festivals, and managed to bring them to a rather wider public. Ernst Krenek wrote his jazz operas *Sprung über den Schatten* (1924) and *Jonny Spielt Auf* (1927), with its negro hero; Wilhelm Grosz (known to us as the composer of 'It was on the Isle of Capri that I met her') wrote a *Jazzband* for violin (1925) and the ballet *Baby in the Bar* (1927), and set Ringelnatz's light verse to some very original music. A jazz class was instituted at the Frankfurt Hochsches Konservatorium under Matyas Seiber, who published a *Jazz Percussion Tutor*. In 1923 Hermann Scherchen introduced *L'Histoire du Soldat* at Frankfurt with Carl Ebert as narrator, later taking it on tour with a cut-down version of Cocteau and Milhaud's short opera *Le Pauvre Matelot* (1926). It was performed at the Berlin State Opera in 1925, and in 1928 was produced there by Brecht's friend Jakob Geis, as part of the première of the Cocteau–Stravinsky *Oedipus Rex*. The Germans not only took the French ideas up; they took them seriously; and they took them to the public. And all this for more than 'purely' musical reasons.[4]

This interest of the Age of Expressionism in jazz was closely allied to that other aspect of the German theatre in the 1920s already noted, namely cabaret. And yet one of the most remarkable features of twentieth-century theatrical history is the attraction which this form of theatre had for almost all intellectuals. Indeed one finds that the most extreme avant-garde artists of the time were fascinated by the possibilities of the cabaret genre. In Berlin Kurt Hiller, one of the initiators of German Expressionism, created literary cabarets, Neopathetisches Cabaret (1909) and Gnu (1911), and being German developed a theory and a programme to go with them:

> We see nothing unworthy and ignoble about mingling the most serious forms
> of philosophy amid songs and (cerebral) jokes: on the contrary precisely
> because for us philosophy is not just something academic, but has a vital
> significance, is not just something to be taught, not just a job, not just
> morality or expenditure of perspiration, but living experience, it seems to us
> to be more appropriate for a *cabaret* than for a lecture-room or a learned
> journal.[5]

The Italian Futurists, who exercised a considerable influence on German Expressionism, were also moving in the same direction as Marinetti's praise of the lowbrow music-hall instead of the classical stage revealed. Apart from totally rejecting the psychological analysis of feelings, Marinetti praised the kind of theatre where the smoke of cigars and cigarettes linked the atmosphere in the audience with that on the stage and went on:

> Variety theatre is naturally anti-academic, primitive and naive...it destroys
> the solemn, sacred, serious and sublime in Art with a capital A. It
> cooperates in the...destruction of immortal masterpieces, plagiarising them,
> parodying them, making them look commonplace by stripping them of their
> solemn apparatus.[6]

Almost more famous was the Cabaret Voltaire (described by Richard Huelsenbeck as a Varieté-Miniatur), which became the centre for the Dadaists in Zurich during the war. That this Dada cabaret was no harmless game can be seen from the proclaimed intentions of one of its main participants, Richard Huelsenbeck:

> Wir wollten das Cabaret Voltaire zu einem Brennpunkt 'jüngster Kunst'
> machen, obwohl wir uns nicht scheuchten, auch hin und wieder den feisten
> und vollkommen verständnislosen Züricher Spiessbürgern zu sagen, dass wir
> sie für Schweine und den deutschen Kaiser für den Initiator des Krieges
> hielten.

> We wanted to make the Cabaret Voltaire into the focal point of modern art
> although we were not afraid to tell the fat and completely uncomprehending
> Zurich bourgeois from time to time that we thought them swine and held the
> German Emperor responsible for starting the war.[7]

The First World War was indeed what laid the firm foundations for the development of German as distinct from French cabaret. In wartime many legitimate theatres shut down and restaurants had to close by ten o'clock in the evening. It was this that gave the café-cabarets a chance to develop and become popular. Then in 1918, when pre-censorship of scripts was removed, they were able to develop even more freely, especially in their treatment of erotic as well as political material. The lead given by the Dadaists in Zurich was taken up and developed in all the major cities of Germany, but nowhere more so than in Berlin and Munich. The talent was obviously there in all the necessary spheres; there were songsmiths, stage-designers, composers and dancers. What was needed was the proper framework in which these could develop and this was first provided by Max Reinhardt, who in December 1919 brought back to life the cabaret Schall und Rauch (Sound and Smoke) in the cellar rooms beneath his Grosses Schauspielhaus. This cabaret had developed out of the circle Die Brille in 1901, a group of young actors from the Deutsches Theater, which put on a show on behalf of the tubercular Christian Morgenstern. It then continued as a purely literary cabaret, often doing take-offs of the highbrow show upstairs. Max Reinhardt was a member from the start and took over the general direction in 1903. With the intention of doing literary parodies (something that Brecht was to continue throughout his whole career as a dramatist), Reinhardt assembled a group of performers and song-writers who were interested in cabaret, among them the composer Friedrich Hollaender and the artist and stage-designer George Grosz. The important development was, however, that literary parody quickly developed into social and political comment. Schall und Rauch (a quotation incidentally from Goethe's *Faust*) thereby became the cradle for a totally new and different kind of revolutionary development in the theatre.

In re-establishing his cabaret Schall und Rauch after the First World War, Reinhardt was able to look back at and build upon a remarkably rich vein of talent, for the sheer quality of the artists traditionally associated with literary cabaret in Germany was astonishing. One of the most astonishing figures of the time, and one who had a powerful influence on Brecht, was Karl Valentin, the popular Munich comedian. The influence of Valentin is particularly noticeable in Brecht's early one-acters, characterized by the grotesque humour which was a feature of the comedian's own sketches. Brecht himself performed in Valentin's sketches which also used the picture-card technique, whereby the speaker indicates the elements in a picture with a pointer, while explaining them in verse or song. Brecht was to develop this technique throughout his life as a dramatist, in just the same way as he never lost his love for Valentin's crazy logic, one of the fundamental elements of his famous alienation effect. Valentin showed that the simplest elements of everyday speech could be exploited in such a way that the fundamental paradox at the heart of things was exposed. What Valentin built up out of these linguistic elements was a new kind of *Volksstück*. Brecht

developed these ideas in connection with his play *Puntila* and formulated them in his essay 'Anmerkungen zum *Volksstück*', ideas which are
applicable as much to his own art as to Valentin. The essence of his
argument is as follows:

1. The situations in the *Volksstück* are grotesque.
2. A story-line as such is monotonous, so it is thrown on the scrap-heap.
    Plays have now no plot, hardly even a thread running through them. As
    far as plot is concerned literary cabaret can give some useful pointers.
    In cabaret the unified, consistent plot is done away with and instead
    there are 'numbers', that is to say sketches loosely connected to each
    other. This is the case particularly in pieces like Valentin's *Tingeltangel*
    and *Oktoberfest*.
3. Of greatest importance is finding a style which is at once artistic and
    natural.
4. This new kind of theatre has the original form of *Gestik*, it has humour,
    imagination and wisdom.[8]

So much for the new dramatic form and language which Brecht
gained from his association with Karl Valentin. Fortunately, however,
he could also approve of what was being put across by this method, for
Valentin had clearly found a way of creating a type of theatre which
was popular in every sense, but still far from harmless or middle class.
Karl Valentin had found a way to speak the unspeakable. He was an
outspoken pacifist, anti-militarist and anti-capitalist and was able despite
censorship and police control to express these sentiments in his amusing
sketches, though even he had trouble with the authorities because of his
stage utterances. In 1917 he incurred a six-week performing ban for telling this story from the public platform:

> Vorgestern bin ich am Hauptbahnhof gewesen, da haben sie die
> Gehirnverletzten von der Front auf die Rotkreuzautos gladen und ins
> Schwabinger Krankenhaus gfahrn. Die Rotkreuzautos haben keine
> Gummiradl mehr ghabt wegen der Rationierung. Grad gscheppert und
> gwackelt habens, diese Krankenautos – aber, es war das reinste Wunder, die
> Verletzten haben's Hirn nicht verloren dabei. Ankommen sind's damit! Und
> gestern hat der König sie besucht. Mit seinem Auto. Das hat natürlich
> schöne Gummiradl ghabt. Der hätt aber keine Gummiradl braucht, denn der
> hätt ja sowieso kein Hirn verlorn.[9]

> The day before yesterday, I was at the station, there they were loading the
> front-line wounded with brain damage into the Red Cross ambulances to
> drive them to the Schwabing Infirmary. Because of rationing the Red Cross
> ambulances had lost their rubber tyres. They really rattled and banged about,
> these ambulances – but despite this it was an absolute miracle, because none
> of the wounded lost their brains! They arrived with them intact! And
> yesterday the king visited them. In his car. Naturally it had lovely rubber
> tyres. It wouldn't have needed rubber tyres, because he wouldn't have lost
> his brain anyway.

It is generally assumed that Brecht was attracted to the sphere of

Valentin's activities because he liked the smoky music-halls in which the comedian performed. Certainly this was no officially approved, solemn, state theatre redolent of court and middle-class culture. But it is clear that Brecht was enamoured not only of the ambience, but also of everything about this kind of theatre. The same is true of what he found in the literary–political cabaret. There he found talent of an extraordinarily high level. Richard Dehmel and Arno Holz (the Naturalist and experimental verse-smith) were associated with cabaret and so too was Detlev von Liliencron, who had introduced a completely new and lively parlando-tone into German verse. However, the guiding spirit of German cabaret from the turn of the century on and the theatrical figure whom Brecht admired more than any other was the German-American dramatist, Frank Wedekind, who has still not been accorded his due by the traditional academic critics. Wedekind was the first real exponent of the anti-art movement, the first to look in his lyrics for a new note consistent with the new century. He found it by turning to the *Moritat*, the moralizing horror-ballad still sung in his day by street-singers and beggars in back yards, at fairs and the like.

This was real folksong as distinct from the idealized *Volkslied* of the Romantics. It was eminently singable and yet sounded improvised and fresh. Eric Singer, who produced one of the first anthologies of such lyrics, has pointed out how far removed they are from any hymnic, odic, or in any way solemn poetry constructed according to a preconceived ethical programme in the artificial atmosphere of the study. Such lyrics have no premasticated problems, no pedagogical perspectives, no insufferable pathos; neither do they aim to 'épater le bourgeois' by distortion of syntax or by the revelation of impossible depths. They are completely non-intellectual, non-scientific. In his anthology of this kind of poetry Eric Singer produces a surprisingly respectable collection of names: Hermann Hesse (winner of the Nobel Prize for Literature); Alfred Kerr, the theatre critic; Franz Theodor Csokor, the Austrian dramatist; and many others. Such literary production cannot simply be regarded as a minor strain in the main stream of German literature. In fact, this stream was not nearly so insignificant as Singer's comments might lead one to think. The songs which Wedekind sang while accompanying himself on the lute were not at all harmless. Songs like 'Ilse' or 'Der Tantenmörder' were clearly felt to be demoniacal attacks on all morality.

This was a new hard note which was to come to full fruition some years later with Brecht's gruesome ballad 'Mack the Knife', though one must not overlook the many minor figures who carried on the tradition – Klabund, Mehring, Tucholsky, Kästner and others. Most of these *Kabarettisten* had close connections with the theatre. Klabund's play based on *The Chinese Chalk Circle* was one of the theatrical events of the age, and was clearly exploited by Brecht who always had a keen nose for promising material. Cabaret was only a small part of Klabund's literary and theatrical activity, yet none the less considerable. Like Brecht, he was an admirer of Villon and saw himself as the same type of social outcast, a 'divine tramp'. His songs were eagerly seized upon by cabaret, and he himself recited them in Schall und Rauch. His real contribution to cabaret however, were his *Bänkellieder* in a kind of elevated dialect or big-city argot. This was to prove an important element in the new wave – the attempt to produce the authentic voice of the big city.

Walter Mehring was also a playwright (his *Kaufmann von Berlin* was produced by Piscator at the Nollendorfplatztheater) who, like Klabund, came from the Expressionist avant-garde and was active in the Berlin Dada movement. Brought into the cabaret Schall und Rauch by Max Reinhardt to write songs, he did it so well, he claims, that his success as a song-writer has resulted in his exclusion from all serious histories of literature ever since. Mehring's songs, however, are probably the best work he ever did. He had no elevated ideas about expressing his lyrical individuality or seducing the people to ART (though he could not always forget his expressionistic technique). In songs like the 'Kartenhexe' he carried on the Wedekind tradition of the gruesome song, the melodramatic horror-ballad using the milieu of East End Berlin for his horrible crimes, improbable denouements and fascinating criminals (so reminiscent of Brecht's) like Bloody Bruno and Squint-eyed Elli. To his work he added the international flavour which has always been a feature of cabaret, as in songs like 'Die kleinen Hotels', which exploit the sordid romanticism of shabby, seedy, fifth-class French hotels, again a milieu like the international dockland Brecht loved.

But the real warrior who exploited the possibilities of cabaret as a weapon against the reactionary aspects of Germany was Kurt Tucholsky. Enormously successful in his own chosen sphere as journalist, novelist and verse-maker, he was the author of two of the great best sellers of the period (*Rheinsberg. Ein Bilderbuch für Verliebte* (*Rheinsberg. A Picture Book for Lovers*), and *Schloss Gripsholm* (*Gripsholm Castle*)), editor of the comic paper *Ulk* (*Joke*), correspondent of the *Vossische Zeitung* and later editor of the radical journal *Weltbühne* (*The World Stage*). Tucholsky was one of the funniest writers Germany has ever seen and also one of the most serious. He was a political pamphleteer of the first water who detested the reactionary, nationalistic, militaristic side of Germany and fought the good fight against the army, the Putschists and the hanging judges not once but five times under his various pseudonyms, only to suffer the fate of all great satirists and Cassandras – he saw his worst predictions come true. Here we are concerned with the war he waged from the stage, and in this he proved to be the master of the sketch and the chanson – a fine tactician who could be the funny and sentimental Berliner as well as the enlightened and aggressive critic. He, too, had no pretension to ART, and as a result his songs are even better than Mehring's, crisper, clearer, with not a word wasted. He could adapt himself to the singer and the composer, and the outcome was a rare combination of music, text and artiste. Tucholsky was a big-city product, a master of the atmosphere of Berlin with its teeming millions, and above all a master of the spoken language, the peculiar argot of the city, which was so curiously lacking in industrial Germany's nature-orientated literary verse. As with the others, cabaret was only a very small part of 'Tucho's' many-sided activities but not the least part. He raised cabaret to be a weapon in the great battle against the powers of darkness in the land. His satire was biting, and he struck home. In his time he was one of the best loved and most hated men in Germany.

One more figure needs to be mentioned – Erich Kästner, a writer known to millions as the author of children's books like *Emil and the Detectives*. Another side of Kästner is that of the fierce satirist and moralist, author of so-called 'functional poetry'. Like Tucholsky he was a best-selling writer and journalist who worked with Nobel Peace Prize winner Carl von Ossietzky on the *Weltbühne*. He too operated from the spirit of the language; he liked to take an idiomatic phrase and develop its possibilities; he could be very hard and very crude, very much aware of the erotic life of the twentieth-century city-dweller, and certainly many of his poems were 'not nice' though they were often sentimental.

Willett sums up the situation: 'The German poet of the twenties could communicate with a large public; and he had to have an ear for music. Nobody thought it profound or clever if he was impossible to understand.'[10] Klabund died young; Mehring left the country and spent the war years in America; Tucholsky committed suicide in Sweden in 1935; Kästner stayed behind in Germany throughout the Nazi period and somehow survived. Apart from his songs and cabaret material like *Leben in dieser Zeit*, it is his novel *Fabian* which gives the best picture of the 1920s. Here in the 'Anonymous Cabaret' the interesting feature apart from the honky-tonk music and the dreadful ballads is the conférencier called Caligula who insults the audience:

'Das geht entschieden zu weit!' rief ein Besucher, dessen Gesicht mit Schmissnarben verziert war. Er war aufgesprungen und zog sich empört das Jackett straff.
'Hinsetzen!' sagte Caligula und verzog den Mund. 'Wissen Sie was sie sind? Ein Idiot!'
Der Akademiker rang nach Luft.
'Im übrigen', fuhr der Kabarettinhaber fort, 'im übrigen meine ich Idiot nicht im beleidigenden Sinne, sondern als Charakteristikum'. Die Leuten lachten und klatschten. Der Herr mit Schmissen und der
Empörung wurde von seinen Bekannten auf den Stuhl gezogen und beschwichtigt.[11]

('That's going too far!', cried one of the audience, whose face was decorated with duelling scars. He sprang to his feet and indignantly pulled down his dinner-jacket.

'Sit down', said Caligula, screwing up his mouth. 'Do you know what you are? An idiot!'

The ex-student struggled for breath.

'I should add', went on the proprietor of the cabaret. 'I should add that I use the word 'idiot' not as an insult, but as a simple statement of fact.'

The audience laughed and applauded. The man of scars and indignation was dragged back to his seat by his friends, and pacified.)

Cabaret we have seen was in a position to introduce certain features which had until then been outside the scope of the traditional theatre. The Naturalists, for example, had made a feature of 'real life' and 'real speech', and this as much as the subject-matter of their plays had been the first great shock to the genteel tradition of literary theatre in Germany. The staccato, quick-moving, revue-type play of the Expressionists was always deliberately unsettling. To this the *Kabarettisten* added the cosmopolitan voice of the big city, great piquanterie, blasé cynicism combined with extreme sentimentality and fierce social criticism expressed in catchy songs. The effect of all this (as in many Expressionist plays) was heightened by the close contact between artist and public. The 'intimacy' of this kind of theatre was exploited for closer combat, more aggressive attack, quicker wit. This was for Germany a great age of satire, especially in the cabaret. It is, of course, a gross simplification to equate cabaret with 'political' or 'satirical' cabaret. 'German cabaret was both more and less than this. It was a member of a vast family including such forms of entertainment as variety, little revue, short operetta etc. . . .'[12] It was a fleeting art of which only printed texts of the songs or sketches and the recordings of the music could have any permanence, yet it can be overlooked at peril.

Apart from its effect in undermining the genteel tradition in the German theatre, cabaret was one more source for the new type of theatre generally associated with Brecht. Brecht himself grew from this background of cabaret to create his great works. He was brought into cabaret by Mehring and gave his *Legende vom toten Soldaten* accompanying himself on the lute as Wedekind had done before him. Needless to say, Brecht was howled down by his reactionary audience. However, he soon developed and was said to have been curiously effective on the cabaret stage. 'There was an unmistakable odour of revolution about him. Clearly it was this way of singing his crude ballads that did it. When he sang them with his shrill voice women swooned.'[13] Brecht lived the anti-art trend of the age, associating as he deliberately did with boxers, professional cyclists, and popular comedians like Karl Valentin. For his first works he used not the loftiest resources of European culture but distinctly anti-literary sources – revue-type Expressionist drama, popular songs, the music-hall, Kipling's barrack-room ballads, doggerel verse, Villon, Wedekind. Somehow out of this subliterary, subcultural material he created great art; and although he moved a long way from his cabaret-like beginnings, he never lost the basic elements of the cabaret, the close contact between artist and public which was marked equally by sentiment and aggressive attack. Brecht is never pompous and often funny, and that is a very rare thing in the German theatre.

Perhaps some examples are in order to demonstrate how Brecht transferred the world of cabaret to his own theatrical works, and a good example appears as early as the *Kleines Mahagonny* (1927), in which Brecht had his singers in a boxing ring dressed as crooks and gangsters singing their crude songs in jazz rhythms to blues saxophone accompaniment:

> Auf nach Mahagonny
> Die Luft ist kühl und frisch
> Dort gibt es Pferd- und Weiberfleisch
> Whisky und Pokertisch.
> Schöner grüner Mond von Mahagonny, leuchte uns!
> Denn wir haben heute hier
> Unterm Hemde Geldpapier
> Für ein grosses Lachen deines grossen dummen Munds. (*GW* 8, 243)

> (Away to Mahagonny
> The air is fresh and cool
> There's horsemeat and female flesh there
> Whisky and poker tables.
> Lovely green moon of Mahagonny show us the way!
> For today we have
> Folding money under our shirts
> For one great laugh from your stupid great mouth.)

Looking back on songs like these from the *Kleines Mahagonny* Brecht was able to discern the first small beginnings of his new theatre for the modern age. Words and music are now integrated not only into a functional form, the song itself and its performances are indicators of the new *Gestus* which is the characteristic of the epic theatre (see also Ch. 3).

> Praktisch gesprochen ist gestische Musik eine Musik, die dem Schauspieler ermöglicht, gewisse Grundgesten vorzuführen. Die sogenannte billige Musik ist besonders in Kabarett und Operette schon seit geraumer Zeit eine Art gestischer Musik. Die 'ernste' Musik hingegen hält immer noch am Lyrismus fest. (*GW* 15, 476)

> (Speaking practically gestic music is music which enables the performer to present basic gestures. So-called cheap music, especially cabaret and operetta, has been a kind of gestic music for a long time. 'Serious' music on the other hand still clings to lyricism.)

Further examples of the cabaret style can be discerned in *Die Dreigroschenoper*. Many traces of the original *Beggar's Opera* of John Gay, which was itself a parody, are still apparent; there are introductions, arias, recitations, ensembles, etc., but the operatic style is largely either abandoned or parodied; cabaret songs now obtrude and Brecht himself encouraged his singers not to sing the songs in the operatic manner but to project them in cabaret style. The whole becomes an experiment in epic theatre, but one in which the socio-political intention is largely diluted by the success of the songs. These have been so successful in themselves that they have gone back to the cabaret whence they came and have been part of the pop repertoire ever since.

Cabaret elements are easily discernible in other of Brecht's early plays, for example, in *Baal*, which has a scene in which the errant genius is expected to perform his songs nightly in public. Act Two of *Drums in the Night*, actually takes place in the Picadilly Bar where the phrase 'die rote Zibebe' (or red raisin) is used for the moon. One day after the première the first production of a dramatic piece called *Die rote Zibebe* was launched. This was a cabaret piece which Brecht wrote as something in the *Bänkelsang* style arising out of the play itself. On the cabaret stage in a circle stood several boxes like bathing huts, closed at the front with curtains. A character called Old Grubb in *Drums in the Night*, the publican who sang *The Ballad of the Dead Soldier* to his guitar, now played the part of the cabaret compère, only without speaking. He stumbled across to one of the cabins and pulled back the curtain with a long teacher's pointer. The character called forth then staggered or rolled out stiffly like a robot to declaim or sing his or her part and then, as it were, when the machinery had run down, slithered back into his cabin, which the compère immediately closed again. In the first production Brecht himself took part. There were also many songs by Klabund who performed them in person dressed in black, pronouncing the words monotonously and lugubriously like an out-of-work grave-digger.

Ich sage es frei von der Leber weg,
zum Feilschen und Fackeln ist keine Zeit.
ein armer wandernder Totengräber
bittet um Arbeit.

(I'm saying it absolutely straight out,
This is no time for messing about,
A poor, wandering grave-digger
Is asking for work.)

He then appealed directly to the audience for anything to bury, any old aunties, any old girl-friends! This was Brecht's own attempt to use the theatre for literary cabaret, apart from the use he put cabaret material to in his own plays. Unfortunately the police withdrew permission for the performances and the project collapsed.

Cabaret of the Tucholsky–Mehring kind was often accused of being merely negative, of not being positive enough, of merely rejecting and criticizing, of soiling the German nest. This view of left-wing intellectual satire was one of which Brecht was aware, and he was always careful in all his works to avoid the dangers of mere negativity. Equally he was aware of the danger exhibited by the other extreme, for example by

171

the Marxist cabaret groups which developed at the time, caricaturing the military, the hanging judges and capitalists in a bludgeoning manner which deadened the main comic appeal of cabaret.

As an antidote against this, Brecht took from Wedekind and Valentin the general theatrical spirit incorporated in the idea that theatre should be fun. Clearly there was a problem here if the aim of didactic theatre in general was to impart a message and that of Marxist theatre in particular was to instil a particular message, but Brecht, despite his comments on 'culinary' theatre (by which was meant empty entertainment), held on to this general principle of 'fun' in the theatre, even in the apparently most arid *Lehrstücke* which he attempted at one stage in his development. In his essay 'Das Theater als sportliche Anstalt' (1920) Brecht asks for 'fun' in the theatre. In the essay 'Über das Theater der grossen Städte' (1924) Brecht again mentions the idea of 'fun' together with the concept of naïvety: 'Das einzige was diese Städte bisher als Kunst produzierten war Spass: die Filme Charlie Chaplins und den Jazz' (The only thing these cities have so far produced by way of art was fun: Charlie Chaplin's films and jazz.'); while in his essay 'Mehr guten Sport' (1926) he said 'Ein Theater ohne Kontakt mit dem Publikum ist ein Nonsens.' ('A theatre devoid of contact with the public is a nonsense.')[14]

Altogether this gradually builds up to his theory of dialectical drama, whereby a certain naïvety is associated with critical distance. The customer should be able to enter the theatre in the same way as he enters any other place of entertainment, be it cabaret, sports arena or planetarium. The attitude of mind is quietly reflective, weighing things up, seeing how things really are. Spass means not just fun or entertainment and amusement, but the pleasure at working things out, the joy of a logical solution, new insights and impulses. Cabaret could provide this. Cabaret could be serious, socially and politically relevant, but never boring. One further feature of cabaret carried over in part from Wedekind to Brecht is the rejection of Naturalism. After his very first dramatic efforts Wedekind, as is well known, turned from Naturalism to a manner of presentation which was at one and the same time realistic and symbolic, absurd and grotesque. Fundamental human issues could be presented in this broken form, which never allowed the audience to pin issues down to those of one particular place and one particular time and render them comparatively safe and harmless in this way. The conflicts between culture and religion, sexual morality and changing social circumstances, the artist and the material world were presented by Wedekind in a manner which became fundamentally disturbing, because they could not be reduced to the conditioning factors of class or milieu, as they tended to be in naturalistic plays. Wedekind and cabaret helped Brecht towards a realization of the importance of the destruction of the illusion of reality: they showed him that this could be done most effectively by the constant use of music and song. In a sense by adopting the little theatre cabaret techniques Brecht was also reacting against the vast totality of the Wagnerian operatic *Gesamtkunstwerk*, which called for nothing less from each individual member of the audience, than total abandonment of the self. Cabaret showed how this kind of illusion could be destroyed by changes of lighting, direct address to the audience, audience participation by means of the refrain, etc. The illusion-destroying song could be sentimental and naïve, but also amusing and aggressive; it could be yet another powerful weapon in the political struggle. Significantly, Brecht did not rest content with the enormously successful association with Weill in earlier works like *Mahagonny, Dreigroschenoper* and *Happy End*, but developed beyond these in later works, into different, more reflective songs composed by other composers for other works. Whatever the phase in his career, a Brecht play is never merely a play, or even an 'opera', but a theatrical experience in which music and song are fundamental elements.

NOTES

1.   Enid Starkie, *From Gautier to Eliot: The Influence of France on English Literature 1851–1939* (London, 1960), p. 135.
2.   Christopher Isherwood, *The World in the Evening* (London, 1954), Part II, Chapter II.
3.   John Mander, *Berlin: The Eagle and the Bear* (London, 1959), p. 106.
4.   John Willett, *The Theatre of Bertolt Brecht* (London, 1967), p. 128.
5.   Quoted from J. M. Ritchie, *German Expressionist Drama* (Boston, 1976) p. 34.
6.   'The variety theatre', from Marinetti, *Selected Writings*, R. W. Flint, ed., (London, 1972).
7.   R. Huelsenbeck, *En avant Dada* (Hannover, 1920). Quoted from Greul, *Better, die die Zeit bedeuten*, Vol. I, p. 177.
8.   See Brecht, *GW* 17, 1162–9. For a fuller discussion of Brecht's use of the *Volksstück*, see Chapter 5.
9.   Helmut Schimmer, *Karl Valentin* (Munich, 1977), pp. 125–6.
10. Willett, op. cit., p. 88.
11. Erich Kästner, *Gesammelte Schriften* (Zurich/Berlin/Cologne, n.d.). Vol. 2, pp. 57–8.
12. J. M. Ritchie, 'German theater between the Wars and the genteel tradition', *Modern Drama* (1965), p. 371.
13. Quoted by Martin Esslin in *Brecht: A Choice of Evils* (London, 1959), p. 11.
14. See *GW* 15, 47–9; 75–7; 81–4; italics are Brecht's.

SELECT BIBLIOGRAPHY

APPIGNANESI, LISA, *The Cabaret*, London, 1975

BUDZINSKI, KLAUS, *Die Muse mit der scharfen Zunge, vom Cabaret zum Kabarett*, Munich, 1961

GREUL, HEINZ, *Bretter, die die Zeit bedeuten. Die Kulturgeschichte des Kabaretts*, 2 vols, Munich, 1971

HOFFMANN, C., 'Brecht's humor. Laughter while the shark bites', *Germanic Review*, 38 (1963), 157–66

McLEAN, SAMMY K., *The Bänkelsang and the Work of Bertolt Brecht*, Paris-The Hague, 1972

RAABE, PAUL, ed., *The Era of German Expressionism*, London, 1974

RIHA, KARL, *Moritat-Song-Bänkelsang*, Göttingen, 1965

RITCHIE, J. M., *German Expressionist Drama*, Boston, 1976

THOLE, BERNARD, *Die Gesänge in den Stücken Bertolt Brechts: Zur Geschichte und Ästhetik des Liedes im Drama*, Göppingen, 1973

Chapter 11

BRECHT IN THE GERMAN DEMO-CRATIC REPUBLIC

RONALD SPEIRS

There was a characteristic mixture of caution and commitment in Brecht's adoption of East Berlin as his last place of residence. He and Helene Weigel arrived in the Soviet-administered sector of the city on 22 October 1948, at a time when the crisis in East–West relations had resulted in the Russians' blockade of the land routes into the city, and in the airlift organized by the Western Allies to provision the sectors of Berlin under Allied control. Brecht's move to the East at this critical juncture was a signal of his support for the Communists and of his readiness to endorse very tough measures in the Communist struggle against the capitalist states of the West. On the other hand, Brecht was careful to ensure that his ideological commitment to Communism remained a voluntary one, made on his own terms.

After four months in Berlin, during which time he and his old collaborator Erich Engel prepared their very successful production of *Mutter Courage und ihre Kinder* (*Mother Courage and her Children*), Brecht returned to Zürich for the next four months. The production of *Mother Courage* was evidently a test-piece, intended to support Brecht's position as he negotiated with the authorities for the establishment in East Berlin of a theatre company under his own direction. In Zürich he busied himself with the recruitment of actors and other theatrical artists for the proposed company in Berlin, awaited official approval of the project, and worked on the play with which he intended to open his new theatre, *Die Tage der Commune* (*The Days of the Commune*). At the same time, however, he was conducting a correspondence with the Austrian composer, Gottfried von Einem, concerning a proposal that Brecht should play a leading role in the revival of the Salzburg festival. As payment for his contribution to the project Brecht asked for 'ein Äquivalent, mehr wert für mich als Vorschuss irgendwelcher Art; das wäre ein Asyl, also ein Pass ('something in exchange that would be more valuable to me than any kind of advance; by this I mean an asylum – a passport').[1] With an Austrian passport Brecht knew that he would be entitled to travel from East to West in order to carry on his

175

work there, even if East–West relations deteriorated yet further; he would also have the right to leave East Berlin if political or personal considerations should make a return to the West advisable. Although he had once defended Stalin's trials of dissidents in Moscow, he sought to ensure that his own support for Communism would not lead to his becoming trapped and persecuted like other intellectual sympathizers with Communism whom he had known and admired.[2]

In addition to his Austrian citizenship (granted on 14 September 1950), Brecht safeguarded his independence in East Berlin by placing the copyright for his work in the hands of a West German publisher, Peter Suhrkamp, by retaining a Swiss bank account, and by refusing any binding contract – or salary even – with his 'own' theatre company, the 'Berliner Ensemble'. Not until 1953 did Helene Weigel, officially appointed as managing director (*Intendantin*) of the ensemble, manage to persuade Brecht, the artistic director of the company, to sign a fairly open-ended form of contract. There is an unpleasant discrepancy between the measures taken by Brecht to preserve a quite unusual degree of independence for himself in East Germany, and his irritation with other Germans, whose residence in the Soviet zone was *in*voluntary, for failing to share his view that 'ein befohlener Sozialismus besser ist als gar keiner' ('imposed socialism is better than none at all') (*Aj*, 864).

Throughout his stay in the GDR, but most particularly in its early years, Brecht was keenly aware of the embattled position of the new socialist republic, and of the consequent need for its supporters to maintain a unified front. In addition to his work in the theatre, which was intended to contribute to the process of German re-education, he took part in public discussions and other propaganda exercises in support of the GDR. He made a number of public statements, for example, endorsing the Soviet–GDR campaign against the remilitarization of Germany, but tactfully avoided any reference to the existence of the Kasernierte Volkspolizei (People's Police in Barracks) from which the Nationale Volksarmee (National People's Army) was subsequently developed. In reply to an enquiry as to the probable outcome of general elections, if these were held throughout both East and West Germany, Brecht expressed the view that the population in each part of Germany would vote for the maintenance of their respective political and economic systems. This reply was not published at the time, nor did Brecht campaign for the holding of elections which would put his surmise to the test. In fact, in 1954, after the uprising of June 1953 had revealed the strength of internal opposition to the policies of the SED (Sozialistische Einheitspartei Deutschlands – Socialist Unity Party of Germany), he came out against the Allied proposals for the holding of free elections throughout Germany. He now used the familiar anti-democratic argument that the concept of 'free elections' is meaningless unless the voter has been given all the facts that would enable him to exercise his choice in an informed way. In other words: no elections before the electorate has received the necessary Marxist–Leninist schooling.

Brecht's plays have earned him the reputation of being a champion of the man in the street, sympathetic to his 'low' preoccupation with satisfying his appetites. It is thus all the more surprising that neither Brecht's public statements nor his private ones during his years in the GDR contain much evidence of concern for the problems of ordinary working people there. Some entries in his *Arbeitsjournal* (*Journal of Work*) from the early months of his stay in East Berlin show him attentive to the concrete details of life in the devastated city – the hunger, the poor clothing, the depradations of the Russians, as well as the festive occasions which seemed to promise a better future for the country. Such observations then disappear until September 1953, when he records a conversation he had with a disaffected plumber who had come to do some work in Brecht's house. If his public reticence on such matters is partly explicable as solidarity with a socialist regime trying to establish itself under very difficult circumstances, the paucity of private commentary is more puzzling and disturbing. His enormous appetite for and dedication to his artistic work in the theatre offers some explanation, as does the fact that Helene Weigel's willing acceptance of the practical burdens of managing the theatre and running the home meant that Brecht had little need to confront the day-to-day difficulties of life in East Berlin. At any rate, it appears to have taken the upheaval of 16 and 17 June 1953 to force Brecht to pay attention to concrete problems once more. However, his political response to the June uprising, which had taken him by surprise, indicates that he was unwilling to undertake any fundamental reassessment of the regime which he had come to East Germany to support.

His first reaction to the demonstrations was to engage in discussions with other members of the Berliner Ensemble, and then to send an open letter of support to the party leader Walter Ulbricht, stating his solidarity with the SED at a time of crisis – and thus implicitly endorsing the intervention of Soviet troops against the crowds on the streets. This letter also qualified Brecht's support by expressing 'confidence' that 'die grosse Aussprache mit den Massen über das Tempo des sozialistischen Aufbaus wird zu einer Sichtung und Sicherung der sozialistischen Errungenschaften führen' ('the great dialogue with the masses on the speed of socialist development will lead to the achievements of socialism being reviewed and secured') (*Aj*: Anmerkungen, 195). When the party newspaper, *Neues Deutschland*, published only the last sentence of his letter, thus making it appear to be a message of unqualified support, Brecht insisted on enlarging on his position in the following terms:

> Ich hoffe jetzt, dass die Provokateure isoliert und ihre Verbindungsnetze zerstört werden, die Arbeiter aber, die in berechtigter Unzufriedenheit

demonstriert haben, nicht mit den Provokateuren auf eine Stufe gestellt werden, damit nicht die so nötige grosse Aussprache über die allseitig gemachten Fehler von vornherein gestört wird. (*GW* 20, 237)

(I now hope that the *provocateurs* have been isolated and their networks destroyed, and that the workers who demonstrated out of justified dissatisfaction will not be put on the same level as the *provocateurs*, so that the great and very necessary dialogue about the mistakes made on all sides is not disturbed from the outset.)

Brecht's emphasis on the role played by 'Fascist troublemakers' in the uprising (an interpretation also favoured by the SED) is partly explained by the fact that he witnessed the disturbances in Berlin, where such penetration by 'class enemies' was possible. Yet he continued to hold to this view after it had become clear that demonstrations had also occurred simultaneously in many other parts of the GDR, where *provocateurs* could not be said to have been 'kolonnenweise eingeschleust' ('flooded in by the column').[3] This interpretation enabled Brecht to maintain that the use of Soviet tanks had been justified, since they had been sent in against the Western troublemakers but 'keineswegs gegen die Demonstrationen der Arbeiter' ('by no means against the demonstrations of the workers') (*GW* 20, 327). Such a categorical pronouncement on a confused situation shows how much Brecht could disregard objectivity where the policies of the SED were concerned.[4]

The *agents provocateurs* theory also suited Brecht's tendency to put the best possible interpretation on events in two other repects. If the blame for any violence and anti-Communism exhibited on 17 June were placed on the shoulders of Western infiltrators, it could be maintained that the basic agreement between party and people remained unimpaired. The unfortunate consequence of the 'mistakes made on all sides', the threat to the security of the republic, could be used as a lever to make the government more responsive to the people. As well as permitting Brecht to urge political reforms, his interpretation of events also sought to cope with his fears about the possible resurgence of Fascist sympathies among the citizens of the GDR. His fear about the long-lasting effects of the Nazi past on the Germans is illustrated by the following observations on the problems of winning over young Germans to the cause of socialism:

von der jugend muss man nicht zu viel erwarten. das ist nicht aus unhöflichkeit gesagt, sondern aus freundlichkeit. sie sind ausgebildet worden zum zertrümmern der welt, aber nicht ausgebildet, in einer zertrümmerten welt zu leben. kurz, unsere jugend ist eine hitlerjugend . . . sie hatten die ehre, die gauleiter und marschalle des kommenden weltreichs zu werden, und vor allem für dieses zu sterben. ihnen wurde der sozialismusersatz chemisch rein zugeführt und der echte stoff ist für sie nun besonders schwer erkenntlich und verdaulich. nicht nur ihre laster, sondern auch ihre tugenden wurden hitlerisiert. sie vereinen das denkvermögen von kindern mit der unbelehrbarkeit von greisen. nur vernunft könnte diese impulse entgiften,

aber vernunft kann nicht einfach, in form von lebensmitteln, geliefert
werden; sie muss produziert werden in dem grossen produktionsprozess der
gesellschaft. nur hier, wo die jugend wieder aufgelöst wird, liegen die
lösungen, und man sollte die bequeme hoffnung aufgeben, diese leute hätten
viel gelernt von ihren erlebnissen katastrophaler art. die erlebnisse lehren nur
den, der lernen will, und gelernt hat, zu lernen.[5]

(One must not expect too much from youth. That isn't said out of
impoliteness, but out of friendliness. They were educated to destroy the
world, but not educated to live in a world that has been destroyed. In short,
our youth is a Hitler Youth. They had the honour of becoming the 'gauleiter'
and marshalls of the coming world empire, and above all of dying for this
empire. Substitute socialism was fed to them in chemically pure form, and
the real thing is particularly hard for them to recognize and to digest. Their
virtues were Hitlerized as well as their vices. They combine the thinking
capacity of children with the ineducability of the senile. Only reason could
take the poison out of their impulses, but reason cannot simply be supplied,
as food can; it has to be produced in the great production process of society,
Only here, where the collective of youth will be dissolved again, are the
solutions to be found, and one should abandon the facile hope that these
people have learned much from their catastrophic experiences. Experiences
only teach the person who wants to learn, and who has learnt how to learn.)

If the Fascist influence on the Germans was still so strong that GDR
workers could easily fall prey to the slogans of the 'class enemy', as
had allegedly happened on 17 June, Brecht could feel justified in continuing to support the authoritarian political system built up by the SED
as being a necessary bulwark against resurgent National Socialism.
Thus, Brecht's interpretation of the uprising enabled him to maintain his
double loyalty to the people and to the government: he could urge political reform without having to argue for a fundamental change in political structures.[6]

If Brecht appears to have put loyalty before criticism in his attitudes
to SED policies in most areas of life, this was not the case in the field
of cultural policy. In this area of vital interest to Brecht as an artist, his
opposition to officially favoured aesthetic doctrines could not be avoided
or hidden. Yet even here he avoided fighting a theoretical battle to
defend his conception of 'epic' or 'scientific' theatre against opponents
who promulgated Stanislavsky's dramaturgical ideas as the only proper
ones for a socialist theatre to follow. His opposition to ruling taste in
theatrical matters was expressed through his work with the Berliner
Ensemble, which he understood as the experimental application of his
theories. He was very fond of saying 'the proof of the pudding is in the
eating', but even after many theatrical successes his work still proved
indigestible to leading theoreticians of drama in the GDR – as became
evident at the Stanislavsky conference in 1953. Brecht did not attend the
conference himself; he sent Helene Weigel to receive the brickbats.

In order to defend his own freedom to experiment, and that of other
modern artists whom he respected, Brecht had to oppose the theory of

'socialist realism' as pronounced by the Stalinist cultural functionary
Zhdanov and embraced by the SED. Initially, he advanced his argu-
ments for greater artistic freedom within the context of controversies
that had arisen around the work of particular artists, such as the sculp-
tor Ernst Barlach and the musician Hanns Eisler, whose opera *Doktor
Faustus* had met with fierce opposition from official circles. After the
events of June 1953 had brought signs of thaw in the political–cultural
climate, Brecht put forward more generally formulated objections to the
party's practice of trying to dictate both the forms and the content of
literature and art.[7]

The Zhdanovite definition of socialist realism demanded that literature
be partisan, optimistic, relevant to topical issues, traditional in form and
easily understood by the broad masses of the working people. In practice 'partisan' meant supportive of current party policy, idealizing in the
portrayal of workers (particularly of party activists), and hostile in its
depiction of 'class enemies'. 'Optimism' meant that any problems raised
in a play should be solved in the course of the action through the efforts
of a 'positive hero' with whom the audience is encouraged to identify
emotionally. There was also a battery of abusive terms to be applied to
works of literature which failed to suit the tastes or purposes of people
in authority. Any work which was experimental in style could be dub-
bed 'formalist' or 'decadent', particularly if it encouraged a coolly intellectual rather than an enthusiastic response in the reader or the audience. A work which gave credit to the spontaneous revolutionary potential of workers, such as Brecht's *Die Mutter* (*The Mother*), could be
accused of 'left-radicalism'.[8] If a work showed that there were serious
problems still to be resolved on the road to socialism the author could
be condemned for 'objectivism' or 'defeatism'. Brecht's *The Days of
the Commune* was criticized in these terms by the central committee of
the SED.[9]

The official, narrowly prescriptive attitude to literature was anathema
to Brecht, who, although an advocate of central planning in the field of
political economy, wanted to preserve for artists their old-fashioned
freedom to experiment. He also wanted to encourage the creativity and
critical independence of his audience. He considered that problems
should be dealt with at a higher level of generality in art than in day-
to-day political reality. He therefore preferred to write parabolic plays
dealing with the principles and structures of social behaviour than with
specific topical issues. He wanted to develop in his audience a *method* of
thinking which could be applied to a variety of situations, not tell them
what they should think about specific issues. In order to encourage the
audience's critical activity, he chose to leave problems apparently unsol-
ved at the end of his plays. Usually he set his plays in historically or culturally unfamiliar contexts because he feared that the immediate rendering
of contemporary reality would only strengthen men in their habitual
responses to the matters at issue. Optimism could be expressed by other

artistic means, he considered, than by presenting facile solutions to difficulties or through a show of all too solid solidarity. It could be expressed better as the confidence to face up to problems, and to seek out the contradictions in social and political life which are both the expression of problems and the source of the impulses necessary to deal with those problems. His kind of hero, so he asserted provocatively, was more depressed by rosy red than by any other colour. These generalizations apply as much to the Marxist works he wrote during his exile as they do to his adaptations for the Berliner Ensemble. However, his theory and practice of theatre acquired a new degree of explosiveness in the GDR through their blatant non-conformity to the theory and practice of socialist realism.

The dogmatism of the proponents of socialist realism in the GDR annoyed Brecht because he saw it as evidence of the undiminished power of familiar German vices, such as conservatism, schoolmasterly authoritarianism, philistinism, prudishness and dry abstractness. He was irritated by the insensitivity to language evident in the continued use by influential critics of terms of abuse which had been current under National Socialism ('decadent', 'unhealthy', 'over-intellectual') and by their arrogant claim to know exactly what the *Volk* wanted, needed or was capable of understanding. Ironically enough, the philistinism of official demands for propagandistic literature drove Brecht, who for years had fought under the banner of the 'use value' of literature, to insist ever more firmly on the importance of the pleasure principle in art. His renewed endorsement, after the asceticism of the early 1930s, of *Spass* (fun) in the theatre, which was already apparent in the 'Anmerkungen zum Volksstück' ('Notes on popular theatre') (1940) became a major element in his polemic against official philistinism. In one prose fragment Brecht satirizes, in unfamiliarly Orwellian vein, the bureaucratic mentality which would like to plan the production of literature as it would plan the production of boots. Here he ironically credits an Institute for the Writing of Books with the achievement of enabling all but 9 per cent of the population to write novels – all of them identical, thanks to the complementary efforts of the Office for Literature.[10]

Brecht's theatrical work in the GDR began with his production of *Mother Courage* in January 1949. After the success of this production, Helene Weigel was charged with the organization of the Berliner Ensemble, and Brecht began to plan his first production with 'his' new company. He wanted to open with *The Days of the Commune*, a play dealing with the strengths and weaknesses of the Paris Commune of 1871, which Brecht had thought relevant to the problems facing the builders of socialism in East Germany. However, Weigel persuaded him to substitute the much less controversial *Herr Puntila und sein Knecht Matti* (*Herr Puntila and his Servant Matti*). *The Days of the Commune* was not performed by the Berliner Ensemble until 1962, six years after

Brecht's death. The opening production of *Puntila* was given a run of 100 performances, thus establishing the company's practice of keeping productions in the repertoire for long periods (wherever possible), and so justifying the long periods of preparation and rehearsal – six or even nine months on occasion. In its first season the Ensemble also performed two other plays, Gorky's *Wassa Schelesnowa* and Brecht's adaptation of *Der Hofmeister* (*The Private Tutor*) by the eighteenth-century dramatist J. M. R. Lenz. These productions also established traditions in the work of the company, since the Gorky play was the first of a series of works by Russian authors performed there, and the adaptation of *The Private Tutor* was followed by a number of such experiments in interpreting works of the past from a Marxist point of view. Brecht hoped to show how to develop a repertoire in which classical works were not treated as museum pieces but as contributions to the historical self-understanding of a present-day audience. The lack of 'piety' evident in his handling of the 'classical heritage', particularly in the Ensemble's productions of Kleist's *Der zerbrochene Krug* (*The Broken Pitcher*) and Goethe's *Urfaust* (the original version of *Faust*), contrasted markedly with the staid and reverent productions of classical plays which were the officially approved staple of GDR theatres in those days, and brought down the wrath of the authorities on the Ensemble. Apart from productions of Brecht's own plays, the company's repertoire was completed by peformances of plays by younger GDR playwrights. This last strand in the pattern was introduced with the production in 1953 of *Katzgraben* by Erwin Strittmatter. The company's efforts in this direction have been intermittent, but were most active in the early 1970s when the company came under the leadership of Ruth Berghaus.

A careful written and photographic record was made of a number of the early productions. The intention was to provide future producers with a *Modellinszenierung* (model production), in which they could study the problems discovered during rehearsals and the proposed solutions to them. These documents of work in progress were part of Brecht's conception of a 'scientific' theatre which should describe both its methods and its results rationally, so that future experiments could rerun, and test and adopt the methods which had been so painstakingly developed.[11] There was much emphasis on the rational and collective character of work at the Ensemble, since this was seen as the way to ensure that the work of the company could continue uninterrupted by changes in personnel. Brecht's success in creating a 'transportable' method of working in the theatre seemed initially to be confirmed by successful new productions at the Ensemble after Brecht's death, such as the production by Benno Besson in 1957 of *Der gute Mensch von Sezuan* (*The Good Person of Szechwan*), the production by Palitzsch and Wekwerth in 1959 of *Der aufhaltsame Aufstieg des Arturo Ui* (*The Resistable Rise of Arturo Ui*) and the production of the adaptation of *Coriolanus* by Wekwerth and Tenschert in 1964. However, each of these men had considerable individual talents and had worked closely with Brecht at the Ensemble. The ability of actors and producers of the 'third generation' to emulate Brecht's ideal of a theatre which is both intellectually and aesthetically rich is much more questionable.[12]

After he was safely dead, Brecht became an officially promoted classic of socialist literature in the GDR. His last house in East Berlin has been converted into the 'Brecht Centre of the GDR' under the auspices of the Academy of Arts. Every possible anniversary is seized on as an opportunity to pay tribute to him as a guiding spirit of the country's cultural life. Schooling in Brecht's methods is part of the education of young actors. During his lifetime the attitude of the authorities to the playwright was a good deal less cordial. His refusal to write plays with a traditional 'dramatic' structure and emotive effect was met with condescension or outright hostility from influential critics, particularly once the campaign against formalism was launched in 1951. At the fifth plenary session of the Central Committee of the SED *The Mother* was attacked for its 'didacticism' and 'formalism'. The most notorious furore concerned the opera *Das Verhör des Lukullus* (*The Trial of Lucullus*) for which Paul Dessau had composed the music. Exception was taken to the playwright's failure to distinguish clearly between wars of aggression and wars of defence, to his use of symbolism, and most vehemently, to the 'dissonances' in Dessau's score. After lengthy discussions with party officials both artists agreed to make modifications.

During the culturally repressive period from 1951 to 1953, official disapproval of Brecht's style of theatre meant that new productions of the Ensemble were not reviewed in East German papers until long after the première. As Brecht complained in 1953, 'unsere aufführungen in berlin haben fast kein echo mehr' ('our performances in Berlin have virtually no resonance nowadays') (*Aj* 1008). The increase of Soviet plays performed to 25 per cent of the GDR repertoire in 1952 is a further sign of the restrictive, Moscow-oriented cultural policy of that period. By 1956 the situation had still improved so little that Brecht counted himself fortunate to have his 'own' theatre where he could at least be sure of having his plays performed: 'Das ist durchaus nötig, denn die Theater der Deutschen Demokratischen Republik gehören – betrüblicherweise von meinem Standpunkt aus – zu den wenigen Theatern in Europa, die meine Stücke nicht aufführen.' ('And that is quite necessary, for the theatres of the German Democratic Republic belong – sadly from my point of view – to the few theatres in Europe which do not perform my plays.')[13] Before the Berliner Ensemble took up permanent quarters in the Theater am Schiffbauerdamm in 1954 Brecht did not even have this degree of artistic security in the GDR – despite the generous terms which had been negotiated for the company.

Initially, Brecht believed that his plays would be better received by audiences of workers than by the traditionally middle-class theatre-going public with its preconceived notions of how theatre ought to be. In

1949, for example, he was encouraged by the response of steelworkers to the early production of *Mother Courage*. However, experience showed that the proportion of workers attending performances never rose above a disappointingly low level. The Ensemble sought to foster interest among the workers by arranging special performances for groups from factories, the army and trades unions. They particularly cultivated relations with the BUNA works, a large chemical concern. To judge by the 'BUNA-Protokoll',[14] a record of discussions held with employees of the firm in 1968–69, the same problems still remained to be solved: only a small proportion of the staff attended the discussions; of those who did there were hardly any who did not have some kind of specialist training; the most active participants were the articulate middle-class employees, and the objections raised to the Brechtian conception of theatre were the familiar ones about not wanting to be obliged to make intellectual efforts during an evening at the theatre.

The statistics of Brecht productions in the GDR show considerable fluctuations in popularity.[15] The following figures refer only to individual plays, excluding the 'Brecht evenings' (selections from his work) which have sometimes enjoyed considerable popularity, and take no account of amateur performances. In the years 1949–51 the number of productions was relatively high (14, 16 and 11 respectively), considering the novelty of Brecht's work for German audiences. In the years 1952–56 there were fewer productions: 7 in 1952, 5 in 1953, 8 in 1954, only 2 in 1955 and 7 in 1956. These fluctuations reflect periods of cultural 'thaw' or hardening; when the atmosphere was repressive it was less easy to produce Brecht. After Brecht's death in 1956 many more theatres in the GDR suddenly began performing Brecht's plays, and the range of his work being performed was extended. The 21 new productions in 1957 were followed by 29 in 1958 (the peak year of Brecht's popularity in the GDR). In 1961, 1962 and 1963 there were 20, 22 and 20 productions, and in the decade 1959–69 the average hovered around 15 plays performed each year. In 1970 there began a new downward trend – 13 productions in 1970, 9 in 1971 and 5 in 1972. The next Brecht anniversary, 1973 (25 years after his move to East Berlin), brought a slight revival with 12 new productions, followed by 14 in 1974 and 7 in 1975 and 1976. By 1977 his work had dropped to twenty-first position in the repertoire. An overall decline in Brecht's popularity is to be expected, since there must be a limit to the public's readiness to watch yet another production of a Brecht play. It appears that the return of Manfred Wekwerth to the Berliner Ensemble in 1977 has resulted in the improvement at least of the company's popularity with audiences.

The relative popularity of individual plays by Brecht in the GDR is perhaps rather surprising, and certainly indicative of a trend in the reception of Brecht's work there. By far the most frequently performed play is *Die Gewehre der Frau Carrar* (*Señora Carrar's Rifles*), an agitational piece designed to enlist active support for the Republican cause in the Spanish Civil War. Exceptionally, Brecht decided to use emotive rather than 'alienating' techniques when writing this play; because of this he later dismissed it as being 'opportunistic'. Ironically, however, it is precisely because the play more closely conforms to the officially approved model of a dramatically effective play than any other play by Brecht that it has enjoyed such resounding success with producers in the GDR. The second most popular play is *Puntila*, which in the years 1949–78 had 61 productions, as compared to 71 for *Carrar*. GDR theatres like to point out the topical relevance of the plays they perform, particularly where Brecht is concerned, but his comedy about life in a pre-revolutionary farming community in Finland is performed more frequently than can plausibly be justified in terms of its unquenchable topicality. The play appeals, rather, because it is a tolerably funny and intellectually not too demanding *Volksstück* (see Ch. 5). What is more, it can be performed successfully even in cultural backwaters by provincial actors not gifted with an excess of talent. As one critic wryly observes, 'weil die Politik schonend serviert worden ist, kommt Brecht auch in Plauen an' ('because the politics were served up gently, Brecht is even successful in Plauen').[16] Even in the case of this play, however, fear of Brecht's dialectical boldness reduces the amount of fun in those productions where the producer does not allow the selfish but vital and charming estate owner to be more than a caricature.

The next most popular piece is *Die Dreigroschenoper* (*The Threepenny Opera*), which comes just ahead of *Mother Courage*. Each of these plays has enjoyed only about half as many productions as *Puntila*. As far as artistic merit is concerned, *Mother Courage* is surely the better play, but *The Threepenny Opera* has the appeal of cynical humour and Weill's music. Concern has been expressed by critics in the GDR about the relatively infrequent performance there of such major plays as *Der kaukasische Kreidekreis* (*The Caucasian Chalk Circle*) or *Leben des Galilei* (*Life of Galileo*). There seem to be a number of plausible reasons for this state of affairs. Each of these plays has enjoyed long and successful runs in the repertoire of the Berliner Ensemble, and these polished productions may well inhibit provincial producers from trying to emulate them. Another problem of making Brecht popular is the length of his plays and their frequently discursive character. The marked unpopularity of *Galileo* in GDR theatres other than the Berliner Ensemble (which draws part of its audience from West Berlin) has surely something to do with the demands it makes on the intellect and the patience of the audience. Producers may also be worried by the problem of controlling the ambiguities in plays where the oppressors of the people are described simply as 'die Oberen' ('the high-ups') or 'die Obrigkeit' ('the authorities') rather than as capitalists or Fascists. Such problems as the freedom and the responsibility of the intelligentsia (the theme of *Galileo*) are still acute in Communist countries as well as capitalist ones, and the audiences are quick to respond to ambiguities or overtones which make a text relevant to their experience. On the other hand, there is some pressure on producers to keep turning to Brecht's plays, since he virtually *is* (apart from Friedrich Wolf) the tradition of German socialist drama. Hence the overworking of his 'safer' plays.

The problem of sustaining interest in and fresh approaches to Brecht's plays has not bypassed his successors at the Berliner Ensemble and was one of the many causes of the 'crisis' at the Ensemble which emerged in 1968–69. During the 1960s the company was dominated artistically by Manfred Wekwerth, whose productions won a mixture of acclaim and disapproval for their 'machine-like' precision. The younger directors resented his domination. After a disagreement with Weigel, Wekwerth left the company in 1969, as did a number of important actors and theatrical artists. When Weigel died, her post as *Intendantin* was filled by her deputy Ruth Berghaus, who hoped to reinvigorate the Ensemble by performing some of Brecht's neglected early plays and more plays by contemporary GDR dramatists. It was hoped that new perspectives for the production of Brecht's 'classic' works would thus be opened. Two dramatists, Karl Mickel and Heiner Müller, were drawn directly into the work of the company. Berghaus permitted various lines of experimentation to run alongside each other, a practice approved of by some, but condemned as 'Pseudo-Vielfalt' ('pseudo-multiplicity') by Werner Hecht, defender of Brechtian orthodoxy. In 1977 Wekwerth returned to the Ensemble, replacing Berghaus and reimposing firm control on the company.

Despite the reverence in which Brecht's name is now held, there is still a residue of suspicion about the validity of his theatrical methods. In his early years in the GDR his theory of 'alienation' was criticized for being an insufficiently positive method of developing the socialist consciousness of an audience. This kind of argument is still in circulation. Nowadays it is conceded that Brecht's conception of theatre *was* a valuable method to use under the pre-revolutionary social conditions in which it was conceived; under the conditions of 'real, existing socialism', however, his themes and methods have become increasingly irrelevant. Defenders of Brecht's legacy, such as Hecht and Wekwerth, argue that it is still important to keep alive the awareness of class struggle even in socialist countries, since the struggle continues on an international scale and the capitalist 'class enemies' are constantly developing ever subtler ways of conducting it. Wekwerth is particularly interested in focusing on the insidious power of capitalism to alienate and manipulate the consciousness of the working class so that the victims of capitalism remain unaware of their oppression. He therefore wants to pay more attention to the inner life of the individual than Brecht did. There is a danger, as far as adherence to Brechtian principles is concerned, that Brecht's stress on the typifying social *Gestus* will be forgotten in Wekwerth's efforts to give his plays the kind of psychological interest that is more acceptable to ruling taste in the GDR.

Brecht's importance for the development of GDR drama has lain in the encouragement his example has given to younger playwrights to deviate from the narrow path of socialist realism in their pursuit of a form of theatre which is both socialist and alive. Whenever the cultural atmosphere has thawed sufficiently, as in the years 1958–59, 1963–66 or in the early 1970s, dramatists have emerged with dialectical dramatizations of current or recent problems in the GDR, which owe their emphasis on contradiction rather than resolution pre-eminently to Brecht. Although Brecht never completed the task of writing a play about life in the GDR, he did make studies and sketches for a dramatization of the life of Hans Garbe, the first of the country's 'heroes of labour'. Heiner Müller's *Der Lohndrücker* (*The Bosses' Man*) took up the task which Brecht left unfinished – and immediately ran into trouble for his pains. The influence of Brecht has not always been strongest where it has been most obvious. Helmut Baierl's *Frau Flinz*, for example, is an attempt to rewrite *Mother Courage* as a socialist realist comedy. However, it fails to do justice to the conflicts of interest between individuals and groups which emerged, or failed to disappear, during the transition to socialism.

Ironically, it is the anarchic hero of Brecht's first play, *Baal* (which has never been performed in the GDR) who has caught the imagination of other dramatists more than any other of his characters. Descendants of Baal are to be found in plays by Müller, Peter Hacks, Volker Braun and Hartmut Lange. This type of character, whose energies and appetites exceed the norms among their compatriots, has proved useful as a means of bringing out the conflicts in the relations between individual and collective. When official hostility to such conflict-ridden views of GDR society has become too great, the playwrights have had recourse to the Brechtian device of writing dramatic parables, which they set in historically or culturally distant surroundings. Greek mythology has proved to be a valuable storehouse of figures and situations for their parables (e.g. Hacks' *Amphitryon*, Müller's *Herakles*, Lange's *Philoktet*). Brecht's influence is also evident in the formal characteristics of many plays – their episodic or 'epic' structure, in the dialectical relationship between scenes, in the use of paradox, deliberately awkward syntax, highly compressed expression, all of them designed to force the audience to engage intellectually with the themes of the plays. One can frequently detect echoes (in the verse style of Hacks, Müller or Lange) of the 'roughened' versification and diction developed by Brecht in his early adaptation of Marlowe's *Edward the Second*. Even Brecht's metaphorical technique in *Die Heilige Johanna der Schlachthöfe* (*Saint Joan of the Stockyards*) seems to have been the model for the clusters of metaphors in Lange's *Marski* or Müller's *Der Bau* (*The Construction Site*). Although the avant-garde Marxist playwrights of the GDR tend nowadays to stress their desire to 'go beyond' Brecht,[17] it is clear that those who are serious about mastering the contradictions in society owe at least their inspiration to him.

NOTES

1. Brecht's correspondence with von Einem is documented in S. Melchinger, 'Bertolt Brechts Salzburger Totentanz', *Stuttgarter Zeitung*, 5, No. 4 (1963).

2. See the essay 'Über die Moskauer Prozesse' (*GW* 20, 111). For a discussion of Brecht's attitudes to Stalinism, see Peter Bormans, 'Brecht und der Stalinismus', in *Brecht Jahrbuch 1974* (Frankfurt am Main, 1975), pp. 53–76.

3. Letter from Brecht to Peter Suhrkamp, quoted by Erwin Leiser in 'Brecht, Grass und der 17. Juni 1953', *Die Weltwoche* (Zurich), 11 February 1966.

4. The poem 'Böser Morgen' (*GW* 10, 1010) suggests that Brecht had difficulties in reconciling his conscience to his attitudes to the victims of political oppression. The poem is from the group of 'Buckower Elegien', which have particularly influenced other lyric poets in the GDR. Brecht's lyrics from his GDR years and their influence on other poets is an important topic which, for reasons of space, this chapter has not attempted to deal with.

5. This is an unpublished text, dated *c.* 1950, from the Bertolt Brecht Archive (ref. BBA 66/45). Material from the Archive will henceforth be referred to with the abbreviation BBA.

6. He proposed a reform of the role of the *Volkskammer* (People's Chamber) in 1954 (*GW* 20, 329). He also hoped that the Party would play a more active role as a mediator between bureaucracy and people: 'die partei könnte viel tun in einer stadt wie buckow. sie müsste sich zum anwalt der kleinen leute machen, ihre interessen durchfechten, ihr vertrauen gewinnen ... überall müsste die partei eingreifen, die paar mann, die den staat vertreten im gegensatz zur beamtenschaft' ('The Party could do much in a town like Buckow. It should make itself the advocate of the man in the street, fight for his interests, win his confidence .... The Party should be active in all directions, these few men who represent the state as opposed to the bureaucracy'.) (BBA 971/22).

7. See particularly the essay 'Kulturpolitik und Akademie der Künste' (*GW* 19, 540–4).

8. F. Oelssner, a member of the Politbüro, is quoted as using this term by Hüttich in *Theater in the Planned Society* (Chapel Hill, 1978), p. 27.

9. See J. Rühle, *Theater und Revolution* (Munich, 1963), p. 186.

10. The archive reference for this fragment is BBA 95/07. Unfortunately it is not possible to reproduce the text here. It is to be published in a collection of miscellaneous prose pieces.

11. Producers expressed very decided opposition to the idea of following models created in the 1950s and 1960s at the 'Brecht 78' conference.

12. Even the sympathetic critic Ernst Schumacher found grave weaknesses in

the Ensemble's new productions of *Puntila* and the *Chalk Circle* in 1975 and 1976, *Brecht–Kritiken* (Berlin, 1977).

13. Address to the 'Sektion Dramatik' of the fourth German Writers Congress, *Protokoll des IV Deutschen Schriftstellerkongresses* (Berlin, 1956).

14. Contained in Hecht, *Brecht: Vielseitige Betrachtungen* (Berlin, 1978), pp. 301–29.

15. The repertoire for the whole of the GDR is published annually in *Theater der Zeit*. Statistics of past performances of Brecht's plays are contained in *Brecht-Dialog 1968* (Berlin, 1968), *Brecht 73* (Berlin, 1973) and *Brecht 78* (Berlin, 1979).

16. *Brecht 73* (Berlin, 1973), p. 63.

17. The playwrights' growing distance from Brecht is illustrated by the contributions of Braun, Müller and Mickel to the 'Brecht 73' conference.

SELECT BIBLIOGRAPHY

BARKER, C., 'Theatre in East Germany', in *The German Theatre*, R. Hayman, ed., London, 1975

Bertolt Brecht und das Theater in der DDR (German/English), published by the Zentrum DDR des Internationalen Theaterinstituts, Dresden, 1967

HECHT, W. ed., *Brecht-Dialog 1968*, Berlin, 1968

HECHT, W. ed., *Brecht 73*, Berlin, 1973

HECHT, W. ed., *Brecht 78*, Berlin, 1979

WYSS, M. ed., *Brecht in der Kritik*, Munich, 1977

ESSLIN, M., *Brecht: A Choice of Evils*, London, 1959

HECHT, W., *Brecht: Vielseitige Betrachtungen*, Berlin, 1978

HUETTICH, H. G., *Theater in the Planned Society*, Chapel Hill, 1978

JÄGER, M., 'Zur Rezeption des Stückeschreibers Brecht in der DDR', in *Bertolt Brecht* I. Special volume in the series Text und Kritik, Munich, 1972

KLUNKER, H., *Zeitstücke und Zeitgenossen*, Munich, 1975

MITTENZWEI, W., *Wer war Brecht*, Berlin, 1977

NÖSSIG, M., *Die Schauspieltheater der DDR und das Erbe (1979–1974)*, Berlin, 1976

PATTERSON, M., *German Theatre Today*, London, 1976

RÜHLE, J., *Theater und Revolution*, Munich, 1963

SCHIVELBUSCH, W., *Sozialistisches Drama nach Brecht*, Darmstadt, 1964

SCHUMACHER, E., *Brecht: Theater und Gesellschaft im 20. Jahrhundert*, Berlin, 1973

SCHUMACHER, E., *Brecht–Kritiken*, Berlin, 1977

SEIDEL, G., *Brecht und die Deutsche Demokratische Republik, Mitteilungen der Akademie der Künste der DDR* Nr. I, Berlin, 1978

SUBIOTTO, A., *Bertolt Brecht's Adaptations for the Berliner Ensemble*, London, 1975

Theater–Bilanz 1945–1969, Berlin, 1969

Theater der Zeit, esp. nos. 19(1964); 14(1966); 2(1968); 2(1973).

Theater in der Zeitenwende, 2 vols, published by the Institut für Gesellschaftswissenschaften beim ZK der SED, Berlin, 1972

VÖLKER, K., *Brecht–Chronik*, Munich, 1971

Chapter 12

THE LEGACY FOR GERMAN-SPEAKING PLAYWRIGHTS

ANTHONY WAINE

Political theatre, of which Brecht's plays are outstanding examples, is not a modern phenomenon. In his survey of the history of this type of theatre Siegfried Melchinger traces its origins as far back as Ancient Greece.[1] According to him the first known political drama is *The Persians*, an anti-war play by Aeschylus, performed in 462 BC. Portentously its author was eventually forced to live (and die) in exile on Sicily, though the move was made to appear voluntary. Some 2,400 years later Bertolt Brecht 'chose' exile as an alternative to the concentration camps of the Nazis.

What characteristics then do political plays of all ages and cultures share? They are political less by virtue of their subject-matter than by virtue of a certain set of assumptions on the part of their creators. The political dramatist is one who views the theatre as a public institution with the same responsibilities and powers that other such institutions possess. He does not regard the audience as a random collection of private individuals, but as a public group with certain common social and historical experiences. His works generally seek to publicize matters which, for whatever reasons, the ruling powers would prefer to suppress. He thus hopes to initiate or participate in a public debate and to influence, if possible, public opinion. Consequently his plays are rarely provincial, but national and international in their import.

Inevitably such theatre is critical theatre, but very often, implicitly, self-critical theatre too. In a note on his play *Der Besuch der alten Dame* (*The Visit*) Dürrenmatt wrote:

> *Der Besuch der alten Dame* ist eine Geschichte, die sich irgendwo in Mitteleuropa in einer kleinen Stadt ereignet, geschrieben von einem, der sich von diesen Leuten durchaus nicht distanziert und der nicht so sicher ist, ob er anders handeln würde.[2]

> (*The Visit* is a story which takes place somewhere in Central Europe in a small town and is written by someone who certainly does not distance himself from these people and is not so certain that he would act any differently.)

Valid political drama is not written from a position of moral superiority but out of a sense of co-responsibility for the fate of a society to which one belongs.

Bertolt Brecht bequeathed to the post-war, German-writing dramatists a modern political theatre, which he had systematically developed both in theory and practice to respond to the great changes and conflicts which the industrialization of society had produced. One might summarize the content of the legacy under the following four headings: the heterogeneity of the dramatic methods; the technical flexibility; the new relationship between actor and audience; and, finally, (though this is speaking within the limited German context only), the use of satire and irony as effective devices for social criticism.

The variety of dramatic methods is an aspect of his legacy which Brecht himself once unwittingly anticipated in an entry in his *Arbeitsjournal*:

24.4.41. wenn ich meine letzten stücke betrachte und vergleiche, GALILEI, MUTTER COURAGE, FURCHT UND ELEND, DER GUTE MENSCH VON SEZUAN, HERR PUNTILA UND SEIN KNECHT MATTI, AUFSTIEG DES UI, so finde ich sie enorm uneinheitlich in jeder weise, selbst die genres wechseln unaufhörlich. biographie, gestarium, parabel, charakterlustspiel im volkston, historienfarce – die stücke streben auseinander wie die gestirne im neuen weltbild der physik, als sei auch hier irgendein kern der dramatik explodiert. (*Aj* 274)

(24.4.41. When I consider and compare my last plays, GALILEO, MOTHER COURAGE, FEAR AND MISERY, THE GOOD PERSON OF SZECHWAN, HERR PUNTILA AND HIS SERVANT MATTI, THE RISE OF UI, I find them extremely lacking in uniformity. Even the genres are constantly changing. Biography, gestus tableau, parable, comedy of character written in popular idiom, historical farce – the plays diverge from one another like the stars in the new picture of the universe that physics has produced, as if here too some nucleus of drama had exploded.)

If one adds to this list the genres of the political revue and musical one realizes how much greater the range of formal possibilities has become for his successors.

It was Brecht too, though here Piscator's legacy was inextricably intertwined with his, who has enabled playwrights tackling large and complex political subjects to do so with considerably more freedom from dramatic conventions than was hitherto thought possible. The present-day playwright can now, like the novelist, skip easily from one year to another, from one town to another, even from one country to another in his epic portrayals of the relationship of the individual to society. To facilitate such manoeuvrability a plethora of techniques were integrated by Brecht and Piscator into the drama, ranging from the simple use of boards informing audiences of the changing time, place and significance of the action they are about to witness, to commentaries, songs, flashbacks. This function was often embodied in the figure of the narrator. Such techniques, however, were employed not only to inform and elucidate, but also to place the acted scenes in a different perspective, thus attempting to compel audiences to reflect critically on the significance of what they had just seen.

This 'manipulation' of the attitudes of spectators constitutes one of the most radically new principles of his theatre. Here actors also had a key part to play. By their very style of acting they were to encourage the spectator to take a critical, intellectual interest in the characters' behaviour. This approach contrasted significantly with the traditional aim of (Western) directors and actors who for centuries had striven to foster only the emotional involvement of audiences (see Ch. 8). By retaining a certain degree of rational control, on the other hand, the spectator would, it was hoped, be receptive to the (political) lessons being taught. The presentation by the actors of the subject-matter was therefore as crucial for the politicization of the spectator as the subject-matter itself.

One way in which actors could help to distance the audience from the character they were playing was to stylize comically aspects of their portrayal. It is well known that two of Brecht's idols were comic actors: Charlie Chaplin and the Bavarian beer-hall clown Karl Valentin. Not only did he publicly acknowledge his indebtedness to these two artists for his new style of acting, but he also admitted:

> Der V-Effekt ist ein altes Kunstmittel, *bekannt aus der Komödie*, gewissen Zweigen der Volkskunst und der Praxis des asiatischen Theaters. (*GW* 16, 652)
>
> (The distance-creating effect is an old artistic device, *familiar to us in comedy*, certain branches of popular art and the methods of the Asian theatre.)

Brecht's deployment of comic techniques permeates through his plays to the very texture of the language itself. His unashamed use of comic forms, two of which, the *Charakterlustspiel* and *Historienfarce* have already been cited, helped to establish comedy as a serious genre in German dramatic history and undoubtedly paved the way for important political comedies and tragicomedies such as Max Frisch's *Biedermann und die Brandstifter* (*The Fire Raisers*) (1958), Peter Hacks' *Die Sorgen und die Macht* (*Anxiety and Power*) (1960), Friedrich Dürrenmatt's *Die Physiker* (*The Physicists*) (1962) and Martin Walser's *Eiche und Angora* (*The Rabbit Race*) (1962).

The dates of the first performances of these plays, particularly the latter two, are significant. They underline the beginning of the fruition of Brecht's legacy for German-speaking drama. Although some of Dürrenmatt's earlier plays and those of his Swiss compatriot Max Frisch had shown unmistakable signs of Brecht's influence – hardly surprising in the case of Frisch who became a close friend of Brecht during his six-month sojourn in Switzerland in 1947–the years 1958 to 1966 saw a whole cross-section of playwrights embracing Brecht's political theatre.

The late 1950s also witnessed a dramatic increase in the number of productions of his works on the German-speaking stage from 31 in the theatre season 1956–57 to 61 in 1957–58 and 69 in the following season. The popularity of Brecht – a posthumous one since he died in 1956 – was even more remarkable in view of the politically motivated boycotting of his plays in Vienna, Zurich, Cologne, Düsseldorf, Hamburg and Berlin. However, it should be added that the majority of theatres playing Brecht at this time deliberately toned down the political resonances of his dramas and emphasized instead their 'theatrical' qualities.

Why though, apart from the increased popularity among dramaturgs, directors and audiences of Brecht's plays around 1957–58, should almost an entire generation of playwrights begin to respond to the theatre of Brecht at this particular juncture? The answer lies in the recent history of German society. The primitive cultural isolationism of the National Socialists, followed by the spiritual shock of capitulation and chaos of the year 1945, the decimation of so many potential writers in the concentration camps and on the battlefields retarded the development of a new, independent literature in both halves of Germany for nearly a decade and a half after 1945.[3] When this generation of writers finally found its feet in the late 1950s and early 1960s it faced stark alternatives. On the one hand there was the unpolitical existentialist theatre of Beckett and Ionesco, so potentially attractive to a post-Auschwitz, post-Hiroshima generation of intellectuals. Diametrically opposed to this was the politically conscious and didactic theatre of Brecht which analysed symptoms and causes of social malaises and proffered remedies.

Despite the flirtation of some playwrights such as Günter Grass, Wolfgang Hildesheimer and Tankred Dorst with the so-called theatre of the absurd, Brecht's theatre of commitment challenged the majority of German and Swiss writers to face up to the political realities of the recent past and present which directly impinged upon their lives; the cold war, the threat of a nuclear holocaust, the mechanical mass butchery of the concentration camps, the Fascist potential latent in democratic societies. Furthermore, certain events with world-wide moral and political implications also occurred between 1958 and 1962 which may well have reinforced the need to confront audiences with national and international issues rather than with more parochial or personal ones. In 1958 the first of several new war trials was held in West Germany of individuals accused of committing atrocities against the Jewish people. This forced public attention (particularly in Germany) away from the obsessive pursuit of economic security and success to memories of the recent past which had been so effectively repressed. In 1960–61 the trial of Adolf Eichmann, one of the most infamous Nazi leaders, was held in Jerusalem. The East–West conflict and its seemingly inevitable nuclear solution reached new peaks in August 1961 with the building of the Berlin Wall, followed one year later by the Cuban missile crisis.

To fellow socialist writers seeking to depict the developing socialist society of the GDR Brecht had issued a quite specific challenge:

> Wir müssen überall, wo wir Lösungen zeigen, das Problem, wo wir Siege zeigen, die Drohung der Niederlage zeigen, sonst entsteht der Irrtum, es handele sich um leichte Siege. Überall müssen wir das Krisenhafte, Problemerfüllte, Konfliktreiche des neuen Lebens aufdecken... (*GW* 16, 800)
>
> (Wherever we show solutions we must also show the problem; wherever we show victories, we must also show the threat of defeat, otherwise the false impression will be conveyed that the victories are easily achieved.
> Everywhere we must uncover the crises, problems and conflicts of the new way of life...)

In this state, whose political leaders demanded (and to a large extent still do) affirmative, and not critical political literature, Brecht's legacy was to prove most embarrassing.

This was particularly true in the case of Peter Hacks (who emigrated from West to East Germany in 1955) and Hartmut Lange (who moved from the East to the West in 1965). In *Die Sorgen und die Macht* by Hacks and in *Marski* by Lange the major problem facing an emergent socialist state is highlighted; the contradiction between the actual existence of a socialist state and the old bourgeois consciousness that still determines the behaviour of some of its citizens. In Hacks' play the central figure is the materialistic, egocentric Max Fidorra, who works in the local briquette factory, while Lange chooses the Puntila-like figure of the former estate owner Marski, whose servants desert him one by one to pool their efforts and resources in the local agricultural cooperative. Both plays in fact paint a more optimistic picture of their socialist society and its development than do their Western equivalents in portraying capitalist society. The individuals, who are out of step with historical and political developments, are not tragically destroyed or isolated. Instead their fellow men and women, either individually or collectively, endeavour to reform and reintegrate them. Despite such commendably socialist features these plays evidently still contained too much of the crises, problems and conflicts of the new society (and probably also too much social satire) for the authorities, who prevented a production altogether or hurriedly had them withdrawn from the repertoire. Not surprisingly the likes of Hacks and Lange (and also Heiner Müller) quickly realized that such vital political *Zeitstücke* (plays about contemporary issues) would never or very rarely be produced in their original version and so began adapting classical myths and literature, in which their political message was camouflaged sufficiently to be relatively harmless and therefore acceptable to the political censor.

If Brecht was a problem, posthumously, for the East German authorities for having handed down a theatre that does not fight shy of revealing conflicts and contradictions, in the West he often became a problem more to the dramatists themselves than to the authorities. The sheer magnitude of Brecht's *œuvre* – in one respect a positive source of ideas and methods – sometimes retarded and frustrated the development of a personal style for many a dramatist. In the heat of a public discussion in 1966 on the subject of contemporary theatre, under the chairmanship of Dr Günther Rühle, one of the participants, Martin Walser, exclaimed: 'Als Dramatiker hat mich Brecht kaputt gemacht!' ('Brecht has destroyed me as a dramatist.')[4] Nor did any German playwright in the 1960s who dealt with political subjects escape the invariably unfavourable comparison with the progenitor of the modern political theatre or the concomitant charge of being an epigone.

The only way to lay the ghost of the man and hence deal productively with his legacy was to question both his methods and his ideas in the light of the historical, social and political events and developments which separated him from the post-war generation of writers, whose reality was that of the second half of the twentieth century. Peter Hacks, one of Brecht's 'pupils' in the GDR, has formulated the challenge laid down by the 'master':

> Brechts Wirklichkeit war die der ersten Hälfte des zwanzigsten Jahrhunderts. Unsere Wirklichkeit ist schon anders; unsere Methoden müssen anders aussehen als die Brechts, wenn sie brechtsche Methoden sein wollen. Wie jede Leistung des menschlichen Geistes bleibt die Leistung Brechts historisch. Sie ist vergänglich und ewig. Ihre Fortsetzung kann nur auf dem Weg der Negation erfolgen, nicht auf dem des Verlängerns.[5]

> (Brecht's reality was that of the first half of the twentieth century. Our reality is already different; our methods have to differ from his if they are to be called Brechtian. Like every intellectual achievement Brecht's remains an historical one. It is both ephemeral and eternal. To take his work further one must negate not prolong it.)

What are the principal, historical, political and social developments which have, arguably, conditioned the outlook of writers born between, say 1916 (e.g. Peter Weiss) and 1931 (e.g. Rolf Hochhuth)? Brecht's age had been dominated by the great ideological struggles between systems of the right, capitalism and Fascism, and that of the left, socialism. But this statement requires immediate qualification. One had capitalism in practice, while socialism was largely theoretical since the Soviet Union was still in its infancy. In addition Brecht and other intellectuals often did not have much knowledge of what was actually happening in the USSR. In the post-1950 era one has the struggle in practice between the so-called capitalist countries and so-called socialist states. Not only has capitalism of the *laissez-faire*, nineteenth-century ilk now long since been overhauled and transformed positively, through a number of social and political reforms, but since Stalin's purges in the 1930s, and the USSR's armed intervention in the GDR (1953), Hungary (1956) and Czechoslovakia (1968), socialism on the Soviet model has also become highly suspect for many Western (and some Eastern) intellectuals. The consequence of this changed historical situation is that Brecht's natural, seemingly unquestioning commitment to revolutionary change is not shared by many of today's writers. Indeed one of the most powerful dramas in the post-war German theatre, Peter Weiss' *Marat/Sade*, is about the dilemma of the intellectual over whether to commit himself politically.

Equally Max Frisch's parable *Biedermann und die Brandstifter* about the responsibility of the individual to act when confronted by a threat to his society is applicable not only to bourgeois democracies such as Weimar which allowed themselves to be undermined by political extremism, but also to socialist democracies like that of Benes' Czechoslovakia which opened its doors to Communists, committed to the destruction of the democratic system. Symptomatic of the new attitude of equivocation towards commitment to a specific doctrine (e.g. Communism) is the un-Brechtian subtitle 'Ein Lehrstück ohne Lehre' ('A Parable without a Lesson') which, on one level, implies Frisch's inability to proffer an ideological alternative to the negative conditions he portrays in the play. Presumably he sees a vigilant bourgeois democracy as the least of all evils.

The progress achieved by Western democracies since the Second World War has also altered the contemporary writer's perspective – and function. Especially the economic boom years of the 1950s and early 1960s have changed the situation of large sections of the working class from one of material insecurity, as was prevalent in the 1920s when Brecht's literary and political ideas were taking shape, to one of relative affluence. The arrival of the so-called 'affluent society' has brought with it an *embourgeoisement* of the values of the working class and a consequent diminishing of their earlier class consciousness. Equally, whereas Brecht could still prick the social conscience of his middle-class audience with slogans such as 'Nur wer im Wohlstand lebt, lebt angenehm' ('Only the prosperous lead pleasant lives'), little political mileage can be gained out of such sentiments nowadays, since the bourgeoisie does not perceive itself to be any longer the exclusive possessor of privilege and prosperity. During the renaissance of the political theatre between 1958 and 1966 hardly any play by its exponents is about class conflict or even class divisions – a fundamental theme running throughout Brecht's dramas. Only one play, Martin Walser's *Überlebensgross Herr Krott* (*Larger-than-life Herr Krott*) devotes itself to the subject, only to prove how socially determined antagonisms are painstakingly suppressed by the petty bourgeoisie, always eager to adapt to the capitalist ethic and ever ready to swear allegiance to its preservation!

It was not just class war which preoccupied Brecht. War in its literal meaning of hostilities between persons and nations is another recurrent theme in his work. Brecht was an avowed pacifist who never ceased to inveigh against the inhumanity and the absurdity of all wars. Essentially his most successful anti-war parables (*Mutter Courage* and *Schweyk im zweiten Weltkrieg*) (*Schweyk in the Second World War*) are about how or how not to survive in circumstances of conventional war. Responsibility for starting such wars and continuing them is shown by him to lie either with the political and military leaders like the *überlebensgross* (larger than life) figures of Hitler, Goering and Himmler in *Schweyk im zweiten Weltkrieg* who impose their will from above on the little man like Schweyk, or else with powerful economic groupings seeking to profit from the spoils of war. *Mutter Courage* was to demonstrate, according to Brecht, 'dass die grossen Geschäfte in den Kriegen nicht von den kleinen Leuten gemacht werden' ('that no great fortunes are made out of war by the little people') (*GW* 17, 1138).

As a Marxist, Brecht saw racism and militarism emanating ultimately from the same source, namely capitalism, and, furthermore, he was analysing these phenomena as they were actually arising. The more detached and ideologically independent post-war generation of German and Swiss intellectuals, studying with hindsight the thematic nexus of the Third Reich, the war and the atom bomb, present a much more differentiated interpretation of the issues. First they concentrate more emphatically on the role of science and technology in military conflict and crimes against man (e.g. the experiments in the concentration camps), though Brecht's *Leben des Galilei* doubtlessly anticipated their discussion. Second they pay greater attention to the social psychology underlying individual and collective acts of aggression and cruelty, and especially man's seemingly limitless potential for sadism – surely symptomatic of this is the choice of the Marquis de Sade himself as the protagonist in Peter Weiss' *Marat/Sade* drama. Third the moral responsibility of every individual, great or small, for his own destiny and that of his fellow men constitutes a major shift in emphasis from Brecht's ideological standpoint. Clearly the most decisive factor behind the changed perspective of the post-Brechtian playwrights towards responsibility was the fate of the Jews in many European countries between 1933 and 1945. How could an entire race be systematically persecuted without the tacit support of the majority and the direct physical involvement of a large minority of non-Jewish citizens? One of the many levels on which Dürrenmatt's *Der Besuch der alten Dame* may be read is of the cowardly opportunism of an entire community in permitting one of its members to be victimized in exchange for its own material well-being. This play was typical of many of the new political dramas in that it demonstrated how present-day societies, despite their democratic veneer, were still highly vulnerable and inflammable (cf. Frisch's *Biedermann und die Brandstifter*!) and thus reminded audiences of the need to learn from the tragic mistakes of the all too recent past.

After that brief adumbration of the changed historical perspective of the post-Brechtian dramatists, the remainder of the chapter will consider some specific examples of contemporary political dramas, assessing to what extent their creators are indebted to Brecht but also examining in what respects, technically and thematically, they differ from his theatre and its ideology. The plays to which I shall refer fall broadly into two categories. There are on the one hand the parables, the direct descendants of Brecht, and on the other the documentary dramas which belong more to the tradition of Piscator's theatre. Indeed Erwin Piscator personally acted as a kind of midwife for the rebirth of this type of play by directing the three most outstanding examples of contemporary German documentary drama himself, Hochhuth's *Der Stellvertreter* (*The Representative*) (1963), Kipphardt's *In der Sache J. Robert Oppenheimer* (In the Matter of J. Robert Oppenheimer) (1964) and Weiss' *Die Ermittlung* (*The Investigation*) (1965). Before considering this response to the legacy of Brecht, three parable plays will be considered in relation to Brecht, all of which, significantly, were premiered in 1961–62. They are Dürrenmatt's *Die Physiker*, Frisch's *Andorra* and Walser's *Eiche und Angora*.

Technically, *Die Physiker* is the furthest removed from Brecht. It has a closed form, rigidly maintaining the unities of time, place and action. Only at the very end of the play when the three scientists step forward and speak directly to the audience is a gesture made towards epic theatre practice. Most un-Brechtian is the play's generating of suspense. After all the play does involve murders, spies and the police. Yet in its subject-matter it is an ambiguous rejoinder to the dispute on the responsibility of the scientist initiated by Brecht in *Leben des Galilei*. This play chronicled the intellectual development and creative life of a great man whose ideas heralded the dawn of the modern age. In contrast to this *Die Physiker* presents the sterile, self-destructive capsule of a world in which one scientist has voluntarily incarcerated himself, because he fears the harm to mankind which his discoveries, should they be exploited by politicians (in the East or the West), could bring in their train. For Galilei knowledge was a formidable weapon for man and his fellow men to improve themselves with. For Möbius knowledge has become a potential weapon with which men can annihilate their fellow men. The historical optimism which rings through in Brecht's play, even allowing for Galilei's self-castigations in Scene 14, is nowhere present in Dürrenmatt's drama. Where Andrea, Galilei's pupil, goes across the border in the last scene of the play, carrying with him Galilei's most recent scientific treatise, Dürrenmatt substitutes a scene with the most macabre implications. Möbius's theories have fallen into the hands of a monstrous crank, who is to use them to effect her domination over the entire world – a veritable Hitlerian fantasy. The setting of his play in a mental asylum is not only a perfectly apposite symbol for his view of the irrationality of the nuclear age, it is the antipode to Brecht's unshakeable belief in the power of reason, so often vaunted by Galilei himself: 'Ja, ich glaube an die Gewalt der Vernunft über die

Menschen. Sie können ihr auf die Dauer nicht widerstehen.' ('Yes, I believe in the gentle force of reason on people. In the long run they cannot resist it.')

Dürrenmatt's fellow countryman Max Frisch finds it equally difficult to hold such a sanguine view as Brecht's when depicting contemporary reality. Not that this is at all surprising. Perhaps nowhere in the history of mankind have man's proclivities towards irrational thought been more apparent than in the racist myths promulgated by the Nazis. In *Andorra* Frisch presents a parable about the racist impulses found to be latent in the most self-respecting, democratic communities, once pressure is brought to bear on them. In this case the pressure comes from the neighbouring bellicose and racist 'Blacks', to whom the Andorrans have always felt morally superior – clearly a parallel to the attitude of the Swiss *vis-à-vis* the Germans. Frisch gives his play one supremely ironic twist. The young man Andri, on whom the townsfolk begin to project their latent anti-Semitic prejudices, is in fact not a Jew, but has an Andorran father and a mother from the neighbouring country of the Blacks. However, by the time this information is revealed Andri's identity has been so conditioned that he refuses to accept himself as anything but Jewish, while his fiancée Barblin, on account of the suffering she bears with Andri, has no identity left at all. At the end of the play she is deranged. In such a depiction of the individual a clear difference from Brecht emerges. Invariably in his plays, even in those such as *Die Rundköpfe und die Spitzköpfe* (*Round Heads and Pointed Heads*) and *Furcht und Elend im Dritten Reich* (*Fear and Misery in the Third Reich*) which deal with the subject of racism, he shows man essentially to be a victim of an unjust economic system. Frisch and many of his contemporaries on the other hand rarely show man in this light. Rather they delineate the mental casualties of an age in which systematically induced fears and prejudices are more potent in influencing human behaviour than material conditions.

Another such casualty is Alois Grübel, the anti-hero of Martin Walser's parable, *Eiche und Angora*. Having undergone medical 'treatment' in a Nazi concentration camp for being a Communist, Alois emerges a model Nazi, though mentally unstable. After the war his relapses into the now defunct Nazi *Weltanschauung* cause his fellow citizens, who have all readjusted from Fascism to democracy with bewildering agility, so much embarrassment that he is twice sent away to a Catholic mental hospital to be re-educated to the new ideology (a mixture of anti-Communism and belief in free enterprise). Anna, his wife, like Barblin in Frisch's *Andorra*, eventually loses her mind as she witnesses first the physical and then the mental emasculation of her husband.

In the three parables chosen as representative of the post-Brechtian didactic theatre one common denominator emerges. All three central figures, Möbius in *Die Physiker*, Andri in *Andorra* and Alois in *Eiche und Angora*, become outsiders of their society. This tragically coloured picture of the individual contrasts markedly with the approach of Brecht, whose overriding interest was in the social and economic laws determining the individual rather than in the individual himself, and who places the interests of the collective before those of the individual. Peter Brook implicitly formulated this contrast between Brecht and the present-day playwrights when he wrote '... the role of the individual in the society, his duties and his needs, the issues of what belongs to him and what belongs to the state, are in question again. Again... man is asking why he has a life and against what he can measure it.'[6]

Nowhere has this issue (raised incidentally by Brook in Ch. 3 ('The rough theatre') of his book, which is one of the most stimulating assessments in English or German of Brecht's legacy) been more fundamentally debated than in *Marat/Sade*, whose author Brook characterizes in the following way: 'Peter Weiss, combining Jewish family, Czech upbringing, German language, Swedish home, Marxist sympathies, emerges just at the moment when his Brechtianism is related to obsessive individualism to a degree unthinkable in Brecht himself.'[7] In this play Marat argues for the use of force to change and improve society while de Sade rejects all causes, asserting monomaniacally: 'Ich glaube nur an mich selbst.' ('I believe only in myself.')

Marat/Sade abounds in distancing effects *à la* Brecht. Indeed they are so frequently employed that some may be taken as a deliberate parody of Brecht, as for example when he entitles one scene quite simply 'Interruptus'! Like Peter Weiss, Walser, Frisch (and Dürrenmatt in most of his other plays in the 1950s) also openly select from the arsenal of techniques Brecht bequeathed them. At the end of almost every scene in *Andorra* Frisch has a character step forward to address the audience directly and assess in retrospect the role which he played in the events leading to Andri's persecution. *Eiche und Angora* is still more reminiscent of Brecht, not least of all through its subtitle 'Eine deutsche Chronik', with its obvious echoing of Brecht's chronicles such as *Mutter Courage*. It also uses scene titles which inform the audience in advance of the quintessence of each scene. Most Brechtian of all are Alois' 'relapses' which not only illustrate his labile psychological state after release from the concentration camp but intentionally function as a juxtaposition to the opportunism and hypocrisy of his fellow citizens, for whom coming to grips with the past is accomplished with relatively little personal discomfort.

However, when one looks at these plays – Weiss' *Marat/Sade* is an exception – and compares them with Brecht's dramas, one finds far fewer 'theatrical' or 'non-dramatic' elements. Songs, particularly those sung to the accompaniment of music, are absent. The play within a play (*Der Kaukasische Kreidekreis*) (*The Caucasian Chalk Circle*) or role-playing (*Der Gute Mensch von Sezuan*) or pantomimic sequences have been rejected by his successors undoubtedly because they were felt to be too aesthetic and thus detrimental to the political message.

Such considerations were certainly uppermost in the minds of the other wave of playwrights whose works represent an even more critical reappraisal of aspects of the legacy of Brecht. For Peter Weiss, Heinar Kipphardt and Rolf Hochhuth the parable itself, as developed and perfected by Brecht, was implicitly considered to be too art-istic, too artificial to deal with the reality of events such as Auschwitz or Hiroshima. They wished to confront audiences with facts, whose authenticity and truth had not been weakened through having first been distilled into fiction, even if it were the indubitably realistic fiction of a Brecht. His often exotic setting in a stylized Soho, Chicago or China, his affection for the spectacular historical setting of a seventeenth-century Italy or the epic tableau of the Thirty Years War were implicitly viewed as too escapist and as too escape-inducing, as Günther Rühle observed:

> In einer Gesellschaft, die so grosse Erfolge darin gehabt hat, das Vergangene zu vergessen oder wegzudrücken, überlegt sich natürlich ein Autor, wie er sein allzu mobiles Publikum zwingt, sich wieder zu stellen und zu hören. Er überlegt sich wie er Belege beibringt, die eines auf keinen Fall mehr zulassen: Ausflüchte vor dem Stoff, Belege, die die Ausreden im Keim ersticken, das Gezeigte sei erdichtet, also unwirklich, pure Poesie.[8]

> (An author, living in a society which has been so successful in forgetting or suppressing the past, naturally thinks about how to compel his all-too-flexible audience to face facts again and listen. He thinks about how to present evidence which above all will stop his audience from evading the facts any longer and which will invalidate from the very start the excuses that what is being presented is invented, pure fiction, and therefore unreal.)

This necessitated a return to a more naturalistic theatre, which Brecht had argued against for most of his life.

Rolf Hochhuth's *Der Stellvertreter* (first performed in 1963) is certainly Brechtian and Piscatorian in its epic sweep with scenes set in Berlin, Rome and, finally, Auschwitz itself. However, no attempt is made to distance the audience from the events being shown or from the main characters. It has the emotional appeal of a political thriller, with characters eliciting a wholly sympathetic response or alienating us altogether. The two principal villains in the play are the concentration camp Kommandant, called the Doktor, and Pope Pius XII. The latter, God's 'representative' on earth, Hochhuth accuses of having remained silent despite knowing about the extermination of Jews by Germans in concentration camps. Hochhuth's argument, voiced through the two heroes Gerstein and Riccardo, is that the Pope, by not publicly censuring the actions of the Nazis, shirked his moral responsibility. The other focal thematic point of the play, personified in the figure of the satanic Doktor, is the psychopathology of cruelty. Neither ethical nor psycho-analytic concerns, perhaps because they were too closely associated with bourgeois culture, played any significant role in the works of Brecht.

The import of such concerns for a post-Brechtian theatre single-mindedly dedicated to the 'investigation' (the title of Weiss' Auschwitz documentary) of the causes and effects of the cataclysms of the years 1933 to 1945 can be gauged by the fact that they are also central to Kipphardt's *In der Sache J. Robert Oppenheimer* and Weiss' *Die Ermittlung*. The latter, modelled closely on the trial held in Frankfurt in 1964–65 of SS officers employed in the Auschwitz camp, confronts villains with victims (those Jews who somehow survived) in the sober setting of a courtroom. An identical location, once again reproducing the authentic circumstances of the hearing of Oppenheimer by an American Senate committee in 1954, is chosen by Kipphardt for his political and psychological study of the American atomic physicist. He is presented both as a mass murderer in so far as he was responsible for developing the atom bomb dropped on Hiroshima but also as a victim himself, for like Galilei he has played into the hands of the authorities and is now at their mercy. The bitter irony of this play is that the hearing is not concerned with Oppenheimer's involvement with the atom bomb but with his refusal to help with the development of the much more devastating hydrogen bomb. His former Communist sympathies are the present concern of the committee. The scientist–intellectual's involvement in the 'real' world of politics has led him into tragic dilemmas from which either self-immurement – the path chosen by Dürrenmatt's Möbius – or a return to pure science, divorced from military and political objectives, are the only escape routes. In the closing lines of the play Oppenheimer announces his choice of the latter: 'Wir haben die Arbeit des Teufels getan, und wir kehren nun zu unseren wirklichen Aufgaben zurück.' ('We have performed the work of the devil and now we shall return to our real tasks.') In this guardedly positive ending Kipphardt (who lived and worked in the GDR until the late 1950s) expresses himself in agreement with Brecht's message delivered via the epilogue in the final scene of *Leben des Galilei*:

> Hütet nun ihr der Wissenschaften Licht
> Nutzt es und missbraucht es nicht
> Dass es nicht ein Feuerfall
> Einst verzehre noch uns all
> Ja, uns all.

> (Now guard the light of the sciences, using it and not abusing it lest it should turn into a conflagration which consumes all of us, yes all of us.)

The dilemma of the artist and intellectual engaged voluntarily or by chance in the political sphere is the subject of a play which also marks the culmination of the process of coming to terms with Brecht. For Günter Grass' *Die Plebejer proben den Aufstand* (*The Plebeians Rehearse the Uprising*) (first performed in 1966) is undisguisedly concerned with Brecht himself and his refusal to lend his prestigious support to the delegation of workers who approached him at his theatre during the uprisings in various East German cities in June 1953. (A detailed account of this can be found in Ch. 11.) The 'Chef' ('boss', i.e.

Brecht) is rehearsing his Marxist adaptation of Shakespeare's *Coriolanus*. A delegation of workers arrives at the theatre asking for the Chef's signature in support of their cause, but he declines, exploiting instead the opportunity to study working-class speech and behaviour and pressing ahead with the theatrical task at hand.

Grass' characterization of the intellectual Brecht for whom theatre was superior to reality and to whom reality was a material to be kneaded into an appropriate and aesthetically satisfying shape, is a conscious expression of what first the parable and then the documentary playwrights subconsciously set out to demonstrate themselves. They strove for a theatre that was far closer to reality, both in its intellectual content, its low-key aesthetic effects and its anti-utopian political tendency. Paradoxically, however, it is probably their greater emphasis on reality at the expense of theatre which has meant that while Brecht's plays continue to be played in Germany and elsewhere many of the plays discussed here are now seen more as historical documents, produced in response to a specific political climate. It is true that after 1966, the year of Grass' play, political plays which conformed to the definition attempted at the beginning of the chapter were performed. Two agitprop plays by Peter Weiss, *Lusitanischer Popanz* (*Lusitanian Bogey*) and *Viet Nam Diskurs* (*Vietnam Discourse*), were more revolutionary than anything that had previously been seen in the non-Communist countries. Hochhuth's anti-Churchill drama *Soldaten* (*Soldiers*) appeared in 1967 and Tankred Dorst's political revue *Toller* about the German revolutionary writer was produced a year later. On the other hand two dramatists, Walser and Frisch, whose names are associated with the Brechtian legacy, had plays performed in 1967, *Die Zimmerschlacht* (*Home Front*) and *Biografie: Ein Spiel* (*Biography: A Game*), which concentrated on the more private aspects of individuals' lives.

What is more significant about the year 1966 as a turning-point in the post-Brechtian theatre is the appearance of a generation in the theatre whose years of birth (invariably between 1942 and 1946) mean that they bypassed altogether the political and social traumas (war and its aftermath, totalitarianism, exile), at least one of which will have conditioned the childhood, the youth and possibly the early adulthood of a Peter Weiss or a Rolf Hochhuth, and which enabled them to share and respond to some of the basic historical experiences which impinged on Brecht's own life. In 1966 Peter Handke's radically subjectivist *Publikumsbeschimpfung* (*Offending the Audience*) and Martin Sperr's *Jagdszenen aus Niederbayern* (*Hunting Scenes from Lower Bavaria*) were performed. The latter play and especially its title are symptomatic of the new trend. If one of the hallmarks of the political theatre is its national and international relevance, then the post-post-Brechtian one is characterized by an unashamed rootedness in the provinces. This is certainly true of Franz Xaver Kroetz, the most successful of the new German playwrights of the 1970s. The 'teacher' figure for Kroetz, Sperr and even Handke was not Brecht but Ödön von Horváth, whose own plays, while heavy in socio-political implications, are intentionally provincial in their ambience and their speech.

In conclusion, when evaluating the legacy of Brecht, one has to start from the general context of a post-war cultural situation beset for almost a decade and a half with discontinuity, disorientation and rootlessness. Brecht (and to an extent the director Piscator) offered a still vital tradition and a healthy and substantial body of theory and praxis that had, like the two men themselves, been enriched by the great upheavals of recent German history. These helped a considerable number of playwrights in the search for their own identity as writers and indirectly gave direction and purpose to German-speaking dramatic literature to a point where, like the German film ten years later, it achieved international fame. The success of plays such as *Andorra* and *Eiche und Angora*, *Der Stellvertreter* and *Oppenheimer* on the stages of major East and West German cities is in no small measure due to their authors' often intensive wrestling with the leviathan legacy of Bertolt Brecht.

NOTES

1. S. Melchinger, *Geschichte des politischen Theaters*, 2 vols (Frankfurt, 1974).
2. F. Dürrenmatt, *Theater-Schriften und Reden* (Zurich, 1966), p. 180.
3. Switzerland, on account of her political neutrality during the war, experienced no major damage to her economic and social structures and no serious break in her cultural traditions. On the contrary, through attracting so many exiled German artists and intellectuals, she actually profited culturally from the political situation in her neighbouring German-speaking states. Zurich in fact became the most prominent theatre of the free German language in Europe. Modern Swiss drama, as represented by Frisch and Dürrenmatt, was already flourishing by the late 1940s.
4. Quoted from a letter by G. Rühle to the present author.
5. P. Hacks, *Das Poetische* (Frankfurt, 1972), p. 45.
6. P. Brook, *The Empty Space* (London, 1972), p. 94.
7. Ibid., p. 94.
8. G. Rühle, *Theater in unserer Zeit* (Frankfurt, 1976), p. 130.

SELECT BIBLIOGRAPHY

BROOK, P., *The Empty Space*, London, 1972
HAYMAN, R., ed., *The German Theatre: A Symposium*, London, 1975
HINCK, W., *Das moderne Drama in Deutschland*, Göttingen, 1973

INNES, C., *Modern German Drama: A Study in Form*, Cambridge, 1979

MELCHINGER, S., *Geschichte des politischen Theaters*, 2 vols, Frankfurt, 1974

MENNEMEIER, F., *Modernes deutsches Drama*, 2 vols, Munich, 1973–75

PATTERSON, M., *German Theatre Today*, London, 1976

RÜHLE, G., *Theater in unserer Zeit*, Frankfurt, 1976

TAËNI, R., *Drama nach Brecht*, Basel, 1968

ON INDIVIDUAL PLAYWRIGHTS

BIEDERMANN, M., *Das Politische Theater von Max Frisch*, Lampertheim, 1974

HILTON, I., *Peter Weiss*, London, 1970

LAUBE, H., *Peter Hacks*, Munich, 1972

TAËNI, R., *Rolf Hochhuth*, Munich, 1977

WAINE, A., *Martin Walser: The Development as Dramatist 1950–1970*, Bonn, 1978

WHITTON, K. G., *The Theatre of Friedrich Dürrenmatt*, London, 1979

Chapter 13

BRECHT AND THE ENGLISH THEATRE

MARO GERMANOU

The relationship of Brecht with the English theatre covers, broadly speaking, almost forty years of theatre history that has yet to be written. As far as dramatic practice is concerned, the relationship began in 1933 when the play *Anna Anna* (later called *The Seven Deadly Sins*) was performed at the Savoy Theatre in London.[1] Since then the history of Brecht's appropriation by English theatre people has gone through several stages. Brecht was translated, directed, adapted; he was criticized, distorted, rejected or glorified. In the number of his plays produced and the amount of secondary literature written on him he can be compared only with Shakespeare. Since the last twenty years of Brecht's relationship with the English theatre have been the most important, the critical work done on the subject is in its infancy. Critics need to distance themselves from the immediate impressions as well as to analyse a long period of theatre practice before they can estimate the repercussions of this relationship.

Now, however, the rise of the 'alternative' theatre movement makes the need for this study pressing and, indeed, imperative. For it is with this movement that Brecht has more affinities since it has defined itself against the mainstream theatre as Brecht did in his own time. Consequently the 'alternative' theatre movement has a lot to learn about theatre practice and theory from Brecht's paradigm. Gradually critics started mentioning Brecht with reference to English playwrights who have been positioned within that movement, for example studies like Albert Hunt's on Arden (*A Study of his Plays*) or Tony Coult's on Bond (*The Plays of Edward Bond*). Also critics and historians of the movement like John Russell Taylor (*Anger and After*, and *The Second Wave*) and Ronald Hayman (*British Theatre Since 1955*) never fail to mention Brecht in their accounts of the English theatre. This chapter is going to give a historical and critical account of Brecht's reception into theatre life in England since the early days of his influence, with the aim of bringing a perspective to attitudes to Brecht to be found in the 'alternative' theatre movement.

Brecht made his appearance in England during the social instability that preceded the outbreak of the Second World War. It was the time when England saw the rise of the Workers' Theatre Movement (1926–36) which almost monopolized the political dramatic scene prior to the emergence of the Unity theatre in 1936. The WTM performed at political demonstrations small, anti-naturalistic sketches which made use of agit-prop and the tradition of nineteenth-century popular English theatre, music-hall and cabaret. But the political motive of their work, which was to intensify class struggle, became outdated with the rise of the Popular Front policy which made unity against Fascism a priority over class struggle. '. . . the WTM was irretrievably associated with what now came to be regarded as sectarianism; its exuberant revolutionism was an embarrassment, its attacks on the Labour Left out of place; proletarianism was an obstacle to building the broad alliance.'[2] Thus on the cultural level it was the Unity theatre that began to carry out the Popular Front policy. In 1938, the Unity performed Brecht's *Senora Carrar's Rifles* while the London Choral Union had presented *The Expedient* only two years before.[3] In the meantime Ewan MacColl, an old member of the WTM, together with Joan Littlewood formed the Theatre of Action in Manchester. In search of a new theatre language they were experimenting with early Brecht around 1934, while two years later they produced the Piscator–Brecht adaptation of *Schweik* which was then considered to be a very avant-garde production. '. . . it was played against black curtains with symbolic drawings pinned to the numerous locations–this was an unusual method of presentation in those days.'[4] In the same period some of Brecht's one-act plays were translated and published in journals, as well as two of his theoretical essays: 'The Fourth Wall of China' and the 'German Drama: Pre-Hitler'.[5]

Once the political climate changed from the upheavals of the 1930s to the reconstruction of the country on the basis of the Welfare State, the era of political experimentation in the theatre ended and Brecht disappeared from the English stage for ten years. Only the *Parables for the Theatre* were translated and an essay on acting technique by Brecht was published in *New Theatre*. The post-war era is usually referred to as one of stagnation as regards theatre. Films competed with theatre for audiences while theatre had also to face increased rent and production costs. In London foreign plays, musicals, revivals and light comedies prevailed. There was a return to conventional forms of theatre with the exception of the verse drama revival – T. S. Eliot and Christopher Fry – which was anti-naturalistic but lacked the political dimensions of the previous decade. According to Jonathan Hammond, the fringe in the 1940s and 1950s took the form of 'private theatre clubs like the New Linsday, the Mercury, the Boltons and the Watergate . . ., frequently presenting plays banned by the Lord Chamberlain because of themes of violence or homosexuality'.[6]

Only two theatres tried to carry on their traditions, the Unity, and the Theatre Workshop founded by Joan Littlewood in 1945. The former concentrated on community theatre and produced plays by foreign progressive playwrights, together with some local ones which aimed to attract a working-class audience. As for Theatre Workshop, ignored by English critics, it was involved in touring activities, usually working in association with unions, till 1953, when it established itself in the Theatre Royal in Stratford, London.

This decade of silence in the relationship between Brecht and the English theatre seems to indicate that because of the brevity of their pre-war relationship Brecht had not managed to establish himself as an important source of stimulation for the English theatre. But the silence has a political dimension as well. It is not accidental that English theatre workers 'discovered' Brecht during the social uncertainty of the 1930s, only to 'lose' him in the quiet, though austere, years that followed the war – even Theatre Workshop and Unity had 'forgotten' him. No doubt this indicates that during periods of intense social contradictions radical forms of cultural expression are likely to emerge and build associations with the social milieu. Post-war England did not seem to provide this opportunity.

There are several reasons to account for Brecht's reappearance in the mid-1950s. The Berliner Ensemble had been formed and had five years' experience of touring abroad to critical acclaim. In England a debate was going on about the foundation of permanent and subsidized companies and the practice of the Berliner Ensemble became a focus of interest. The campaign developed with Kenneth Tynan, the drama critic of the *Observer*, as its most dedicated advocate. At the Paris Drama festival in 1955 Tynan was impressed by the facilities of Brecht's Company:

> My first impression was of petrified amazement at the amount of money involved. From East Berlin Brecht has transported dozens of impressionistic settings, hundreds of costumes, a new revolving stage for the Sarah-Bernhardt, a new curtain and seventy-six actors – fewer than half of his permanent Company.[7]

But Tynan did not propagate Brecht only as the director of a subsidized company. In his articles he invoked Brecht as the solution to many sorts of problems in the theatre. For Tynan Brecht had initiated changes in the art of the theatre that English people were unaware of. Thus Brecht became the 'most original dramatist'[8] and in his articles Tynan propagated him as such. In his review of *The Caucasian Chalk Circle* as performed by the Berliner Ensemble at the Paris Drama Festival in 1955 Tynan glorifies the play's originality, measuring it against the English plays of the period.

> But if I felt unmoved by what Brecht had to say, I was overwhelmed by the way in which he said it. It was as shocking and revolutionary as a cold shower. In the British theatre everything is sacrificed to obtain sympathy for the leading characters: Chez Brecht, sympathy is nowhere; everything is sacrificed for clarity of narrative. No time is wasted on emotional climaxes.[9]

In the meanwhile Brecht was reapproached by English theatre practitioners who had come in contact with him before the war. In 1955 Joan

Littlewood directed and played the title role of *Mother Courage and her Children* at the Devon Festival of the Arts. The same year Oscar Lewenstein, an old member of the Unity theatre, visited Brecht in East Berlin and produced *The Threepenny Opera* in 1956 at the Royal Court. Finally John Fernald who had worked on the Unity's production of *Señora Carrar's Rifles* went to Berlin as well to see Brecht and produced in July 1956 *The Caucasian Chalk Circle* for RADA.

A new director to approach Brecht in Berlin was George Devine who was at that time involved in the creation of the English Stage Company. His impressions from his attendance at the Ensemble's production of *The Caucasian Chalk Circle* show an interest in the idea of the permanent, subsidized company focusing on the method of working on plays.

> Under its neon sign, the atmosphere of the theatre is quiet and informal. The group appears to function in a natural and unneurotic manner, and by West End standards, the kind of theatre they believe in seems carefree and dedicated, but without polish. To watch a Brechtian production is to stumble upon the agreeable chaos of an artist's studio, to have the artist turn up a picture and tell you, 'This – this is more or less finished.' Such an ability to work in a truly artistic manner is unique in the theatre of the world, and most enviable. But underlying the informality is something vital and real. The audience makes this a people's theatre . . . Brecht's dedicated public give the production an air of religious ritual . . . . Although the actors seemed like children playing, they gave the impression that they worked because they liked and believed in what they had to portray . . . Brecht often rehearses his plays for months and if, when the time comes, a production is not ready, another play in the repertory is substituted until it is ready . . .[10]

In this account, Devine as a director does not show much interest in the play itself; still, certain important points concerning the making of theatre are implied, points which stimulate debates within the 'alternative' theatre companies in England even now. The long rehearsal periods, the lack of anxiety, the informality of the production, the emphasis on the play as part of a long-term process rather than as an end-product, the general idea of the theatre being associated with constant work and production; the importance of a group of people permanently working together and committed to what they were doing; finally the achievement of producing progressive plays for a proletarian audience.

In addition the theatre journal *Encore*, founded in 1954, propagated Brecht's work and provided initial information about it; but these articles were mostly based on second-hand accounts of what Brechtian theatre was about and misunderstandings were inevitable. Despite the mistreatment of Brecht's work due to the lack of knowledge concerning his theory and practice and the reservations about the kind of theatre he wanted to establish, the admiration for a genius director and playwright who brought something intrinsically new to the theatre is present in all these articles.

The greatest impact made on the relationship between Brecht and the

English theatre was the visit of the Berliner Ensemble to London in August 1956 when they performed *Mother Courage and her Children*, *The Caucasian Chalk Circle* and *Drums and Trumpets*. Brecht's plays being largely unknown to the English audience, which in addition had no knowledge of the German language, encountered an immediate problem of reception. Spectators and critics noticed more the way things were said and acted in the plays and less, if at all, what was said. Brecht (who died only two weeks before that visit) was aware of this problem himself.

> For our London season we need to bear two things in mind. First: we shall be offering most of the audience a pure pantomime, a kind of silent film on the stage for they know no German. Second: there is in England a long-standing fear that German art must be terribly heavy, slow, laborious and pedestrian. So our playing needs to be quick, light, strong. This is not a question of hurry, but of speed, not simply of quick playing, but of quick thinking.[11]

Because of the linguistic unfamiliarity, the first thing that audiences noticed in these productions was the physical appearance of the set and the actors. Subsequently influences were first noticed among stage-designers and directors. This becomes evident in the reviews written on the occasion of these productions. For those who did not see the plays, and even for some of those who did, the way critics received the Company's work determined to a great extent the framework within which Brecht was to be placed and appropriated by English theatre people.

Tynan, reviewing the plays, notices the physical presence of the actors and the set.

> Brecht's actors do not behave like Western actors; they neither bludgeon us with personality nor woo us with charm; they look shockingly like people – real potato-faced people such as one might meet in a bus-queue . . . I defy anyone to forget Brecht's stage pictures. No steps or rostra encumber the platform; the dominant colours are brown and greys; and against a high, encircling, off-white backcloth we see nothing but solid, selected objects – the twin gates in *The Caucasian Chalk Circle* or Mother Courage's covered wagon. The beauty of Brechtian settings is not the dazzling kind that begs for applause. It is the more durable beauty of use.[12]

And Harold Hobson, writing in the *Sunday Times* about the Company's season at the Palace Theatre, remarked:

> . . . the Berliner Ensemble does not seek emotion: it seeks understanding. It therefore constantly reminds the audience that what it sees on the stage is not real, but only a fictional entertainment intended to illuminate the mind . . . . Instead of life, it (the audience) is offered an explanation of life.[13]

Hobson, however, contradicts himself by the end of the review, claiming that despite everything theatre is not a place suited to thinking.

> I do not believe that fundamentally there is any more rational illumination in

Mother Courage or the other plays of Brecht than there is in *Uncle Tom's Cabin*.[14]

Hobson does not give up his principles about the nature of theatre despite the practice of the production whose effects he felt himself. Chained to his set ways of thinking, Hobson basically gave up dealing with Brecht who was mainly appropriated by Tynan. It was he who played the leading role in the formulations of opinions about Brecht. He made him known to the English people as the humanist, the genius of stagecraft and the director of a subsidized company. Most people were to see Brecht on this basis.

Reviewing the Berliner Ensemble's productions, Tynan defined Brechtian theatre in terms of the economy in staging, and the lack of emotion, illusion and identification; he emphasized the structure of the plays, the narrative element. Brecht and his company came to stand for the potential for aesthetic plurality and novelty in the theatre. The disregard of the significance that Brecht's theory and politics had for his theatre practice, and their absence from the evaluation of his artistic work, gave rise to the intrinsically aesthetic framework within which Brecht was placed and on the basis of which he was going to be read, seen and directed. Deprived of their political dimensions Brecht's 'novelties' were treated as isolated artistic devices that could be incorporated unquestioningly into the dominant bourgeois theatre in order to revitalize it, while originally they were meant to work against it. Brecht's Marxist views, rarely mentioned by Tynan, are seen as the result of a free choice that any individual has the right to make about the 'doctrine' he is going to adopt. This is applied to the plays' ideas in the context of humanist morality: 'How to improve the human condition'. This is not surprising because whenever Tynan or other critics wanted information about the theory or the politics they referred mainly to Esslin's book *Brecht: A Choice of Evils* (1959). This book and Willett's *The Theatre of Bertolt Brecht* (1959) were the first systematic studies to appear and the most influential in formulating opinions about Brecht.

It is primarily Esslin's book that provides those distortions of Brecht's work that are going to follow Brecht in his appropriation in England. Esslin's study, though psychological, has important political implications. According to him an opposition exists between Brecht's reason and emotions. As soon as he turned to Marxism, the argument goes, Brecht tried to give a rational and scientific dimension to his plays, suppressing the emotions. But the emotions do manage to appear on stage and even prevail in some of the plays, which can thus join the tradition of the great tragedies of the past. So Brecht's plays are good, despite Brecht, his theory and his politics. By depriving the practice of its theory which is not only dramatic but philosophical as well – it includes Brecht's Marxist views on the changeable nature of man, of society seen on the basis of historical contradictions – Brecht's politics are excluded and what we are left with is Brecht 'the dramatist' and his plays as an achievement on their own. It is significant that the theory is treated more as an aesthetic position and less as an attempt to give effective dramatic form to a very specific conception about the world. Thus the theory is reduced to devices – the songs, the masks, the breaking of the illusion. 'The technical elements of alienation' is a phrase that no critic will fail to use. Furthermore, Esslin fails to read Brecht's work historically. Had he done so, he would have noticed that by the end of his life Brecht had developed ways for the audience to criticize the characters while at the same time feeling sympathy for them, i.e. reason and emotions combined.

But it was not only Esslin who promoted distortions of Brecht. *Encore*, which helped to keep the interest in Brecht alive, did so on similarly false grounds. There are articles like Ernst Bornemann's according to which Brecht's theatre was 'a place of utter magic – but only for those who loved Brecht as a lyric poet and were sensitive to that inexplicable gift in him which transformed everything that he touched'.[15] Robert Bolt's admiration of Brecht is based on a division between Brecht the artist and Brecht the Communist: '... theatrically I think he was right... he knew it all instinctively. I just regret that the particular philosophy to which he was wedded happened to be one that was grossly inadequate to our situation.'[16] On this basis, Brecht's name tended to creep into any article that dealt with popular or experimental theatre and into any review of plays that showed signs of escaping from naturalism.

It was within this climate that English theatre practitioners started working on Brecht. The work of Neher, Otto and von Appen became the main source of inspiration for English stage-designers. 'The principal lessons learned concerned the lightness of construction of Brecht's sets, their flexibility and mobility and above all their marvellous use of texture of the materials employed.'[17] Integrating Brecht's forms and aesthetic designs, performances were characterized by productions alienating the central character, while naturalistic plays were produced with minimum sets with no pretence to stage illusion. An increased literarization of the theatre was noticed as well as a move towards history for subject-matter. Brecht's plays were also occasionally produced on the TV and the radio.

A number of directors are associated with Brecht. George Devine's production of *The Good Person of Szechwan* followed immediately the visit of the Berliner Ensemble. The director made use of Teo Otto's setting, but his effort was nevertheless considered a failure by Tynan, who glorified the play on humanistic grounds but rejected the production for failing to incorporate the Brechtian style of acting:

> Honourably bent on directing his cast along cold, detached Brechtian lines, Mr. Devine forgets that the Brechtian method works only with team actors of great technical maturity. With greener players it looks like casual

dawdling . . . . All the same, the production must not be missed by anyone interested in hearing the fundamental problems of human (as opposed to Western European) existence discussed in the theatre.[18]

William Gaskill has been considered to be the warmest advocate of British Brecht. He directed *The Caucasian Chalk Circle* in 1962 for the RSC at the Aldwych, then *Baal* in 1963 and *Mother Courage* at the National in 1965. In addition he directed a Brechtian production of Far-quhar's *The Recruiting Officer* in 1963 where the effort to make the cos-tumes 'look worn and used'[19] was meant to be Brechtian. There was also an attempt to emphasize the social elements in Farquhar's play, and develop a new attitude towards the direction of classical works. His Brechtian *Macbeth* at the Royal Court in 1966 seems to have been a less ambitious production which concentrated mainly on breaking the illusion and was 'staged deliberately against a light-coloured, sandy background, with full stage lighting, to avoid Gothic effects . . . . The ghosts, the witchcraft, the delusions of Macbeth were all to be watched with clinical detachment.'[20] Present also was the minimal set – the economy of staging – that became the hallmark of Gaskill's produc-tions.

The Caucasian Chalk Circle was the work by Gaskill that was most welcomed both by Tom Milne, 'a remarkable Brechtian performance'[21] and by Tynan. The latter, however, had a reservation about the produc-tion which was inevitable given the aesthetic viewpoint from which he was working – that is the tendency to focus on the artist–genius as the sole source for the production of the artistic work:

> I endorse the play's message, but no message can confer greatness on a play unless a man of genius delivers it. The touchstone, in other words, is not what Brecht says but the fact that it is Brecht who says it.[22]

Tynan had also expressed a slight dissatisfaction about Brecht adapt-ing another genius, Shakespeare, giving a materialistic outlook to his tragedy *Coriolanus*. According to Tynan, above everything else, *Coriolanus* 'is the work of a man who genuinely believed heroes *were* indispensable. Brecht's anti-hero is historically convincing; but after the banishment, stripped as he is of emotional complexities, he becomes theatrically uninteresting, if not redundant.'[23] This tendency of tradi-tional aesthetics treats the text as the end-product arising from the mind of the writer whose psychology and life become the basic elements upon which the text is going to be interpreted and directed. It can thus lend support to museum-like productions of plays.

With Brecht there is the traditional problem of the Berliner Ensem-ble's productions which were used as a prototype to be imitated. This tendency of directors to imitate the Company's versions of the plays was aggravated by the fact that the main translations were of the plays. The theory, till 1964 when Willett translated it in a systematic way, was largely unknown, since only a small number of arbitrarily selected theoretical essays had been translated in journals. Thus there grew an attitude that emphasized Brecht's plays rather than his theory, and a habit that dissociated the one from the other. The critics themselves worked on the same assumption and treated the English productions as try-outs of the prototype. Therefore the best performance must be a museum piece – Gaskill's productions were praised on this basis.

If, however, directors had been able to forget Brecht 'the person' and the plays as 'the product of the person and his company', and instead situated his work within the framework of the social and economic relationships that determine them, a different way of producing Brecht could have been developed. For placing Brecht's work within its German social context of the period would have inevitably raised the question whether his work can meet the social and dramatic demands of the present. The question of adapting Brecht to contemporary situations remains open for the future, a question to be faced by the 'alternative' theatre movement. The absence of this movement at the time when Brecht was introduced in England, gave all the rights to the mainstream theatre to perform Brecht as a classic, next to the other 'geniuses' of the past. It was a theatre that wanted productions 'theatrically interesting' but 'historically unconvincing'.

At the time when Brecht was being introduced into England, another kind of theatre appeared on the English cultural scene, that of Artaud and the theatre of the absurd. The year 1955 saw the premiere of Beckett's *Waiting for Godot* and 1956 Ionesco's *The Bald Prima Donna*. Examining the coexistence of two new and radically different traditions within the English theatre, which was at that moment in search of a new theatre language, may illuminate some of the ways in which Brecht was seen by many theatre workers. An interesting example is Peter Brook. He never directed Brecht but he advised all the theatres of the world 'to look at the affirmations of Artaud, Meyerhold, Stanislavsky, Grotowsky, Brecht then compare them with the life of the particular place in which we work'.[24] Equating Brecht and the other directors is dangerous, for it disregards the fact that Brecht tried to create a 'popular and realistic' theatre that was meant to intervene politically in capitalist society; and this differentiates him radically from the other directors. Brecht's dramatic experiments were of use whenever they could serve his social intentions; they were not meant to satisfy his aesthetic curiosity. What Brook is doing here is to deprive Brecht's theatre of its social context and perceive it as an intrinsically artistic work. He refuses to see the different forms of politicization which have determined the aesthetics of each director. In his introduction to *Marat/Sade* he repeats his claim that there is not much difference between the shock tactics of Artaud and Brecht's alienation effect. The play itself makes use of both directors. In his version of *Lear* Brook followed the same process. The production was based on a Beckettian interpretation of the text. But this did not concern 'the actual technique of staging, which was

most Brechtian both in the decor (a background of burnished copper –
as in the Berliner Ensemble *Galileo*) and in the acting: unheroic,
relaxed'.[25]

Perhaps Brook is an extreme example of the way Brecht was received
in England. Going back to Gaskill's career will only help to intensify
the present doubt, whether or to what extent English theatre people ever
understood Brecht's theory and politics in a way that could be made
significant for dramatic practice. In 1970 Gaskill gave an account of his
development, starting by acknowledging Brecht's importance for his
work:

> Brecht was the great formative influence on my work . . . Brecht showed us
> that theatre could be partly a question of economy; reducing things to their
> simplest visual statement, with the minimum of scenery, the minimum of
> furniture, necessary to create an expression in the theatre. You could also
> say this was true of Beckett (Gaskill's production of three Beckett plays
> recently opened at the Court's Theatre Upstairs) – that Beckett's work was
> essentially a reduction down to elements, to what theatre actually is, the least
> one needs to be theatrical. The influence of Brecht was also connected with
> a sense of moral and political direction . . . I do think we all feel a bit
> differently now. There is a tendency today amongst younger playwrights to
> what we used to call amorality . . . I don't think I could ever exist in a theatre
> which had nothing to do with words or a theatre in which words were
> debased. That's the chief link between the work I do in Restoration Comedy
> and, say, Edward Bond . . . Beckett is the great archetypal figure in modern
> theatre. He concentrates theatre into a statement which many people can
> recognise and accept.[26]

Language and the economy of the stage seem to be the main attractions
that Gaskill found in these three playwrights. Still Brecht is associated
with a 'political and moral' direction, Bond's language expresses the
growing 'amorality' of our society and Beckett is beyond both. Gaskill
seems to be interested in the fact that the director has to establish a
relationship between an essential object and action or language of the
play; whatever the action might indicate or the language claim. His passage from Brecht to Beckett via Bond in the above account demonstrates an aesthetic programme that was not associated with any specific
political direction or problematic.

On the other hand in Theatre Workshop, productions of realistic
plays were adapted by Joan Littlewood, giving them Brechtian nuances.
She had developed a kind of work that minimized the importance of the
finished text in order to give the opportunity to the actors to contribute
to the making of it. Plays underwent alterations during rehearsals finally
coordinated by the director. '. . . music-hall tricks of presentation –
direct addresses to the audience; musical entrances and exits'[27] were her
most usual alterations. In Brechtian theatre, however, the introduction
of a song, the interruption of a scene or the use of dance were ways of
signifying something of importance in relation to man and the world.

217

And this has to be incorporated into the written text whose importance she tried to minimize. As they stand her adaptations were aesthetic attempts to escape from the realistic, well-made structure of the plays.

Perhaps it has become evident by now that to many English theatre people Brecht's theatre meant that they could break through the three-dimensional stage, destroy the limits of the naturalistic text and be free to pursue any kind of experimentation. The simultaneous appearance of the epic theatre and the theatre of the absurd provided equal opportunities for experimentation by using Brecht or Artaud or both. English theatre people who found themselves under the spell of Brecht at some time in their career did not differentiate Brecht's theatre from other ways of doing theatre, nor did they give priority to it. Failing to see the necessary association of Brecht's political and dramatic theory with his practice, they assimilated his theatre by depriving it of its political implications and affinities; what remained from Brecht's theatre were isolated dramatic forms dissociated from their political effect and problematic.

The year 1956 also saw the emergence of a new generation of English playwrights who found a home at the English Stage Company at the Royal Court. The company was founded mainly by George Devine, Tony Richardson and Oscar Lewenstein, and it aimed not only to encourage new playwrights whose plays could not be performed in the West End but also to experiment in order to find 'a contemporary style in dramatic work, in acting, decor and production'.[28] At a later stage the company was joined by Gaskill, Lindsay Anderson, John Dexter and Anthony Page, who were to direct mainly the plays of this generation: Osborne, Wesker, Jellicoe, Simpson, early Arden and Bond. Shelagh Delaney and Brendan Behan were two other new playwrights who found a home at the Theatre Workshop at the same time.

What was received as revolutionary in their plays was their content rather than their form, which largely remained within the framework of the well-made play; but this did not prevent them from becoming successful commercially. Fighting against a stagnated theatre that was more associated with the past than with present England, this generation claimed to put on stage real people facing contemporary problems. It was on that basis that their work was welcomed both by Tynan[29] and the left which nevertheless had some reservations concerning the writers' 'failure to break through the liberal individualism which is the characteristic outlook of the petit-bourgeoisie'.[30] In most cases the plays concentrated on the condemnation of an 'intolerable' society. But this condemnation is motivated more by a sense of personal frustration than by a criticism of that society that could have led to the affirmation of the possibility of change. The lack of development in some of them is indicative. *Look Back in Anger* and Wesker's *Trilogy* end in failure or with a return to the initial situation from which the characters wanted to escape, intensifying the sense of their hopelessness. On the other hand some of them end on a humanistic note. In a *Taste of Honey* a new baby is born out of the disorganized family life, while in *Chicken Soup with Barley* despite everything there is a final affirmation of brotherhood.

The English Stage Company also founded in the late 1950s a workshop for writers which was joined by Wesker, Arden and Jellicoe and later by Bond. The group was to operate as a stimulus for the writers' creativity, working on improvisation and acting. With William Gaskill the writers worked on 'Brechtian improvisation based on the short didactic plays of Brecht'.[31] At that time the company had no great experience of Brecht. *The Threepenny Opera* and *The Good Person of Szechwan* directed in 1956 were the only Brecht productions until Gaskill's *Caucasian Chalk Circle* in 1962. It would be dangerous to claim that Gaskill's courses shaped in a specific way the company playwrights' conception of Brecht. Some of them never attended the group and there was an already formulated opinion about Brecht among theatre people as has already been indicated. But as Gaskill said it was a period when everybody was 'aware of influences' and it is not accidental that as a result of these courses Bond 'wrote two short plays...one of which was Beckett-like and the other rather Brecht-like in style'.[32] Nor is it accidental that at the same time Ann Jellicoe, who co-directed with Devine her play *The Sport of my Mad Mother*, justifies her use of Brechtian devices in the play in the following way:

> Whatever Brecht's theory may say, it is still true that his theatre is more theatrically moving than anything my generation has yet seen. His device of constantly breaking the illusion merely serves to stimulate the audience to participate in the action.[33]

Perhaps these examples are enough to indicate that the company's treatment of Becht is the familar one; the emphasis is on Brecht's work as one more stylistic technique in the practice of writing.

Whether or not the company can be held responsible, this generation of playwrights did not differ from other theatre workers in the way it used Brecht. Many of them tried their hand at him in order to escape from the confines of naturalism by imposing on their plays Brechtian elements that gave to the texts an air of renewal. Osborne's *Luther*, a history play that tried to follow the model of Brecht's *Galileo*, is a characteristic example. Osborne builds together a series of tableaux and uses a knight to announce the place and time of the action in some scenes. The use of these devices, however, does not prevent the play from being a psychological treatment of one individual that has no comment to make on present reality.

John Arden and Edward Bond are two playwrights who during their early period, before the rise of the 'alternative' theatre movement, were already positively associated with Brecht by critics. In referring to Arden, Esslin defined the concept of Brechtianism formally on the basis of some devices similar to Brecht's which if adopted could label a play as Brechtian.

> The linking of scenes by songs in *Live Like Pigs*, the use of folk songs in *Seargent Musgrave's Dance*, the masks in *Happy Haven*, the whole structure and technique of the *Workhouse Donkey* (with a narrator and copious musical interludes), the parable technique of *Armstrong's Last Goodnight*, all show a genuine affinity with Brechtian concepts.[34]

Hayman defines Bond's Brechtianism on the same basis. According to him in Bond's *Lear*,

> ... the succession of more or less disconnected episodes and the vignette characterisation of peasants who appear only briefly are reminiscent of *Mutter Courage*. In his original production of *Lear* at the Royal Court, William Gaskill followed Brecht's Berliner Ensemble by creating a locale through foreground object rather than background decor, and in the style of the groupings, lighting, costumes, and overall visual economy.[35]

It seems that critics will never go beyond this formalism unless they examine the political effect of these Brechtian usages in relation to the cultural and social formation of present society. In addition it seems that playwrights integrated Brechtian devices into their dramatic practice, treating them as a fetish. *Live Like Pigs* is a slice of working-class life destroyed by a disorganized way of living; it is more an exposition of a situation rather than an analysis and criticism. The alternation of songs and prose is a formal escape from naturalism (but offers no critical perspective on the play's substance). Naturalism is basically a question of content. The play, locked into its descriptive exposition, fails to give a socially significant perspective to its characters; the contradictions of the play are resolved against them.

Brecht developed his devices within his own historical and cultural context which regulated their validity. So it should be evident that nobody can use a Brechtian device expecting the effect to be still the same, not even such a central thesis as that of disrupting the illusion, which has been heavily used by the English theatre. This device in pre-war Germany was seen as a direct attack on bourgeois theatre and the class that supported it; then its dynamic function was to displace the familiar view of taking the appearance for the reality and thereby to expose the artifice. The present generation of audiences which have been brought up within a modernist cultural context, conceive as familiar both the illusory nature of theatre and any sort of disruption, provided it is not associated with a political point as well.

It has been claimed so far that English theatre did not manage to appropriate Brecht's work in its political dimension. True enough, the social and political indifference that prevailed in England in the 1950s and 1960s did not encourage a different approach to Brecht. Instead it cultivated an aesthetic approach that did revitalize the English theatre and served to stimulate experimentation in dramatic form. For what

English theatre did assimilate in a broad way was the whole range of Brechtian formal categories – songs, music, titles, mixing different forms of writing, the literarization of the theatre, the anti-illusionistic effects. These have become, in many quarters, the iron principles of the English theatre, what many people have come now to recognize as 'cliche', the established way of making theatre. This series of cliches that have been associated with Brecht have to be given up if theatre in England is to move forwards and make use of its potential for social action.

The political upheavals of the late 1960s in Western Europe that brought to the surface the previously well-concealed social contradictions of capitalism, provided the ground for the development of a more profound political awareness in theatre workers. In many ways the emergence of the 'alternative' theatre movement was a rupture with the past. Thus Brecht himself was sometimes seen in a perspective that placed him in the right context. But the new cultural developments carried within them elements of the past; there was an already formulated approach towards the appropriation of Brecht by the mainstream theatre which the 'alternative' theatre inherited and in most cases accepted instead of reacting against it.

The number of Brecht productions in England doubled after 1968. The 'alternative' theatre showed a preference for the didactic plays of Brecht which were meant to be more overtly political while his later ones joined the repertoire of the subsidized companies. Nevertheless, these didactic plays were often performed as museum pieces; the contemporary relevance of their politics was not questioned. The belief that there is something intrinsically new in Brecht's plays and that they could still work in England today as they had worked in the past still prevailed.

The playwrights, on the other hand, kept themselves mainly attached to the set of Brechtian cliches and the fetishization of his formal devices. Howard Barker's *Fair Slaughter* has a 'Brechtian' structure built on a series of disruptures. A story is told in flashbacks where the present constantly alternates with the past. Still the overall effect is that of a long narrative; cause and effect follow each other and the interruptions between them can only intensify the very linear exposition of a biographical and psychological portrait of a helpless man.

The search by theatre workers for similarities between Brecht and themselves has compelled them to stress so far only their affinity with him. However, instead of emphasizing similarities, and thereby depriving their own texts of that historical, cultural and social context which had imbued them with a very specific political value, it would seem wiser to emphasize these differences with the Brechtian view of the world which had resulted from changed social forces. Then it would become evident that for a Brechtian writer or director it is not a question of how similar he is to Brecht but of how different he is from him. If one agrees that Brecht wanted to develop a theatre of political intervention in a historically determined set of circumstances, the idea of being Brechtian while different from Brecht becomes crucial. For theatre has to intervene in different historical sets of circumstances by which it is also determined; the mere fetishization of formal devices is thus inadequate; instead the techniques are readapted to the new historical context.

It was this kind of theatre that Brecht focused on and wanted to develop towards the end of his life but only touched upon in both theory and practice. It was the theatre that was going 'to make use in its representations of the new social scientific method known as dialectical materialism'.[36] It is significant that Brecht did not give a formal definition for dialectical theatre as he had often done with the epic. This time the definition is scientific, theoretical and heavily political rather than aesthetic. This theatre is going to treat its object as articulated by the discourse of dialectical materialism, which is also going to define the way dramatic forms are to be used. It is this less developed part of Brecht's theatre that has to be carried further by English theatre workers.

On this basis a new attitude began to develop in the 1970s concerning the direction of Brecht's plays. It was an approach that did not concentrate on the play as the end-product of the writer and his company but on the position that the text occupied as regards the economic relationships of its time. This implies a rereading and understanding of Brecht's theory and practice not in order to reproduce them but to see their limits and historical inability to meet present demands, and thus to move beyond them. The need to revitalize and adapt Brecht to new circumstances was a challenge that some theatre people chose to take up. 'To develop Brecht's own ideas' was the pronouncement of the Foco Novo Company when in 1975 it produced *A Man's Man* adapted by Bernard Pomerance and directed by Roland Rees.

> The prologue is full of fears of Soviet agitation, compounding the role of British imperialism in India. Bloody five becomes an instigator of the original pagoda robbery, and is involved in illicit elephant traffic. There are scattered references to the General Strike back home, and attempts to relate these to questions of colonialism vaguely hinted at by Brecht. More serious a breach with Brecht is the addition of psychoanalytic flesh. Galy Gay is protrayed as a 'dreamer' and his child-like awe of the army explains its ability to run circles round him . . . When he has doubts, the soldiers resort to force, rather than Brecht's 'scientific' logic, to turn him into Jip . . . . With the taking of the Tibetan fortress he finds a sudden conscience and, in remorse, renounces both Jip and that side of himself that has opted for 'dream rather than reality' . . .[37]

Some English playwrights, too, resorted to the idea of a dialectical theatre to fight not only against the established Brechtian cliché plays but also the sort of theatre, deriving from the mid-1950s, but still alive today, and which treats as humanistic and moral problems which are of a political and economic nature. Particularly some of the later plays by

John Arden and Edward Bond and others by David Edgar, Alfio Bernabei, Steve Gooch, Roger Howard, John McGrath, David Rudkin, and Caryl Churchill do attempt to practise the concept of dialectical theatre using its dynamic and productivity to generate that kind of social criticism which could lead to constructive political change.

NOTES

1. N. Jacobs and P. Ohlsens, eds., *Bertolt Brecht in Britain* (London, 1977), p. 87.
2. Raphael Samuel, 'Workers' Theatre Movement: editorial introduction', *History Workshop* No. 4, Sally Alexander et al., eds (Oxford, 1977), p. 108.
3. Jacobs and Ohlsen, op. cit., p. 87.
4. Reminiscence from Connie Williams in Ewan MacColl's 'Grass roots of Theatre Workshop', *Theatre Quarterly*, **3** No. 9 (1973),p. 64.
5. Jacobs and Ohlsen, op. cit., p. 93.
6. Jonathan Hammond, 'A potted history of the Fringe', *Theatre Quarterly*, **3** No. 12 (1973), p. 37.
7. Kenneth Tynan, *Curtains* (London, 1961), p. 389.
8. Ibid., p. 318.
9. Ibid., p. 390.
10. George Devine, 'The Berliner Ensemble', *Encore*, **3**, No. 2 (1956),p. 11.
11. Bertolt Brecht, 'Our London season, 1956' in *Brecht on Theatre*, p. 283.
12. Tynan, *Curtains*, p. 452.
13. Harold Hobson in Jacobs and Ohlsen, op. cit., p. 80.
14. Ibid., p. 81.
15. Ernst Bornemann, 'The real Brecht', *Encore*, **5**, No. 2 (1958),p. 33.
16. Robert Bolt, interview with the editors, *Encore*, **8**, No. 2 (1961),p. 27.
17. Martin Esslin, 'Brecht and the English theatre', *Tulane Drama Review*, **11**, No. 2 (1966), p. 65.
18. Tynan, *Curtains*, pp. 147–8.
19. William Gaskill, 'Finding a style for Farquhar', *Theatre Quarterly*, **1**, No. 1 (1971), p. 16.
20. John Elsom, *Post War British Theatre* (London, 1979), pp. 124–5.
21. Tom Milne, *'The Caucasian Chalk Circle'*, *Encore*, **9**, No. 3 (1962), p. 46.
22. Kenneth Tynan, *Tynan Right and Left* (London, 1967), p. 123.
23. Ibid., p. 162.
24. Peter Brook, *The Empty Space* (Harmondsworth, Middlesex, 1979), p. 96.
25. Esslin, op. cit., p. 66.
26. William Gaskill interviewed by Peter Ansorge, *Plays and Players*, **17**, No. 8 (1970),p. 53.
27. John Russell Taylor, *Anger and After* (London, 1978), p. 122.
28. Terry Browne, *Playwrights' Theatre* (London, 1975), p. 12.

29. See Tynan in *Curtains* reviewing Osborne's *Look Back in Anger*, p. 131, Delaney's *A Taste of Honey*, p. 213, and in *Tynan Right and Left* Wesker's *Chicken Soup with Barley*, p. 33.
30. Arnold Kettle, 'Rebel and causes: Some thoughts on the Angry Young Men', *Marxism Today*, **2** (March, 1958), p. 68.
31. William Gaskill interviewed by Irving Wardle, *Gambit*, **5**, No. 17 (1970), p. 39.
32. Ibid.
33. Anne Jellicoe 'Something of sport', *Encore*, **5**, No. 1 (1958), p. 26.
34. Esslin, op. cit., p. 70.
35. Ronald Hayman in *British Theatre since 1955*, Keith Thomas and J. S. Weiner, eds (Oxford, 1979), p. 48.
36. 'A Short Organum for the Theatre', in *Brecht on Theatre*, p. 193.
37. David Mairowitz, 'A Man's Man', *Plays and Players*, **23**, No. 3 (1975), p. 20.

SELECT BIBLIOGRAPHY

BRADBY, DAVID and JOHN MCCORNICK, 'Brecht and his influence,' in *People's Theatre*, New Jersey, 1978

COULT, TONY, *The Plays of Edward Bond*, London, 1974

ELSOM, JOHN, 'Brecht: cool ambiguity', in *Post War British Theatre*, London, 1979

ESSLIN, MARTIN, 'Brecht and the English theatre', in *Tulane Drama Review*, **11**, No. 2 (1966)

GRAY, RONALD, 'Epilogue: Brecht and political theatre in America and Britain', in *Brecht: The Dramatist*, Cambridge, 1976

HAYMAN, RONALD, 'Brecht in the English theatre', in *German Theatre: A Symposium*, R. Hayman, ed. London, 1975

HAYMAN, RONALD, *British Theatre since 1955*, London, 1979

HINCHCLIFFE, ARNOLD, 'European influences', in *British Theatre, 1950–1970*, Oxford, 1974

HOLLAND, PETER, 'Brecht, Bond, Gaskill and the practice of political theatre', in *Theatre Quarterly*, **8**, No. 2 (1978)

HUNT, ALBERT, *Arden: A Study of his Plays*, London, 1974

JACOBS, NICHOLAS and PRUDENCE OHLSEN, eds, *Bertolt Brecht in Britain*, London, 1977

TAYLOR, JOHN RUSSELL, *Anger and After*, London, 1962

TAYLOR, JOHN RUSSELL, *The Second Wave*, London, 1971

WILLETT, JOHN, 'The English aspect', in *The Theatre of Bertolt Brecht*, London, 1977

INDEX

Absurd, theatre of the, 195, 216, 218
Aeschylus, 192
Agitprop theatres, 125, 209
Die Aktion, 91
Aldwych Theatre, 215
Anderson, Lindsay, 218
Anzengruber, Ludwig, 21, 73
Appen, Karl von, 214
Arco-Valley, Count, 93
Arden, John, 208, 218, 219, 220, 223
Aristotle on drama, 12, 13
Art Soviet (Arbeitsrat für Kunst), 96
Artaud, Antonin, 216, 218
Auden, W. H., 160

Bab, Julius, 120
Baierl, Helmut, 187
Balázs, Béla, 114, 146
Balzac, Honoré de, 100
Barker, Howard, 221
Barlach, Ernst, 26, 180
Barney, Ludwig, 110
Bäuerle, Adolf, 71
Bauhaus, 95–6, 97, 101
Bavarian Soviet Republic, 93
Becher, Johannes R., 103, 122, 145
Beckett, Samuel, 142, 195, 216, 217, 219
Behan, Brendan, 218
Behne, Adolf, 96
Bentley, Eric, 142
Berghaus, Ruth, 182, 186
Bergson, Henri, 64
Berliner Theater, 110
Bernabei, Alfio, 223
Besson, Benno, 182
Billinger, Richard, 74
Bismarck, Otto von, 4, 108, 113
Bleibtreu, Karl, 22
Blumenthal, Oscar, 110

Bölsche, Wilhelm, 22
Bolshevik Revolution, 92
  art and, 101–2
Bolt, Robert, 214
Bond, Edward, 208, 217, 218, 219, 220,
  223
Bornemann, Ernst, 214
BPRS (League of Proletarian-Revolutionary
  Writers), 103
Brahm, Otto, 109–15, 119
Brando, Marlon, 134
Braun, Volker, 187
Brecht, Bertolt, viii–ix, x, xi–xii, 2, 3, 5,
  6, 7, 8–9, 87, 91–2, 96, 97–101,
  102, 103–4, 114, 145, 146
  acting style, 129, 134–9, 142, 154,
    157, 183, 194, 214–15
  *The Adventures of the Good Soldier
    Schwejk*, 146–7, 156–7, 158,
    209; *see also* Piscator, Erwin
  alienation, or distancing effect, 36–7,
    39–40, 41, 63–4, 65, 66–7,
    135–6, 138, 141, 164. 185,
    186, 194, 202, 216
  'Alienation effects in Chinese acting',
    36, 137
  Anna Anna (later called *The Seven
    Deadly Sins*), 208
  Arbeitsjournal (*Journal of Work*), 177,
    193
  art and entertainment, 108, 172, 181
  Baal 45–7, 52, 62, 98, 117, 171, 187,
    215
  Berliner Ensemble, viii, 137, 138, 156,
    157, 176, 177, 179, 181–6,
    210, 212, 213, 215, 217, 220
  Boom, 147–8
  and Cabaret, 160–73
  The Caucasian Chalk Circle, ix, 77,

Index

161, 166, 185, 202, 210, 211, 212, 215, 219
and comedy, 63–4, 65, 66–7, 79
and Communist Party (KPD), 52–3, 83, 98, 99, 176
and (East German) Communist Party (SED), 176–80, 183
Coriolanus, 182, 215
Days of the Commune, 175, 180, 181
Drums and Trumpets, 212
Drums in the Night, 6, 98, 117, 157, 171
Edward II, 119, 187
epic theatre, 11–12, 13, 14, 16, 18, 20, 22, 25, 27–8, 30–44, 111, 115, 120, 125–6, 134–5, 137, 139, 141, 142, 145, 146, 150, 154, 170–1, 179, 187, 193, 218, 222
The Exception and the Rule, 36
in exile, viii, 7–8, 156
The Expedient (The Measures Taken), 209
'on experimental theatre', 134
and Expressionism, 63, 97–8, 100–1, 103, 117, 161–2
Fear and Misery of the Third Reich, 7–8, 68, 157, 193, 201
and the Federal Republic, viii, 8, 176, 195
Galileo, ix, 8, 185, 193, 199, 200, 204, 217, 219
and the German Democratic Republic, viii, xi, xii, 8, 43–4, 104, 175–89, 196, 204–5
The Good Person of Szechwan, 37, 60–1, 66–7, 77, 182, 193, 202, 214, 219
Happy End, 173
and Heisenberg Uncertainty Principle, 40–1
Herr Puntila and his Servant Matti, 37, 43, 56–7, 67, 69, 77–9, 165, 181, 182, 185, 193, 196
In the Jungle of the Cities, 2, 3, 47
individual and society in plays of, 45–62
Joe P. Fleischhacker, 148–9, 150
and his legacy, 192–207, 208–24
Legend of the Dead Soldier, 5, 117, 169
Lehrstücke (Didactic Plays), 37, 51–3, 124–5, 154, 172, 221
Little Mahagonny, 170
Mahagonny notes, 11–12, 32–3, 111, 118

A Man's a Man, 47–9, 62, 99, 156, 222
and Marxism, 33, 37, 38, 39, 41–2, 43, 50, 51, 54, 55–6, 62, 77, 83, 98–9, 149, 158, 172, 181, 182, 213
The Measures Taken, ix, 51–3, 62, 98
Messingkauf dialogues, 37, 40, 51, 53–4, 134–5
The Mother, ix, 141, 180, 183
Mother Courage, ix, 57–60, 77, 139, 141, 158, 175, 181, 184, 185, 187, 193, 199, 211, 212, 213, 215, 220
and naturalism, 31, 42, 134, 136, 149, 172, 203, 214, 219, 220
and Nazism, 48, 66, 69, 178–9, 181
and New Objectivity, 96, 117, 162
New Technique of Acting, 39
The Private Life of the Master Race, see under *Fear and Misery of the Third Reich* above
realism, concept of, 42–3, 100–1, 103
The Recruiting Officer (adapted from Farquhar)
Refugee Dialogues, 40
The Resistable Rise of Arturo Ui, 37, 66, 182, 193
Rise and Fall of the City of Mahagonny, 173
Round Heads and Pointed Heads, 8, 66, 201
St. Joan of the Stockyards, 2, 7, 37, 66–7, 85, 187
Schwejk in the Second World War, 77, 157, 199 (*see also* Hasek, Jaroslav)
Senora Carrar's Rifles, 43, 184–5, 209, 211
Short Organon for the Theatre, 37, 38–41, 42, 51
and Socialist Realism, 103, 180–1, 187
The Street Scene, 31, 34–5, 36, 136
The Threepenny Opera, 43, 77, 99, 120, 170, 173, 185, 211, 219
The Trial of Lucullus, 183
USA, fascination with, 47, 48
and *Volksbühne* (People's Theatre), 122, 123, 127
and *Volksstück*, 63, 67–9, 72, 73, 75, 77–9, 164–5, 181, 185
Die Brille, 164
Broch, Hermann, 86
Brod, Max, 146, 147
Brook, Peter, 202, 216–7

Bruckner, Ferdinand, 123, 150
Büchner, Georg, 2, 19, 20–1, 25, 28, 115, 118, 154
cabaret, 160–73, 209
    Cabaret Voltaire, 102, 163
    Neopathetisches Cabaret, 163
    Gnu, 163
    Schall und Rauch, 115, 164

Cabaret (United Artists' film), 160
Carl, Karl, 71
Cartel of Productive Estates (*Kartell der schaffenden Stände*), 4
Cézanne, Paul, 86
Chaplin, Charlie, 136, 172, 194
Chekhov, Anton, 130, 133
Chronegk, Ludwig, 110, 113
Churchill, Caryl, 223
Claudel, Paul, 36
Communist International, 97, 103
Communist Party, German (KPD), 6, 7, 92, 93, 94, 95, 98, 127, 147
    and amateur and workers' theatres, 124–6
    Brecht and, 52–3, 83, 98, 99, 175
    and intellectuals, 92, 94, 97, 98, 102–3, 198
Communist Workers Party (KAPD), 94
Comte, Auguste, 22
Constructivism, 101
Coult, Tony, 208
Councils of Intellectual Workers, 93–4, 95
Courbet, Gustave, 86
Coward, Noel, 142
Credé, Carl, 124, 156
Csokor, Franz Theodor, 166
Cubism, 89

Dada, 102, 118, 163–4
Darwin, Charles, 22, 114
Dehmel, Richard, 166
Delaney, Shelagh, 218
Dessau, Paul, 183
Deutsches Theater, 110, 112, 113, 116, 164
Deutschnationale Handlungsgehilfenverband, 4
Devine, George, 138, 211, 214, 218, 219
Dexter, John, 218
Diderot, Denis, 100
Döblin, Alfred, 100, 145
Dorst, Tankred, 195, 205
Dos Passos, John, 100
Durieux, Tilla, 147, 148
Dürrenmatt, Friedrich, 192, 194, 199, 200, 201, 202, 204

Edgar, David, 223
Eichmann, Adolf, 195
Einem, Gottfried von, 175
Eisler, Hanns, 98, 156, 180
Eisner, Kurt, 93
Eliot, T. S., 83, 209
Encore, 211, 214
Engel, Erich, 120, 175
Engels, Friedrich, 19, 113
English Stage Company, 211, 218, 219
Enlightenment, the, 12, 84, 100
Ernst, Paul, 24
Esslin, Martin, 213–14, 219
Ettlinger, Joseph, 116
Expressionism, 12, 20, 24, 25–7, 28, 63, 73, 89, 91, 92, 96, 115–18, 125, 161–3, 169
    activist wing, 89–90, 91, 92–4, 98
    Brecht's view of, 63, 97–8, 100–1
    Dada and, 102, 167
    and SPD, 89

Farquhar, George, 215
Fauvism, 89
Federal Republic of Germany, 8, 195
Fehling, Jürgen, 117, 124
Fernald, John, 211
Feuerbach, Ludwig, 19
Frank, Bruno, 73
First World War, 3, 5, 25, 46
    and literati, 91–2
Foco Novo Company, 222
Fontane, Theodor, 111
Förster, August, 110
Frankfurt School (Frankfurt Institute for Social Research), 76, 88, 101
Franz, Ellen, 110
Freie Bühne, Die (Independent Theatre), 110, 112, 113, 114
Freie Volksbühne (Independent People's Theatre), 114, 115, 116, 117, 120–3, 125, 127, 145, 156
Freud, Sigmund, 18, 25
Freytag, Gustav, 21
Frisch, Max, 194, 198, 199, 200, 201, 202, 205, 206
Fry, Christopher, 209
Futurism, 89, 163

Gasbarra, Felix, 145, 146, 147
Gaskill, William, 215, 216, 217, 218, 219, 220
Gay, John, 170
George, Stefan, 88
George II, Duke of Saxe-Meiningen, 110
German Democratic Republic, viii, 8, 9,

Index

43–4, 97, 104, 116, 175–89, 196, 204–5
German National Theatre, 108
German Popular Front (Volksfront), 97
Gleich, Josef, 71
Goering, Reinhard, 116, 118
Goethe, Johann Wolfgang von, 14–15, 20, 28, 85, 115, 120, 150, 164, 182
Goetz, Curt, 73
Gooch, Steve, 223
Gorky, Maxim, 115, 133, 182
Gottsched, Johann Christoph, 12–13, 28, 109, 111
Grabbe, Christian Dietrich, 19–20, 25, 28, 117
Grass, Günter, 195, 204–5
Grieg, Nordahl, 157
Gropius, Walter, 95, 96
Grosses Schauspielhaus (Berlin), 115, 117, 118, 121, 164
Grosz, George, 102, 116, 146, 147, 156, 164
Grotowsky, Vladimir, 216
Gutzkow, Karl, 21, 28

Hacks, Peter, 64, 187, 194, 196, 197
Halbe, Max, 23
Hammond, Jonathan, 209
Handke, Peter, 76, 205
Hart, Heinrich, 22
Hart, Julius, 22
Hasek, Jaroslav, 146
Hasenclever, Walter, 26, 89, 92, 97, 117
Hauptmann, Gerhart, 23–4, 28, 111–12
Hayman, Ronald, 208, 220
Hazlitt, William, 64
Heartfield, John, 102, 118
Hebbel, Friedrich, 21–2
Hecht, Werner, 186
Heine, Heinrich, 2
Herder, Johann Gottfried, 14
Herzfeld(e), Wieland, 102, 156
Hesse, Hermann, 166
Heym, Georg, 89
Hildesheimer, Wolfgang, 195
Hiller, Kurt, 92, 94, 95, 97, 163
Hinrichs, August, 74
Hitler, Adolf, 6, 7, 66
Hobson, Harold, 212–13
Hochhuth, Rolf, 197, 200, 203, 205, 206
Hoffmann, Joseph, 109
Hofmannsthal, Hugo von, 24, 46
Hölderlin, Friedrich, 85
Holl, Fritz, 123
Hollaender, Friedrich, 164
Holz, Arno, 22–3, 166

Horváth, Ödön von, 75–7, 124, 206
Howard, Roger, 223
Howerd, Frankie, 78
Huelsenbeck, Richard, 163
Hunt, Albert, 208
Hurwicz, Angelika, 139

Ibsen, Henrik, 22, 26, 110, 111, 112, 114
Iffland, August Wilhelm, 17
Imperial Germany, see Second Reich
Independent Social Democratic Party (USPD), 5, 92, 94, 97, 124
  and intellectuals, 92, 97
Ionesco, Eugène, 195, 216
Isherwood, Christopher, 160

Jacobsohn, Siegfried, 97
Jahn, Alfred, 124
Jellicoe, Ann, 218, 219
Jessner, Leopold, 119–20, 150
Jhering, Herbert, 116, 117, 118, 123
Johst, Hanns, 117
Joyce, James, 86, 100
Jung, Franz, 102
Jünger, Ernst, 91–2
Junges Deutschland, 21

Kafka, Franz, 86, 100
Kainz, Josef, 110
Kaiser, Georg, 3, 26–7, 28, 89, 100, 117
Kampfbund für deutsche Kultur, 98
Kandinsky, Wassily, 89, 96
Kant, Immanuel, 33, 84, 85
KAPD (Communist Workers Party), 94
Kapp Putsch, 6, 96
Kästner, Erich, 166, 168
Kayssler, Friedrich, 123, 155
Kean, Charles, 110
Kerr, Alfred, 151, 166
Kessler, Harry Graf, 92
Kipling, Rudyard, 169
Kipphardt, Heinar, 200, 203, 204, 206
Klabund, Alfred, 166, 167, 168, 171
Kleist, Heinrich von, 18–19, 182
Kokoschka, Oskar, 26, 89
Kornfeld, Paul, 26, 117
Korsch, Karl, 7
Kortner, Fritz, 119
Kotzebue, August, 18
KPD, see Communist Party
Krauss, Werner, 118
Kroetz, Franz Xaver, 76–7, 205

Lampel, Peter, 6, 150
Landauer, Gustave, 93
Lange, Hartmut, 187, 196

Lania, Leo, 145, 146, 147, 153
L'Arronge, Adolph, 110, 112
Lassalle, Ferdinand, 113
Laube, Heinrich, 21, 28, 109, 110
League of Proletarian-Revolutionary
    Writers (BPRS), 103
Lenya, Lotte, 137–8
Lenz, J. M. R., 14, 20, 28, 118, 182
Lessing, Gotthold Ephraim, 12–14, 16,
    28, 67, 100, 108, 115
Lessing Theater, 110, 113, 148
Leviné, Eugen, 93
Lewenstein, Oscar, 211, 218
Liebknecht, Karl, 92, 94
Liliencron, Detlev von, 166
Die Linkskurve, 98
Lissitzky, El, 101
Littlewood, Joan, 209, 210–11, 217
Lorca, F. Garcia, 157
Ludwig, Otto, 21
Luxemburg, Rosa, 92, 94

MacColl, Ewan, 209
McGrath, John, 223
Malik Verlag, 102
Mallarmé, Stéphane, 86
Mann, Heinrich, 4, 5, 90–1, 92, 94, 95,
    97
    Geist und Tat, 90–1
Mann, Thomas, 2, 93, 95
Marc, Franz, 89, 91
Marinetti, Filippo Tomaso, 163
Marowitz, Charles, 142
Martin, Karl Heinz, 116, 118, 119
Marx, Karl and Marxism, 19, 33, 39,
    41–2, 65–6, 94, 113, 114, 154,
    172, 202
Mayakovsky, Vladimir, 101
Mehring, Walter, 116, 145, 149, 158, 166,
    167, 168, 169, 171
Meiningen Players, 110–11, 115
Meisl, Karl, 71
Melchinger, Siegfried, 192
Meyerhold, Vsevolod, 101, 102, 216
Mickel, Karl, 186
Milne, Tom, 215
Minelli, Liza, 160
Molière, Jean-Baptiste, 12, 25, 70
Morgenstern, Christian, 164
Moscow Art Theatre, 130, 133–5, 136,
    142
Mühsam, Erich, 91, 93, 97, 124, 146
Müller, Heiner, 186, 187, 196
Müller, Traugott, 151
Müller-Schlosser, Hans, 74
Musil, Robert, 86

National Socialist German Workers Party
    (NSDAP), 3, 7, 8, 23, 48, 66,
    67–8, 74, 75, 87, 95, 124, 126,
    127, 160, 161, 195, 199, 201, 203
    Brecht and, 48, 66, 69, 192
    and intellectuals, 96, 97
National Theatre, 215
Naturalism, 20, 22–4, 28, 109–15, 155,
    169, 172
    and SPD, 88
Nazism *see* National Socialist German
    Workers Party
Neft, Heinrich, 116
Neher, Carola, viii
Neher, Caspar, 119, 214
Nemirovich-Danchenko, Vladimir, 130,
    133
Neo-Classicism, 12–13, 28
Nestriepke, Siegfried, 115
Nestroy, Johann, 71–2, 73
Neuber, Friederike Caroline, 109, 111
Neue Freie Volksbühne (New Independent
    People's Theatre), 115, 116
New Objectivity (Neue Sachlichkeit), 95,
    96, 117, 160
Nietzsche, Friedrich, 18, 22, 25, 63,
    87–8, 89, 90, 94
November Revolution, 5, 6
    intellectuals and 92–4

O'Casey, Sean, 157
Osborne, John, 218, 219
Ossietzky, Carl von, 97, 168
Otto, Teo, 214
Ottwalt, Ernst, viii

Page, Anthony, 218
Palitzsch, Peter, 182
Pallenberg, Max, 146
Paquet, Alfons, 125
Pfemfert, Franz, 91, 92, 94
Picasso, Pablo, 86
Pinthus, Kurt, 26
Piscator, Erwin, 31–2, 96, 101–2, 114,
    115, 117–18, 120, 121–3, 125–7,
    145–59, 161, 167, 193, 200, 203,
    206, 209
    and Dada, 102
Plautus, 78,
Die Pleite, 102
Pomerance, Bernard, 222
Pound, Ezra, 83
Proletkult, 101, 102
Proust, Marcel, 86

Raimund, Ferdinand, 71

Index

Realism, German nineteenth-century, 18, 19–22, 28, 100–1
Rees, Roland, 222
Rehfisch, Hans J., 122, 124
Reich, Bernhard, 148, 149
Reimann, Hans, 146, 147, 153
Reinhardt, Max, 115–19, 123, 126, 161, 164, 167
Renn, Ludwig, 98
Die Revolution, 91
Richardson, Tony, 218
Rix, Brian, 64
Rolland, Romain, 117
Romanticism, 18–19, 84–5, 166
Rosenberg, Alfred, 98
Die Rote Fahne, 102
Royal Court Theatre (London), 138, 211, 215, 218, 220
Royal Shakespeare Company, 215
Rubiner, Ludwig, 92
Rudkin, David, 223
Rühle, Günther, 108, 197, 203

Sachs, Hans, 70
Savoy Theatre (London), 208
Schall und Rauch, 115, 116, 167
Die Schaubühne, 97
Schickele, René, 91
Schiller, Friedrich, 15–17, 28, 85, 87–8, 108, 111
    The Robbers (*Die Räuber*), 120, 145
Schiller Theatre, 113
Schlaf, Johannes, 23
Schlegel, Friedrich and August Wilhelm, 18
Schnitzler, Arthur, 24
Schoenberg, Arnold, 86, 89
Schönherr, Karl, 74
Schönlank, Bruno, 125
Schröder, Friedrich Ludwig, 17
Second Reich, 2–5, 22
    middle class in, 87
    writers in, 88
Seghers, Anna, 98
Shakespeare, William, 13, 14, 18, 20, 21, 28, 31, 115, 119, 208
    Romeo and Juliet, 64
    Coriolanus, 120, 205, 215
    Hamlet, 120, 150
    Macbeth, 132, 215
    King Lear, 216
Shaw, George Bernard, 112
Shchegolev, Peter, 151
Simpson, Norman, 218
Singer, Eric, 166
Social Democratic Party, German (SPD), 3, 4, 6, 92, 94, 95

and amateur and workers theatre, 124–6
    and intellectuals, 89, 94, 97
    and Naturalism, 88, 113, 114, 115
    and People's Theatre, 113–16
Socialist Realism, 68–9, 100, 103
Sorge, Reinhard Johannes, 26, 89, 117
Spartacists, 6, 92
Sperr, Martin, 73, 205
Staatliches Schauspielhaus (Berlin), 119, 120, 145, 156
Stadler, Ernst, 89, 91
Stalin, Josef, 97, 103, 176, 197
Stanislavsky, Constantine, 111, 128–43, 179, 216
Stavenhagen, Fritz, 73
Sternberg, Fritz, 7, 157
Sternheim, Carl, 25, 100
Storm and Stress (*Sturm und Drang*), 12, 14–15, 16, 17, 25, 28, 46
Stramm, August, 91
Stranitzky, Josef, 70, 73
Strasberg, Lee, 138
Strauss, David Friedrich, 19
Stravinsky, Igor, 86
Strindberg, August, 26, 110, 112, 115
Strittmatter, Erwin, 182
Sturm group, 96
Sturm und Drang see Storm and Stress
Sudermann, Hermann, 23
Suhrkamp, Peter, 176
Suprematism, 89
Symbolist movement, 88
Das Tage-Buch, 97, 121

Taut, Bruno, 96
Taylor, John Russell, 208
Tenschert, Joachim, 182
Theater am Nollendorfplatz (Berlin), 146
Theater am Schiffbauerdamm (Berlin), 146, 183
Theatre of Action (Manchester), 209
Theatre Royal (London), 210
Theatre Workshop, 209, 217
Thoma, Ludwig, 73
Tieck, Ludwig, 18
Toller, Ernst, 3, 6, 26, 27, 28, 89, 92, 93, 97, 100, 116, 117, 118, 121, 122, 123, 124–5, 126–7, 146, 155, 158
Tolstoy, Alexey, 151
Tolstoy, Leo, 22, 100, 110, 114
Trakl, Georg, 89
Tretyakov, Sergei, viii
Tucholsky, Kurt, 97, 98, 117, 146, 166, 167–8, 171
Türk, Julius, 115

Tynan, Kenneth, 134, 138, 210, 212, 213, 214, 215, 218

Ulbricht, Walter, 177
Unity Theatre (London), 209, 211
Unruh, Fritz von, 26, 92, 116
USA
  Bertolt Brecht in, 9
  Heinrich Mann in, 97
  Stanislavsky and, 134
USPD *see* Independent Social Democratic Party
USSR
  avant-garde in, 103
  Brecht visits, 103
  Heinrich Mann's support for, 97

Valentin, Karl, 164–6, 169, 172, 194
Vienna Burgtheater, 109, 111, 115
Villon, François, 167, 169
Vitus, Maximilian, 74
Volksbühne (People's Theatre), 120–3, 127, 145 *see also* Freie Bühne *and* Freie Volksbühne
Vormärz, 2

Wagner, Richard, 88, 109, 173
Walser, Martin, 62, 194, 197, 198, 200, 201, 202, 205, 206
Wandervogel youth movement, 91
Wangenheim, Gustav von, 125
Weber, Carl, 137
Weber, Max, 2, 93
Wedekind, Frank, 24–5, 28, 112, 116, 117, 118, 166, 167, 169, 172
Weigel, Helene, 138, 141, 157, 175, 176, 177, 179, 181, 186
Weill, Kurt, 120, 137, 157, 173
Weimar Classicism, 12, 15–17, 85, 87
Weimar Republic, 3, 6–7, 95, 115, 118, 120, 125, 127, 160, 198
  intellectuals in, 87
Weiss, Peter, 197, 198, 199, 200, 202, 203, 204, 205, 216
Die weissen Blätter, 91
Wekwerth, Manfred, 182, 184, 186
Welk, Ehm, 122, 145
Die Weltbühne, 95, 97, 167, 168
Werfel, Franz, 26, 89
Wesker, Arnold, 218, 219
Wilde, Oscar, 112
Wilder, Thornton, 36
Wilhelmine Germany, 4–5, 25, 115, 120, 123
  avant-garde in, 88, 90–1
  see also Second Reich
Wille, Bruno, 114, 115
Willett, John, 154, 162, 168, 213, 215
Wolf, Friedrich, 98, 118, 123, 125, 156, 186
Workers' Theatre Movement, 209

Zeitstück, 123–4, 125, 156, 196
Zhdanov, Andrei, 180
Das Ziel, 94
Zola, Émile, 22, 90, 114
Zuckmayer, Carl, 73, 75, 76
Das Zwanzigste Jahrhundert, 90